Business Law

John Ellison LLB (Hons), Grad Cert Ed, MA (Dunelm)
Tom Harrison BA (Hons), Grad Cert Ed, LLM (London)
With contributions by Jim Bedingfield

Harrison Law Publishing 2000

© Tom Harrison   John Ellison

ISBN 0-9538720-0-9

First Edition 1987
  Reprinted 1989, 1990
Second Edition 1991
  Reprinted 1992, 1993
Third Edition 1994
  Reprinted 1995
Fourth Edition 1997
  Reprinted 1998
Fifth Edition 2000
  Reprinted 2002

Published in Great Britain by
Harrison Law Publishing
53 South Street
Durham City
DH1 4QP

Tel: 0191 3846218
Fax: 0191 3846218

British Cataloguing-in-Publications Data
A catalogue record for this book is available from the British Library

Printed and bound in Great Britain at Athenaeum Press, Gateshead

Preface

This well established student text, used by students on degree sub-degree and professional programmes, is now in its fifth edition. We do recognise that the book has grown significantly over the years, edition by edition, and has become a little unwieldy. As a consequence we have made a determined effort to restructure Business Law and effectively reduce it's size. Inevitably then, some areas of the subject have been reduced, in particular the chapters on employment law. We believe however that students will find the new edition a more manageable learning resource which contains a comprehensive coverage of the principles of business law. Popular assignments, with some additions, have been retained, with a reordered glossary of terms.

We hope that the style and approach of the book is student friendly, making the law as accessible as possible so that the study of business law is enjoyable as well as informative. The direct impact that business law has on our personal experiences as consumers and employees should ensure that the book remains of practical value as a reference source long after your formal legal studies have been completed.

For ease of expression the book adopts, in general, the practice of using 'he' for 'he or she' and 'his' for 'his and hers'.

J E
T H

Acknowledgements

Many thanks to Moira Page who has the ability to decipher woefully handwritten text and had the sole responsibility for the design and type setting of the text and the book cover.

TH JE
Durham June 2000

The Authors

John Ellison and Tom Harrison are both law teachers at New College Durham.

John Ellison is Programme Manager for higher education at New College and Director of the full-time HND programme. He is also chairman of the AEB committee responsible for 'A' Level Law.

Tom Harrison is course leader for the Music Industry Management stream on the HND course at New College. He is also a visiting lecturer in employment law at Durham University.

Table of Contents

Table of Cases

C

D

E

F

G

H

I

J

K

L

M

N

O

P

R

Table of Statutes, Statutory Instruments and Treaties

Glossary of Legal Terms

Acceptance	• an unconditional assent to an offer
Actus reus	• guilty act for the purposes of crime
Adjudicate	• to settle a legal problem by giving judgment
Advocacy	• the activity of pleading a case before a court
Agent	• person empowered to make contracts on behalf of another
Appeal	• asking a higher court to change the decision of a lower court
Appellant	• a person who appeals
Arbitrate	• to settle a dispute without court action
Articles of Association	• rules concerned with the internal administration of a company
Ascertained goods	• goods which were unascertained and have been identified
Auditor	• independent financial investigator of a company
Bankruptcy	• personal insolvency
Barrister	• lawyer who is an advocate for a client in any court
Bill	• draft legislation
Binding precedent	• a precedent which has to be followed
Capacity	• requirement that parties be capable of contracting
Capital	• funds raised to finance an organisation
Causation	• link between harm suffered and an unlawful act
Cause of action	• reason why a case is brought to court
Civil action	• a case brought by an individual against another alleging a civil wrong
Civil law	• law dealing with the personal rights and obligations of individuals
Claimant	• a person or organisation bringing a civil action
Code of practice	• a statement of trading behaviour produced by a trade association

Codification	• bring law together in a formal code
Collective agreement	• the product of collective bargaining
Company dissolution	• striking a company off the register of companies by the Registrar
Company secretary	• the senior administrative officer of a registered company
Compensation order	• court order requiring a payment of money to the victim of a crime
Complainant	• an individual presenting a complaint to a tribunal
Compulsory winding up	• winding up by an order of the court
Conciliation	• bringing together the parties to a dispute
Conditions	• major terms in a contract
Consensus ad idem	• a meeting of the minds
Consideration	• the idea that the parties to a contract must exchange promises of value
Consolidation	• bring a number of statutes together into one
Constructive dismissal	• a contract of employment terminated by the employee because of the employers repudiatory conduct
Consumer goods	• goods which are ordinarily intended for private use or consumption
Contract	• legally enforceable agreement
Contract for services	• a contract between an employer and a self employed contractor
Contract of adhesion	• contract under which a party offer terms which are not up for negotiation
Contributory negligence	• partial defence to a negligence claim
Cooling off	• a period provided for under statute within which a consumer who has entered into a credit transaction can cancel the agreement
Corporation	• an organisation treated as an artificial legal person
Criminal law	• a branch of public law describing rules whose breach results in criminal proceedings
Damages	• contractual remedy under which a monetary award is made
Data protection	• legal protection granted to individuals in relation the collection, storage and distribution of personal data about them, using computers
Debentures	• written statement acknowledging a company's indebtedness and

	usually supported by some security
Defendant	• a party against whom a civil claim is brought
Delegated legislation	• law produced by individuals and organisations granted the power by Parliament
Deliverable state	• goods which are in such a condition that the buyer would be bound to accept them
Delivery	• the voluntary transfer of physical possession of the goods from the seller to the buyer
Dictum	• judicial statement in a judgment
Direct discrimination	• less favourable treatment against a particular group
Directive	• a type of EC law which is in effect an instruction to member states to pass a law giving effect to the rules set out in the directive
Director	• person responsible for the management of a registered company
Disability	• a physical or mental impairment which has a substantial long term affect on the person's ability to carry out normal day to day activities
Discharge of contract	• bringing a contract to an end
Disqualification order	• court order issued against a named person preventing them from acting as a director or company promoter for the duration of the order
Doctrine	• general principle of law
Duress	• use of threats to force someone into making a contract
Duty of care	• principle of the tort of negligence recognising the circumstances under which one party has a legal responsibility to another
Economic duress	• using improper economic pressure to induce a contract
Equitable	• literally fair and just, but in a legal sense
Estoppel	• rule of evidence under which a person is prevented from denying the truth of a previous statement of fact
European Union	• an organisation of 15 European member states which consists of the European Community and two other elements or pillars
Exclusion clauses	• contract terms seeking to eliminate specified or general contractual liabilities
Express dismissal	• a contract of employment terminated by the employer with or without notice
Express Terms	• contractual undertakings expressly agreed orally or in writing by the parties to a contract

Extortionate credit bargain	• a credit contract which requires repayments which are grossly exorbitant
Fault liability	• liability associated with evidence of blameworthiness
Force majeure	• clause in a contract making provision for events which would otherwise frustrate the contract
Freedom of contract	• the notion that parties to a contract should be allowed to make their deal without legal interference
Frustration	• a change in circumstances making contractual performance radically different from that envisaged
Gross misconduct	• grave misconduct which constitutes a repudiatory breach of the contract of employment
Implied terms	• contractual obligations which are implied into a contract by operation of the common law or statute
Improvement notice	• an order served by a health and safety inspector requiring a contravention of safety law to be remedied within a specified time
Injunction	• court order requiring someone to do something or not to do something
Insolvency	• condition under which the liabilities of a business exceed its assets
Interlocutory injunction	• temporary injunction
Judicial precedent	• a court decision which will act as a guide for future courts and can only be overruled by a higher court
Jurisdiction	• legal powers of a court or tribunal over particular types of disputes
Law report	• published report of court proceedings containing the court's judgment
Legal aid	• state funded scheme providing financial assistance for legal claims
Legislation	• law made by Parliament
Legislature	• formal law making body of a state in the UK Parliament
Lien	• the unpaid seller's right to keep possession of goods against payment in the event of the buyer's insolvency
Liquidated damages	• claim for damages where the amount being sought has been quantified
Liquidation	• corporate insolvency
Liquidator	• person responsible for managing a company winding up
Litigant	• a party involved in civil proceedings

Member	• a company shareholder
Memorandum of Association	• constitutional document of a company establishing its name, objectives and capital structure
Mens rea	• 'guilty mind', state of mind required for a criminal offence
Misrepresentation	• remedy available to a person induced into making a contract by a false statement
Mutual termination	• a contractual agreement to terminate a contract of employment
Negligence	• a legal claim for damages based upon the plaintiff establishing that the defendant has caused loss by breach of a duty of care
Occupiers liability	• tort imposing a duty on occupiers of premises towards their visitors
Offer	• an unequivocal undertaking to be bound by an acceptance
Official receiver	• an officer attached to al courts with insolvency jurisdiction, employed by the DTI and responsible for insolvency matters
Package holidays	• combination of holiday components in the Package Travel Regulations
Parol contract	• oral contract
Partnership	• an unicorporated business association often referred to as a 'firm'
Passing off	• a legal action in tort available where a business represents its goods or services as those of another business
Persuasive precedent	• a precedent which a court does not have to follow but should take account of in reaching its decision
Plaintiff	• person or organisation bringing a civil action (now a claimant)
Price variation clause	• an express term of a contract which allows one of the parties to change the price in certain circumstances after the contract has been concluded
Prima facie case	• "on the face of it" a case to answer
Principal	• person who appoints an agent to act on his behalf for the purpose of making contracts
Private company	• registered company prohibited from selling its shares to the public
Product liability	• legal basis upon which a person who suffers harm as a result of a defective product can be compensated
Prohibition notice	• a statutory notice served on a trader requiring him to stop trading in unsafe goods of a particular description

Prohibition notice	• an order served by a health and safety inspector requiring that an activity that contravenes safety law should be terminated
Promoter	• someone involved in setting up a company
Property	• ownership
Property misdescription	• expression used to describe the making of false misleading statements by estate agents
Prospectus	• document providing information to the public about a company which is offering its shares
Protected goods	• statutory protection granted to debtors under consumer credit agreements
Public company	• registered company able to sell its securities publicly
Public policy	• concept guiding judicial decision making based on consideration of the public interest
Punitive damages	• damages awarded to punish the defendant for the losses caused
Quantum meruit	• 'as much as he has deserved'
Quoted company	• company whose securities are traded on the Stock Exchange
Receiver	• person appointed to take control of specified property of a company
Reckless statement	• a statement made regardless of whether it is true or false
Registered company	• a corporate body formed under the registration procedures of the Companies Act 1985
Reinstatement	• to re-employ an employee following a dismissal and treat him as if there had been no dismissal
Representation	• statement which induces the making of a contract
Repudiatory breach	• a serious breach of contract which allows the innocent party to accept the breach and regard the contract terminated
Rescind	• to annul or cancel for instance a contract
Res ipsa loquitur	• 'let the thing speak for itself' Rule of evidence under which the claimant is relieved of the burden of proof
Respondent	• an individual defending a complaint before a tribunal or the party
Restitutio in integrum	• returning everything to the state as it was before

Retention of title clause	• an express term of a contract under which the seller retains the ownership of goods until certain conditions, such as full payment, have been met
Rights issue	• an issue of new shares offered first to existing shareholders
Risk assessment	• a comprehensive survey of organisational, job, workplace and individual factors that affect health and safety at work
Sale of goods	• a contract involving the exchange of the ownership of goods in return for money
Satisfactory quality	• statutory standard of quality demanded of goods sold by a seller in the course of business
Securities	• investments in a company
Sexual harassment	• conduct of a sexual nature that is unwanted, unreasonable and offensive to the recipient
Shareholder	• person holding shares in a company who enjoys all the rights attached to the shares
Shares	• a unit of company capital which a member can own
Solicitor	• lawyer who is a general practitioner of the law and who has limited rights of audience to represent a client in court proceedings
Specific goods	• goods which have been identified and agreed upon at the time the contract is made
Specific performance	• equitable remedy under which the court orders a contracting party to carry out their promises
Statute	• an Act of Parliament
Strict liability	• liability imposed without fault
Balance of probabilities	• standard of proof, "more likely than not"
Tort	• a civil wrong, the remedy for which is an award of damages
Trade descriptions	• descriptions applied to goods or services by business sellers
Transfer of risk	• the passing over from the seller to the buyer the risk of accidental loss or damage to goods
Trespasser	• an entrant onto land without legal authority
Trust and confidence	• implied term in a contract of employment signifying mutual respect
Uberrimae fidei	• a state of utmost good faith

Ultra vires	• legal doctrine expressing the proposition that corporate bodies cannot act outside their powers
Unascertained goods	• goods which have been generally described but not specifically identified or singled out at the time the contract is made
Unconditional appropriation	• a final irrevocable setting aside of goods to be used in the performance of a contract, for example by an act of delivery
Undue influence	• unlawful pressure put on someone when they make a contract
Unfair dismissal	• dismissal without good reason contrary to statute
Unilateral action	• an act done by one party only
Unliquidated damages	• claim for damages where the amount is not quantified
Vicarious liability	• legal liability imposed upon one person for the unlawful act of another
Victimisation	• less favourable treatment because a person has given evidence or brought proceedings under the discrimination legislation
Visitor	• person lawfully present on land or premises
Volenti non fit injuria	• defence in tort when the claimant has accepted the risk
Warranties	• minor terms which if broken enable only a claim for damages to be brought
Winding up	• process by which registered company is brought to an end
Working environment	• arrangements of a workplace including physical and psychological conditions of work
Wrongful dismissal	• dismissal in a wrongful manner by contravening notice requirements in breach of contract

Chapter 1
The Legal System

The Legal Framework

The principal objective of a legal system is the establishment of rules designed in the broadest sense to regulate relationships. Human societies are highly complex social structures. Without systems of rules or codes of conduct to control them, such societies have difficulty in maintaining their cohesion, and gradually break up. The interdependence of each member of a community with its other members creates a continuous interaction between individuals and groups and this contact inevitably can lead to occasional disagreement and conflict. In a Western culture like ours, which recognises that people should have the freedom to express their individualism, the realisation of that freedom can result in the infringement of the rights of others. Someone operating a commercial enterprise by selling second hand cars in the street outside his house, or building an extension, or holding regular all night parties may treat these activities as the exercise of basic personal freedoms. They will however give rise to conflict if neighbours resent the street being turned into a used vehicle lot, or find the light to their windows and gardens cut out by the new building, or that they cannot sleep at night for noise. Where interests conflict in this way the law attempts to reconcile differences by referring their solution to established principles and rules which have been developed to clarify individual rights and obligations. The relationships between neighbours are but a small part of the complex pattern of relationships most people are involved in and which the law attempts to regulate.

Moral Rules

However the law is not the sole binding agent of our social structure. It is not only legal rules which are responsible for guaranteeing social cohesion. Institutions which create legal rules are merely one facet of the wider institutional structure of our society. Political, economic, commercial, cultural and religious institutions are amongst those located in the broader social fabric and which contribute to what we term our *society*. Their contribution also includes the development of rules. Schools and religious institutions for instance recognise a responsibility for the teaching of ethics and morality, and this reminds us that we should not assume rule making to be the sole prerogative of the law. The rules and codes of conduct developed from our sense of moral justice and our perceptions of fairness and unfairness are important determinants of our behaviour. Like legal rules, moral rules guide our conduct and inform us how we should behave in given circumstances. Rules of this kind are described as *normative*. They indicate how we ought to conduct ourselves.

A major difference between legal and moral rules is seen in the sanctions which apply if they are broken. Breach of legal rules carries a potential formal sanction, proceedings before a court followed by a court order. Breaching the moral code does not of itself trigger any formal consequence; we may however feel personally discredited by how we have behaved and find that others who are aware of our conduct avoid or criticise us. So it may be that our neighbour keeps the noise down at night motivated more by a sense of what is fair and reasonable than through any concern over legal sanctions.

In business, ethical considerations also play a role in informing organisational behaviour, although usually in a more diluted form, for the personality of the individuals making up the organisation has a tendency to be subsumed within the personality of the organisation itself. Cynics may argue that businesses which appear to be guided by ethical standards in their business dealings are simply recognising the value of goodwill and cost of legal sanctions and are thus, in effect, protecting their profits. It has also been argued that businesses are keen to self regulate as a way of avoiding the imposition of legal controls which take away their freedom of action by determining their behaviour for them.

The Business Environment

Our study of these legal rules is of course constrained by the particular field of law we are concerned with, the law applying to the business environment, and a book devoted to a study of this kind focuses specifically on the legal relationships that are a product of business activity and the legal rules which have developed in response to it. Essentially businesses are provider organisations, selling goods and services to anyone who requires them. The customers of a business are usually referred to as consumers. They may be other businesses themselves, but they also include of course individuals, *ultimate consumers*, who use the goods and services for their own private benefit. Examining the business world in any detail reveals far more complex legal relationships than the simple neighbour example given above. We discover an environment in which a richly diverse range of transactions are constantly performed; where resources of labour, capital, and land are being acquired and disposed of, various forms of property are being bought and sold, information and advice is given and sought, and decisions are regularly being made which have an impact on the owners, managers and customers of the organisations with which they are associated. In short we are seeing a sophisticated market economy conducting its operations.

At first glance the business environment may appear to have little relevance to anyone other than those who are directly associated with it, such as business managers. In practice the impact of business is experienced by everyone. We can see this when we consider ourselves in our role as consumers, that is as users of products and services. Whether we are buying clothes, household goods, holidays, shares, having the car repaired, opening a bank account, taking a job or renting a flat we participate in a business relationship. It does not always have to be a formal matter, and usually will not be. But all these activities are carried on within a legal framework which attempts to set out the responsibilities and obligations of the participants.

Business organisations sit at the centre of a web of relationships which have a strong legal dimension to them. For instance, a business may take decisions on the basis of expert advice provided by a professional advisor in return for payment of a fee or charge. Inaccurate or incomplete advice relied upon by the business may cause it to suffer commercial damage. If this occurs the business may have a legal remedy against the advisor, and will seek to recover any losses it has sustained. Similarly, within the organisation legal relationships exist between managers, owners and staff. Thus, to take one example, directors of a limited company are accountable to the shareholders in general meeting, and can be dismissed from their office by a company resolution in circumstances where they have been guilty of commercial incompetence or malpractice. Exploring the law as it applies to business thus involves examining the legal framework within which all businesses, from the multinational corporations to the one member businesses, pursue their commercial objectives. We have noted that this framework has to do with the relationships their business activity creates, but what are the purposes which underpin legal intervention in business affairs?

The Purpose of a System of Business Law

Complex, affluent, property owning societies develop detailed and sophisticated rules to regulate themselves, and in the United Kingdom as in most modern states almost every aspect of human activity is either directly or indirectly affected by law. These laws seek to achieve different purposes. One major classification in any legal system involves distinguishing between those legal rules which are concerned with private rights and obligations, a branch of law referred to as *civil* law, and those whose primary purpose is the welfare of society generally, and its protection by means of rules that seek to prevent anti-social forms of behaviour, supported by the power to punish those who break them. This is the *criminal* law.

Legal rules in the field of business are designed to fulfil certain primary purposes. These include the remedying of private grievances, the control of anti-social activities and the regulation of harmful activities.

The remedying of private grievances

Various branches of law are concerned with recognising personal rights which can be enforced by means of legal proceedings if they are infringed, or where there is a threat to infringe them. One of these branches is the law of *tort*. It is based upon the existence of a set of obligations referred to as *torts*, or civil wrongs, which have been evolved by the courts as a response to the need for established codes of conduct to protect people from certain types of harm. Tortious obligations are imposed by law, rather than arising by agreement between the parties as is the case with contractual obligations. In effect the law of tort recognises specific legal rights, which entitle anyone for whom those rights have been infringed to sue the wrongdoer for compensation. The most significant civil wrong is the tort of negligence which can provide a remedy when an individual suffers harm as a result of the *fault* of another e.g. medical negligence, careless driving. (see Chapter 7)

The law of contract is a further example of a branch of law dealing in private rights and obligations. Contractual agreements involve the making of promises which are legally enforceable. A party to a contract therefore has the right to take legal action against the other party to the agreement in the event of that person being in breach of his contractual obligations. We will examine the principles of the law of contract in Chapters (8-10).

Both the law of contract and the law of tort are crucial to the effective functioning of the business environment. Without the ability to enter into binding agreements businesses would be left fully exposed to the risk of their transactions being unilaterally terminated by the other contracting party. Such vulnerability would seriously undermine business confidence and would hamper economic activity generally, and without the ability to seek compensation and redress for wrongs committed against them businesses could suffer significant economic harm. Consider for instance a situation where a small under-insured business could obtain no compensation following the total destruction of its stock and premises due to negligent repair work carried out to an adjoining gas main by the gas company, or where a supplier of goods has delivered them only to find that the buyer refuses to pay for them.

The control of anti-social activities

This is essentially the task of the criminal law. Whilst it is not possible to prevent crimes from being committed, the presence of penal sanctions, such as imprisonment and fines, which are used to support the criminal code, can act as a deterrent to the commission of an offence.

There is no adequate definition of a crime. Lord Diplock in *Knuller v. Director of Public Prosecutions* 1972 attempted to pin-point the essential differences between civil and criminal law when he said, *"Civil liability is concerned with the relationship of one citizen to another; criminal liability is concerned with the relationship of a citizen to society organised as a state."*

Businesses, like individuals, are subject to the criminal law. Of the wide range of offences that an organisation might commit in the course of its business, the following provide some illustrations:

- offences in the field of consumer protection. These are many and varied. They include offences connected with false trade descriptions applied to goods and services, consumer credit arrangements such as engaging in activities requiring a licence but where no licence has been granted, and safety obligations for certain manufactured items, for instance oil heaters and electric blankets, which must meet standards laid down under government regulations; (considered in Chapter 12)

- offences in the field of employment, such as a contravention of the obligations owed to employees under health and safety legislation; (considered in Chapter 7)

- offences connected with the operation of registered companies, such as failure to file accounts or the insertion of untrue statements in a prospectus; (considered in Chapter 4)

- offences in relation to tax liability, such as the making of false returns.

Enforcement of the criminal code is a duty imposed upon a range of agencies. The *Crown Prosecution Service* (the CPS), set up in 1985, is responsible for the prosecution of all criminal offences which have resulted from police investigations. Investigation of potential liability in certain specific fields of the criminal law, and the bringing of prosecutions where appropriate, is placed in the hands of specialised agencies. *Trading Standards Officers* employed by local authorities are responsible for investigation and prosecution of that part of the criminal code dealing with consumer protection, the *Health and Safety Executive* through its inspectorate, deals with criminal aspects of health and safety law, and the *Department of Trade and Industry* has the task of investigating breaches of company legislation where criminal offences are involved. These agencies investigate complaints made to them. They also rely on inspection as a method of systemised investigation.

The regulation of harmful activities

Methods of legal regulation include licensing, registration and inspection. These are useful mechanisms for exercising effective control over a range of activities, which, if uncontrolled, could be physically, economically and socially harmful. As we have noted above powers of inspection, supported by enforcement mechanisms, are granted to factory inspectors working for the Health and Safety Executive. The inspection of work places such as factories and building sites enables inspectors to ascertain whether safety legislation is being complied with, and that employees' physical requirements are thus being met. Certain types of trading practices which are potentially anti-competitive can only be pursued legitimately if the agreements in which they are contained are registered with the Director General of Fair Trading, under the Restrictive Trade Practices Act 1976. Even then they are only legally permissible if they are approved by the Restrictive Trade Practices Court. Additionally anyone in the business of providing credit facilities is obliged to register under the Consumer Credit Act 1974 with the Director General of Fair Trading before being legally permitted to lend money. The aim is to eliminate unscrupulous finance dealers from the credit market, overcoming the social problems which arise when poorer members of society borrow at high rates of interest which they are unable to afford, often in an effort to extricate themselves from other debts. And in cases of alleged malpractice in the management of registered companies the Department of Trade and Industry has the power to carry out investigations into the affairs of companies, for instance to establish the true ownership of shares in a company.

The Importance of Law to Business

The legal system affects businesses and individuals alike. Every aspect of business life, from formation and operation to dissolution, occurs within an environment of legal regulation. We have seen that many purposes are being pursued in applying legal regulation to business activity. In broad terms the underlying characteristics of business law may be seen as the dual aims of:

(a)   providing a practical and comprehensive framework of legal rules and principles to assist the organisation in its commercial affairs; whilst at the same time

(b)   ensuring a sufficient level of protection for the legitimate interests of those who come into direct contact with it. This includes not only members of the public in their capacity as consumers, but also business creditors and the employees and owners of business enterprises.

There appears to be one fundamental and compelling reason why business organisations are likely to seek to comply with the law. If they fail to do so it will cost them money, either directly or indirectly. A business which is in breach of law, whether the civil law or the criminal law, will in most cases suffer from the breach commercially.

The commercial consequences to an organisation which has been found to have broken or otherwise failed to comply with the law includes the possibility of:

- an action for damages against the business, brought by someone seeking financial compensation from it. Such an action may be the result of a breach of contract committed by the business, or be in respect of some form of tortious liability it has incurred. An alternative claim brought against it could be for an injunction restraining it from pursuing a particular course of action;

- a claim that the action of the business is devoid of legal effect because it has failed to follow procedures which bind it. For instance, a limited company cannot act unless it has correctly followed the registration procedures laid down by statute, and has received a certificate of incorporation. Nor can it alter its own constitution, its memorandum and articles of association, unless this is done in accordance with relevant statutory procedures regarding notice periods, the holding of a meeting and the need to secure an appropriate majority of votes cast;

- the loss of an opportunity to take some form of legal action, because the time limit for doing so has passed, for instance bringing a late appeal against an unfavourable planning decision;

- a prosecution brought against it alleging breach of the criminal law, resulting in a fine, or in certain circumstances the seizure of assets;

- the exercise of enforcement action against it for its failure to comply with some legal requirement, for example to take steps to remedy a serious hazard to health, as a result of which its business operations are suspended;

- the bringing of a petition to have the organisation brought to an end. A registered company can for example be wound up compulsorily by its unpaid creditors.

As most commercial enterprises are profit maximisers these outcomes can be seen as interfering in the pursuit of basic organisational aims.

Thus at an organisation level there are sound commercial reasons for keeping properly informed about the law and complying with it, apart from any moral or social responsibility for acting within the law. Moreover, legal proceedings often attract public attention and result in adverse publicity. Also individuals engaged in managing a business may find themselves dismissed and facing civil and/or criminal liability if they are responsible for serious errors of judgment which carry legal consequences, such as negligent or dishonest performance in handling a company's financial affairs.

Developing Legal Knowledge and Skills

Usually it is not possible for people in business to find the time to develop the skills to cope with all the legal demands of operating a business, however there will remain sound reasons for acquiring at least a basic level of legal knowledge and skills and devoting some time to legal issues as and when they arise. This is because:

- many straightforward legal problems can be resolved simply by means of a letter or a telephone call to the other party involved. Legal advice has to be paid for, and in some situations will be both an unnecessary expense, and a time consuming activity;

- certain legal problems require immediate action, for example, what rights the employer has to dismiss an employee against whom an allegation of sexual misconduct has been made; or what rights a buyer has to reject goods delivered late by the seller;

- the daily routine of a business involves frequent encounters with matters of a legal nature, such as examining contracts, signing cheques, health and safety, negotiating deals and organising the workforce. It would be impractical to seek professional advice regularly in these routine areas;

- many business activities are closely legally regulated, and a working knowledge of them is essential if the business is to function effectively. For example a business providing credit facilities needs to employ staff who are fully aware of the strict legal requirements regulating such transactions;

- when expert advice and assistance is being sought the effectiveness of the process of consultation is assisted if the precise issues can be identified from the outset, and relevant records and materials can be presented at the time. In addition, when the advice is given it will be of little value in the possession of someone who can make no real sense of it;

- managing a business effectively demands a working knowledge of the legal implications not only of what is being decided, but also of the processes by which it is decided. For instance company directors ought to be familiar with the basic principles of the law of company meetings, since it is by means of such meetings that important decision making is achieved.

Law Making Institutions

Until the 1st January 1973 English law was created by two, separate, law making institutions, the courts and Parliament. However in 1973 the United Kingdom became a member of the European Economic Community, the effect of which in legal terms was to introduce a new, third, law making source. The impact of this fundamental change has been considerable, even though there are many areas of activity which remain outside the jurisdiction of the law making bodies of the European Union (EU). Business operations however fall squarely within the remit of the work of the European Union. The European Union is considered in Chapter 2.

To acquire a proper understanding of the law it is necessary to consider the work of the law makers, and examine the methods by which they create law. In an historical context it was the courts which laid down the original foundations of our law, and so it is appropriate to consider their law making role before examining the contribution of Parliament as the supreme UK law maker.

The Courts of England and Wales

For the purpose of the administration of justice in England and Wales two separate court structures exist, one dealing with civil law matters and the other criminal matters. Some courts exercise both a civil and criminal jurisdiction. An example is provided by the Magistrates courts, which are primarily criminal courts but which also exercise a limited but nevertheless important civil jurisdiction in family matters.

An appeals structure gives the parties involved in any form of legal proceedings the opportunity to appeal against the decision of the trial court on points of law or fact. The trial court is the court in which the case is first tried, and in which evidence is given on oath to the court by witnesses appearing for the parties involved, to enable the court to establish for the purposes of the case the relevant material facts. The court in which a case is first tried is known as a court of *first instance*. Usually *leave to appeal* must be granted either by the trial court or the appellate court although certain appeals are available as of right.

The Civil Courts

In a civil court an action is commenced by a *plaintiff* (now a claimant) who sues the other party, called the *defendant*. If either party takes the case before a higher court on appeal that party is known as the *appellant* and the other as the *respondent*.

Before commencing proceedings the plaintiff must decide whether the case is worth bringing. This is likely to involve a number of considerations including costs, time, the complexity of the action, and the resources of the defendant. In 1999 new procedures were introduced to promote early settlement of cases and where possible direct cases from the courts towards cheaper and quicker resolutions. The main thrust of the reforms is to encourage greater openness between opponents and require lawyers to follow agreed steps from the moment a claim is envisaged. The aim is to reduce spiralling costs and delays in legal action. Judges as trial managers are required to set strict timetables for cases and ensure that deadlines are met. In an attempt to make the administration of justice more understandable to the layman, new terminology has also been introduced for example:

- a *plaintiff* is now a *claimant*;

- a *High court writ* is now a *claim form*;

- *minors* are now called *children*;

- witnesses are no longer *subpoenaed* but *summoned*;

- *pleadings* are replaced by a *statement of claim*.

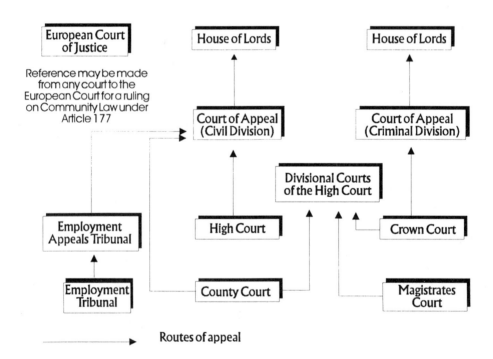

Figure 1.1   *Civil and Criminal Courts structure in England and Wales, including Employment Tribunals*

Law Making by the Courts

The two major domestic sources of law making are the courts and the legislature. Whereas the legislature creates law through the introduction of statutes, the law making role of the courts is quite different. Parliament enjoys a virtually unlimited lawmaking capacity. The courts on the other hand are subject to significant restrictions in their role as lawmakers. This is entirely proper since the courts are manned by members of the judiciary, the judges, who are neither elected by the public to this office nor are accountable to the public for the way in which they discharge their responsibilities.

The primary role of the courts, and the various tribunals which supplement the courts system, is the resolution of legal disputes which are brought before them. This process has a history dating back to Norman times.

In order to resolve a dispute it is necessary to have a reference point; some identifiable rule or principle which can be applied in order to solve the problem. One approach is simply to treat each case on its own merits, but such a system would hardly be just for decisions would turn on the character of the individual judge, whose values, prejudices, qualities of analysis and reasoning power would dominate the decision making process. Such a system would be unpredictable and capricious. English law, in common with other law making systems, adopted an approach that sought to achieve a level of certainty and consistency. It did this by means of a process referred to as *stare decisis*, literally *standing by the decision*. Today we talk of the doctrine of judicial precedent. Under the doctrine of judicial precedent, the successor to the stare decisis system, judges when deciding cases must take into account relevant precedents, that is earlier cases based upon materially similar sets of facts. Whether a court is bound to follow an earlier case of a similar kind can be a matter of considerable complexity, however the general rule is that the decisions of higher courts are binding on lower courts within the hierarchical courts structure seen. This structure can be seen in Figure 1.1.

English law became enshrined in the precedent system, and much of our modern law is still found in the decisions of the courts arrived at by resolving the cases brought before them. Not surprisingly this body of law is referred to as case law. It is these cases, or precedents, which make up the contents of the law reports, the published reports of court proceedings containing the judgment given in the case. The bulk of the law of contract (Chapters 8-10) and the law of tort (Chapter 7) is judge made law, or, as it is more usually known, the common law.

In addition to developing and refining the common law, the judges in modern times have played an increasingly important role in the task of interpreting and applying statutory provisions.

The meaning of common law

In its modern usage the expression common law has come to mean law other than that contained in statutory provisions. Common law in this sense means judge made law embodied in case decisions. However, the expression common law is also sometimes used to describe, in a broader sense, the *type* of legal system that operates in England and Wales, a system which has been adopted by countries all over the world and especially those in the Commonwealth.

The common law of England dates back to the Norman Conquest and has its origins in the decisions of the royal judges who attempted to develop and apply principles of law *common* to the whole country. This they did by modifying and adapting rules of Norman law, and rules contained in Saxon local custom. The development of the common law has involved an evolutionary process extending over hundreds of years. Through the process England and Wales was rewarded with a unified and coherent body of law which remains the foundation upon which significant areas of our law, such as the law of contract and tort are based.

The judgment of the court

Whatever the nature of a case coming before a court the most vital legal aspect of the legal proceedings comes at the end of the trial when judgment is delivered. Whereas certain parts of the judgment will be binding for the future, other parts of the judgment will have merely persuasive authority whenever the case is considered by a future court. These ideas need further explanation.

When a decision is reached on a dispute before a superior court, such as the High Court, Court of Appeal or House of Lords, the judges will announce their decision by making speeches known as judgments. Within a judgment, the judges will refer to numerous matters, such as the relevant legal principles which are drawn from existing cases or statutes, a review of the facts of the case, their opinion on the relevant law, their actual decision and the reasons for it. For the parties to an action, the matter they are most concerned with is the actual decision, that is who has won the case. The main issue of relevance to the law, however, is the reason for the decision. This is known as the *ratio decidendi* of the case (the reason for deciding). The *ratio* expresses the underlying legal principle relied on in reaching the decision and it is this which constitutes the binding precedent. As we have seen this means that if a lower court in a later case is faced with a similar dispute it will in general be bound to apply the earlier *ratio decidendi*.

All other matters referred to in a judgment are termed *obiter dicta* (things said by the way). The *obiter* forms persuasive precedent and may be taken into account by a court in a later similar case, however the court is not bound to follow it.

The decision of the House of Lords in *Smith v. Stages and Another* 1989 illustrates the distinction between *ratio* and *obiter*. In this case it was necessary to determine the extent to which an employer may be made liable for the actions of an employee, and in particular when an employee can be said to be acting in the course of his employment. The action was brought on behalf of an employee, who as a passenger in the defendant's car, suffered personal injuries as a result of the negligent driving of the defendant, a fellow employee. Despite the fact that the employers neither required nor authorised the journey by car to and from their particular workplace they were joined as second defendants on a claim that they were vicariously liable for the driver's negligence. The House of Lords held that here the employers were vicariously liable for the employee's negligent driving. The court decided that employees who are required to travel to and from non regular workplaces, and are in receipt of wages for doing so, remain within the course of their employment, even if they have a choice as to the mode and time of travel. This statement forms the *ratio* of the judgment and is binding on a lower court if faced with a similar factual situation.

In the course of the judgment however a number of suggestions were made by the House of Lords in relation to the question as to when an employee is acting in the course of his employment during travelling time. The receipt of wages would indicate that an employee was travelling in his employer's time, and acting in the course of his employment. Equally so would an employee travelling in the employer's time between different workplaces. An employee travelling in his employer's time from his ordinary residence to a workplace, other than his regular workplace, to the scene of an emergency such as a fire, accident or mechanical breakdown of plant, would also be acting in the course of his employment. Deviations or interruptions of a journey undertaken in the course of employment unless merely incidental would normally take an employee outside the course of his employment. All of these suggestions are *obiter dicta,* persuasive authority which may or may not be followed by a lower court dealing with a similar case.

A court with suitable jurisdiction has the power to declare the decision in a previous case no longer good law. This can be done when there is evidence that the previous court did not accurately interpret the law, or when the later court is of the view that the ratio of the earlier case is no longer sustainable or desirable. Where overruling takes place, the case which has been overruled is considered 'bad law' and does not have to be followed by the present court or any future court.

Reversing occurs when an appeal court overturns the decision of the court below it from which the appeal came. If the appeal court agrees with the lower court's decision it is said to affirm it.

Statute

Within the United Kingdom the primary source of law is made by Parliament in the form of Statutes. Statutes or Acts of Parliament are also referred to as legislation and in the fields of commercial, company and consumer protection law there are numerous examples of major statutes that contain the fundamental rules. The Sale of Goods Act 1979, the Trade Descriptions Act 1968, the Supply of Goods and Services Act 1982, the Consumer Protection Act 1987 and the Data Protection Act 1998 all contain provisions conferring rights on consumers in commercial transactions. The Companies Act 1985 contains the rules relating to the formation and operation of companies. These statutes are referred to throughout the book.

While primary legislation is a major source of law, many statutes contemplate further law making by means of delegated legislation. Numerous Statutory Instruments contain a multitude of regulations which have the force of law, and provide a convenient means of amending previous statutory provisions. Under the umbrella of the Health and Safety at Work etc. Act 1974 the Secretary of State for Employment is given authority on the advice of the Health and Safety Commission to make regulations on a wide range of matters. It is by this means that the previous law on health and safety at work is in the process of being replaced and refined.

In Chapter 2 we will focus on how Statutory Instruments may be used to incorporate European Community legislation into the domestic law of the United Kingdom. The Unfair Terms in Consumer Contract Regulations 1994 (1999) were introduced to give effect to the 1993 European Directive on Unfair Terms in Consumer Contracts. The Package Travel, Package Holiday and Package Tours Regulations 1992 are designed to implement the EC directive on Package Holidays (see Chapter 11). Statutes and Statutory Instruments are only enacted of course after undergoing a strict parliamentary process. In addition, draft Codes of Practice require the approval of both Houses of Parliament and only come into effect on such date as the Secretary of State appoints.

Codes of Practice have an increasingly important role in the regulation of business. Their primary function is to provide guidance. While a failure to observe the provision of a code of practice does not of itself make a person liable to legal proceedings before a court or tribunal, compliance or non compliance with a code is admissible in evidence.

When a dispute comes before a court it is the task of the court to hear the evidence, identify the relevant law and apply it. The legal principles which the court has to apply may be common law principles. Often however they will be principles, or rules, which are contained in statutes. Where this is so, the court has to ascertain the meaning of the statute in order to apply it, and sometimes this can cause problems for a court because it discovers that the language of the statute is not entirely clear.

The courts take the view that their responsibility is to discern Parliament's will or intention from the legislation under consideration.

Statutory Interpretation

In relation to statutes the primary role of the courts and tribunals is to apply the legal rules within them to conflict situations. Inevitably this function involves interpreting the meaning of particular legal rules and so setting precedents which provide guidance to future courts and tribunals as to how these rules should be applied. The task of the courts in interpreting statutory provisions is to attempt to discover Parliament's intention and this should be achieved primarily by examining the specific words of the statute.

An example of a statutory provision may help to illustrate this judicial function. In the Employment Rights Act 1996 there are numerous provisions which confer rights on employees. In particular if a qualified employee believes that he has been dismissed without good reason he may under section 111 present a complaint of unfair dismissal against his employer before an Employment Tribunal. The Act provides however that there are strict time limits to be complied with, otherwise the right to present a complaint will be lost.

Section 111(2) of the Act states that .... *"an employment tribunal shall not consider a complaint under this section unless it is presented to the tribunal before the end of the period of three months beginning with the effective date of termination or within such further period as the tribunal considers reasonable in a case where it is satisfied that it was not reasonably practicable for the complaint to be presented before the end of the period of three months."*

The legal rule is stating therefore, in relatively straightforward terms, that if a dismissed employee wants to complain of unfair dismissal before an Employment Tribunal he must start the proceedings within three months, but if he fails to do so the tribunal still has a discretion to hear the case if it was not reasonably practicable for him to present it within the time limit. If a legal dispute arises over whether an unfair dismissal claim has been presented within the time limits it is the function of the courts and tribunals to attempt to resolve the conflict by applying the exact wording of s.111(2) to the factual situation before it. The subsection requires the Employment Tribunal therefore to ask itself one or possibly two questions:

1.   Has the complaint been brought within the three months time limit prescribed in the section?

2.   If not, was it reasonably practicable to present the complaint within the time limit?

If the answer to the first question is no and the answer to the second question is yes then the tribunal should not proceed to hear the complaint of unfair dismissal. If the reverse is true however and either the complaint is within the time limits or it was not reasonably practicable to present it in time then the tribunal does have jurisdiction to proceed.

There are many case decisions which over the years have provided guidance to Employment Tribunals as to the approach to be adopted in addressing these questions.

If a tribunal decide that the complaint was not presented within the time period it would still proceed to hear it if it was not reasonably practicable to present the complaint in time. Parliament has left it to the courts and tribunals therefore to determine the issue of reasonable practicability in any given case. Reasons for late claims brought before tribunals have included postal delays, bad advice from lawyers or civil servants, and obstructive employers. Case decisions made in relation to these reasons provide guidance and in some cases lay down precedents for future cases.

To summarise therefore it is possible to say that the law on time limits for presenting a complaint of unfair dismissal is most certainly contained within s.111(2) of the Employment Rights Act 1996 but also as interpreted in the numerous precedents of our courts and tribunals.

The Resolution of Business Disputes

While the High Court has an important role to play in hearing civil disputes concerning large sums of money the vast majority of civil legal actions which go to court are dealt with at County Court level. Changes in the jurisdiction of the County Courts, has increased their workload by passing over to them cases which previously would have been heard before the High Court.

Not all civil disputes however are resolved by means of court proceedings. Many cases are dealt with instead before tribunals. The workload of tribunals has been steadily increasing. Collectively tribunals now handle in the region of six times more work than the High Court and County Court combined. One important field in which they are used is in the handling of employment disputes. These are heard before Employment Tribunals.

We begin by looking at the organisations and individuals who are available to assist those with a legal problem.

Sources of Legal Advice and Information

Many sources of legal advice and information are available to a consumer or a trader who has a legal problem. He may be able to research it himself by looking at law books in a library, but more usually he will seek outside help. If the trader is a member of a trade or professional association it is probable that he will be able to obtain legal guidance from such a body, particularly if the question is one which is closely associated with the operation or regulation of his business.

In relation to legal enquiries of a general nature, the Citizen's Advice Bureau (CAB) may be able to point a consumer in the right direction, or provide the information which he requires. In addition, there are a number of law centres which provide a similar, though more specialist, role in giving legal advice and acting on behalf of clients. Law centres, however, tend to deal with legal problems arising in relation to social issues such as housing, immigration, consumer and employee rights. They do not usually take on the role of advising businessmen in relation to commercial matters.

Lawyers

The most obvious source of advice and legal information is the solicitor. Larger business organisations may have their own legal department or in-house solicitor to provide a comprehensive legal service for the business. These permanently employed lawyers will deal with such matters as conveyancing, drawing up contracts, registering intellectual property rights, advising management on day to day legal matters, designing procedures to ensure compliance by the business with its legal requirements and conducting litigation on its behalf.

Smaller business organisations cannot usually justify the expense of a legal department and will use *solicitors* in private practice to deal with their legal affairs. Solicitors are the general practitioners of the law, although within any particular firm individual solicitors will usually specialise in one or two areas of law. If a businessman refers a legal problem to solicitor and the solicitor requires further specialist help or advice in order to deal with it, the solicitor can obtain the opinion of a *barrister*. The barrister, or counsel, usually specialises in a much narrower field of law than the solicitor. A businessman cannot approach a barrister directly for legal help but must first use a solicitor. The solicitor can refer the matter to a barrister if he feels that it is necessary. The main functions of the barrister are to provide legal opinions, to draw pleadings in preparation for litigation, and to act as an advocate in court. A solicitor cannot always act as an advocate without a barrister because the solicitor has only limited rights of audience before the courts. He is allowed to appear before a Magistrates Court, a County Court and, in certain circumstances, a Crown Court without a barrister. He is unable to appear in the

High Court or any of the appeal courts and must use a barrister if he intends to conduct a case in one of these courts.

Communications between a client and a solicitor or barrister are subject to legal professional privilege. This means that the lawyer is duty bound not to disclose the communication to any other party without the authority of the client. In practice the effect of legal professional privilege is that the client can disclose all of the information which is relevant to his legal problem without fear that the information may be used against him at some later stage. The purpose of the rule is to ensure that the client does not hold back information which might be relevant to the legal problem which has arisen. This allows the lawyer to have all of the facts and to make a proper decision as to the course of action which is in the client's best interests.

In July 1995 *conditional fee arrangements*, often referred to as no win no fee arrangements became available for personal injury, insolvency and human rights cases. If the case is won solicitors can charge a success fee of up to double their normal fee. This is to compensate for the risk of not being paid if they lose. The amount of the success fee is reflected by the degree of risk involved. Should the case be lost the plaintiff, under conditional fee arrangements, will have no liability for his own solicitors costs but is still potentially liable for his opponent's costs. This risk for prospective plaintiffs can and should be covered by after-the-event insurance. The Law Society has developed and approved an insurance package called Accident Line Protect, designed to be used in conjunction with conditional fees. At the cost of £85 this insurance cover is however only available where the solicitors are members of the *Law Society's Accident Line Scheme so* guaranteeing that they are experts in personal injury work .The Law Society recommend that the conditional fee charged should not in any event exceed 25% of the damage recovered. There is no doubt that through this scheme many more accident victims particularly those at the workplace, have been encouraged to seek and obtain legal redress, when otherwise they would have been discouraged to do so because of the risk of substantial legal costs. One notable case commenced in September 1996 under conditional fee arrangements was personal injury claim brought against the tobacco industry. Here solicitors had been prepared to accept the risk of an estimated two million pounds in costs in proceedings which are expected to take years to get to court.

Suing in the County Court

Before a business takes a decision to sue in the County Court, for example for an outstanding debt, there are a number of matters which must be considered carefully. Probably the most important factor will be that of cost, both in terms of money and in terms of the time and resources which must be invested in legal proceedings. Most of the plaintiff's costs will eventually be payable by the defendant if the plaintiff wins his case. However the plaintiff has a contract with his solicitor and is bound under that contract to pay the solicitor's fees, and disbursements such as court fees, regardless of the outcome of the case. The plaintiff must therefore spend all of this money himself in the hope of later recovering it from the defendant. Even if the plaintiff is successful, he may not be able to obtain an order that the defendant pays all of his legal costs because a defendant can challenge the amount of a successful plaintiff's legal bill. This is done in a *taxation of costs* in which the court will require the defendant to pay only those costs which were reasonably and necessarily incurred by the plaintiff in the action. After a taxation, the plaintiff will usually have to pay some part of his own legal costs. These in effect are deducted from whatever damages he has recovered from the defendant.

Another important consideration, closely associated with the question of costs, is whether the defendant will actually be able to satisfy any judgment which is eventually made against him. If the defendant is a "man of straw", and has no resources, the plaintiff will be wasting his money by pursuing him in the courts. He may end up by having to pay all of his own legal costs and by getting them back from the defendant by instalments of one a month, or by not getting them back at all. For this reason it is essential that the financial circumstances of the potential defendant are investigated before proceedings are issued against him. There is no formal procedure for this type of investigation, so the plaintiff will simply have to conduct it in the best way that he can.

In making the decision to sue someone, a business must also be aware that the legal process is slow. It may take one to four years to obtain judgment against a defendant, depending on the complexity of the case and its particular circumstances. In extreme cases, litigants have suffered mental illness or depression as a result of involvement with litigation. There is recognised mental condition called litigation neurosis. Involvement in litigation over a long period of time is certainly a drain on the resources of the parties in terms of time, money and mental energy.

Publicity is another important factor. Proceedings before the courts are held in public and can be attended by anyone, including the press. Depending on the circumstances, a business may be inviting adverse publicity and a loss of goodwill by taking legal proceedings. If the legal action is being taken against an important customer, the damage to ongoing business relationships can be substantial.

In addition to these factors, it is self evident that the plaintiff must have a sound legal basis for his claim and sufficient evidence to support it. This evidence may be documentary or may be provided by witnesses. In the case of the verbal evidence by witnesses, the credibility of the witnesses will be an important consideration. It may also be necessary to employ expert witnesses if the subject matter of the dispute is technical in nature, for example if it centres around a mechanical or electrical problem.

Negotiation, compromise and settlement

For one or more of the reasons given above, the parties to a dispute will usually try to reach a settlement without the necessity of taking legal proceedings. Negotiations will take place before legal proceedings are issued and will usually continue as an ongoing process right up to the date of the trial. If both parties are prepared to litigate, this is probably an indication that there is some merit in the case that each of them is arguing. If a compromise can be agreed this will probably result in the saving of costs, time and adverse publicity.

Employment Tribunals

Tribunals are an alternative method to the courts used to handle certain types of specific disputes. In general they tend to be quicker, less formal and therefore cheaper than the ordinary courts. The vast majority of individual employment rights and duties are legally enforceable by means of presenting a complaint before an Industrial Tribunal. Originating under the Industrial Training Act 1964 with only a restricted function, the Employment Tribunal is now the focus for dealing with statutory employment law disputes. Employment Tribunals have a wide jurisdiction extending to unfair dismissal, redundancy, wage deductions, discrimination and numerous other statutory employment rights. The Industrial Tribunals (Extensions of Jurisdiction) (England and Wales) Order 1994 provides that Tribunals may also determine wrongful dismissal claims which previously were exclusively heard in the County Court. The Tribunal is composed of three members, a legally qualified chairman and two lay members, one of whom is usually a nominee of an employer's organisation, and the other the nominee of a trade union.

County Court or High Court?

The decision whether to bring proceedings in the County Court or the High Court will be based upon a number of factors.

(i)   **Convenience**. There are over 400 County Courts in England and Wales. This means they are readily accessible to plaintiffs. A County Court can usually hear those cases where the cause of action arose in its own district, or where the defendant either resides or carries on his business. Thus it is possible that a plaintiff might have the choice of three courts in which to commence proceedings. By contrast the High Court sits in London, and only rarely hears civil cases outside London.

(ii)   **Costs**. Court costs are much cheaper in the County Court than the High Court. Bringing a High Court action may involve the payment of additional lawyers, for instance a firm of solicitors acting as the London agents for the local firm who originally handled the case. Lawyers' professional charges, like those of other professionals, vary not only according to the nature of the work involved but also according to where they carry out their work. Legal charges in London and other major cities for example are generally significantly higher than those of lawyers working elsewhere.

(iii)   **Quality**. It is very dangerous to make comparisons about the quality or standard of justice as between courts. Sometimes it may be felt that the complexity of a case makes it a more suitable candidate for consideration before a High Court judge than before a circuit judge in a County Court. Equally it may be the case that a plaintiff's lawyer is entirely confident that the case should go before the local County Court. It is worth remembering that the legal complexity of a case is not necessarily related to the amount of the claim involved.

(iv)   **Jurisdictional limitations**. As we saw above because of the geographical distribution of County Courts there are jurisdictional rules as to which court can hear the case. No such limitations apply to the High Court. However there are further jurisdictional considerations that need to be borne in mind in the decision about which court should hear the case. These concern the type of action that is being dealt with and the financial value of the claim involved. Over certain kinds of action the County Court has exclusive jurisdiction, such as applications for the renewal of a business lease and in consumer credit cases such as the repossession of goods subject to a hire purchase agreement. With respect to the financial value of a claim, regulations introduced under the Courts and Legal Services Act 1990 have made it possible for the County Courts to deal with many more actions than was previously the case. To cope with the increased workload there are now 72 continuous trial centres. In general, cases with a value of below £25,000 will be heard in the County Court, and with a value of more than £50,000 in the High Court. For those between £25,000 and £50,000 the case will be allocated to either the County Court or the High Court on the basis of financial substance, complexity, importance and the need for the matter to be dealt with as quickly as possible. When a legal claim is brought it is, of course, not always possible to quantify in advance the amount the plaintiff is claiming. A claim for compensation for personal injuries will be for an unspecified sum, or in legal terminology an unliquidated amount, it being left to the court to decide on the evidence the figure which should be awarded. A claim for loss of profits on the other hand can be expressed in a quantified or liquidated form. In the past plaintiffs would often seek to overcome financial allocation requirements by overvaluation of claims. The value to be attached to such claims is now to be the amount in money which the plaintiff could reasonably state the case to be worth to him.

Small Claims Arbitration

For the purpose of determining small claims, that is those claims not exceeding £8,000, rules made under the County Courts Act 1984 require that the matter must be referred to the arbitration procedure operated by the County Courts. In brief this provides for a relatively informal method for considering the claim, which will usually be heard before a district judge (previously known as a Registrar) rather than a circuit judge, the title given to the senior judge attached to the Court. Although the parties may be legally represented they must normally pay for their own lawyers' fees themselves, whatever the outcome of the case. This is sometimes referred to as the *no costs* regime. Thus a successful plaintiff cannot recover from the defendant the costs of being legally represented.

Most claims can be dealt with under the arbitration procedure if the claim can be quantified in financial terms, and it is not considered that the factual issues are too complex or the point or points of law too difficult. If they are the case is referred to a full trial. A claim for more than £8,000 may be reduced by the party bringing the action to keep the matter within the arbitration procedure. A claim in excess of £8,000 can only be heard within the procedure if both parties agree. The loser will usually bear the costs of the action. This is not the case where the claim is within the £8,000 limit. A sting in the tail for plaintiffs who successfully bring a county court claim estimated as in excess of £8,000, but which is found to be within the small claims jurisdiction, is that such plaintiffs may find that they are not awarded their costs.

The High Court of Justice

The Supreme Court of Judicature is the collective title given to two superior civil courts, the High Court of Justice and the Court of Appeal (Civil Division). These courts sit in London at the Royal Courts of Justice.

The High Court of Justice is for administrative convenience separated into three divisions, each with its own particular jurisdiction. These are the Queen's Bench Division, the Chancery Division and the Family Division. In addition to the cases which are heard in London, High Court cases are also heard at certain centres outside London. These centres are known as High Court and Crown Court Centres, and they include Birmingham, Bristol, Manchester, Leeds and Cardiff.

The Queen's Bench Division hears contractual and tortious actions and any claim not specifically allocated to the other divisions. This makes it the busiest division of the High Court. There is no financial upper limit on its jurisdiction, so it is competent to deal with claims for any amount, though it does not normally try matters which the county court is competent to hear. Two specialised courts within the Queen's Bench Division are the Admiralty Court, which has jurisdiction over shipping matters, and the Commercial Court, which hears only commercial actions and has the advantage for businesses of using a simplified form of procedure. The Queen's Bench Division is headed by the Lord Chief Justice, abbreviated to LCJ.

The Chancery Division has as its nominal head the Lord Chancellor (who is also the head of the Judiciary); however, in practice, the organisation of the work of the court is carried out by the Vice-Chancellor. The jurisdiction of the division includes company law and partnership matters, mortgages, trusts and revenue disputes.

When the High Court deals with a case at first instance exercising what is known as its *original jurisdiction* a single judge is competent to try the case. Each division possesses an appellate jurisdiction which is exercised by three judges (sometimes only two) sitting together, and when it is being exercised the court is known, rather confusingly, as a Divisional Court. The work of the Divisional Courts of the Queen's Bench Division is of considerable importance, and covers the following matters.

- Hearing criminal appeals from Magistrates Courts and the Crown Court by means of a *case stated*. This is a statement of the lower courts' findings of fact which is used by the Divisional Court for redetermining a disputed point of law.

- Hearing civil appeals from certain tribunals.

- Exercising a supervisory jurisdiction over inferior courts and tribunals. This is carried out by means of applications made to the court for the issue of the prerogative orders. These orders provide remedies to protect people and organisations from various forms of injustice. There are three of them; certiorari, prohibition and mandamus.

  Certiorari brings before the court cases from inferior courts and tribunals that have already been decided, or are still being heard, to determine whether the inferior body has exceeded its jurisdiction or denied the rules of natural justice. (An example of these rules is one which provides that both parties in a case must be given the opportunity to be heard.) If such an injustice has occurred the earlier decision will be quashed.

  Prohibition is used to prevent inferior courts, tribunals and other judicial and quasi-judicial bodies from exceeding their jurisdiction.

Mandamus is a command used to compel performance of a legal duty owed by some person or body. It may be used against a government department, a local authority, or a tribunal which is unlawfully refusing to hear a case.

The Divisional Courts of Chancery hear appeals on bankruptcy matters from County Courts with bankruptcy jurisdiction.

The Court of Appeal (Civil Division)

Acting in its civil capacity this court has the Master of the Rolls as its president (referred to in written form as MR). Its judges are called Lord Justices of Appeal (referred to as LJ or LJJ in plural), and the quorum of the court is three.

The court can hear appeals from all three divisions of the High Court and appeals from the County Courts. It also deals with appeals from certain tribunals, such as the Employment Appeal Tribunal.

The appeal is dealt with by way of a rehearing, which involves reviewing the case from the transcript of the trial and of the judges' notes. The court may uphold or reverse the whole or any part of the decision of the lower court, alter the damages awarded, or make a different order concerning costs.

The House of Lords

The House of Lords fulfils two functions, for it is not only the upper chamber of Parliament, but also the final appellate court within the United Kingdom. In the exercise of this function it is said to sit as the judicial committee. When it sits as a court its judges are those peers who hold or have held high judicial office. By convention lay peers do not sit. The judges are known as Lords of Appeal in Ordinary or, more commonly, Law Lords, and they are presided over by the Lord Chancellor. Although the quorum of the court is three, usually five judges sit. Majority decisions prevail in cases of disagreement.

The House of Lords hears appeals from the Court of Appeal, but only if that court or the Appeals Committee of the House has granted leave.

The Administration of Justice Act 1969 enables certain appeals from the High Court to be heard by the House of Lords without first passing through the Court of Appeal. This is known as the *leap-frog* procedure, and it is available only where the appeal involves a point of general public importance, for example on a question of the interpretation of a statutory provision, and then only if the parties consent, and if the House of Lords grants leave for the appeal. It has been used only rarely.

Chapter 2

The European Union

European Community Law

The United Kingdom has been a member of the European Community since January 1st 1973. Following the Maastricht Treaty in 1992 the European Union was created of which the European Community is a part. When we refer to European Law we use the expression European Community or EC Law. Currently the European Union has fifteen member states, with a population of 370 million, which form a single economic region in which goods, services, people and capital can move almost as freely as they do within national boundaries.

As a Member State of the European Union the United Kingdom is bound by European Community Law. In the field of business this is of enormous significance because the European Union is essentially economic in nature, and the community objective of the completion of a single European market is based upon the actual harmonisation of laws relating to business and trade between Member States.

Inevitably therefore there are significant examples of measures which have been adopted and implemented by the UK government as a consequence of European legislation. Examples can be seen in the fields of:

- company law harmonisation and investor protection;

- consumer rights and consumer protection;

- data protection;

- environmental protection;

- intellectual property rights;

- employment law.

In each of these fields European law has been active in amending and adding to existing UK law, as well as requiring the introduction of new law. For example in employment law the Community has been active in the following areas:

- pregnancy dismissals and maternity and parental leave;

- statutory rights for part-time and fixed term workers;

- collective redundancy procedures;

- dismissals and detrimental conduct relating to health and safety;

- acquired rights on a business transfer;

- health and safety at work regulations;

- sex discrimination and equal pay.

The framework of European law is set out in the Treaty of Rome 1957 as amended by the Single European Act of 1986 and the Treaty of European Union signed at Maastricht in 1992 and the institutions of the Community must operate within and give effect to these Treaties. Later in the chapter the legislative process of the Community Institutions is considered and the means by which Community law becomes incorporated into the domestic law of Members States.

Treaty of Rome 1957

The Treaty of Rome 1957, as amended by the Single European Act and the Treaty of European Union signed at Maastricht, sets out the tasks and objectives of the European Community and defines the policy areas within which the community has competence to legislate.

Article 2 of the Treaty of Rome, as amended, sets out the general aims of the Community" *The Community shall have as its task, by establishing a common market and an economic and monetary union and by implementing the common policies or activities referred to in Articles 3 and 3a, to promote throughout the Community a harmonious and balanced development of economic activities, sustainable and non-inflationary growth respecting the environment, a high degree of convergence of economic performance, a high level of employment and of social protection, the raising of the standard of living and quality of life, and economic and social cohesion and solidarity among Member States. "*

These aims are supplemented by other broad statements of intent set out in the preamble to the treaty, that the member states are determined to lay the foundation of an ever closer union among the peoples of Europe and are resolved by pooling their resources to preserve and strengthen peace and liberty. Together they have been important in providing the impetus for closer European integration and by providing an important statement of principles which are taken into account by the Court of Justice in interpreting the treaties themselves and the laws made under them.

Article 3 sets out the activities which are to be undertaken by the Community in order to fulfil its objectives. Each of the activities is further defined in subsequent articles of the Treaty.

The Single European Act 1986

Although the original Member States had hoped to establish the Common Market fully within twelve years, progress towards that aim was in fact much slower than anticipated. This was a product partly of the conflicting national interests involved and the fact that proposals could be blocked by any member state which thought its vital national interests to be at stake.

One of the principal effects of the Single European Act was to lay down the timetable for the completion of the single European market. A White Paper issued by the Commission in 1985 had identified that 282 proposals for new legislation would need to be introduced in order to complete the internal market. The Single European Act provided that these measures should be adopted by the 31st December 1992 in order to create a single internal market comprising a geographical area without internal frontiers in which there would be a free movement of goods, persons, services and capital. In order to facilitate the adoption of all of the measures necessary to complete the single market within the time limit, the Single European Act provided for qualified majority voting in the Council of Ministers in relation to single market measures.

The Single European Act also extended the Community's competence to legislate by setting out additional objectives in relation to economic and monetary co-operation; the health and safety of workers; economic and social cohesion involving the reduction of differences between various regions in the community and policies to reduce the backwardness of the least favoured regions; research and technological development and environmental protection. It also put onto a formal basis, though outside the framework of Community law, the emerging practice of political co-operation in the sphere of foreign policy.

The Single European Act was implemented in the UK by the European Communities (Amendment) Act 1986 which came into effect on 1st July 1987.

The Treaty on European Union

The Treaty on European Union which was negotiated in Maastricht in November 1991 came into effect at the beginning of November 1993, after completing the difficult process of ratification in each of the member states. It survived a second Danish referendum and challenges to its constitutional validity in the German and UK courts.

The Treaty creates a European Union which has three main elements, often described as *pillars*. The first is the European Community itself, the powers and decision making procedures of which are extended and modified. The second element relates to foreign and security policy, and the third to justice and home affairs. The second and third pillars operate outside of the formal institutional framework of the European Union and are based on new inter-governmental arrangements between the member states. As such their decisions do not form part of the body of European law, which is created by the Council of Ministers acting with the Commission and European Parliament, and are not subject to the jurisdiction of the Court of Justice.

In the present context we are concerned only with the first pillar of the Treaty which expands the areas of Community activity. Under the Treaty the task of the European Community will be to promote a harmonious and balanced development of economic activities, sustainable and non-inflationary growth respecting the environment, a high degree of convergence of economic performance, a high level of employment and of social protection, the raising of the standard of living and quality of life, and economic and social cohesion and solidarity.

The UK, however, originally negotiated to opt out of two important parts of the Treaty, the *Social Chapter* and the third stage of economic and monetary union which is the adoption of a single currency. The remainder of the Treaty applies with full effect to the UK and now the Social Chapter has been adopted. One of the main consequences of adopting the Social Chapter is that the UK government is immediately subject to the European Directives which were previously not binding due to the UK opt out under the Maastricht Treaty. A good example is the European Union Parental Leave Directive which the UK government was required to adopt by the 15 December 1999. This has now been adopted and provisions in relation to parental leave are found in Schedule 4 of the Employment Relations Act 1999 which adds a new ss.78-80 to the Employment Rights Act 1996 The Act is also supported by the Maternity and Parental Leave Regulations 1999.

The Treaty on European Union formally extends the legal competence of the EC in a number of areas. In some respects this is simply a confirmation of competence in areas where the Community already takes action, for example its long standing practice of bringing forward consumer protection proposals as single market measures or under broader powers to eliminate distortions in competition. The Treaty on European Union gives or extends European Union competence in the following areas:

- Citizenship of the European Union

- Transport policy

- Research and technological development

- Culture

- Public health

- Consumer protection

- Trans-European networks in the areas of transport, telecommunication and energy

- Industry

- Education

- Civil protection

- Development co-operation with third world countries

- Environment

- Economic and monetary policy

The Treaty operates, like the Single European Act, by inserting amendments into the Treaty of Rome. The structure which it establishes is contained in Figure 2.1.

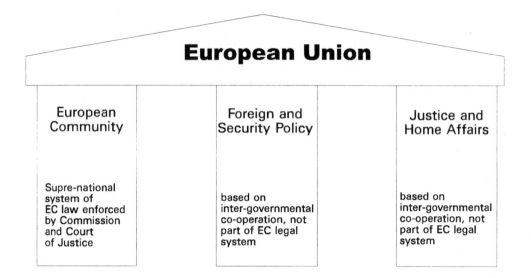

Figure 2.1 *Structure of the European Union*

The Treaty on European Union makes express provision for the principle of *subsidiarity*. Under this principle the Community will act within the limits of the powers conferred upon it and of the objectives assigned to it. In areas which do not fall within its exclusive competence the Community can take action only if and in so far as the objectives of the proposed action cannot be sufficiently achieved by the member states and can be better achieved by the Community. Thus action should only be taken at European Union level where such action if taken at the national or regional level would be inadequate or inappropriate. Any action by the Community must not go beyond what is necessary to achieve the common objectives of the treaties. The principle of subsidiarity is designed to safeguard the residual powers and competences of the member states.

The Amsterdam Treaty 1999

On the 1 May 1999 the Amsterdam Treaty came into force. Its main significance is the introduction of the revised Social Chapter which formally ends the UK opt out from the Community Social Policy. It also creates a legislative case for the introduction of measures to combat discrimination beyond the spheres of nationality and gender. There are proposed Directives on parental leave, works councils, part-time work, fixed term workers and the burden of proof in sex discrimination cases. The European Commission has more room to manoeuvre in proposing legislation under the new Social Chapter in fields such as working conditions information, consolidation of workers and equal pay. Importantly decision making will be by qualified majority vote for a number of issues. A new Article 13 allows the Council on the European Union to take appropriate action (national legislation) to combat discrimination based on "sex, racial or ethnic origin, religion or belief, disability, age or sexual orientation." The appropriate actions would include encouraging legislation at national level on equal opportunities.

It is clear from an examination of the major European treaties that the Community has power to legislate over a very broad range of issues which embrace the entire area of business law. It is in practice by far the most important source of new law in this sphere. It should also be appreciated, however, that there are areas of legal regulation which remain exclusively within the domain of national law making powers. These include, for example, major parts of the criminal law, control over the direct taxation of income, family law, the law of inheritance and numerous other important fields of law.

The Community Institutions

The Community Institutions are:

- the Commission

- the Council of Ministers/Council of the European Union

- the European Parliament

- the Court of Justice of the European Communities.

The Commission

The Commission consists of 20 Commissioners, two from each of the larger EC states and one from each of the others. They are nominated by their governments and appointed by the unanimous agreements of the governments of the member states for a renewable period of four years. The term of office is increased to five years under the Treaty on European Union which also provides that their appointment shall be subject to the approval of the Parliament. Once appointed they must act with complete independence in the interests of the Community. In the performance of their duties they must neither seek not take instructions from any government or any other body. The main functions of the Commission are to initiate policy and proposals for legislation for ultimate adoption by the Council. It is the executive arm of the EC, with responsibility for ensuring the implementation of agreed policies and managing the community's budget.

As *the guardian of the treaties* it must ensure full compliance by member states with Community obligations in accordance with EC law. The Commission has powers to investigate an alleged infringement of the Treaty by a member state and, under article 169, where it considers that the member state has failed to fulfil an EC obligation, the Commission will issue a reasoned opinion on the matter after giving the member state an opportunity to submit its observations. The member state must comply with the reasoned opinion before the deadline stated in it. Where it fails to do so the Commission may refer the matter to the Court of Justice. This procedure is often used where a member state either fails to implement a directive within the given time limit, or implements it incorrectly.

> In *Commission of the European Communities v. United Kingdom of Great Britain and Northern Ireland* 1994 the European Court of Justice ruled against the UK government in two cases brought by the Commission where it was alleged that the UK had failed to properly transpose Directives on collective redundancies and acquired rights. By failing to ensure worker representation in a workplace where there is no recognised trade union the community law obligation to ensure that worker's representatives are informed and consulted on business transfers and collective redundancies had not been complied with. Most of the criticisms were accepted by the UK government and rectified by specific provisions in the Trade Union Reform and Employment Rights Act 1993.

The Commission also has some direct legislative powers which are conferred by the Treaty and others which are delegated to it by the Council. It administers and enforces Community competition policy and has power to impose fines and penalties on organisations or individuals for breach of competition law. In 1992, for example, a fine of 75 million ECU was imposed on Tetra Pak by the Commission for breaches of EC competition law.

The work of the Commission is divided into twenty four Directorates General, each dealing with specific aspects of Community activity and policy under the control of an individual Commisioner. Each Commissioner heads a department, and is known as a Director General (DG). For employment matters there is a Commissioner for Employment, Social Affairs and Education.

Council of the European Union

The Council of the European Union (previously the Council of Ministers) is the EC's principal decision making body with the final say on most secondary legislation. The Commission initiates proposals for legislation as the Council does not have power to do this itself. It can, however, request the Commission to submit to it proposals on matters which may be desirable in order to achieve the objectives of the Treaty. The Council consists of one government minister from each member state and its membership varies according to the nature of the matter under discussion. When the Council is discussing the common agricultural policy, for example, the member states are represented by their ministers of agriculture, for transport matters their ministers of transport and so on. The presidency of the Council and therefore of the Community is held by each member state in rotation for a six month term. Towards the end of each term the heads of state will meet for a summit to discuss major current issues and to chart the future course of the Community. When it involves a meeting of the Heads of State the Council is known as the *European Council*.

The Council is the one institution which is common both to the European Community and to the Foreign Affairs and Home Affairs pillars of the European Union. Most European Union business is conducted at meetings of the Council of Ministers. Shortly after the coming into force of the Treaty on European Union, the Council announced its formal decision to change its name to the Council of the European Union. The other EC institutions, however, have little or no role in the procedures for conducting foreign and home affairs, and it is therefore inaccurate to refer to them as institutions of the European Union. Only the Council has this dual role.

The UK Parliament has the opportunity to assess the legal and political implications of a proposal for EC legislation before the Council votes on it. This is carried out by the *Scrutiny Committees* of the Commons and the Lords who are given copies of the proposals with an explanatory memorandum. The Scrutiny Committees have power to call for written or oral evidence, consult with government departments, call for a debate and if necessary request that amendments to the proposal be negotiated. Once the Scrutiny Committee has cleared a proposal then the minister is free to accept it in the EC Council of Ministers.

The method of voting used in the Council is of particular importance as the Council is the main legislating body in the community. Clearly if all decisions were taken on the basis of a unanimous vote, each member state would have a veto over every Community decision. On the other hand if some form of majority voting system was used, a member state's interests could be overridden and laws introduced against its wishes.

Article 148 of the Treaty of Rome provides that voting may be by a simple majority, a qualified majority, or on the basis of unanimity. Very few decisions are ever taken by a simple majority. The Treaty originally provided for unanimous voting on all important matters, and envisaged a move towards qualified voting after a defined period of time. This did not happen, however, principally as a result of objections by France. In 1965 the French boycotted Community meetings in protest at the introduction of qualified majority voting. The so-called policy of the empty chair resulted in a crisis for the Community which was finally settled by the adoption of the Luxembourg Accords. Under the Luxembourg Accords a member state has the right to insist on a unanimous vote where it considers that its vital national interests are at stake in the matter under discussion. The Accords are in the nature of a political convention without formal legal standing. They have been used on numerous occasions to justify a veto, sometimes on matters of relative unimportance. The increase in Community membership coupled with the use of the veto in this way meant that progress towards the objectives of the Community was extremely slow. It became increasingly recognised that significant changes were necessary in the decision making procedures of the Community if real and substantial advances were to be made in meeting those objectives.

These changes were made in the Single European Act which introduced qualified majority voting for all measures required to complete the single market, with certain exceptions. These related to approximation of indirect taxes, free movement of persons, and matters affecting the rights of employees, which are still subject to voting by unanimity. Measures related to the health and safety of workers, however, are subject to qualified majority voting procedure. Under the Treaty on European Union qualified majority voting has been extended further, into areas such as consumer protection, health, education and environmental programmes

The European Parliament

Members of the European Parliament, MEPs, are the directly elected representatives of the citizens of the European Union. The Parliament sits for a five year term and is based partly in Strasbourg and partly in Brussels. Its powers include the right to dismiss the whole of the Commission on a motion of censure by a two-thirds majority. It has no power to dismiss individual commissioners. MEPs can ask oral or written questions of the Council or the Commission, which must be answered. The answers to written questions are published in the Official Journal of the Community. In respect of the Community's budget, the Parliament has a final say over certain items of expenditure, and has the ultimate power to reject the budget as a whole. In terms of law making power, the European Parliament is markedly different from the UK Parliament, having a relatively minor role in the legislative process.

Its powers have been progressively strengthened by the Single European Act and the Treaty on European Union, in response to a fundamental criticism of the lack of democratic accountability of the Community Institutions. This so-called *democratic deficit* has been characterised by a concentration of power in the hands of the unelected Commission, the practice of the Council to take its decisions behind closed doors, the inability of the Parliament to initiate proposals for new legislation, and the limited role of Parliament within the legislative process.

The Treaty on European Union has gone some way towards addressing the democratic deficit, although it may be argued that the criticism remains valid. The increased power of the Parliament is reflected in the three different Community law-making procedures. The *consultation procedure*, under which the Parliament gives its opinion but has little real power, was laid down in the original Treaty of Rome. The *co-operation procedure*, in which it has power to make amendments but not to veto, was introduced by the Single European Act. The *co-decision procedure*, in which it has power to make amendments and a right of veto, is contained in the Treaty on European Union.

The powers of the Parliament have been strengthened in a number of other ways by the Treaty on European Union. Under article 158 the appointment of the Commission and its president is subject to the approval of Parliament.

By virtue of article 138b the Parliament may, acting by a majority of its members, request the Commission to submit a proposal for new legislation where it considers that this is required. The interpretation of this provision is a matter of some debate, in particular the question whether the Commission has a legal duty to carry out the request. If so, the Parliament has in effect a new right to initiate legislation.

The European Court of Justice

The Court of Justice sits in Luxembourg and is composed of 15 judges who are appointed by the mutual agreement of the member states for renewable periods of six years. They must be persons of absolute independence who are qualified to hold the highest judicial office in their own country or who are legal experts of recognised competence. The court is assisted by nine Advocates-General, who must hold similar qualifications to the judges and are appointed on the same basis. It is the duty of the Advocate-General, acting with complete impartiality and independence, to make reasoned submissions in open court as to the application of Community law to the questions posed in the case before the court. The opinion of the Advocate-General is not binding on the court, which may decide the case in a different way, although this is unusual. There is no equivalent to the Advocate-General within the English legal system.

The Court of Justice has power to hear the following types of case:

- *Actions against member states* Where it appears that a member state has failed to fulfil an obligation under Community law the Commission may take infringement proceedings under article 169. Other member states are also able to bring this type of case, under article 170, provided that they first bring the matter to the attention of the Commission. Prior to the Treaty on European Union the powers of the Court of Justice in such cases were limited to making a declaration requiring the defaulting member state to take the necessary measures to comply with its judgment. There was no effective sanction, other than political pressure, to enforce compliance. Under the new Treaty, however, a member state may ultimately be fined if it fails to comply with the court's ruling.

- *Actions against community institutions* The Court of Justice has power to review the legality of acts of Community Institutions, or their failure to act. The court may declare void any illegal action, award damages and review decisions.

- *Employment disputes between the Community and its employees* The Court of Justice acts as an industrial tribunal for the employees of Community institutions. Cases of this type account for just under a quarter of its case load.

- *Preliminary rulings under article 177* Any court or tribunal in a member state may request a preliminary ruling from the Court of Justice as to the meaning or interpretation of an aspect of Community law. Such a request may be made where the ruling is required to enable that court or tribunal to give judgment in a case before it. Where there is no appeal from its decision, the court or tribunal must request a preliminary ruling if it considers this necessary to enable it to give judgment. This procedure provides an important bridge between the legal systems of member states and that of the Community. It is designed to ensure that European law is applied and interpreted in a uniform manner throughout all member states. The function of the Court of Justice is simply to rule on the interpretation of European law, in the light of which the domestic court or tribunal will decide the case before it.

The Single European Act made provision for a *Court of First Instance of the European Community,* to be attached to the Court of Justice in order to deal with certain categories of case. The need for such a court arises as a result of the growth of the number of cases referred to the Court of Justice, and the likelihood of a continued growth in its workload due to the expansion of the Community itself and to a significant increase in Community legislation related to the completion of the Single Market. It is hoped that the Court of First Instance will reduce the period of time taken to dispose of cases which, before its introduction, averaged 18 months to two years.

The Court of First Instance, established in 1989, has twelve members. They usually act in a judicial capacity, although they are also called upon to undertake the task of Advocate-General. The Court has jurisdiction to hear claims for damages and judicial reviews against Community Institutions, and hear employment cases involving Community employees. There is an appeal on a point of law to the Court of Justice, although a decision of the Court of First Instance on a matter of fact is final. Significantly the Court of First Instance has no jurisdiction to hear cases brought by member states or by Community Institutions, or to deal with references by national courts or tribunals under article 177 for preliminary rulings.

Primacy of European Law

It is a central feature of European law that it takes precedence over any conflicting provisions in the national law of member states. This feature has been strongly developed by the Court of Justice in a series of cases as the issue of priority is not addressed directly in the Treaty of Rome. In *Van Gend en Loos v Nederlands Administratie der Belastingen* 1963 the Court of Justice described the relationship between Community law and domestic law in the following way: *"By creating a community of unlimited duration, having its own institutions, its own personality, its own legal capacity and capacity of representation on the international plain and, more particularly, real powers stemming from a limitation of sovereignty or a transfer of powers from the states to the community, the member states have limited their sovereign rights albeit within limited fields, and have thus created a body of law which binds both their nationals and themselves."*

The principle of supremacy of Community law was clearly affirmed by the Court of Justice in the case of *Costa v ENEL* 1964 in which it held that a provision in the EC Treaty took precedence over a rule in a subsequent Italian statute. The Court relied on the statement in *Van Gend en Loos*, together with the duty imposed by article 5 on each member state to ensure that their obligations under the Treaty are fulfilled, and stated *"The law stemming from the Treaty, an independent source of law, could not, because of its special and original nature, be over-ridden by domestic legal provisions, however framed, without being deprived of its character as Community Law and without the legal basis of the Community itself being called into question."*

The pervasive nature of Community law was described by Lord Denning MR in *Bulmer Ltd. v. Bolinger SA* 1974 in a famous passage. *"When we come to matters with a European element, the Treaty is like an incoming tide. It flows into the estuaries and up the rivers. It cannot be held back. Parliament has decreed that the Treaty is henceforward to be part of our law. It is equal in force to any statute."*

In *Internationale Handelsgesellschaft mbH* 1970, the Court of Justice, in a case which involved a conflict between an EC regulation and the provisions of the German constitution, decided that the EC rule took precedence. *"The validity of a community instrument or its effect within a member State cannot be affected by allegations that it strikes at either the fundamental rights as formulated in that State's constitution or the principles of a national constitutional structure."*

The significance of these decisions in UK law is underlined by s.3(1) of the European Communities Act 1972, which provides *"For the purposes of all legal proceedings any questions as to the meaning or effect of any of the Treaties, or as to the validity meaning or effect of any community instrument, shall be treated as a question of law and, if not referred to the European Court, be for determination as such in accordance with the principles laid down by and any relevant decision of the European Court."*

This section represents the acceptance by the UK government in the 1972 Act of the principles developed by the Court of Justice in its decisions, including those relating to the supremacy of Community law.

The position of EC law within the English legal system is established by the European Communities Act 1972 which, in s.2(1), gives legal effect to the Community law within the UK. It states *"All such rights, powers, liabilities, obligations and restrictions from time to time created or arising by or under the Treaties, and all such remedies and procedures from time to time provided for by or under the Treaties, as in accordance with the Treaties are without further enactment to be given legal effect or used in the United Kingdom shall be recognised and available in law, and be enforced, allowed and followed accordingly, and the expression "enforceable community right" and similar expressions shall be read as referring to one to which this subsection applies."*

This gives legal force to those provisions in the Treaties and in secondary legislation which are directly applicable. This occurs automatically without the need for further UK legislation. The words from time to time make it clear that future as well as existing Community laws are within the scope of s.2(1). In relation to those Community measures which do not have direct applicability, s.2(2) gives power to make delegated legislation for the purpose of giving them effect within the UK. This power is often used to make Statutory Instruments in order to implement Community directives. The Employment Protection (Part-time Employees) Regulations 1995 were made under s.2(2) to bring the legal position of part-time workers in the UK in line with Europe.

The 1972 Act states that where there is a conflict between domestic law and Community law, the latter will take priority. This is laid down in s.2(4) which provides *"... any enactment passed or to be passed shall be construed and have effect subject to the foregoing provisions of this section."*

The effect of s.2(4) has caused much controversy and debate as to its impact on the unwritten constitution of the UK. This debate centres around the constitutional doctrine of parliamentary supremacy. One of the principal features of this doctrine is that Parliament cannot bind its successors by passing legislation restricting the absolute freedom of a future parliament to repeal or amend existing laws or create new ones. The effect of s.2(4) however is that no future Parliament can validly create legislation which conflicts with Community law.

An example of the primacy of community law is provided by the important decision of the House of Lords in *R v. Secretary of State for Employment ex parte Equal Opportunities Commission* 1994. Here their Lordships ruled by a majority of four to one that UK legislation that gives part-time workers (most of whom are women) less protection in relation to unfair dismissal and redundancy than full-time workers (most of whom are men) is indirectly discriminatory and therefore incompatible with European Union Law as to equality between employees.

The issue of supremacy was clearly illustrated in a series of cases known as the *Factortame* cases. The cases centred around a challenge to the validity of the Merchant Shipping Act 1988. The Act was introduced to prevent fishing companies from one EC state establishing themselves in another and registering their vessels there in order to qualify for part of that state's fishing quota, a practice known as quota-hopping. Spain had not been a member of the EC when a system of fishing quotas designed to conserve fish stocks was introduced. On accession the Spanish did not secure a large allocation of quotas. A number of Spanish fishing companies, including the plaintiff, set up subsidiary companies in the UK and claimed a share of the British quota by re-registering their ships under the British flag. The Merchant Shipping Act 1988 was introduced in order to prevent this from happening. By s.14 of the Act a vessel would only qualify for registration as British if it was owned by a British citizen, domiciled and resident in the UK; or, in the case of a company, if 75% of its shareholders and directors were British citizens, domiciled and resident here. Further, the vessels had to be managed and its operations directed and controlled from the UK. The validity of the Act was challenged by the plaintiff on the grounds that it was inconsistent with a number of articles in the Treaty of Rome. In particular, article 52 guarantees to nationals of one member state the right to take up and pursue activities as self-employed persons in another member state, a right known as freedom of establishment. This right extends to companies under article 58. In addition article 7 prohibits discrimination on the grounds of nationality in relation to areas covered by the Treaty.

In the first case, *Factortame Ltd. v. Secretary of State for Transport* 1989, the applicants sought a judicial review challenging the validity of the 1988 Act. The Divisional Court requested a preliminary ruling from the Court of Justice on the compatibility of the 1988 Act with the relevant provisions of the treaty. As it was likely that the Court of Justice would take up to two years to rule on the issue, the applicants requested the Divisional Court to suspend the provisions of the 1988 Act until the judgment of the Court of Justice was delivered. The Divisional Court granted an interim injunction disapplying the relevant parts of the 1988 Act and restraining the Secretary of State from enforcing them in respect of the applicants until the Court of Justice had given its ruling. The injunction was discharged, however, on appeal to the Court of Appeal whose decision was confirmed by the House of Lords. The Lords accepted that directly effective EC law takes priority over later national legislation on the basis of s.2(4) of the European Communities Act 1972, but held that until a ruling was given by the Court of Justice there was a presumption that the 1988 Act was valid. It further held that English Courts have no jurisdiction to suspend the operation of an Act of Parliament or grant an injunction against the Crown. At the same time, however, the House made a second reference to the Court of Justice requesting a preliminary ruling on the question of whether EC law enabled national courts to grant an interim injunction in these circumstances.

In a separate action the EC Commission took infringement proceedings against the UK in relation to the nationality requirements in section 14 of the Merchant Shipping Act. In *Commission v. UK re Merchant Shipping Rules* 1989 the Court of Justice held that the UK was required to suspend the application of the offending parts of the Act. The decision in this case was given effect by a statutory instrument, the Merchant Shipping Act 1988 (Amendment) Order 1989.

In *Factortame Ltd. v. Secretary of State for Transport (no.2)* 1991 the Court of Justice ruled on the questions which had been referred to it by the House of Lords. It held that a court in a member state must set aside any rules of national law which prevent directly effective Community law from having effect. In the circumstances of the present case the UK courts were therefore required, as a matter of EC law, to set aside the rule of English law that the courts had no jurisdiction to grant an interim injunction disapplying an Act of Parliament. The House of Lords then had to consider, given that it had the power to suspend an Act of Parliament, the circumstances in which it would be appropriate to do so. The House decided that it would only be appropriate to take this exceptional course of action where the challenge to the validity of the Act was so firmly based as to justify the suspension of the provision in question. On the facts it was held that the case made out by the applicants had a strong basis and the offending provisions of the Act should therefore be suspended. The case may be regarded as a major landmark in the development of this area of law in confirming the power of the courts to suspend the operation of an Act of Parliament. Whilst the decision was greeted with surprise from some observers, many regarded it as the logical consequence of the 1972 Act. This view was expressed by Lord Bridge in his judgment *"If the supremacy within the European Community of community law over the national law of member states was not always inherent in the EEC Treaty it was certainly well established in the jurisprudence of the Court of Justice long before the United Kingdom joined the Community. Thus, whatever limitation of its sovereignty Parliament accepted when it enacted the European Communities Act 1972 was entirely voluntary."*

Types of Community Law

The major sources of Community law are *primary* legislation found in the treaties establishing and developing the EC; *secondary* legislation made on an ongoing basis by the Community institutions; judgments of the Court of Justice and unwritten general principles of law. In relation to treaty provisions and secondary legislation it is useful to distinguish between the concepts of *direct applicability* and *direct effect*.

A Community law is said to be directly applicable when it is of a type which is directly incorporated in its entirety into the laws of the members states without the need for further legislative or administrative action on the part of the member state or the Community institutions. Such rules create immediate rights and obligations as between individuals and or organisations and as against member states. These rights or obligations are directly enforceable in the ordinary courts within the member states. Article 189 states that EC regulations are directly applicable. Certain provisions of the treaties have been held to be directly applicable, although they only come within this category where they are:

- clear and unambiguous;

- unconditional;

- precise;

- self-contained - i.e. requiring no further action to put them into effect.

Directly applicable Community laws will automatically take effect within the UK by virtue of s.2(1) of the 1972 Act.

A Community law which is not directly applicable may nonetheless have direct effects in terms of conferring rights upon individuals which may be enforced in the domestic courts. Such provisions usually will not have direct applicability because they are not self-contained, in the sense that they require some action, usually by the member state, in order to implement them. Typically this will apply where directives have not been implemented in full or at all, and the deadline for implementation has passed. In these circumstances the directive may produce direct effects provided it is sufficiently clear, unconditional and precise. One significant limitation on the doctrine of direct effects is that directives are only directly effective as against the state. This is known as *vertical direct effect* and is examined below in the context of the defective implementation of directives.

It may be seen that whilst all directly applicable provisions will have direct effects, the reverse will not be true so that a rule may be directly effective without being directly applicable. Not surprisingly, the two are often confused and even the courts tend to use them interchangeably.

The Treaties

The primary legislation of the EC consists of the European Treaties and associated documents, agreements and protocols. These include:

- The Treaty of Paris 1951, establishing the ECSC;

- The Treaty of Rome 1957;

- The Euratom Treaty 1957;

- The Merger Treaty 1965 which established common institutions for all three communities;

- Treaties of Accession on the admission of new member states to the Community;

- Association agreements with non-members;

- The Single European Act 1986;

- The Treaty on European Union 1992;

- The Treaty of Amsterdam 1999.

Under the UK constitution each new treaty requires an Act of Parliament to give it effect within the national legal system. This was achieved by the European Communities Act in 1972 in relation to the treaties which pre-dated it. Separate legislation has been introduced for each subsequent treaty so that, for example, the European Communities (Amendment) Act 1993 gives effect to the Treaty on European Union.

The European Treaties set out the framework of Community law, create the institutions and lay down the procedures for making secondary legislation on an ongoing basis.

Whilst certain provisions in the treaties lay down broad or vague policies which need to be fleshed out in secondary legislation, the Court of Justice has held that others can be directly applicable. Article 119 of the Treaty of Rome, for example, provides that " *Each member state shall ... maintain the application of the principle that men and women receive equal pay for equal work"*. In *Defrenne v. Sabena* 1976 the Court of Justice held that article 119 imposed on member states " *A duty to bring about a specific result to be mandatorally achieved"* and that it could be relied on in an action between a private individual and her private sector employer. Defrenne, an air hostess, claimed to be entitled to the same pay as a male steward whose duties were identical to hers. It was held that she could rely on article 119 even though it was addressed to the member state and was not framed as a rule giving rights to individuals. In so far as it relates to direct discrimination and equal work it was held to be directly applicable.

> In *Barber v. Guardian Royal Exchange* 1990 the Court of Justice applied article 119 in its decision that occupational pension schemes, as opposed to state retirement pension, and the benefits conferred under them on employees, are pay for the purpose of article 119. It is therefore unlawful to discriminate between men and women in relation to them. Mr Barber claimed to be entitled to benefit under his company pension scheme on the same basis as female employees and objected to the fact that he could not receive benefits under the scheme until he reached the age of 65 whereas his female counterparts could benefit at 60. The Court of Justice's decision in his favour caused major changes in many occupational pension schemes to give effect to the equalisation of pension ages and benefits as between men and women.

Many articles of the Treaty have been held to be directly effective, including, for example, article 12 prohibiting member states from introducing new customs duties on imports or exports from other member states, articles 85 and 86 prohibiting anti-competitive practices, article 37(2) on the abolition of customs duties and quantitative restrictions on imports, article 53 on the right of establishment and a number of others.

Secondary Legislation

The Treaties confer significant law making powers on the Institutions of the Community. These powers are limited in that they extend only to areas where the Community has competence to legislate. There are some areas which remain within the exclusive domain of the national sovereignty of the member states. As we have seen, however, the Community's law making competence extents to virtually all aspects of business law.

Article 189 of the Treaty of Rome states *"In order to carry out their task the Council and the Commission shall, in accordance with the provisions of this Treaty, make regulations, issue directives, take decisions, make recommendations or deliver opinions"*. The article goes on to define each of them.

Regulations

A *regulation* has general application. It is binding in its entirety and directly applicable in all member states. Regulations are the equivalent of UK statutes on a community scale. They apply to everyone in all fifteen member states and there is no requirement for action at a national level to bring them into effect. This occurs on the 20th day following their publication in the Official Journal where no other date is specified in them. Council regulation No.295/91, for example, deals with the situation where passengers are denied access to an overbooked scheduled flight for which they have a valid ticket and a confirmed reservation. It establishes common minimum rules applicable in that situation.

Directives

A *directive* shall be binding, as to the result to be achieved, upon each member state to which it is addressed but shall leave to the national authorities the choice of form and methods. Directives are the major instrument for achieving the harmonisation of national laws as between the member states. They operate by setting out the objectives which the proposed new laws must achieve, giving a time limit within which member state governments must achieve them. The resulting law will be in the form of a domestic law within the member state. In the UK directives are implemented either by a new Act of Parliament or by delegated legislation using the enabling powers in s.2(2) of the 1972 Act. The Treaty gives some discretion as to the manner of implementation, provided that the result is achieved. This allows for a certain degree of flexibility, for example, in relation to the consequences for breach of a particular rules which need not be identical in each member state. Breach of the same substantive rule may, for example, give rise to criminal liability in the UK and civil liability in France. There are many examples of directives and their implementation throughout this text, notably in such areas as company law, consumer protection, employment rights and health and safety at work.

Decisions

A *decision* is binding in its entirety upon those to whom it is addressed. They may be addressed to a member state, a business or other organisation or an individual. There is no discretion as to the manner of implementation, and decisions take effect upon notification. They may be used, for example, to enforce Community competition policy.

Recommendations and Opinions

Recommendations and *opinions* are not legally binding or enforceable. They are often addressed to member states and may give a view on a particular matter or set out guidelines to be followed in relation to an issue, sometimes with the implication that if they are not followed proposals for a stronger type of Community law may be made at a later date.

General principles of law

These are an unwritten source of Community law whose existence and validity derive from article 215 which recognises as part of Community law the general principles common to the laws of member states and article 164 which requires the Court of Justice to ensure that in the interpretation and application of this Treaty the law is observed. These provisions enable the Court of Justice to draw from the legal traditions of the member states in developing the jurisprudence of Community law.

Defective implementation of Directives

Where a member state has failed to implement a directive within the specified time period, or where implementation has taken place in part only, there are a number of possible consequences:

- *Infringement proceedings may be taken by the Commission against the member state.* This process is outlined above and ultimately results in a ruling against the member state by the Court of Justice. One problem with this process had been the lack of any power to enforce the judgment of the Court of Justice. Since the coming into effect of the Treaty on European Union however, as we have seen, the Court of Justice has power to fine a member state which fails to comply with a judgment against it.

- *A directive may have direct effects in a case involving the state as defendant.* By definition a directive cannot be directly applicable as it requires some action on the part of the member state to give it effect in national law. Where the member state fails to do this, either in whole or in part, the principle of *vertical direct effect* may come into play. This will prevent the member state from using its own wrongful act of failing properly to implement the directive as a defence to a legal action taken by someone who wishes to enforce the rights contained in the directive against it. In order to be directly effective, the rights set out in the directive must be clear, unambiguous, unconditional and precise.

In *Marshall v. Southampton and South West Hampshire Area Health Authority (Teaching)* 1986, the Health Authority operated a retirement policy for employees under which the normal retirement age was 60 for women and 65 for men. This was consistent with s.6(4) of the Sex Discrimination Act 1975, and in line with state retirement pension ages. An employee's retirement could be postponed by mutual agreement and Miss Marshall continued to work until she was dismissed at age 62. The sole reason given for her dismissal was that she had passed the normal retirement age. She claimed that her dismissal was an unlawful discrimination because men could not be dismissed on grounds of retirement at that age. Her claim was based upon the following articles of the Equal Treatment Directive:

"1(1). The purpose of this directive is to put into effect in the member states the principle of equal treatment for men and women as regards access to employment, including promotion, and to vocational training and as regards working conditions...

2(1). The principle of equal treatment shall mean that there shall be no discrimination whatsoever on grounds of sex either directly, or indirectly by reference in particular to marital or family status.

5(1). Application of the principle of equal treatment with regard to working conditions, including those governing dismissal, means that men and women shall be guaranteed the same conditions without discrimination on grounds of sex."

The Court of Appeal sought a preliminary ruling from the Court of Justice as to whether the retirement policy of the Health Authority constituted discrimination on grounds of sex contrary to the directive; and if so, whether article 5(1) could be relied upon as against a state authority acting in its capacity as employer, in order to avoid the application of s.6(4) of the Sex Discrimination Act 1975. The Court of Justice ruled that the difference in compulsory retirement ages as between men and women was discriminatory and that article 5(1) was clear, unconditional and sufficiently precise to be directly effective. As the date for implementation had passed, it could be relied upon so as to avoid the application of s.6(4) as against the Health Authority, a public sector organisation *"Where a person involved in legal proceedings is able to rely upon a directive as against the state, he may do so regardless of the capacity in which the latter is acting, whether employer or public authority. In either case it is necessary to prevent the state from taking advantage of its own failure to comply with Community Law".*

So the provisions of a directive are capable of direct enforcement against an emanation of the State if there has been a failure to implement the directive into domestic law. The directive will of course have primacy in the event that its provisions conflict with contractual terms.

A good contemporary example of contractual conflict and direct enforceability is provided by *Gibson v. East Riding of Yorkshire Council* 1999 a complaint about the failure to enact Article 7(1) of the Working Time Directive providing that workers are entitled to four weeks annual leave. The EAT held that during the period the directive had not been implemented it had direct effect and an *"employee of an emanation of the State was able to take advantage of its protection."* The directive was clear and precise with no conditions and *"although it as argued that the complainant expressly contracted on the basis that she would receive no paid annual leave her contractual rights were varied by the directive"*. Parties are not entitled to contract out of the entitlement conferred upon them by European Directives, save to the extent that the directive may permit.

The Court of Justice made it clear that directives can only have vertical direct effects in favour of the individual enforceable against the state. They cannot impose obligations on individuals and therefore are not, without full implementation, capable of horizontal direct effect. The *Marshall* case does not, however, make clear exactly which public bodies or manifestations of the state are subject to the rule of vertical direct effect.

In *Foster v. British Gas plc.* 1990, the factual situation was similar to that in Marshall. The sole issue was whether the British Gas Corporation, a nationalised industry, came within the definition of the state for the purposes of the rule. The Court of Justice formulated a broad definition of the state for these purposes. It ruled that the directive could be relied upon in an action for damages against *"... a body, whatever its legal form, which has been made responsible, pursuant to a measure adopted by the state, for providing a public service under the control of the state and has for that purpose special powers beyond those which result from the normal rules applicable in relations between individuals"*.

In the light of this definition, the House of Lords held that the British Gas Corporation was part of the state, and the directive could be relied upon in an action for damages against it.

In *Marshall v. Southampton and South West Hampshire Area Health Authority (No.2)* 1993 a further issue arose as to the amount of compensation recoverable from her employers. The Sex Discrimination Act laid down a statutory maximum award of £6250 under s.65(2). Mrs. Marshall claimed that her full loss amounted to £19,405. Relying on the principles of vertical direct effects developed in the earlier case, she argued that the statutory financial limit was inconsistent with article 6 of the Equal Treatment Directive which in effect requires member states to provide an adequate remedy to a complainant who suffers loss as a result of discriminatory treatment. The House of Lords referred the question to the European Court of Justice for a preliminary ruling under article 177. It ruled that the financial limit conflicted with the requirements of article 6 to provide a real and effective remedy which ensured full compensation for the loss or damage actually sustained. The article had vertical direct effect as against the Health Authority, which as a public body is treated as being part of the State, and which was therefore obliged to pay her compensation in full. The financial limit has now been removed in relation to all sex discrimination claims.

In *Karella v. Ministry of Industry, Energy and Technology* 1994 two shareholders in a Greek company, Klostiria Velka AE, successfully challenged action taken by a Greek government authority, the OAE, which affected their company. The OAE had been given powers under Greek legislation to take over the control of a company, and to increase its capital. Using these powers the OAE took control of Klostiria, and increased its capital from 220m drachmas to 4000 m drachmas. The Court of Justice found that these powers were contrary to the second EC Company Law Directive which provides that other than in special circumstances an increase in capital can only be achieved through a resolution of the shareholders.

- *Member state courts have a duty to interpret national law in the light of the wording and purpose of a relevant directive, not only where the national law in question was introduced in order to give effect to the directive, but also where it pre-dates the directive if no further implementing measure has been introduced and the date for implementation has passed.*

In *Marleasing SA v. La Comercial Internacional de Alimentacion SA* 1992 the Court of Justice held that a national court must interpret national law in conformity with an unimplemented directive after the date for its implementation had passed. On the facts this had the effect of disapplying part of the national law which was inconsistent with the directive. The Court of Justice stated *"the obligation of member states under a directive is to achieve its objects, and their duty by virtue of article 5 of the Treaty to take all necessary steps to ensure the fulfilment of that obligation, binds all authorities of member states, including national courts within their jurisdiction. It follows that in applying national law, whether the provisions concerned pre-date or post-date the directive, the national court asked to interpret national law is bound to do so in every way possible in the light of the text and the aim of the directive to achieve the results envisaged by it and thus to comply with article 189 of the Treaty".*

- *A member state may be liable in damages to an individual for any loss suffered as a result of the state's failure to implement a directive.* This important principle was established by the Court of Justice in the case of *Francovich v. Italian State and Bonifaci* 1992. Liability will arise as against a member state which has failed to implement a directive where the following conditions are met:

(a)   the result to be achieved by the directive includes the creation of rights in favour of individuals;

(b)   the content of those rights are sufficiently defined in the directive; and

(c)   the individual's loss is caused by the failure of the state to implement the directive.

In the *Francovich* case, the Italian government had failed to implement directive 80/987 on the protection of employees in the event of the insolvency of their employer. Under the directive it had been required to ensure that a guarantee institution was in place from which employees could claim payments which could not be met by insolvent employers. Francovich was owed 6 million lire which he was unable to recover from his insolvent employer. He sued the Italian government for damages for its failure to comply with the directive and the Court of Justice gave a preliminary ruling on an article 177 reference that the government was liable in damages for its failure to set up the guarantee institution.

The development of the rule that a member state may be liable to pay damages where it has failed properly to implement a directive is significant in a number of ways. Firstly because the rule of vertical direct effect established in the *Marshall* case does not provide a remedy against a private sector defendant. As a result of the *Francovich* decision, a plaintiff who is unable to sue such a defendant may now be able to sue his government for its failure to legislate. On a broader front the decision is significant because it demonstrates the ability and willingness of the Court of Justice to develop creatively the principles of Community law and new mechanisms for ensuring its effectiveness in areas where the Treaties provide little or no guidance.

- *Damages for other breaches of community law*. The principle established in the *Francovich* case has now been extended to cover the situation where an individual or organisation suffers loss as a result of national legislation which is contrary to EC law, for example because it is incompatible with a provision of the Treaty of Rome. The member state will be liable in damages where the following conditions are met:

(a)   The provision in community law was intended to create rights in favour of individuals;

(b)   The breach of community law is a serious breach; and

(c)   The loss is directly caused by the member states breach of EC law.

These principles have been established by the European Court of Justice through its decisions in a number of cases including *R v. Secretary of State for Transport, ex parte Factortame (No.4)*1995 and *Brasserie du Pecheur SA v. Federal Republic of Germany* 1996.

From the foregoing it will be clear that the European Community law making activities have had enormous impact upon individuals and organisations in the United Kingdom over the nearly three decades of UK membership. The law making competence of the Community has extended into areas affecting the rights and lives of citizens and organisations. Which goes well beyond the notion of the EU as a purely economic market. The United Kingdom was sufficiently anxious about the development of a social dimension to the jurisdiction of the EU, under the Maastricht Treaty, that it negotiated an opt-out from the Social Chapter of the Treaty. The current government has however signed up to the Social Chapter, although it remains ambivalent about UK entry to the European Monetary Union (EMU), with its consequence of the substitution of the Euro for the pound.

The drive towards closer European integration, which the French and German governments in particular favour, remains for the United Kingdom an unresolved political dilemma.

Chapter 3

Business Organisations: Partnerships

Introduction

Business is a broad and loosely defined term. Perhaps it is most generally understood to mean a commercial enterprise which aims to generate a profit for its owners, a profit achieved by the sales of its goods or services. But like most simple definitions this one is not entirely satisfactory. There are business enterprises which certainly aim to trade profitably, but whose overriding purpose is charitable, or educational, and which therefore do not seek to distribute profits to their members. The National Trust is just one example.

Whatever the economic or social objectives a business organisation is established to pursue, the one common characteristic they all share is that they trade, and subsequent chapters will be exploring the range of legal considerations applying to the trading activities undertaken by business organisations. This chapter and the next three, however, take as their theme the organisations themselves, looking at how they are set up and run, and how they come to an end. This is a study which is crucial to an understanding of business law, for without trading organisations the only economic activity that would remain would be between individuals, the kind of activity associated with simple agrarian societies.

Trading is an economic activity, and as such is undertaken in accordance with the principles and practices of economics. The legal implications of trading emerge from legal recognition of different forms of trading organisations, and the consequential rules and principles applicable to such organisations which the law imposes upon them.

Businesses of all kinds reveal certain common characteristics, and it is useful to note these characteristics for they assist in understanding the organisational framework around which the law is constructed.

Common Characteristics of Business Organisations

The following characteristics are exhibited by most businesses:

(a) *Defined business aims and objectives*. In general organisations are set up for a specific purpose; selling particular products, providing a service, and so on. Successful businesses are those which evolve as the commercial environment changes and new commercial opportunities present themselves;

(b) *A distinct identity*. This identity is associated with who owns the organisation, who it employs, what it calls itself, who it trades with and what its markets are;

(c) *An organisational structure displaying levels of authority*. Leadership will be provided in the form of a system of management with senior management levels located at the top of the structure;

(d) *Accountability for its actions*. The organisation as a whole will possess accountability. It will be accountable to those who own it, those whom it employs, and those with whom it trades. Similarly those people it employs are legally accountable to the organisation to fulfill their obligations towards it. This idea of accountability is a key legal concept.

The Classification of Business Organisations

As a starting point in classifying business organisations a simple diagram showing how these organisations relate to each other is useful. The figure on the next page does so. It distinguishes organisations according to ownership and then breaks down private sector business organisations, into their specific legal categories.

Two features of the figure require special attention. These are the distinctions between:

- corporate and unincorporated bodies; and

- private and public sector organisations.

It is not necessary to examine the differences between public and private sector organisations in any detail, however it is important to be clear about the significance of the distinction. Essentially what distinguishes a public sector from a private sector organisation is who owns, and therefore controls it. Whereas in the public sector this will be either directly or indirectly the state, in the private sector it will be private individuals and other organisations.

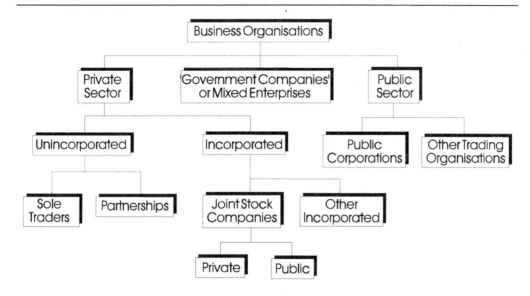

Figure 3.1 *General Classification of Business Organisations*

Most of the work carried out by organisations in the public sector is not principally concerned with commercial trading, but rather with the provision of public services such as health, education and housing, and the management of a wide range of social welfare benefits such as state pensions. The state does however engage in limited commercial trading. Despite privatisation plans the Post Office remains a state trading organisation; so too is Her Majesty's Stationery Office (HMSO). Much of the law contained in this book is as applicable to these state organisations as to those trading in the private sector.

A further distinguishing feature is the method used to create public sector organisations. Usually they are created by a specific Act of Parliament. For example local authorities in England and Wales are established under the Local Government Act 1972. The use of an Act of Parliament to create a private sector organisation, although possible, is most unusual.

Corporate and Unincorporated Bodies

Under English law all business enterprises can be classified into one of two basic legal forms. They are either *corporate* or *unincorporated* bodies. An unincorporated body is usually a group of individuals who have joined together to pursue a common business purpose. The body, and the individuals who compose it, are not separate from each other under the law. They may however trade under a business name, rather than using their own names, creating the appearance that the business is in some way separate from them. The most important example of the unincorporated association is the *partnership*.

A corporate body, or *corporation*, is also generally made up of a group of individuals who have joined together for a common purpose, but who through the process of legal incorporation have created an artificial person which has a legal identity separate from themselves. The distinction between corporate and non-corporate bodies is fundamental to understanding the law as it applies to organisations.

Registered companies are the dominant form of corporate enterprise in the United Kingdom, and therefore warrant particular attention. They are examined in detail in the next chapter. Unincorporated businesses remain however the significant form of business in a number of fields, notably the professions, in consultancy, and in relation to many small business operations. The remainder of this chapter examines these businesses.

There are two types of unincorporated business we need to consider, the sole trade and the partnership.

Sole Traders

The term *sole trader* describes a person operating an unincorporated business alone and thus having sole responsibility for its management. In such a business people rarely work entirely alone and will usually employ staff to assist them in the operation of the business. There are no specific legal formalities relating to the creation of such businesses. The law which a sole trader needs to be aware of is that associated with trading, employing staff and acquiring and operating business premises. Some types of business enterprise must also acquire a licence to permit them to operate. For instance a publican requires a licence to sell intoxicating drinks and a turf accountant a betting and gaming licence.

Such a business will normally be financed by the owner himself, which means that the opportunities for raising business capital are necessarily restricted. The sole owner is entitled to all the profits of the business, but also has unlimited liability in relation to its losses and so must bear them personally. The sole trader form of business is therefore most suitable for an individual who wishes to retain absolute control of the sort of business enterprise which requires only a modest amount of financial investment. Obvious examples include retail shops and service trades such as plumbing and hairdressing. Collectively, sole traders provide a valuable service to the community by making a wide range of goods and services available in a personal way, meeting needs which might otherwise be unfulfilled.

Responsibility for decision making in such a business rests with the owner. There is no individual or group to whom the trader is directly accountable. This is very attractive to those who wish to *be their own boss*. Of course there are those who will be affected by the owner's actions; the customers or clients, the creditors to whom the business owes money, and the employees of the business. Such groups have a valid interest in the decisions made by the sole trader and may ultimately seek to hold the trader legally accountable for the unlawful consequences of commercial decision making. An employee may claim infringement of employment rights, or a customer that consumer rights have been abused. Ultimate accountability arises where the sole trader becomes insolvent, that is unable to meet the debts of the business, and has bankruptcy proceedings commenced against him or her by a creditor.

Partnerships

The other major form of unincorporated business organisation is the partnership. Lawyers refer to partnerships as *firms* for the Partnership Act 1890, which is the main source of partnership law, states under s.4 that: *"Persons who have entered into a partnership with one another for the purposes of this Act are called collectively 'a firm', and the name under which their business is carried on is called the firm-name"*.

There are no detailed legal formalities required when individuals agree to operate a business together and thus form a partnership, and the advantages to a business enterprise of forming a partnership are somewhat similar to those enjoyed by the sole trader. The partners are capable of managing their own firm as they see fit, of sharing the profits and being able to deal directly with their customers or clients.

A partnership provides the compromise of allowing an extension of skill and expertise and the possible influx of additional capital by the introduction of extra partners. This extra potential for capital allows many partnerships to grow to become substantial business enterprises.

Although it has always tended to be overshadowed by the limited company, the partnership remains a significant form of business organisation in the United Kingdom, and is the choice of many people either setting up a new business or modifying an existing one.

Forming a partnership

An agreement between two or more persons to form a partnership constitutes a contract between them but there is no legal requirement as to the form of this contract, so it can be oral, in writing, contained in a deed, or even implied by the law from the surrounding circumstances. The Partnership Act 1890, which contains most of the legal rules relating to partnerships, defines a partnership under s.1 simply as the *"relation which subsists between persons carrying on business in common with a view of profit"*. This definition shows that it is possible for a business to be run as a joint venture without the participants being aware that their business is in law a partnership. This may be of no consequence to them as long as they are able to work together in harmony, but in a dispute it is important to them to ascertain whether their relationship constitutes a partnership. If it does the provisions of the 1890 Act will apply, carrying significant consequences regarding the rights and obligations the partners owe each other.

The main risk in operating a business as a firm is that if the business should get into financial difficulties, the liability of the partners is not limited or restricted in any way. The individual members are liable to the extent of their personal wealth to pay off partnership debts. In extreme cases they may loose almost all their personal property through bankruptcy proceedings.

Although the 1890 Act lays down no formation requirements, it is of course commercially desirable, and certainly common practice, for partners to execute a deed of partnership, in which they provide for matters such as the capital contribution required from each member of the firm, and how profits and losses are to be divided. If the partners do *not* agree such details then the rights and duties laid down under the Act will apply to the partnership.

S.716 Companies Act 1985, provides that a partnership cannot validly consist of more than twenty members. An exception is made however for certain professions, such as accountants and solicitors, who are prevented by statute from practising as limited companies. No restriction is placed upon the size of such firms. Some of the largest firms of lawyers and accountants have hundreds of partners.

Partners can choose any name they please for their firm provided it is not similar to an existing name and therefore not likely to mislead others. However the name cannot end in the word *limited* or any abbreviation of it, for this would indicate that the organisation is a company having limited liability. The words *and Co* at the end of the partnership name usually refers to the fact that there are partners in the firm whose names do not appear in the firm name. If a firm uses a trading name which does not consist of the surnames of all the partners, the Business Names Act 1985 requires that their names must appear on their business stationery, and their true names and addresses must be prominently displayed at their business premises in a place to which the public have access. Non-compliance with these provisions is a criminal offence.

The definition of partnership

Under the s.1 definition there must be:

- a business;

- carried on in common by its members;

- with a view to making a profit.

Under the Act *"business"* includes every trade, occupation or profession. Although as we have seen business is a broad term, it does imply the carrying on of some form of commercial activity. This may be for a single purpose. It is the court, looking at the facts, to resolve any doubt about whether a business is being conducted.

In *Spicer (Keith) Ltd. v. Mansell* 1970 the Court of Appeal held that two persons who were working together for the purpose of forming a limited company, and had opened a bank account and ordered goods in this connection, were not in partnership prior to the incorporation of the company (which in fact was never formed). The reason was that at the relevant time they were preparing for business, rather than operating an existing one.

A thin line often exists between a mere hobby and a business. The following two cases which involve individuals, illustrate this clearly.

In *Eiman v. London Borough of Waltham Forest* 1982 the issue was whether the defendant had been rightly convicted in the Crown Court of the offence of making a demand for unsolicited goods *"in the course of a trade or business"*, contrary to the Unsolicited Goods and Services Act 1971. As a full time employee of the local authority the accused had, as a hobby, composed and published a book of verse. He had then sent out copies of the book to local libraries and made a demand for payment. The High Court held that the Crown Court was entitled to convict the defendant as what had started as a hobby, had become a *"business"* as defined by the Act and therefore the Unsolicited Goods and Services Act did apply. The court found it possible to reach such a conclusion despite the fact that this was an isolated incident without any intention to make a profit.

In *Blakemore v. Bellamy* 1983 the question was whether the accused's spare time activity of buying and selling motor cars through advertisements, contravened the Fair Trading Act 1973, and the Business Advertisements (Disclosure) Order 1977. This is because in the course of a business it is an offence to *"advertise goods for sale"* without making it clear that the goods were sold in the course of a business. Offences under the Trade Descriptions Act, 1968 were also alleged which involved applying false trade descriptions to two of the vehicles in the course of a business. Despite the number of transactions involved, eight in all, the High Court agreed with the magistrates' finding that the defendant's activity was merely a hobby rather than a business. Accordingly the statutory provisions had not been infringed, for the sales were merely private bargains. This was despite the fact that the defendant's objective in making the sales was to achieve gain or reward and as a seller he had clearly demonstrated skill and expertise in the business of buying and selling cars.

For a partnership the business must be a joint venture, which implies mutual rights and obligations existing between the members of it. There may still be a joint venture even though one (or more) of its members is a sleeping partner who does not take an active part in the management of the business but simply contributes capital, and receives a share of the profits in return.

There must also be a profit motive underlying the business. It will be a question of fact whether the partners aim to make a profit. For these purposes the fact that the business fails to make the profit it intended, or indeed makes a loss is not relevant.

Help in determining when a business may be treated as a partnership is provided by s.2. It says that where a person receives a share in the profits of a business, this will be *prima facie* evidence that he is a partner, although the presumption can be shifted by other conflicting evidence. The section goes on to state a list of situations which do not, of themselves, make a person a partner, for instance: where a person working as an employee or agent of the firm is paid out of a share of its profits, or when people are co-owners of land, even where profits are shared from the use of the land.

Two further situations are specified by s.2 which it indicates do not automatically give rise to a partnership. Firstly co-ownership of land, even where profits are shared from the use of the land. Secondly the sharing of gross returns even if the people sharing the returns have a common right or interest in the property which is yielding the income. This draws a distinction between returns and profit. A return is the revenue obtained by some business activity, such as the receipts obtained from the sale of a book over a fixed period, whilst the profit is the sum left after deducting costs from revenue. In the example these would include printing and transport costs.

Managing the Partnership

The background to the relationship of the partners

Unlike the management arrangements which operate in registered companies, in a partnership every partner is entitled to participate in the management of the business unless the partnership agreement provides otherwise. The partners are managing the business not for others, there are no shareholders, but for themselves. There are obvious problems inherent in attempting to reach the sort of joint decisions which are thus necessary to successfully manage a partnership, and it is not uncommon for partners to disagree. There are also risks involved, both in having unlimited liability, and in the fact that individual partners may be responsible for the acts and defaults of their co-partners. Each partner is an agent of the co-partners and as such has an agent's power to bind the partnership by his acts undertaken within the ordinary course of the business. It is crucial therefore that each partner has trust and confidence in his co-partners, the relationship being one of the utmost good faith. This is sometimes given its latin name and is known as a relationship *uberrimae fidei*. Each partner is therefore under a duty to make a full and frank disclosure to the firm of any matters affecting it that come to the partner's attention.

The power of a partner to bind the other members of the firm by his actions illustrates how important it is that each partner should trust and have confidence in his co-partners, not only in regard to their business ability but also as to their business ethics. In *Helmore v. Smith* 1886 Bacon V-C remarked that, *"mutual confidence is the life-blood"* of the firm, whilst in *Baird's Case* 1870 James LJ stated:

> *"Ordinary partnerships are by the law assumed and presumed to be based upon the mutual trust and confidence of each partner in the skill, knowledge and integrity of every other partner. As between the partners and the outside world (whatever may be their private arrangements between themselves), each partner is the unlimited agent of every other in every matter connected with the partnership business, or which he represents as the partnership business, and not being in its nature beyond the scope of the partnership".*

In the course of business, partnerships enter into transactions with other organisations and individuals and inevitably such transactions are negotiated and executed for the partnership by individual partners, rather than by the firm as a whole. It has already been noted that each partner is an agent of his co-partners. *"In English law a firm as such has no existence; partners carry on business both as principals and as agents for each other within the scope of the partnership business; the firm-name is a mere expression, not a legal entity"*, stated Lord Justice Farwell in *Sadler v. Whiteman* 1910.

Under the law of agency, the person who appoints an agent is called the principal. The principal is bound by contracts made within the agent's actual and apparent authority. If the agent acts within either of these two spheres the contract concluded between the agent and the third party becomes the principal's contract, and hence it is the principal and the third party who become bound to each other. The *actual* authority of an agent is the express power given by the principal. A firm may for instance expressly resolve in a partnership meeting that each partner shall have the power to employ staff. Authority may also arise where the agent's power to make a particular contract or class of contracts can be implied from the conduct of the parties or the circumstances of the case. The *apparent*, or ostensible authority of an agent is the power which the agent appears to others to hold. Of a partner's apparent authority s.5 Partnership Act, 1890, says:

> *"Every partner is an agent of the firm and his other partners for the purpose of the business of the partnership; and the acts of every partner who does any act for the carrying on in the usual way business of the kind carried on by the firm of which he is a member bind the firm and his partners, unless the partner so acting has in fact no authority to act for the firm in the particular matter, and the person with whom he is dealing either knows that he has no authority, or does not know or believe him to be a partner".*

The implications of s.5 are potentially very far reaching and reinforce the judicial comment made above that the essence of a sound partnership is the mutual confidence of the partners. To be in a business with someone who can legally bind you by the business contracts they make is only viable if you have complete confidence in their commercial ability and ethical integrity.

Whether a particular contract is *one "carrying on in the usual way business of the kind carried on by the firm"* is a question of fact.

> In *Mercantile Credit Co. Ltd. v. Garrod* 1962 the court had to decide what would be considered as an act of a *"like kind"* to the business of persons who ran a garage. It was held that the sale of a car to a third party by one of the partners bound the other *partners.* This was despite an agreement between them that provided for the carrying out of repair work, and the letting of garages, but expressly excluded car sales.

A private limitation of the powers of an agent is not an effective way to bring the restriction to the notice of an outsider dealing with the agent, and the law recognises this. In a partnership such limitations may result from restrictions placed upon the capacity of the partners contained within their formal partnership agreement, or alternatively be a restriction agreed upon at a meeting of the partners. But if, for example, a partner has acted as an agent for his firm in the past with a particular third party, and he carries out a further transaction of a similar kind with the third party after the firm has taken away his express authority, the third party can nevertheless hold the firm bound, unless he knew at the time of contracting of the partner's lack of authority.

The exact scope of an agent's apparent authority under s.5 has been the subject of much litigation. In any partnership partners will usually have the apparent authority to: sell the goods or personal property of the firm; purchase in the firm's name goods usually or necessarily used in the firm's business; receive payments due to the firm; and employ staff to work for the firm. In a trading partnership (where the business is buying and selling goods) partners will additionally have authority to:

borrow money for a purpose connected with the business of the firm; and deal with payments to and from the firm.

Since a partnership has no separate legal identity it is the individual partners who are ultimately accountable for all the firm's debts. Under the Partnership Act every partner is jointly liable with the other partners for all the debts and obligations of the firm incurred whilst being a partner. A legal action by a creditor seeking to recover money owed to him may be brought against any one or more of the firm's partners. However if the judgment obtained in the court does not satisfy the creditor he cannot then sue the remaining partners for having sued one partner, he is precluded from suing the others for the same debt. Nevertheless the creditor, if he had chosen to do so, could have sued the firm in its own name rather than suing an individual partner of the firm. This has the effect of automatically joining all the partners in the action, and means that the judgment will be met out of assets of the firm as a whole and, if there is a shortfall, out of the property of the individual partners.

The Act goes on to provide that the firm is liable for *"the wrongful act or omission of any partner"* committed within the ordinary course of the firm's business. The term *wrongful* covers tortious acts, although it appears that it does not extend to criminal acts.

An exception however occurs in relation to fraudulent acts carried out within the scope of the firm's business.

In *Hamlyn v. Houston & Co.* 1903 the defendant firm was run by two partners as a grain merchants. One of the partners bribed the clerk of a rival grain merchant, and obtained information from him which enabled the firm to compete at greater advantage. The Court of Appeal held that both partners were liable for this tortious act. Obtaining *information* about rivals was within the general scope of the partners' authority, and therefore it did not matter that the method used to obtain it was unlawful. In the words of Lord Collins, M.R: *"It is too well established by the authorities to be now disputed that a principal may be liable for the fraud or other illegal act committed by his agent within the general scope of the authority given to him, and even the fact that the act of the agent is criminal does not necessarily take it out of the scope of his authority"*.

It is no defence for a firm to show that it did not benefit from the unlawful act of its agent.

The House of Lords in *Lloyd v. Grace, Smith & Co.* 1912 held a solicitor's firm liable for the fraud of its managing clerk who induced one of the firm's clients to transfer certain properties into his name. In advising the client the clerk was acting within the scope of his authority, and that alone made the firm liable for his acts.

Although the Act does not apply to criminal matters two points should be noted. Firstly, there may be occasions when one partner may be held vicariously liable for an offence committed by another. Vicarious liability is considered in Chapter 7. Secondly, a partner may be a party to an offence committed by another simply because it is in the nature of that partnership that they work together.

In *Parsons v. Barnes* 1973 where two partners worked together in a roof-repairing business, one of them was convicted of an offence under the Trade Descriptions Act 1968, by being present when his co-partner made a false statement to a customer.

If a partner acting within the scope of his apparent authority receives and misapplies the property of a third person while it is in the firm's custody the firm is liable to meet the third person's loss. Similarly when the firm has received property of a third person in the course of its business, and the property has been misapplied by a partner while in the firm's custody, it must make good the loss. The liability of partners for misapplications of property, or wrongs of the firm, is stated by the Act to be *joint* and *several*. This means that if a judgment is obtained by a plaintiff against one partner, this does not operate as bar to bringing a further action against all or any of the others if the judgment remains unsatisfied. Where liability is merely joint this is not possible. Compare liability for debts, which was discussed earlier.

In *Plumer v. Gregory* 1874 two of the partners in a firm consisting of three solicitors accepted on the firm's behalf and subsequently misappropriated money entrusted to them by the plaintiff, a client of the firm. The third member of the firm was unaware of these events, which only came to light after the other partners had died. The plaintiff's action against the remaining partner succeeded, for the firm was liable to make good the loss, and liability of the members was joint and several.

Changes in membership

The membership of a firm may alter from time to time. The firm may wish to expand its business by bringing in new partners to provide the benefit of additional capital or fresh expertise. Existing partners may leave the partnership to join a new business, or to retire. A changing membership poses the question of the extent to which incoming and outgoing partners are responsible for the debts and liabilities of the firm. Although partners are responsible for any matters arising during their membership of the firm, incoming partners are not liable for the debts incurred before they joined, nor outgoing partners for those incurred after they leave, provided the retiring partner advertises the fact that he is no longer a member of the firm. This involves sending notice to all customers of the firm while that person was a partner, and advertising the retirement in a publication known as the *London Gazette*. If this is not done a person dealing with the firm after a change in its membership can treat all apparent members of the old firm as still being members of the firm. With regard to existing liabilities the partner may be discharged from them when he retires through the agreement of the new firm and the creditors.

Rights and duties of the partners

Ideally the partnership relationship should be regulated by a comprehensive partnership agreement. If it is not, the provisions of the Partnership Act will apply when the parties are in dispute as to the nature of their duties and are unable to reach agreement amongst themselves. In a business enterprise of this sort, where a member's entire wealth lies at stake, it is clearly of great value to execute a detailed agreement setting out in precise form the powers and responsibilities of the members. For instance it would be prudent for such an agreement to provide grounds for the removal of partners, since the Act makes no such provision. Because the members of the firm have the freedom to make their own agreement, without the statutory controls imposed upon other forms of business organisation, such as the registered company, the partnership stands out as a most flexible form of organisation.

The duties that the Act sets rest upon a single principle, namely that the relationship between the parties is of the utmost good faith.

> In *Law v. Law* 1905, a partner sold his share in the business to another partner for £21,000, but the purchasing partner failed to disclose to his co-partner certain facts about the partnership assets, of which he alone was aware. When the vendor realised that he had sold his share at below its true value he sought to have the sale set aside. The Court of Appeal held that in the absence of such disclosure the sale was voidable, and could be set aside. The purchasing partner had a duty to disclose, which he had not fulfilled.

A partner is under a duty to his co-partners to render true accounts and full information of all things affecting the partnership. Personal benefits can only be retained with the consent of the other partners. This parallels the position directors are in.

> In *Bentley v. Craven* 1853 one of the partners in a firm of sugar refiners, who acted as the firm's buyer, was able to purchase a large quantity of sugar at below market price. He resold it to the firm at the true market price. His co-partners were unaware that he was selling on his own account. When they

discovered this they sued him for the profit he had made, and were held to be entitled to it. It was a secret profit and belonged to the firm.

A partner is under a duty not to compete with his firm by carrying on another business of the same nature unless the other partners have consented. If a partner is in breach of this duty he must account to the firm for all the profits made and pay them over. If the partnership agreement prohibits the carrying on of a competing business, the court may grant an injunction to stop a partner who disregards the limitation.

Further rights and duties are set out in the Act which states that, in the absence of a contrary agreement:

- all partners are entitled to take part in the management of the partnership business;

- any differences arising as to ordinary matters connected with the partnership business are to be decided by a majority of the partners, but no change can be made in the nature of the partnership business without the consent of all the partners;

- no person may be introduced as a partner without the consent of all existing partners;

- all partners are entitled to share equally in the profits of the business irrespective of the amount of time they have given to it, and must contribute equally towards any losses. The Act does not require the firm to keep books of account, although this will normally be provided for in the partnership agreement, together with specific reference to the proportions of the profit each partner is entitled to. If however there are partnership books they have to be kept at the principal place of business, where every partner is entitled to have access to them for the purpose of inspection and copying;

- if a partner makes a payment or advance beyond the agreed capital contribution he is entitled to interest at 5% p.a.;

- a partner is not entitled to payment of interest on his capital until profits have been ascertained;

- the firm must indemnify a partner in respect of payments made and personal liabilities incurred in the ordinary and proper conduct of the business of the firm, or in or about anything necessarily done for the preservation of the business or property of the firm (e.g. paying an insurance premium);

- a partner is not entitled to remuneration for acting in the partnership business.

In cases where the firm consists of active and sleeping partners the partnership agreement will often provide that as well as taking a share of the profits the active partners shall be entitled to the payment of a salary.

If any of the terms of the partnership agreement are broken, damages will be available as a remedy, and where appropriate an injunction may be granted.

Partnership property

It can be of importance, particularly to the partners themselves, to establish which assets used by the partnership actually belong to the firm itself, rather than to themselves as individuals. Mere use of property for partnership purposes does not automatically transfer ownership in it to the business.

> In *Miles v. Clarke* 1953 the defendant started up a photography business which involved him in acquiring a lease and photographic equipment. After trading unsuccessfully he was joined by the plaintiff, a free-lance photographer, who brought into the firm his business connection which was of considerable value. The partners traded profitably for some time, on the basis of equal profit sharing. Later, as a result of personal difficulties, it became necessary to wind up the firm. The plaintiff claimed a share in all the assets of the business. The court held that specific assets of the business other than the stock-in-trade, which had become partnership property, belonged to the particular partner who had brought them in.

The Act provides that all property and rights and interests in property originally brought into the partnership or subsequently acquired by purchase or otherwise on account of the firm, must be held and applied by the partners exclusively for the purpose of the partnership and in accordance with the partnership agreement. Such property is called *partnership property* and will normally be jointly owned by the partners. Because a partner is a co-owner of partnership property, rather than a sole owner of any particular part of the partnership's assets, he may be guilty of theft of partnership property if it can be established that his intention was to permanently deprive the other partners of their share.

Under the Act property bought with money belonging to the firm is deemed to have been bought on account of the firm, unless a contrary intention appears.

Choosing the Legal Form for a Business

This chapter has examined the partnership as a form of private sector enterprise. The next two chapters explores the other major type of private sector trading organisation, the registered company. The difference between these types of organisation is significant not only from a legal standpoint but from a commercial one as well.

It is useful to examine the main distinguishing features of a partnership and companies, before going on to look at the law as it applies to companies in more detail. For those about to set up a business organisation the legal question they face is whether to operate in partnership or form a registered company, that is whether or not to incorporate.

Partnership or registered company?

There are two circumstances in which the opportunity for choosing the legal form of the business is illusory.

(i)   Sometimes people drift into business relationships rather than discuss and plan them in advance. Perhaps what began as a mere hobby pursued by two friends develops into a money making venture, and they find themselves in a business relationship without any conscious decision on their part. If their relationship satisfies the definition of a partnership contained in s.1 Partnership Act 1890, then the law will regard them as partners. They do not need to have entered into a written agreement. They many not even be aware of their legal status. In law however they are now operating as a firm.

(ii)   If professional people, such as accountants, architects, doctors or lawyers seek to carry out their work in combination with co-professionals, the law prevents them from incorporating their business. It is only permissible for them to carry out their work collectively in partnership so the opportunity of incorporating is denied them.

Assuming however that like-minded people are anxious to establish a joint business venture, what factors are likely to influence them in deciding whether or not to incorporate? The following checklist of points covers all the major factors, and illustrates the essential legal and commercial differences between the partnership and the registered company.

Registered companies and partnerships compared

(i)   *Legal status*

A registered company is a corporate body once its certificate of incorporation is granted to it. It is an artificial entity and is required to establish its nationality, a registered office where it can be served with formal notices, and provide itself with a name which it must use for the purpose of conducting business. It is legally separate from its members, who may make contracts with it, for example by selling to it a business previously operated as a partnership or on a sole trader basis.

A partnership is not a corporate body. It is no more than the sum total of the individuals who make it up. Although it must register under the Business Names Act 1985 any name it uses to trade under which does not consist of the surnames of all the partners, this name (e.g. Smith and Co.) does not give it any special persona, although for practical convenience Rules of the Supreme Court enable proceedings by and against the firm to be brought in the firms name.

(ii)   *Members' liability*

In a company, the financial liability of the members for any legal liabilities of the business such as trading debts ends when they have fully paid for their shares. There are however particular circumstances where members may still face personal liability, although these are restricted. An example is the potential personal liability of directors who continue to run the company in circumstances where they know or ought to realise the company is unlikely to avoid an insolvent liquidation, and it subsequently goes into an insolvent liquidation (wrongful trading). Essentially however a shareholder has limited liability.

The liability of partners for the debts of a firm is unlimited. If the assets of the firm are insufficient to meet the liability the creditor can look to the personal property of the individual partners. They may have bankruptcy proceedings brought against them. Limited liability is however available in a limited partnership, a special form of partnership which may be established under the provisions of the Limited Partnership Act 1907. There are however very few limited partnerships in operation.

(iii)   *Agency*

In a company, mere membership does not of itself invest the shareholder with the power to act as an agent for and on behalf of the company. Agency powers are contained in the articles of association of the company and these powers are the principal agency source. Articles normally grant full powers as agents to the board of directors. In a firm however each partner is an agent of the other partners and of the partnership as a whole (s.5 Partnership Act 1890).

(iv)   *Management*

Whereas companies are managed by those granted the power to do so under the articles – the directors of the company, in a firm all the members have the full right to take part in its management. Denial of this right would entitle the aggrieved partner to petition to have the firm dissolved. Thus whilst ownership and management are often in separate hands in the case of a registered company, this is never the position in a firm. Consequently the means available to company members to require directors to account for their actions are of crucial importance, and company law provides that certain decisions, such as alterations to the articles, can only legitimately be carried out at a general meeting of the company where all the membership is entitled to be present.

(v)   *Membership*

There is no limit placed on the number of members a registered company may have. New members can join the company with little restriction, although the directors may have the power to refuse a share transfer in some cases. In a firm however a new partner can only join with the consent of all the existing members, emphasising the close commercial relationship of the partners. Moreover normal trading partnerships are restricted to a maximum of twenty partners. There is no limit however placed on the size of a professional partnership. A private company can have a single member but a firm must have two members.

(vi)   *Taxation*

A company pays corporation tax on a flat rate basis on its profits. Currently the rate is 29%. Shareholders are taxed on the dividends the company pays them.

In a partnership partners pay tax on the apportioned profits they receive from the business under Schedule D. This covers earnings from a trade, profession or occupation and enables them to pay tax on a preceding year basis and claim allowances against their tax liability for expenses incurred in their work for the business, e.g. costs of running a car.

(vii) *Borrowing*

Companies, particularly larger ones, have much greater borrowing capability than partnerships. They can raise loan capital by issuing debentures and provide security by way of floating charges, neither of which partnerships can do.

(viii) *Formalities and public inspection*

Whereas a firm can maintain complete secrecy over its affairs (other than providing details of its proprietors where the Business Names Act 1985 applies) a registered company must provide the Registrar of Companies with a wealth of detail about itself on a regular basis. All of this information is held on its file and is available for public inspection. Thus its membership, its annual accounts, and details of the property it has charged, are amongst the long list of details which the Registrar must be provided with. There are also fees to be paid when such documents are delivered e.g. £25 on filing a copy of the annual return, and also of course a considerable internal administration burden for the company in satisfying the extensive information demands of company legislation. Financial penalties can be exacted against companies in default. Moreover company legislation in general is highly prescriptive, demanding particular procedures to be followed, and forms to be used, if a company is to lawfully conduct its affairs.

(ix) *Contractual scope*

Despite the dilution of the ultra vires principle as it applies to registered companies some limited aspects of it remain. A firm on the other hand is not subject to ultra vires. A partnership can make any contract which the partners so choose. A registered company however must determine the scope of its contractual capacity in its constitution, and its directors are under a duty of contract only within these constitutional limitations.

(x) *Capital*

There are stringent rules controlling the way in which registered companies use capital. In particular it is a general principle of company law that capital investment be maintained and not reduced. A firm however has complete freedom over the way in which it uses its capital.

Assignment - The Firm

Charlotte, Peter and Gareth became friends at University whilst studying on a business management degree programme. After completing their studies, and being unable to find the kind of jobs they were looking for, they decided to set up a management consultancy business. They saw this as a very temporary business arrangement, and, at least initially, regarded it in Peter's words "as a bit of a joke." They adopted the title CPG Management Consultants, rented a room in Nottingham which would serve as an office and their business address, and placed advertisements in local newspapers offering their management services. Two years later their business was trading profitably, and at the end of the years trading each of them received in the region of £10,000 out of the profits of the business.

There were however tensions. Gareth was very keen to allow his wife Liz to join the partnership; as an accountant he felt Liz would bring valuable financial expertise into the business. Charlotte in particular was opposed to Liz joining since she did not get on with her.

Peter who had expertise in the marketing field, was of the opinion that the business should expand its services into marketing consultancy work as well, but whenever he raised the issue at the fortnightly management meetings held by the firm, his ideas were firmly put down by Charlotte and Gareth, who were not marketeers and did not want the business to diversify.

Charlotte wanted the business to invest in a very expensive and sophisticated computer system for the business, but at management meetings Peter and Gareth had consistently rejected such investment on the grounds that the firm neither needed nor could afford the system proposed by Charlotte.

Despite being blocked by her co-partners, two weeks ago Charlotte ordered the computer system she believes the firm needs from the office suppliers they normally deal with. Yesterday the suppliers delivered the system, and sought to install it. Gareth, who was in the office at the time, advised the office supplier that Charlotte had no authority to make the purchase, and that CPG would not be paying the invoice. Gareth has also discovered, through the grapevine, that Peter has being carrying out some private marketing consultancy work from the office in the evenings after Gareth and Charlotte have returned home.

Task

Advise Gareth; whether Charlottes contract is binding on the partnership; what the legal consequences, if any, result from the private work being undertaken by Peter; and whether Liz can be introduced to the partnership without the approval of the other partners.

Chapter 4

Registered Companies: Establishing and Funding

Introduction

The previous chapter explained that for legal purposes business organisations can be divided into those which have corporate status, *corporations*, and those which do not, *unincorporated associations*. In this chapter corporate business enterprises are examined.

Corporate bodies are formed for different purposes. Our focus is upon those created for carrying out commercial business activities.

The Companies Act 1985 and the Company Registration System

The expression *company* is used to describe a business organisation that has been created by following the registration system contained in the Companies Act 1985. The 1985 Act is the latest in a series of statutes stretching back over a century and a half. The present Act contains the main legal framework of English company law, supplemented by additional company legislation passed since 1985, and by a substantial body of common law. Company law is a field in which the European Union has also been an active law maker, and many aspects of contemporary English company law are a result of European Company Law Directives. At European level one of the driving forces in introducing legal change has been the need to achieve a harmonisation of company law regimes in each of the member states.

Statutory registration was first introduced under the Companies Act 1844, to provide a method of which was less expensive and cumbersome than obtaining a charter or sponsoring legislation through Parliament. The system of statutory registration proved immediately popular and helped to provide the capital which the growth of business activity at that time urgently needed. Capital was provided by investors attracted not only by the investment prospects offered by newly formed registered companies but also by the financial protection available through limited liability. The registered company remains just as popular with investors today, and has been further stimulated by the privatisation programme pursued by the Thatcher and Major governments during the 1980s and 90s, under which many previously state owned businesses were sold off to the public, such as Jaguar Cars, British Telecom, British Airways, the electricity and gas undertakings and British Rail which was broken and sold off as a series of separate undertakings.

Types of registerable company

The 1985 Act permits different types of company to be registered. It is for those setting up the company, its *promoters,* to decide which type of company is appropriate to the nature and scale of the business they are intending to conduct. The different types of company registerable allow for different levels of liability on the part of the members of the company, that is the *shareholders,* as they are more commonly known.

The liability of the members of a registered company may be limited either by shares or guarantee, or in rare cases be unlimited. This is provided for by s.1(2) of the Companies Act 1985 which states that a company may be:

(i)   limited by *shares,* where the liability of the company members, the shareholders, is limited to any amount as yet unpaid on their shares; or

(ii)   limited by *guarantee,* where the members' liability is limited to an amount they have guaranteed to contribute in the event of the company being brought to an end, a process known technically as winding up; or

(iii)   *unlimited,* where the members are fully liable for the debts of the company, in the event of it being wound up.

Unlimited companies can only operate as private companies. They are used primarily as service and investment companies.

Limited liability means that where a company is unable to pay its debts its shareholders' legal liability to contribute to the payment of debts is limited to the amount, if any, unpaid on their shares. Thus, if an individual purchases twenty £1 shares in a company and pays 25p on each share (these are called partly paid shares) he is only liable to contribute the amount of the share value remaining unpaid, in this case 20 x 75p, a total of £15.

It is of course only the shareholders whose liability is limited. The company itself is fully liable for its debts, and may be brought to an end through the process of winding-up if it cannot meet them.

A further classification divides companies up into those which are *private* and those which are *public*.

Although the number of public limited companies is relatively small (they are numbered in thousands, whilst private companies are numbered in hundreds of thousands), their commercial importance places them at the heart of the private sector economy. They include the major banks, multinational organisations such as ICI, Glaxo and Marks and Spencer, and a range of other household names. Commonly, public companies began life as private companies, becoming sufficiently successful commercially to warrant *going public,* and thus able to offer their shares on the open market.

Thousands of registered limited companies function in the UK between them employing the majority of the nation's workforce and generating about two thirds of the income made by the private sector. Companies can be formed which have only one member. They can also develop into massive multi-national UK registered enterprises which have thousands of shareholders. Such is the diversity of these organisations that it is difficult to generalise on their structure and behaviour but most have been formed with the expectation of future expansion financed by the raising of capital through the issue of shares. As separate legal entities they also give the owners the protection of limited liability and it is this feature more than any other that has contributed to their popularity. Another appealing feature is that ownership can be divorced from management, thus an investor can stake capital in a company without having to be involved in the actual running of it, whilst maintaining control over the managers by means of their accountability in the general meeting.

Companies can expand and diversify by raising additional capital when it is needed, through the issue of more shares, and hence large scale commercial organisations have evolved with thousands of shareholders holding between them millions of shares. The growth of this form of business enterprise and the recognition of the company as a separate legal entity has however posed many problems and led to many abuses. The law has recognised these difficulties. Various Companies Acts, now consolidated in the Companies Act 1985, have sought to regulate corporate behaviour, bearing in mind not only the interests of the shareholders themselves but also the interests of outsiders who trade with them.

The concept of corporate personality

As an artificial legal person, the registered company has many of the legal attributes of a natural person. It can own property, make legally binding agreements to buy or sell goods and services, execute contracts of employment, and sue or be sued in its own name. But its artificial nature imposes obvious limitations upon its legal capacity. It cannot vote for example. Nevertheless sometimes the collective intention of the board of directors can be regarded as expressing the will of the corporation. Lord Denning has spoken of the company as having a human body, the employees being the hands that carry out its work while *"others are directors and managers who represent the directing mind and will of the company and control what it does"*. As a corporate body, a company may be prosecuted where it is alleged to have committed a criminal offence. For a company to be convicted the court must be satisfied it is responsible in some way for the offence. In effect this means that the liability arises through the unlawful actions of human agents acting in its name and on its behalf. Usually these people will be its employees.

Corporate criminal liability can occur in two ways. Firstly it can occur where a company is held liable for a criminal act under the principle of *vicarious*, or substituted, liability. This means that the company is being treated as though its employees criminal action is its own. Usually such liability can only be established where the offence is one of strict liability, that is to say an offence which can be committed without evidence of fault on the part of the wrongdoer. Examples of offences of strict liability include many of the road traffic offences; driving a vehicle with worn tyres or defective brakes is an example.

However more serious criminal offences usually contain as part of their definitions, a component known technically as the *mens rea* of the offence. The mens rea, literally "guilty mind", is the state of mind the wrongdoer has to have possessed to be convicted. Examples of mens rea components include intention, recklessness, wilfulness, and negligence. In the case of these more serious offences, liability on the part of the company has to be *direct* liability. A company can be convicted in this way for any offence except murder.

It cannot be convicted of murder as this offence carries a mandatory life sentence, and a corporation cannot be imprisoned. Direct or primary liability for criminal acts has only been recognised by the courts in more modern times.

> In *Lennard's Carrying Company Co. Ltd. v. Asiatic Petroleum Co. Ltd.* 1915, Viscount Haldane remarked that, *"A corporation is an abstraction. It has no mind of its own any more than it has a body of its own; its active and directing will must consequently be sought in the person of somebody who…is really the directing mind and will of the personality of the corporation."* This suggests someone at the very top of the organisation, someone who, in Viscount Haldane's words is the essence of corporation itself since, *"his action is the very action of the company itself."*

It was upon the basis of this line of legal reasoning that a charge of manslaughter was brought against P&O Ferries Ltd. in respect of the 192 deaths resulting from the Zeebrugge disaster in 1987. Although the company was not convicted it is apparent that there is no technical bar to the bringing of a prosecution for *corporate crimes* of this kind. The company escaped conviction when the trial judge, Turner J. directed the jury to find it not guilty. This direction was based upon the failure of the prosecution to show that any of the five senior managers, who were also tried for manslaughter with the company, had the necessary state of mind (the mens rea) to be convicted of manslaughter. Only if at least one of them could be found guilty of the offence could the company be found guilty as well. Thus corporate guilt would automatically follow from the guilt of an individual representing the guiding mind and will of the company, a test known as the "identification doctrine". Such a person would normally be either a director, or a senior officer of the company. The judge rejected the argument that the guilt of the company could be established through the collective fault of those responsible for managing it - sometimes referred to as the principle of aggregation.

> In a well publicised prosecution, *R v. OLL Ltd.* 1994, the requirements identified by Turner J. for the successful prosecution of a company for 'corporate' manslaughter were for the first time met. The company operated an activity centre. Evidence showed that the company routinely employed unqualified instructors. Canoes being used by sixth formers capsized whilst they crossed Lyme Bay. Four of them drowned. They had all been instructed, wrongly, not to inflate their life jackets in the event of a capsize. The managing director of the company, Peter Kite, was convicted of manslaughter and given a three year sentence. His *mens rea* was imputed to the company, which was also convicted of manslaughter and fined £60,000, a sum which allegedly represented its total assets.

Whilst the conviction of *OLL Ltd.* demonstrated that a corporation *could* be convicted of manslaughter, the law in this area was still felt to be unsatisfactory. A company whose management of safety was negligent, or even reckless, could not be convicted unless there was sufficient evidence to convict a senior officer. Such evidence might be difficult to obtain, since directors are not subject to duty of safety at law, and since in many companies responsibility for safety matters is delegated to lower levels of management. A spate of high profile cases since *OLL,* such as the Southwell and Paddington rail crashes, have resulted in the government announcing in Spring 2000 that legislation will be introduced to create a new offence of corporate killing and to impose liability upon culpable directors.

Since the members of the company and the company itself are legally separate, changes in the membership, including the death or bankruptcy of members, have no legal effect upon the company. It may have an almost perpetual life span if there remain investors willing to become or to remain members of it.

> The legal separation of a company from its members was confirmed in the leading case of *Salomon v. Salomon & Co.* 1897. Salomon owned a boot and

shoe business. His sons worked in the business and they were anxious to have a stake in it so Salomon formed a registered company with himself as managing director, in which his wife, daughter and each son held a share. The company's nominal capital was £40,000 consisting of 40,000 £1 shares.

The company resolved to purchase the business at a price of £39,000. Salomon had arrived at this figure himself. It was an honest but optimistic valuation of its real worth. The company paid him by allotting him 20,000 £1 shares treated as fully paid, £10,000 worth of debentures (a secured loan repayable before unsecured loans) and the balance in cash. Within a year of trading the company went into insolvent liquidation owing £8,000 to ordinary creditors and having only £6,000 worth of assets. The plaintiff, Mr. Salomon, claimed that as a debenture holder with £10,000 worth of debentures he was a secured creditor and entitled to repayment before the ordinary unsecured creditors. The unsecured creditors did not agree. The House of Lords held that although following the company's formation Salomon had continued to run the business in the same manner and with the same control as he had done when it was unincorporated, the company formed was a separate person from Salomon himself. When the company was liquidated therefore, and in the absence of any fraud on the creditors and shareholders, Salomon, like any other debenture holder, was a secured creditor and entitled to repayment before ordinary creditors. The court thus upheld the principle that a company has a separate legal existence from its membership even where one individual holds the majority of shares and effectively runs the company as his own. In his leading judgment Lord Macnaghten stated, *"The company is at law a different person altogether from the subscribers to the memorandum; and, though it may be that after incorporation the business is precisely the same as it was before, and the same persons are managers, and the same hands receive the profits, the company is not in law the agent of the subscribers or trustee for them. Nor are the subscribers as members liable, in any shape or form, except to the extent and in the manner provided by the Act."*

Many consequences flow from this fundamental proposition of company law. For example the company's bank account is quite separate and independent from the account of the majority shareholder.

In *Underwood Ltd. v. Bank of Liverpool & Martins Ltd.* 1924 it was held that a managing director who held all except one of the shares in his company was acting unlawfully in paying company cheques into his own account, and drawing cheques on the company's account for his own personal benefit.

The application of the *Salomon* principle also makes it possible for a shareholder/director to be convicted on a charge of theft from his own company: *Re: Attorney General's Reference (no. 2 of 1982)* 1984.

A company is the owner of its own property and in which its members have no legal interest, although clearly they have a financial interest.

> In *Macaura v. Northern Assurance Co. Ltd.* 1925 it was held that a majority shareholder has no insurable interest in the company's property. A fire insurance policy over the company's timber estate was therefore invalid as it had been issued in the plaintiff shareholder's name and not the company's name.

Lifting the corporate veil

Both the courts and Parliament have accepted that in some situations it is right and proper to prevent the members from escaping liability by hiding behind the facade of the company. The result has been the creation of a number of exceptions to the principle of limited liability. These exceptions seem to be based broadly upon public policy considerations, and many of them are associated with fraudulent practices. If for instance a company is wound up, and the court is satisfied that the directors have carried on the business with an intention to defraud the creditors, they may be made personally liable for company's debts.

The common law position

The courts are prepared to disregard the separate legal personality of a company where the company has been formed or used to facilitate the evasion of legal obligations. This is sometimes referred to as lifting the veil of incorporation, meaning that the court is able to look behind the corporate, formal identity of the organisation to the shareholders which make it up. It is a very significant step, since stripping away the corporate facade removes the protection which the members have sought to obtain by incorporation.

> In *Gilford Motor Co. Ltd. v. Horne* 1933 the defendant had been employed by the plaintiff motor company and had entered into a valid agreement not to solicit the plaintiff's customers or to compete with it for a certain time after leaving the company's employment. Shortly after leaving the employment of the motor company, the defendant formed a new company to carry on a similar business to that of his former employers and sent out circulars to the customers he had previously dealt with whilst working for the old business. In an action to enforce the restraint clause against the new company the court held that as the defendant in fact controlled the new company, its formation was a mere *"cloak or sham"* to enable him to break the restraint clause. Accordingly an injunction was granted against the defendant and against the company he had formed, to enforce the restraint clause.

Similarly in *Jones v. Lipman* 1962 the defendant agreed to sell land to the plaintiff and then decided not to complete the contract. To avoid the possibility of an order to specific performance to enforce the sale the defendant purchased a majority shareholding in an existing company to which he then sold the land. The plaintiff applied to the court for an order against the defendant and the company to enforce the sale. It was held that the formation of the company was a mere sham to avoid a contract of sale, and specific performance was ordered against the vendor and the company.

In *Re: Bugle Press Ltd.* 1961 the company consisted of three shareholders. Two of them, who together had controlling interest, wanted to buy the shares of the third, but he was not willing to sell so the two of them formed a new company which then made a take-over bid for the shares of the first company. Not surprisingly the two shareholders who had formed the new company accepted the bid. The third did not. However since he only held 1/10 of the total shareholding, under what is now s.428 Companies Act 1985, the new company was able to compulsorily acquire the shares. The Court of Appeal however held that this represented an abuse of the section. The minority shareholder was in effect being evicted from the company. The veil of the new company was lifted and, in the words of Harman LJ: this revealed a *"hollow sham"*, for it was *"nothing but a little hut built round"* the majority shareholders.

The courts are sometimes prepared to lift the veil in order to discover the relationship within groups of companies. It is a common commercial practice for one company to acquire shares in another, often holding sufficient shares to give it total control over the other. In these circumstances the controlling company is referred to as a *holding* or *parent* company, and the other company its *subsidiary*. In appropriate cases a holding company can be regarded as an agent of its subsidiary, although it is more usual to find the subsidiary acting as an agent for the holding company.

In *Firestone Tyre & Rubber Co. Ltd. v. Llewellin (Inspector of Taxes)* 1957 the appellant company was a subsidiary of an American company which made and sold branded tyres and had a world-wide organisation. The British subsidiary manufactured and sold tyres in Europe. The House of Lords held that the appellant company was in fact not trading on its own behalf but as agent of the parent company and the parent company was consequently liable to pay United Kingdom income tax.

In *DHN Food Distributors Ltd. v. Tower Hamlets LBC.* 1976 an arrangement under which two subsidiaries of the holding company were wholly owned by it and had no separate business operations from it, was held by the Court of Appeal to constitute a single corporate body rather than three separate ones. It is difficult to see how this case can be reconciled with the basic principle in *Salomon*.

In *Woolfson v. Strathclyde Regional Council* 1978 the House of Lords, on similar facts came to the opposite conclusion, although it was not prepared to overrule the *DHN* decision. In *Adams v. Cape Industries plc* 1990 the Court of Appeal however made clear that ???? because a parent company and its subsidiaries might be regarded as a single corporate entity for economic purposes, this should not mean that they can be automatically treated as a single entity for legal purposes.

In some cases the courts have disregarded the separate legal personality of a company and have in the public interest investigated the personal qualities of the shareholders. It is in the public interest that an enemy alien is unable to sue in British courts.

In *Daimler Co. Ltd. v. Continental Tyre and Rubber Co. (Gt. Britain) Ltd.* 1916 the tyre company, which was registered in England, and had its registered office there, sued Daimler for debts incurred before the war with Germany had been declared. Daimler claimed that as all the members of the tyre company except one were German nationals and the directors were German nationals resident in Germany the claim should be struck out because to pay the debt would be to trade with the enemy. The House of Lords held that although the nationality of a company is normally decided by where it is incorporated, in some cases the court has power to consider who was in control of the company's business and assets in order that it might determine its status. Here, those in control of the company were enemy aliens and the action was struck out.

It is clear however that the circumstances in which the courts will be prepared to lift the corporate veil remain very limited, a point reaffirmed by the Court of Appeal in *Ord v. Belhaven Pubs Ltd.* 1998. In this case Mr and Mrs Ord bought a pub lease, relying on representations about its profitability and turnover by the vendors, Belhaven. The Ords subsequently claimed that all the representations were false, and some of them were fraudulent, and they sued Belhaven. However by the time the claim was brought, the group of companies of which Belhaven was a member had undergone a rationalisation. All Belhavens assets had been transferred to a sister company and to its parent company. The Ords thus sought to claim against both the sister and parent company instead. The court refused to allow this. Belhaven was still a company, albeit dormant. If the sister or parent company were to be substituted as defendants this would really be a new action against the shareholders of the company, rather than the company itself. In effect it would be lifting the veil of incorporation, and in the absence of any fraud or impropriety, such a step would not be allowed.

The statutory position

In addition to this common law approach there are a number of provisions contained in the Companies Act 1985 which have the effect of lifting the veil.

(a)   Under s.24, if a public company has only one shareholder for more than six months, then that sole shareholder becomes personally liable for the company's debts incurred after that time. Note that to be a member of a company it is only necessary to hold a single share.

(b)   Under s.349(4) if an officer of a company or any person on its behalf:

  (i)   uses the company seal and the company name is not engraved on it;

  (ii)   issues or authorises the issue of a business letter or signs a negotiable instrument and the company name is not mentioned;

  (iii)   issues or authorises the issue of any invoice, receipt or letter of credit of the company and again the company name is not mentioned;

  that person shall be personally liable for debts incurred unless the company agrees to pay them.

In *Penrose v. Martyr* 1858 a bill of exchange was drawn up with the word 'limited' omitted after the company's name and the company secretary who had signed the bill on the company's behalf was held to be personally liable for it.

In *Hendon v. Adelman* 1973 directors of a company whose registered name was L & R Agencies Ltd. signed a cheque on behalf of the company omitting the ampersand between 'L' and 'R'. The bank failed to honour the cheque and the directors were held personally liable on it.

(c)   Under powers granted to the Department of Trade and Industry to investigate the affairs of any company within the same group as one primarily under investigation by a DTI Inspector.S442(1) provides that where there appears to be good reason to do so, the Department may appoint inspectors to investigate and report on the membership of any company in order to determine the true identity of the persons financially interested in its success or failure, or able to control or materially influence its policy.

(d)   Under sections 213 and 214 Insolvency Act 1986. These important provisions are considered later in the chapter.

Public and Private Companies

S1 Companies Act 1985 provides that a registered company limited by shares may be either a *public* or a *private* one. The most significant distinction between them is that a public limited company is permitted to advertise publicly to invite investors to take shares in it. A private company cannot advertise its shares in this way. Once purchased, shares in a public company can then be freely disposed of by the shareholder to anyone else who is willing to buy them. By contrast private companies commonly issue shares on terms that if the member wishes to dispose of them they must first be offered to the existing members. Where such rights are available to members they are known as *pre-emption* rights.

All companies are now treated as though they are private ones, unless certain requirements have been met which allow the company to be registered as a public limited company. This change was introduced to make it easier to define public companies for the purpose of complying with EC company law directives applicable to public companies.

Registration as a public limited company

This can be achieved by satisfying the following requirements:

(i)   stating both in the company name, and in its memorandum, that it is a public company. Thus its name must end in the words *"public limited company"* or the shortened form *"plc."* The name of a private company will end with the word *"limited"* or *"Ltd."*;

(ii)   registering a memorandum of association which is in the form contained in Table F of the Companies (Tables A to F) Regulations 1985;

(iii) meeting the requirement of s.11 of the 1985 Act, which states that the company must have an authorised share capital figure of at least £50,000. The memorandum of association always contains a capital clause stating the amount of capital a company can raise by issuing shares, and it is in this clause that the authorised share capital amount appears. At least one quarter of this amount must be paid up before the company can commence trading, or exercise its borrowing powers, and the company must have allotted shares up to the authorised minimum (ss.101 and 107). Consequently a plc. must have at least £12,500 paid up share capital before it starts trading, and be able to call for an additional £37,500 from its members.

An explanation of the terms regarding company capital may be helpful here.

The *nominal share capital* is the amount that the company is legally authorised to raise by the issue of shares, the *paid-up share* capital is the amount the company has received from the shares it has issued, and the *uncalled capital* is the amount remaining unpaid by shareholders for the shares they hold; e.g. a company may issue £1 shares but require those to whom they are allotted to pay only 50p per share for the present.

The expression *allotment of shares* describes the notification by the company, usually in the form of a letter, that it has accepted an offer for the shares, and that the new shareholders name will be entered on the register of shareholders.

A registered company which does not meet the three requirements listed above is treated as a private company. Private companies differ from public companies in a number of respects. Examining the advantages and disadvantages of a private company over a public one is a way of exploring these differences.

The advantages of a private company

In contrast to a public company a private company enjoys the following advantages:

- it does not require a minimum level of share capital either to register or to commence trading. Its share capital could legitimately comprise of 1p made up by a single share held by a sole member;

- it can avoid s.89 Companies Act 1985, which provides that ordinary shares issued for cash by the company must first be offered to existing ordinary shareholders in proportion to the nominal value of their existing holdings - a *rights issue*. S.91 provides that s.89 can be excluded by a private company in its articles;

- it has a much greater freedom to issue shares in return for assets other than cash than a public company has (for instance where it purchases property which it pays for by transferring fully paid shares to the vendor);

- the directors have greater freedom in their financial dealings with the company and need not disclose as much information about such dealings in the company accounts as is the case for directors of public companies;

- it can be formed and operated with a single member (see below);

- subject to its size it may be excluded from publishing of some or all of its accounts;

- no special qualifications are required of the company secretary;

- it has power to purchase its own shares, and may do so out of capital;

- it can use procedures to avoid the need to hold meetings and satisfy various other statutory obligations. These procedures were introduced by provisions contained in the Companies Act 1989, designed to make it easier for private companies to comply with the substantial level of statutory regulation imposed upon registered companies. The objective has been to further deregulate the private company, thereby assisting it in the conduct of its business affairs. What the Act does is to permit private companies to *deregulate* themselves by means of the use of two types of resolution, the written resolution and the elective resolution.

The written resolution

By using the written resolution procedure a private company is able to do anything which would otherwise require a resolution of the members in a general meeting of the company. The written resolution must be signed by or on behalf of all the members of the company, who, at the date of the resolution, would be entitled to attend and vote at the meeting which would otherwise have to be held to conduct the business. If their approval is obtained a copy of the proposed resolution has to be sent to the company auditors, who must decide whether it concerns them in their capacity as the auditors. If it does they must then indicate whether they are willing to give it their approval. If they approve it the resolution is effective as if it had been passed in general meeting, but if it is not granted the company must hold a general meeting to conduct the business in the ordinary way. This procedure is not available in certain circumstances e.g. to remove a director, and in other cases there are further formalities which must be complied with.

The elective resolution

An elective resolution can be used by a private company as a means of avoiding a number of formalities that it would otherwise have to observe under company legislation. Such a resolution can dispense with the need to obtain the authority of the members before the company issues shares, the need to lay accounts and reports before the general meeting, the need to hold an annual general meeting, and to reappoint auditors annually. Like the written resolution, the elective resolution requires the unanimous approval of all the company members entitled to attend and vote at a general meeting. There are certain qualifications attached to the use of an elective resolution. For instance if it is used to dispense with the need to hold an annual general meeting, a member may serve written notice on the company no later than three months before the end of the year to which the meeting relates, requiring that it be held. In addition an elective resolution can be revoked by means of an ordinary resolution (which requires a simple majority) passed by the members in general meeting.

The disadvantages of a private company

The only major disadvantage it suffers is that it cannot advertise its securities to the public through the issue of a prospectus or other advertising device. S.170 Financial Services Act 1986 however does enable the Secretary of State to make regulations allowing for purely private advertisements between the issuer and the recipient. This lack of capacity to raise capital through the public issue of shares can really only be regarded as a disadvantage if the growth of the business needs to be financed in this way, when the company faces a choice between remaining privately owned and seeking finance by other means, or of going public and reducing the level of control exercisable by the original members over the new business as new members are brought in. It is worth bearing in mind that in general, company survival is achieved by growth. Such growth may be through the expansion of its core business. Alternatively it may occur through mergers with other companies, or, most commonly, where one company acquires another through a *take-over*. But however growth occurs it must always be financed.

Single Member Companies

The Companies (Single Member Private Limited Companies) Regulations 1992, implementing the Twelfth Company Law Directive, allow for the formation and operation of private limited companies having a *single* member. This amends s.1 CA 1985 which requires a company to have at least two members. Now the rule only applies to public companies. The register of members of a single member company must state that it is such a company, and provide the name and address of the sole member; company resolutions must be evidenced in writing; and any contract between the sole member and the company (unless made in the ordinary course of its business on the usual terms and conditions) must be expressed in writing.

The result of the Regulations is that neither s.24 CA 1985 nor s.122 Insolvency Act 1986 apply any longer to private companies. Under s.24, where company membership falls to one, the sole remaining member can become personally liable for the debts of the company; s.122 enables the court to wind up a company if its membership falls below two.

S.283 CA 1985 is not however affected, so even a single member company must still have two officers, a director and a secretary. Normally the sole member is likely to be the director, and the non-member the secretary.

The meaning of the expression public company

As we have seen a public limited company is one which satisfies certain statutory criteria. However the expression public company is sometimes used in a commercial rather than a legal sense to denote companies whose shares are dealt with on the Stock Exchange; major United Kingdom organisations such as ICI and Marks and Spencer are examples. Technically such companies are *listed* or *market* companies. Not all public limited companies are quoted i.e. listed on the Stock Exchange, but only the largest ones which are able to meet the stringent entry requirements the Stock Exchange demands. Those public limited companies which are not quoted on the Stock Exchange will offer their securities in one of the intermediate securities markets, such as the Unlisted Securities Market (the USM) a *junior league* of the Stock Exchange set up in 1980. The other intermediate securities markets are the Over the Counter Market and the Third Market. Thus public and private companies can be classified by reference to the method by which their shares can be issued. Company financing is considered later in the chapter.

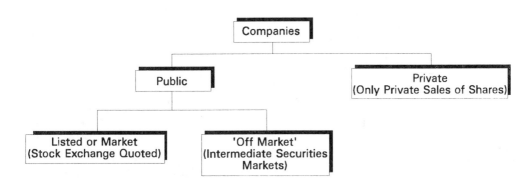

Figure 4.1   *Classification of Companies by Market*

Formation of a Registered Company

A company is incorporated and so comes into being when the Registrar of Companies issues it with a document called the certificate of incorporation. This certificate is issued following an application by the persons who wish to form the company. They are known as the company's *promoters* and they are considered in more detail a little later. The two main documents which must be included in the application are the *memorandum of association* and the *articles of association*. Once the certificate of incorporation has been granted a private company can commence trading immediately, however a public company must be issued with a further document, a *trading certificate*, before it is authorised to start trading.

The Memorandum of Association

The memorandum of association and the articles of association set out the constitution of a registered company. They are the two major documents within a group of documents to be sent to the Registrar of Companies prior to incorporation. A memorandum is required by the Companies Act 1985 which specifies that it must include the following matters:

(i)   the name of the company with *limited* as the last word in the case of a private company, or *public limited company* in the case of a public company;

(ii)   the situation of the registered office identifying whether the company is situated in England or Scotland;

(iii) the objects of the company;

(iv)   the liability of the members;

(v)   the nominal capital of the company and its division into numbers of shares and denominations.

The Registrar of Companies maintains a file for all registered companies, which is open to public inspection on payment of a fee. The file for each company includes the company memorandum. The contents of the memorandum are of importance to the members of the company itself (the shareholders), and especially to those who deal with the company commercially. The indication that the company has limited liability shown by the inclusion of the word `limited', serves as a warning to outsiders that in the event of the company being unable to meet its financial liabilities at any time, its shareholders, can only be called upon to make good any loss up to the value which remains unpaid to the company on their shares. Once however the shares have been fully paid the shareholders' financial liability ceases. Of course the liability of the company, as opposed to its members, is not limited in any way and if it is wound up all its assets will be used to meet the claims of the creditors.

Stating the country in which the company is situated determines whether it is an English or Scottish company. Usually a Notice of Situation of Registered Office, giving the company's full address is sent to the Registrar together with the Memorandum. It must, in any event, be sent to him within fourteen days of incorporation of the company. The registered office is important since documents are effectively served on the company by posting or delivering them to this address. A *writ* (a document used to commence legal proceedings) served on the company will be effectively served if delivered to the registered office.

The *objects clause* sets the contractual limits within which the company can validly operate. The need to state the company's objects may be seen as a protection to shareholders by giving them some reassurance as to the ways in which their capital may be used by the directors. It also acts as a potential control over the powers of the directors. A company, can, however, resolve to alter its objects, and in any event it is usual to draft the objects clause very widely. Furthermore even if a company acts outside its objects clause the transaction will in most cases be binding on it, although the members may seek to censure the authorising directors. This matter is considered in more detail below.

The *liability clause* is a formality which merely states the nature of the shareholders' liability, that is whether it is limited by shares, by guarantee, or unlimited.

The *capital clause* sets out the amount of capital the company is authorised to raise by the issue of shares, and the way in which the shares are to be divided. This amount can be raised by the agreement of the shareholders without difficulty, although a reduction in the share capital, whilst possible, is more strictly regulated. It is a basic principle of company law that share capital should be maintained to protect the interests of the company's creditors.

The memorandum concludes with the names and addresses of those people agreeing to take shares in the company on its formation, indicating how many shares each will take. These people are called *subscribers*. The subscribers for the shares in the memorandum will often be appointed as directors. As the statutory minimum membership of a private company is one, a single subscriber to the memorandum will suffice to form the company. The minimum membership for a public company is two. Each subscriber will agree to take a certain number of shares on incorporation of the company, and the subscribers are therefore the first members of the company. Subsequently new members will join the company as and when it allots shares to them and their names are entered on the register of members. Every company must maintain a register of members which is open to public inspection. Usually the subscribers will have been the company promoters - the people engaged in setting up the company.

Company name

Generally a company is free to choose the name it wishes to adopt, although as we have seen the word *limited* for a private company or *plc* for a public company must be inserted at the end of the company name. This is required by s.26 Companies Act

1985, which also provides that the name cannot be the same as one already held on the index of company names kept by the Registrar. Nor can a name be used which would in the opinion of the Secretary of State constitute a criminal offence or be offensive.

It is a tort for a person to represent his business as that of another and thereby obtain profit from that other's business goodwill. In such circumstances the injured business can claim under the tort of passing off against the business guilty of the deception, and recover damages and obtain an injunction, by way of a remedy.

> In *Ewing v. Buttercup Margarine Co. Ltd.* 1917 the plaintiff, who carried on business using the name Buttercup Dairy Co., obtained an injunction against the defendant company on the grounds that the public might be confused as to the identity of the two organisations.

It makes no difference whether the name is real or invented.

> In *Exxon Corporation v. Exxon Insurance Consultants International Ltd.* 1981 the plaintiffs obtained an injunction to prevent the defendants from passing off its goods as the defendant's by the use of the word *Exxon*. The plaintiffs, formerly the Esso Company, had invented the word *Exxon* as a replacement name. They were however unsuccessful in seeking an injunction for breach of copyright. The court held that the word *Exxon* was not an *"original literary work"* under the Copyright Act 1956, since, in the words of Stephenson LJ a *"literary work is something intended to afford either information and instruction or pleasure in the form of literary enjoyment"*.

The objects clause and the ultra vires doctrine

Being a corporate body the registered company can only lawfully do those things which its constitution allows it to do. It is a direct consequence of the artificiality of corporations which, being purely creations of the law, only possess a restricted capacity. As a condition of incorporation every registered company must include a statement in its memorandum which sets out what the company has been formed to do. The scope or extent of this statement, known as the company's *objects clause*, is initially decided by the people setting up the company, its promoters. They will often become the company's first directors following its incorporation.

The details contained in the objects clause provide shareholders with a description of the range of activities their company can legitimately undertake. It is right that, as investors, a company's shareholders should know the purpose for which their financial contribution can be used. A rational investor will want to establish how well the board of directors manages the company, something which can be achieved by looking at the company's past and present trading performance in its particular line of business. An investor may be less willing to put money into an enterprise where the board has a wide freedom under the company's objects clause to pursue diverse commercial activities, some of which may fall well outside their experience as managers. This is particularly likely in the smaller private companies, for whereas the boards handling the affairs of public companies will include executive directors having wide commercial experience, in small private limited companies directors will sometimes have at best only a rudimentary knowledge of business management, and at worst none at all.

If a company acts outside the limits of its permissible activities as expressed in the objects clause it is said to be acting *ultra vires*, that is beyond its powers. At common law an ultra vires transaction has always been treated as a nullity, consequently an ultra vires contract entered into by a company was neither enforceable by it or against it. Even if the other contracting party was unaware that the company was exceeding its powers as expressed in the memorandum this would provide no relief, for under the doctrine of *constructive notice* a person dealing with a company was deemed to be aware of its public documents and hence of any restrictions on the company's capacity contained in them. Nor could the company subsequently ratify in general meeting an ultra vires transaction made on its behalf by the directors. Ratification has the effect of retrospectively validating a transaction, but in the case of an ultra vires contract this is not possible since the contract is a nullity.

> The application of these principles is seen in *Ashbury Railway Carriage Co. Ltd. v. Riche* 1875. The company's objects included the power to manufacture or sell rail rolling stock and carry on business as mechanical engineers and general contractors. The company purchased a concession to finance the building of a railway in Belgium, but later the directors repudiated the contract. In an action for breach of contract against the company, the House of Lords held that the contract was ultra vires and void from the outset. Lord Cairns expressed the law when he said, *"This contract was entirely beyond the objects in the memorandum ... If it was a contract void at its beginning, it was void because the company could not make the contract".*

When the United Kingdom became a member of the European Community on 1st January, 1973, the European Communities Act 1972, by which entry was effected, in a hurried attempt at providing for some measure of harmonisation between English company law and company law as it applied in the other member states, introduced an important statutory modification to the ultra vires doctrine. This modification, which was contained in s.9(1), and was subsequently incorporated unchanged into the Companies Act 1985 as s.35, provided that in favour of a person acting in good faith with a company, any transaction decided on by its directors was deemed to be within the capacity of the company to make. Whilst not eliminating the doctrine of ultra vires s.35 went some way towards reducing its impact. The

Companies Act 1989, which more fully implemented the first EC directive on company law, introduced a new s.35 which goes much further towards eliminating ultra vires as it affects the registered company. However the doctrine is still not completely dead.

The present law

The present s.35 states that, *"The validity of an act done by a company shall not be called into question on the ground of lack of capacity by reason on anything in the company's memorandum."* In other words it validates transactions which would otherwise be void on the grounds of breaching the company's constitution as expressed in the memorandum. The section goes on to say that anyone making a transaction with the company is not obliged to check the memorandum to ascertain whether it authorises the transaction. A further provision, s.711A, abolishes the doctrine of constructive notice of matters which would be disclosed by a company search. Previously, as we have seen, a person dealing with a company was in some circumstances deemed to have knowledge of information contained in the public file of the company held at the Companies Registry. This principle no longer applies.

The changes introduced under the Companies Act 1989 do not however completely eliminate the application of ultra vires to registered companies. In this context three matters need to be noted:

(i)   a shareholder still retains the power to seek an injunction to restrain the company from entering into an ultra vires transaction, although this opportunity is lost once the transaction has been made, whether or not it has been carried out;

(ii)   directors are still obliged to act within their company's constitution. S.35(3) says, *"it remains the duty of the directors to observe any limitations on their powers flowing from the company's memorandum"*. The company can now however ratify action taken by directors in excess of their powers by means of a special resolution, thus reversing the position in the *Ashbury Railway Carriage* case, and an additional special resolution may be passed to relieve the directors of any liability they may have incurred for breach of duty as a result of exceeding the company's powers;

(iii)   as a result of s.109 Companies Act 1989, if a director exceeds his powers and the other party to the contract is a director of the company or the holding company, the company can if it chooses avoid the contract. The section is an attempt at preventing directors defrauding the company using the provisions of the new s.35.

Whilst the powers of a company are found in its memorandum, the rules regulating the way in which these powers should be exercised are usually contained in the articles of association. Articles may, for example, cut down on the general powers enjoyed by directors to make contracts within the company's authorised areas of business, by requiring that transactions involving more than a certain amount of money be approved by the members through an ordinary resolution passed at a meeting of the company. This can give rise to circumstances where an outsider enters into a transaction with a company which its memorandum authorises, but where the company's internal rules have not been complied with. Internal rules contained in a company's articles of association, being contained in its public file, came within the doctrine of constructive notice: the outsider was deemed to be aware of them. What he could not know was whether they had in fact been complied with when a company decision was made.

For instance, he would have no way of discovering whether a resolution *required* to be passed by the company under the articles *had* been passed. As a response to this difficulty the rule in *Royal British Bank v. Turquand* 1856 provided that an outsider was entitled to assume that the necessary rules of internal management had been complied with.

The rule in *Turquands Case* is affected by the Companies Act 1989. It provides that a third party dealing in good faith with a company can treat the company's constitution as imposing no restrictions on the power of the board of directors or persons authorised by them to bind the company. This provision thus supersedes the rule in *Turquands Case*. A third party is assumed to be acting in good faith, unless the contrary can be shown. Knowledge that the directors are acting beyond their powers does not, in itself, amount to bad faith.

Alteration of the objects clause

By virtue of s.4 Companies Act 1985, a company may by means of a special resolution alter its objects clause at any time and for any reason. The alteration is effective so long as no application is made to the court to cancel it within 21 days of the special resolution, and the company sends the Registrar within a further 15 days a copy of the altered memorandum. A special resolution involves a vote being taken at a company meeting in which at lest ¾ of those eligible to vote, vote in favour of the resolution. An application to cancel can be made by the holders of at least 15% of the issued share capital of any class, and the alteration is only effective in these circumstances where the court confirms it. It is relevant here to note in connection with the alteration of objects that a company can now adopt a single object to carry on business as a general commercial company (s.3A). A company formed with such an object will be able to carry on any business or trade, and do anything incidental or conducive to such a business or trade.

The Articles of Association

The articles of association of a registered company must be supplied to the Registrar of Companies prior to incorporation. Like the memorandum of association the articles will then be included in the company's file kept at Companies House in Cardiff.

The articles are concerned with the internal administration of the company, and it is for those setting up the company to determine the rules they consider appropriate for inclusion within the articles. The Companies Act 1985 does however provide a set of model articles which a company can adopt in whole or in part if it wishes. If a company fails to provide a set of articles then the model articles contained in the 1985 Act automatically apply to the company. They are known as *Table A* Articles. Matters which are normally dealt with in the Articles include the appointment and powers of the board of directors, the rules in relation to members' meetings and voting, and the types of shares the company can issue and the rights attaching to them.

Other registration documents

In addition to the memorandum and articles of association there are certain other documents which must be supplied to the Registrar prior to incorporation. These include a statutory declaration that all the requirements of the Act have been complied with. Fees must also be paid.

Having examined all the documents filed and ensured that they are in order, the Registrar then issues a certificate under official seal which certifies that the company is incorporated. The certificate is conclusive evidence that all the requirements of the Companies Act 1985 have been complied with and that the company is a company authorised to be registered and duly registered under the Act. A private company can enter into contracts, borrow money, and carry on business immediately on incorporation. However a public limited company registered under the 1985 Act cannot commence business until a certificate is issued by the Registrar that the share capital of the company is not less than the authorised minimum (i.e. £50,000 with at least one-quarter paid up). If more than a year after the incorporation of a public company it has not been issued with such a certificate the Secretary of State may petition the court for the company to be wound up.

Promoters

Promoters are people involved in the setting up of registered companies. The term is a wide one and does not appear to have any special technical meaning. Bowen LJ in *Whaley Bridge v. Green* 1880 stated:

"The term promoter is a term of business not of law, usefully summing up in a single word a number of business operations familiar to the commercial world by which a company is generally brought into existence".

The types of operations carried out by promoters include not only the registration of the memorandum and articles but also arrangements for obtaining capital, identifying people suitable to act as directors (head hunting), the negotiation of preliminary agreements and, in the case of a public company, the preparation and issue of a prospectus. Once the company commences business the role of the promoter is at an end. Following the incorporation of the company the promoters will frequently take over its management in the capacity of directors.

Although the activities of promoters are essentially commercial, there are legal consequences attached to the relationship between a promoter, the company that has been set up, and the members taking up shares in it. These consequences all stem from the common law view of a promoter as someone who stands in a fiduciary position towards the company. A considerable body of law has developed around the function of promoter, and this has sought to emphasise the importance of being able to identify who qualifies to be treated as a company promoter.

Who is a promoter?

Although the expression promoter crops up in legislation (it is, for example, used in the Financial Services Act 1986), statute provides us with no definition to work from, and it has been left to the courts to provide a judicial interpretation. As long ago as 1877 Cockburn LJ, in *Twycross v. Grant,* spoke of a promoter as:

"one who undertakes to form a company with reference to a given project and to set it going, and who takes the necessary steps to accomplish that purpose."

Thus a promoter will be:

- anyone giving instructions for preparing and registering a memorandum and set of articles;

- a person who, whilst not actively involved in such activity, is associated with those who are, and the understanding is that he or she will obtain a profit from the setting up of the company;

- anyone involved in pre-trading activities on the company's behalf; for example, by seeking to secure resources such as capital and labour for the prospective company.

It is lawful for one company to be the promoter of another, provided, of course, the promoting company is already in existence. Such promotions will occur where a company decides to form a subsidiary.

Professional people such as solicitors and accountants, who are involved in setting up companies acting on instructions received from their clients, are acting simply as agents and will not, without more, be regarded as promoters themselves.

The definition is thus a flexible one, and it is of considerable importance to anyone associated with the process of company formation to identify whether they fall within it. The reason for this is clear. As a company promoter a person becomes subject to the duties and responsibilities imposed by law on such people, which may give rise to financial penalties if they are not met.

The position in law of a promoter

As soon as a person takes steps to set up a company, and with that object in mind, his or her legal duties as a promoter emerge. We noted earlier that these duties are based on a fiduciary relationship with the company about to be formed. This means no profit may be made from the promotion which is not disclosed to the company once it is set up. Undisclosed profit is referred to as *secret profit*. The rule regarding secret profits is a clear indication that the courts view the relationship between a promoter and the company in the same way as the relationship between an agent and a principal, for agents have a duty to their principals to account for any profits they make personally. Such profits are the property of the principal. However, a promoter is not an agent of the company for an obvious reason. A person cannot act as an agent for someone who does not exist and so, until the company is formed, its promoters are acting on behalf of a non-existent principal. The consequences of this position we shall consider shortly. Before doing so we need to explore more fully the consequences of the fiduciary relationship.

The promoter as a fiduciary

The expression *fiduciary* signifies a sort of trusteeship. You may have come across before in other legal contexts. For instance, it appears in the expression *bona fide* meaning good faith, and in *uberrimae fidei* which describes certain types of contracts which are said to be based upon the utmost good faith of the parties making them. Insurance contracts are a good example. As a fiduciary, a promoter has an obligation to disclose fully to the company all relevant matters associated with transactions made between the promoter and the company; in particular, any profit made. There is nothing unlawful in promoters profiting from setting up a company and then selling assets to it. This was exactly what happened in *Salomon's case*, where Salomon set up the new company and then sold his business to it at an inflated price. What is unlawful is the failure to disclose the profit to either an *independent board* or to the existing and any intended shareholders.

Disclosure to an independent board is often impossible since promoters frequently take up office as directors of the newly formed company, especially where private companies are involved. In such circumstances full disclosure must instead be made to the existing shareholders and also, where appropriate, to any intended shareholders. For example, disclosure to intended shareholders could be achieved by information provided in a company prospectus. In this way the promoters will have fulfilled their duty since, in the words of Lindley MR in *Lagunas Nitrate Co. v. Lagunas Syndicate* 1899: *"the real truth is disclosed to those who are induced by the promoters to join the company"*

The idea underlying this basic principle is that a company has the right to receive a full account of a promoter's interest in any transaction with the company, thus enabling it to arrive at a proper decision whether or not to proceed with the transaction.

Company remedies for breach of promoters duties

A company may have a number of alternative remedies available to it in the event of a promoter being in breach of his fiduciary duty. These are:

Rescission

Rescission is an equitable remedy, which seeks to restore both parties to their pre-contractual positions. It is available in the case of any contract made as a consequence of non-disclosure or misrepresentation. It cannot be used where the company is in liquidation, or where any of the following bars apply:

- The contract has been affirmed, i.e. accepted by the company in knowledge of the breach that has occurred.

- There has been delay in bringing the claim.

- Third party rights have been acquired.

- Substantial restoration of the parties to their pre-contractual position is not possible.

- The court has applied its powers under s.2(2) Misrepresentation Act 1967, to declare the contract subsisting and to award damages in lieu of rescission.

Accounting for any undisclosed profit

Generally, it is not possible for a company to keep the property which is the subject of the transaction and reduce the price paid for it to the extent of the promoter's secret profit. The only circumstance in which this will be possible is where the contract was made by someone acting as an agent of the company at a time when it was formed.

> Making a claim for the promoters' profit can be difficult, as illustrated in *Re: Cape Breton Co.* 1887. Here coal mines were bought by six partners for £5,500. They extracted coal from the mines, later deciding to form a company to conduct their commercial operations. Two of the six partners became directors. The company bought the mines for £42,000 from the vendor, who was one of the six original partners and was acting as a trustee for all of them. The company went into liquidation and a claim was brought for the undisclosed profit made by the two directors, there having been no disclosure to an independent board. Rescission was impossible as the company was in liquidation. The court dismissed the claim for the profit, on the grounds that the mines had not originally been purchased to sell to the company, and therefore had not been bought on its behalf.

Damages

Damages – the award of a sum of money by way of compensation – is not available for breach of fiduciary duty, but may be claimed where the contract has been induced by misrepresentation. This is an indirect means of obtaining damages for breach of duty.

> In *Re: Leeds and Hanley Theatre of Varieties* 1902 an existing company bought two music halls for £24,000 which were then conveyed to a nominee. The intention was to form a new company which would buy the halls. The directors of this new company, after it was formed, issued a prospectus to raise money for the purchase of the halls at a price of £75,000. They did not constitute an independent board. The prospectus made no reference to the promoting company but indicated that the nominee was the vendor. It was held that the promoting company was the real vendor and should have been disclosed. Damages would be awarded representing the difference between the market price and the contract price, i.e. the profit.

Further remedies

Damages may also be available in cases of fraud and, under the rule in *Hedley Byrne v. Heller and Partners* 1964, in cases of negligent misrepresentation, on the grounds that a promoter owes the company a duty of care.

The Insolvency Act 1986 allows for a claim to be brought in a winding up under s.212 where a promoter can be shown to have misapplied property or acted in breach of duty. A promoter will also be liable for loss or damage caused to a subscriber of a company's shares resulting from an untrue statement in the prospectus to which the promoter was a party.

Promoter remuneration

Payment for the work performed by the promoter can be legitimately made by any of the following methods:

(a) by a sale of the promoter's own property to the company for cash, or for fully paid shares at an overvalue of which proper disclosure has been made;

(b) by the promoter being given an option to take up further shares in the company at their nominal (par) value. If the market value of the shares is higher than the par value when the option is exercised, the promoter will make a profit;

(c) by inserting a provision in the articles providing for the payment of a fixed figure to the promoter. This cannot create a binding contract between the company and the promoter. However, it will usually be possible for the promoter to ensure the company makes such a payment and it cannot recover the payment made once it has been made.

Disqualification of promoters

A disqualification order can be made against a promoter by the court under s.1 Company Directors Disqualification Act 1986. This can prohibit him or her from taking part in the promotion of company for up to 15 years. The grounds on which the court can apply the provisions of the Act are considered later.

Pre-Incorporation Contracts

No company can be bound by a contract made on its behalf, or by someone acting as a trustee for it, before it has been incorporated. Such contracts are referred to as *pre-incorporation contracts*. They do not bind it for the simple reason that at the time they are made the company lacks all legal capacity, being for the present non existent. In agency terms anyone purporting to act as the company's agent is acting on behalf of a non-existent principal. The consequences of this proposition of law can be significant for those dealing with the promoters of the company.

In *Re: English & Colonial Produce Co. Ltd.* 1906 the company was held not to be liable to pay solicitors their fees for work carried out in setting it up. The work had been carried out on the instructions of the promoters, who subsequently became the directors of the company. Similarly the company is unable to sue on such contracts. In *Natal Land v. Pauline Colliery* 1904 the appellant company, Natal Land, entered into an agreement to grant a mining lease to the respondent, Pauline Colliery. The respondent had not, at that time, been incorporated and the agreement was made with a third party acting on the respondent's behalf. The respondent was subsequently incorporated, and discovered coal on the land subject to the lease, at which point the appellant refused to grant the lease. It was held that the respondent could not force the appellant to do so.

Furthermore, it is not possible for a company to *ratify* – that is to adopt – a contract made on its behalf before it was formed. Ratification operates retrospectively and is, therefore, also caught by the fact that the company was not in law a person at the relevant time. However, whilst a company cannot be bound by a pre-incorporation contract, the promoter who is responsible for making the contract can be. In this way the other party may have a remedy. The position is governed by s.36(4) of the Companies Act 1985. The section provides that any contract made by or on behalf of a company as yet unincorporated has the effect of binding the contract maker personally, unless the agreement provides otherwise

The effect of the section was considered by the Court of Appeal in *Phonogram v. Lane* 1981. The defendant signed an agreement *"for and on behalf of"* the proposed company. However, the company was never formed and the plaintiffs now sought to recover money they had advanced, repayable under the terms of the agreement. They claimed the defendant was personally liable under what is now s.36(4) of the Companies Act 1985. On the defendant's behalf it was claimed that signing as an agent was a way of excluding personal liability. The court disagreed, finding the defendant personally liable. In Lord Denning's words, *"There must be a clear exclusion of personal liability"*.

The court also suggested a promoter can be made personally liable where the company in question is not as yet even in the process of being formed, and both sides are aware the company is not yet in existence.

Novation

Once a company has been incorporated however, it may take up contracts made for it prior to incorporation by means of a process known as *novation*. Novation involves the discharge of the original contract and its replacement with a new one, to which the company is a party. This relieves the promoter of the personal liability which existed under the original pre-incorporation contract. Unlike ratification, novation does not operate retrospectively. It can also be inferred from the conduct of the parties, in other words it does not have to be expressly agreed.

> In *Howard v. Patent Ivory Manufacturing Co.* 1888 a company resolution to adopt a pre-incorporation agreement was held to be sufficient evidence of intention of novation even though the outsider, as the other party to the transaction, was never informed. However, a mistaken belief of the company that it is bound by a pre-incorporation contract is not sufficient to infer novation (*Re: Northumberland Avenue Hotel* 1886).

When a person acts as an agent for an unformed company a very valuable protection for the agent is to include a clause into the agreement stating that personal liability is to cease when the company enters into a fresh contract with the other party on the terms of the original agreement. The clause should further provide for rescission of the original agreement if novation fails to take place. There is, of course, no way a company can be forced to adopt a pre-incorporation contract. In the case of a public limited company, s.117 of the Companies Act 1985 contains an important provision dealing with contracts made by the company after incorporation but before its trading certificate is issued. Such contracts, says the section, are validly made but if the company fails to meet its obligations within 21 days of being asked to do so, its directors become jointly and severally liable to compensate the other party for any loss or damage sustained as a result of its failure to commence business.

Financing the Company

For any company the raising of money for trading purposes is essential to its ability to carry on trade. The capital so acquired is a fundamental resource of the company.

Companies are able to raise the capital in different ways. The methods available and the legal rules and principles associated with them, are examined below. Essentially, this examination focuses upon two ways in which companies acquire capital, namely, through the issue of shares, and by means of borrowing through the issue of debentures. Shares and debentures are often referred to collectively as *company securities*.

Capital

Before examining company securities it may be helpful to say a few words about the expression of capital. In a legal sense, capital is something positive. It is what the company has raised and can use for doing things, to buy business premises for instance, which are then referred to as fixed capital, or to purchase stock, which is referred to as circulating capital. In an accountancy sense, however, capital is something negative, appearing in a balance sheet under the heading of *liabilities*. Thus, to an accountant the money raised by issuing shares – *share capital*, issuing debentures - *loan capital,* as well as, the amount of money owed by the company to its trade creditors, is all regarded as part of the company's indebtedness. This is capital as a *debt*. All these items are owed.

The expression capital is such an important one that it has found its way into a variety of technical terms used in company law. The most important of these terms are:

- *Share capital*
  This is capital raised by the issue of the company's shares, and is often used as a way of distinguishing capital gained in this way, from capital gained through borrowing.

- *Loan capital*
  This is capital acquired by means of borrowing.

- *Nominal (or authorised capital)*
  This expression refers to the value of shares a company is authorised to issue, and it appears in the capital clause of the memorandum of association.

- *Issued capital*
  Usually this term is used to describe the value of capital in the form of shares which have actually been issued to the members.

- *Paid-up capital*
  This is the amount which has been paid to the company by its members for the shares they hold. Companies do not always require immediate payment in full for issued shares. Under s.351 of the Companies Act 1985, if a company makes a reference to share capital on its business stationery or order forms, this must be a reference to its paid up capital.

- *Unpaid capital*
  If shares have been issued which have not been fully paid for, the amount outstanding is referred to as *unpaid capital*. For example, if 5,000 issued shares have a nominal value (that is a face value, sometimes referred to as *par* value) of £1 each and shareholders have been required to pay only 40 pence per share, then the paid up capital is £2,000 and the unpaid capital is £3,000. Shareholders may be required to pay up the outstanding amount on their shares by the company making a *call* on them to do so. The unpaid amount is the extent of the shareholders' liability to the company.

- *Reserve capital*

  Under s.120 of the Companies Act 1985, a company may, by means of a special resolution, determine that any portion of its unpaid capital shall not be called up except if the company is being brought to an end by being wound up. Such a sum is referred to as *reserve capital*. Once created it is no longer under the control of the company's directors. Consequently, the company cannot charge it, that is, use it as a security (for raising a loan, for example). To do so would be to damage the position of the company's creditors. The only way the special resolution can be revoked is with the consent of the court under a scheme of arrangement. Unlike reserve capital, mere uncalled capital can be charged by the company.

In company law references to capital are usually references to share capital.

Share Capital

We have seen that issuing shares is one way of financing a company. How far a company is willing to use this method is likely to depend upon many factors. A private company may be willing to issue more shares because existing members are not in a position to invest further in the company, yet do not wish to dilute their control over the running of the company by issuing shares which grant votes to new members. A public company may avoid a share issue if its present investment potential is unlikely to attract the market. An alternative approach is to borrow money, that is raise loan capital, usually by means of the issue of debentures. Again, a company may be reluctant to use this approach, since it will have the effect of tying it down, and at times of high interest rates such borrowings may not be commercially advisable.

Further alternatives used by companies are:

(a)   to obtain goods and services on credit; for instance, by leasing vehicles or obtaining machinery on hire purchase terms;

(b)   to retain profits - which simply involves holding back profits made by trading, the effects being borne by the shareholders whose *dividends*, (their return on their investment), will be reduced accordingly.

For the moment, however, we shall concentrate on the use of shares as a way of raising money, considering how share capital is raised; and how it can be altered. Before examining these issues however we need to say a little about shares themselves.

Classes of shares

Essentially a share is a unit of company ownership and a shareholder, as a stakeholder in the organisation, is a company member. Sometimes companies, particularly smaller ones, will issue only one type, or class, of shares. If they do, all the shares will carry equal rights. But in larger companies different classes of shares are usually issued with varying rights attaching to them relating such matters as voting, payment of dividends and return of capital on liquidation. The two main types of shares are:

(a) *Preference shares*

The main characteristic of a preference share is that it will carry a preferred fixed dividend. This means that the holder of a preference share is entitled to a fixed amount of dividend, e.g. 6% on the value of each share, before other shareholders are paid any dividend. They are presumed to be cumulative which means that if in any year the company fails to declare a dividend, the shortfall must be made up out of profits of subsequent years. A preference share is therefore a safe investment with fixed interest, no matter how small or large is the company's profit. As far as return of capital on a winding up is concerned, the preference shareholder will rank equally with ordinary shareholders for any payment due, unless the preference shares are made preferential as to capital. Normally, preference shares do not carry voting rights and therefore the preference shareholder has little influence over the company's activities.

(b) *Ordinary shares*

Ordinary shares are often referred to as the *equity share capital* of a company. When a company declares a dividend and the preference shareholders have been paid, the holders of ordinary shares are entitled to the remainder. It follows therefore that an ordinary shareholder in a well-managed company making high profits will receive a good return on his investment and consequently the value of his shares will rise. In this way a share can have a much higher market value than it's face value. Unfortunately, the reverse is also true and they may fall in market value so that ordinary shares inevitably carry a certain risk. This risk is reflected in the amount of control that an ordinary shareholder has over the company's business. While voting rights are not normally attached to preference shares, they are attached to ordinary shares enabling the ordinary shareholder to voice an opinion in a general meeting and vote on major issues involving the running of the company. Ordinary shareholders thus have the capacity to remove directors who have mismanaged the business of the company. An ordinary resolution is required in order to do so.

Where a company's share capital is divided into different classes, statutory provisions apply which limit the ability of the company to alter the rights attached to the classes of shares. S.125 provides that the written consent of three quarters in *value* of the shares of the class, or alternatively their approval by way of an extraordinary resolution of a meeting of the shareholders of that class, is needed for an alteration to be validly made. Even then a 15% or more dissenting group of shareholders of that class have 21 days in which to challenge the variations before the court (s.127).

Raising share capital

Private companies and public companies

One of the fundamental differences between private and public companies lies in their ability to raise share capital. Public companies usually seek to raise capital, whether through the issue of shares or debentures, by advertising their securities to the public, hence their designation as public companies. Their ability to do so has led to a range of statutory provisions designed to protect the investing public from being misled about the financial condition and future prospects of a business in which prospective investors are considering making an investment. Over the past few years there have been a number of well publicised cases involving public companies which have collapsed causing financial distress to small investors, often retired people, who have little or no chance of recovering their investment. Sometimes the Government has been prepared to provide financial assistance, as in the *Barlow Clowes* case. In most cases however, investors simply have to suffer the loss themselves. The *Barings* collapse, which resulted from the activities of the rogue trader Nick Leeson, is a reminder that even public companies which are regarded as rock solid national institutions are not free of investment risk. Large institutional investors, such as pension funds, are of course much better placed to assess the potential and the risks involved in investing in public companies. The general law dealing with investor protection is contained in the Financial Services Act 1986, and statutory references included below are references to the 1986 Act unless stated otherwise.

As to the position of private companies and their ability to raise capital, there are only two significant provisions:

(a)   under s.143, a private company must not apply for its shares to be listed on the Stock Exchange; and

(b)   under s.170, a private company must not issue any advertisement offering its securities, unless the circumstances under which the advertisement is issued are covered by an order made by the Secretary of State for Trade and Industry, exempting the company from the section.

The effect of these two provisions is that, subject to the s.170 exception a private company cannot raise money by selling its securities on the open market. Obviously this limitation restricts the growth of a private company's capital acquired through the issue of its securities, and consequently of limiting the size of its membership. Whereas in a public company the membership will often be measured in thousands, the membership of private companies is inevitably much smaller. Thus, whilst private companies frequently operate under arrangements in which all the members are also directors, in a public company ownership and management is usually found in separate hands.

The development of a company

The investment risks involved make it most unusual for a public company to be formed from scratch and immediately seek to raise capital from the public to finance the new business. Usually, the growth of a company will follow the kind of pattern indicated below.

- A private company is formed, which either establishes a new business or acquires an existing one. Its share capital will be small, and will be contributed by a group of shareholders, who are likely to become the company's directors and managers. Loan capital will come from overdraft arrangements made with banks, which are secured by means of directors' personal guarantees. Most companies do not progress beyond this stage.

- The private company is converted into a public one to enable it to raise more capital from the public and from financial institutions. This move will be motivated by the need to expand and by the ambitions of its owners. Its securities will not be sold on the Stock Exchange, because it is not yet large enough to meet the listing requirements (see below), but instead will be traded in the *intermediate securities markets*, such as the Unlisted Securities Market (USM).

- The company becomes listed on the Stock Exchange. By now it is a very successful commercial organisation. Future expansion will usually be by means of *rights issues* of its shares.

Flotation

Flotation is a term used to describe the process by which a company seeks to raise capital through offering its securities on an established market. A company flotation took place in the example given above, when the company first sought capital by offering its securities in one of the intermediate securities markets. There are a number of these markets, the most important being:

(a) **the Unlisted Securities Market**

This was set up in 1980 by the Stock Exchange to provide a regulated securities market for companies not yet able to meet the full listing conditions to become a company quoted on the Stock Exchange. It is sometimes referred to as the 'junior league' of the Stock Exchange;

(b) **the Over the Counter Market**

This is an alternative to the markets controlled by the Stock Exchange. It is operated by authorised dealers in securities;

(c) **the Third Market**

This was established by the Stock Exchange in 1987 to pick up the securities being dealt with in the Over the Counter Market. Its rules simply require that sponsorship of a member of the Stock Exchange be obtained. Once this has occurred, admission to the market is available.

The legal, as opposed to the commercial, significance of these markets is that the 1986 Act draws an important distinction between *listed securities* – those submitted to the Official List of the Stock Exchange - and those which have not been so admitted – *unlisted securities*.

The legal controls imposed upon both types of securities as part of the process of financial market regulation is one of the objectives of the Financial Services Act.

Securities

There are five methods which may be used by a public company to invite the public to subscribe for, that is to take up, its securities.

(a) *By making a direct invitation to the public.*

This is achieved by the company issuing a prospectus, a document by which the company advertises the securities it wishes to sell. The prospectus is published and distributed to anyone wishing to take a copy. It may appear in newspapers. The privatisation of state-owned industries during the 1980s was handled in this way.

(b) *By means of a rights issue.*

Well established public companies normally raise additional capital by this method. The company sends each of its members a letter informing them they have been provisionally allotted new shares. If the member pays the price for these shares, the issue price, he or she is registered as the new holder. Alternatively, the member may sell the right to subscribe on the share market. The price at which the shares will be offered by the company will be below their current open market value, making them a more worthwhile proposition to the existing members. The number of shares provisionally allotted under a rights issue is related to the number of shares being held at the time by the member. Thus one share may be offered for every two presently held. The letter of provisional allotment is treated as a prospectus, since it is not possible to predict who may end up taking the shares, the member or someone buying the right to subscribe from the member.

(c)   *By an offer for sale.*

Here the company disposes of the shares through an intermediary, an *issuing house* which buys the shares and then re-sells them at a higher price to the public. The public offer is made by means of a document referred to as an *offer for sale*, which is treated as a prospectus, and for whose contents both the company and the issuing house are responsible. The issuing house is usually a merchant bank. It will provide the company with advice and assistance to ensure that the issue is successful. An offer for sale is the method generally used for a flotation when a company is being launched as a listed or USM company for the first time. One of the requirements of a flotation is that a substantial number of shares are available to be taken up by new rather than existing investors.

(d)   *By a placing.*

Here the securities are initially allotted in large *blocks to a limited number of financial institutions, for resale by these institutions* at a profit. Debenture stock is often issued in this way. The expression *placing* is derived from the institutions taking the securities, which are referred to as *places*.

(e)   *By an offer by tender.*

This involves the company or an issuing house inviting tenders for fixed numbers of new shares. Usually a specified price is indicated, and the bidders will put in bids above this figure, shares being allotted to the highest bidders.

Whatever method a company uses to issue its securities, the decision made by the potential investor whether or not to take up the company's securities will be dependent upon whether the investor is satisfied, on the basis of the available information, that the investment is a sound one. An investor will generally be looking for a good potential return from the company, some growth over a given period, and the ability to dispose readily of the interest on the market should he or she choose to do so. Investment decisions, indeed the whole system under which a market for company shares can operate effectively, must be based upon a flow of reliable, accurate and up to date information concerning those companies whose securities are publicly available. Investors are interested not only in the current health of the company, but also its trading record and the forecasts of its future prospects and potential. Of course, it is the companies themselves which are best placed to provide this information. Likewise, they are also best placed to manipulate such information, to distort the true picture and mislead the investor by false and inaccurate statements, by half truths and omissions. Not surprisingly, therefore, it has long been the law that certain standards of accuracy must be met in the publication of company prospectuses. The issue of a prospectus, however, is a *one-off* event. If it has done its job the share issue will be fully subscribed. It should be borne in mind that this is not the end of the story as far as the shares themselves are concerned, since over the lifetime of a company they may be bought and sold on numerous occasions.

One further source of information which may be relied upon by the prospective investor is the audited accounts of the company. The extent to which auditors are liable for this information is considered in the next chapter.

When a company is seeking to issue new new securities it will use a prospectus. If, however, it is a company quoted on the Stock Exchange, the potential investor has the re-assurance of knowing that in order to obtain a Stock Exchange quotation the company has had to meet the demanding listing requirements set out under the Stock Exchange rules. For the company, a Stock Exchange listing means that its securities are being traded on a highly respected and closely controlled market. One effect of this is on the value of the securities themselves. Listing significantly increases their market value.

The control of listed securities

The Stock Exchange is the leading UK securities market. The admission of a company's securities into this market through a Stock Exchange listing, i.e. being *quoted* on the Stock Exchange, increases the market price of the securities because they can readily be bought and sold. Up to 1984 in order to grant a listing the Stock Exchange required to see the draft prospectus before publication, to satisfy itself that the document met the requirements applied to prospectuses under company legislation then current and that it contained the detailed and demanding information required by the Stock Exchange itself. However, the decision regarding a listing was essentially a private matter between the company and the Stock Exchange.

This position was changed in 1984 by the introduction of statutory regulations which gave effect to three European Community Directives. The Directives demanded a much broader system for the regulation of securities markets than existed under UK domestic law on prospectuses. The system is now controlled by the Financial Services Act 1986, Part IV. The effect is that a listing can only take place of the requirements if the so called 'Yellow Book' (The Admission of Securities to Listing) containing the Stock Exchange regulations are met. These regulations are given the force of law under the 1986 Act. The new system of control has two main features:

(a)   the requirements that listing particulars must be published before the securities are listed. The Companies Registry must have a copy of these particulars delivered to it for filing, in effect making the listing particulars a form of prospectus; and

(b)   the imposition of continuing obligations upon the company, for example, to tackle the possibility of directors using inside information to their advantage by buying or selling the company's shares in the period preceding the publication of its results. Admission rules require disclosure of such dealings. Thus admission has the effect of exposing the company to Stock Exchange supervision after the relevant securities have been issued.

Admission to list

The Stock Exchange is allowed a maximum of six months to consider an application, although a decision is normally made in a much shorter time. Application procedures and the conditions to be fulfilled by applicants are contained in the Yellow Book.

Under s.144 it is provided that a transaction involving a listed security is not to be treated as void or voidable solely on the grounds of a breach of listing particulars. However, a claim for damages to recover losses resulting from untrue or misleading statements or the omission of information by the company is not prevented under the section.

Under s.145 the Stock Exchange has the power to suspend a listing. This power is sometimes exercised where take-over rumours are distorting the normal functioning of the market in the company's shares.

Contents of the listing particulars

S.146 requires the company to provide information regarding its *financial condition*. The section defines this as information which investors and their professional advisers would reasonably require in order to make an informed assessment of the company's financial position, its assets and liabilities, its profits and losses, its prospects, and the rights attaching to the securities it is offering.

Less information may be provided to more sophisticated investors.

The Yellow Book contains further requirements.

The effect is that under the listing rules, a company in supplying the Stock Exchange with the listing particulars is really furnishing it with a prospectus.

Supplementary listing particulars

Under s.147 further particulars – *called supplementary particulars* – must be approved by the Stock Exchange and registered with the Registrar of Companies, if any of the following circumstances have occurred:

- there has been a significant change affecting any matter included in the original particulars;

- a new matter has arisen which would have been included in the original particulars if it had been present at the time;

- a significant mistake, i.e. not a trivial change or mistake, has been made in the particulars.

Remedies

S.150 allows *"any person who had acquired any of the securities in question and suffered loss in respect of them"*, the right to claim compensation. The claim may be brought against those responsible for the listing particulars in cases of material mis-statements, material omissions and misleading opinions. The word *'material'* appears to be related to the loss sustained, and a subscriber may thus bring a claim under the section when he or she was not aware of the error, or had not even seen the particulars at all.

The section specifically states that any other civil or criminal liability arising from errors in the listing particulars is not defeated, that is replaced, by it. Consequently, a claim can be brought on grounds of fraud, or in respect of any of the forms of misrepresentation.

Under s.47 criminal liability is imposed upon anyone making false statements in particulars. The section grants the court power to impose a fine and/or up to seven years imprisonment. Civil liability under s.150 is attached to, amongst others, the issuing house and its directors, and anyone expressly taking responsibility for any part of the particulars (s.152).

Defences

S.151 provides that a person who has contravened s.150 shall not be liable if it can be shown:

(a)   that he or she had a reasonable belief in the truth of the statements, or that it was reasonable to allow the relevant omission;

(b)   that the statement was by an expert and that he or she had a belief in the expert's competence, and of that expert's consent to the inclusion of the statement in the particulars;

(c)   when (a) and (b) cannot be established, that the person published a correction or took reasonable steps to have one published and reasonably believed it had been.

The control of unlisted securities

Part V of the Financial Services Act 1986 is designed to replace the provisions regulating prospectuses contained in the Companies Act 1985. At present most offers of unlisted securities are subject to detailed USM (Unlisted Securities Market) regulations, and Part V is simply designed to give these rules statutory force.

Under these arrangements control applies only to *offers of unlisted securities*. Thus there is no provision made for continuing control. The provisions apply largely to the issue of *company prospectuses*, the word *prospectus* being specifically referred to in the relevant sections of the Act. S.160 provides that no advertisement affecting any securities can be made unless a prospectus has been delivered to the Registrar of Companies, or the advertisement is such that no agreement can be entered into as a result of it until a prospectus has been delivered to the Registrar. S.163 specifies the information to be contained in the prospectus. It is the same as that specified in s.146 for listing particulars. S.164 provides for the issue of a supplementary prospectus, a parallel provision to s.147 (see above). Compensation is dealt with under s.166 (paralleling s.150), and defences under s.167 (paralleling s.151). Those responsible for issuing a prospectus are defined in s.168, which is an analogue of s.152.

Exemptions from S.160

The old law on prospectuses required that a prospectus was only needed when an offer was made to the public. This expression caused the courts some difficulty. The position under the 1986 Act is to specify three main areas in which exemption from the need to provide a prospectus in the issue of company securities will apply. These are:

- advertisements of a *private character*. Orders will be made to specify what these are to include, e.g. a rights issue;

- advertisements where investment is a merely incidental aspect of the arrangement; an example would be a scheme under which tenants take shares in the management company which manages their properties;

- offers to professionals in the securities markets.

The securities of private companies

We have seen that private companies cannot offer their securities to the public (s.190). One of the problems this raises is the question of trying to define the expression *offer to the public*, a point referred to above. How widely can a private company offer its shares before it falls foul of s.170? The Department of Trade and Industry has the power to make regulations excepting certain categories of offer from the s.170 provisions.

These categories are:

(a)   advertisements of a private character;

(b)   advertisements which deal with investment only incidentally;

(c)   advertisements addressed to persons who appear to the DTI to be sufficiently expert to understand the risks involved.

Common Law Remedies for Defects in Listing Particulars and Prospectuses

We have seen that the 1986 Act provides compensation for breach of statutory duty in failing to meet the information requirements demanded of listing particulars and prospectuses under its relevant provisions. Nowadays, thorough scrutiny of draft prospectuses by merchant banks and the Stock Exchange generally identifies errors before publication - usually referred to as the *pre-vetting procedure*. The statutory remedies do not in any case apply to securities issued by private companies where individuals have suffered loss as a result of misleading statements. Here the injured party must rely on common law remedies. This involves an examination of the law of misrepresentation.

Misrepresentation

A misrepresentation is a material mis-statement of fact which induces the making of a contract. Misrepresentations may be fraudulent, negligent or innocent. The remedy of misrepresentation is available to the subscriber against the person from whom the shares were acquired, that is either the company itself or an issuing house. If misrepresentation can be established, the injured party may rescind the contract or bring a claim for damages.

Rescission

Rescission is an equitable remedy. Under it the parties are restored to their pre-contractual position. The shareholders name is taken off the register and the company returns to the shareholder any money paid for the shares plus interest. Rescission is available in respect of any of the forms of misrepresentation referred to above, but the problem with it is that the right to rescind is lost if the action is not brought quickly, or if the contract has been affirmed. Usually, in the case of contracts for shares, the right to rescind has been lost before it can be exercised.

The remedy of rescission is only available against the company and not, for example, against its directors. It can only be obtained if the following conditions are met, namely;

(a)   that the company had either actual or constructive knowledge that the contract was made on the basis of the misrepresentation; and

(b)   that it was made by someone having authority to act as an agent of the company: *Lynde v Anglo-Italian Hemp Spinning Co* 1896. On this point it should be noted that:

   (i)   a promoter cannot be an agent of the company before its formation;

   (ii)   the person misled may still rescind if the company is aware of the promoter's misrepresentation when the shares are allotted: *Re: Metropolitan Coal Consumer's Association* 1892;

(iii)   a company will be liable for an experts report concerning it unless the company clearly states it cannot verify the accuracy of the report: *Re: Pacaya Rubber Company* 1914.

Damages

The remedy of damages may be sought at common law in the tort of deceit for fraudulent misrepresentation, and under the principle in *Hedley Byrne v. Heller and Partners* 1964 in the tort of negligence for negligent mis-statements.

In the leading case of *Derry v. Peek* 1889 deceit was defined as, *"a false statement made knowingly, without belief in its truth, or recklessly, careless whether it be true or false"*. It thus covers not only the deliberate lie, but also the statement which the maker thinks might be untrue. Both forms of conduct involve deception. Of course, it is the task of proving this state of mind that is most difficult to establish in bringing a claim. Moreover, a claim can only be brought where:

- the plaintiff was a person intended to rely on the statement; for example, when shares are bought on the open market. A statement made in the prospectus which was published to induce subscriptions for the shares will not give rise to liability, for the method of acquisition is a different one (*Peek v. Gurney* 1873);

- the plaintiff was induced by the statement to take the shares, even if it was only one of the factors that influenced the subscriber (*Edgington v. Fitzmaurice* 1885). When the plaintiff has made independent enquiries and relied on them in arriving at the decision to take shares, the misleading statement is irrelevant.

If a plaintiff is awarded damages, their membership of the company is not terminated. This is based on the principle that capital should not be returned to the company's members, because to do so would be to reduce the fund available to the company's creditors (*Houldsworth v. City of Glasgow Bank* 1880). Such a condition does not apply where the successful claim has been brought against a party other than the company, for instance against a director who authorised the fraudulent statement.

In order to bring a successful action for negligent misrepresentation under the *Hedley Byrne* principle, it will be necessary for the plaintiff to show that the defendant owed him or her a duty of care, which has been broken causing economic loss suffered by the plaintiff. There need not be a contractual relationship between the plaintiff and the defendant. There is some doubt about the application of the principle in a company law context. It is not clear whether company directors or the company itself owes a duty of care to persons subscribing for its securities. Some members of the House of Lords in *Hedley Byrne* felt that such a duty might arise in certain circumstances, such as a rights issue where the offer of securities is being made to existing members. Section 2(1) of the Misrepresentation Act 1967 allows for damages to be claimed in cases of pre-contractual negligent misrepresentations made by one of the contracting parties to the other. Its advantage over the common law remedy is that the burden of proof (i.e. that there was no negligence) lies with the defendant.

Criminal liability

Criminal liability for false statements arises under s.47 Financial Services Act 1986. The section applies to a statement, promise or forecast which is misleading, false or deceptive, where the person making it knows it is misleading, etc., or makes it recklessly.

It is also an offence under s.19 Theft Act 1968 for an officer of a company knowingly to make a statement which is false, misleading or deceptive, with intent to deceive the members or creditors of the company. In the case of a prospectus, s.19 can only apply to a rights issue since the section applies to persons who at the time of the offence were members.

A further example of the use of the criminal code in relation to securities is contained in the statutory rules relating to insider dealing.

Insider Dealing

Shares are commodities which are bought and sold in the market in much the same way as other products. The Stock Exchange is the established market place for this commercial activity. For the Stock Exchange to function as an effective market there has to be confidence that the value of the securities being traded on it reflects their true value. Neither buyers nor sellers of securities will be willing to trade freely if they face the prospect of buying, or selling, for less than the real value of the securities in question. How, then, can a real value be arrived at? The answer is through a process of valuation based upon all the relevant information available at the time. Share values are a reflection of general information regarding national economic performance, the condition of the particular market a company deals in, and specific information about the fitness of the company itself.

Whilst general information is usually available to all market participants, for instance by following the financial press, information specific to the company itself inevitably is held by those who are closest to the company, either because they work for it, or through their association with it as advisors, or as friends or relations of its employees. Such people can gain information about the company before the rest of the market, giving them advance access to the value of its securities, and enabling them to buy or sell advantageously. Such a practice is known as *insider dealing*. In the United Kingdom it is regarded as unethical, as likely to undermine market confidence in the Stock Exchange, and in cases where the insiders are the directors, as a breach of trust.

Legislation was introduced in 1980 making insider dealing a criminal offence. The United Kingdom was the first European country to respond in this way. Financial markets had up to that time regarded it as quite proper for those with access to specific financial information to use it to their own advantage. It was a perk of the job. The new legislation not only removed this perk; it made it a criminal offence, and thus raised one of the continuing arguments about the proper role of business law: is it to facilitate wealth creation or to set standards of business behaviour? In practice it usually seeks to balance these conflicting pressures.

The present law is contained in the Criminal Justice Act 1993, which defines the offence of insider dealing by restricting what an insider can do. Only an individual can commit an offence, not a company. The essence of the offence involves defining insider information, considering how that information may be gained, and restricting its use.

S.56 of the Act treats as insider information, information which:

- relates to particular securities or to a particular issuer of securities (i.e. thus excluding general securities and their issuers);

- is specific or precise;

- has not been made public; and

- if it were made public would be likely to have a significant effect on the price of any securities.

Price-sensitive information is the term used to describe inside information which would be likely to affect significantly the price of securities if it were made public, and such securities are hence termed *price-affected securities*. Information is regarded as publicly available if it has been published for investors or it can be found in public records such as the companies file. It is treated as in the public domain even though it can only be obtained using diligence and expertise or observation, or has been communicated to a section of the public rather than generally, or has been published outside the UK.

The Act seeks to restrict identified categories of people from making use of inside information by way of dealing in (i.e. buying or selling) price affected securities.

Crucial therefore is the way in which the Act describes who these *insiders* are. A person has information as an insider only if they know it is inside information which they have obtained from an inside source. It comes from an inside source if it is obtained by them through their position as a director, employee or shareholder of an issuer of securities, or through their employment office or profession. This latter category is a wide one. Professional advisors, financial journalists, and even staff working for the printer who puts out price sensitive information are swept up by it. All these people are classed as primary insiders.

The legislation also extends to secondary insiders, that is people who either directly or indirectly get the information from a primary insider. For example if a director was to give a friend inside information about the company concerning a possible take-over the friend would become a secondary insider, or tippee i.e. someone who has been tipped off. If however the director had publicly disclosed the information it would no longer be *inside* information, and anyone using it would not consequently be regarded as a secondary insider.

The basic aim of the 1993 legislation is the protection of markets rather than individuals. It creates criminal offences, carrying a maximum of seven years imprisonment, and unlimited fine, which are committed by an insider who deals on a regulated European market in price affected securities, or who encourages another person to deal, or who simply discloses to a person inside information other than in the proper performance of the function of the discloser's employment, office or profession. Only individuals can be prosecuted, not companies, and the decision to prosecute must be made by the Secretary of State or the Director of Public Prosecutions.

The Act does not grant any civil remedy. A director who is in breach may be liable to account to the company for any profit made, as in *Regal (Hastings) Ltd. v. Gulliver* considered in the next chapter, but generally in insider dealing cases it will not be the company who is the loser, but rather the market participants deprived of the inside information

The Alteration of Share Capital

The memorandum of association of a company with a share capital has to include a capital clause specifying the amount the company is authorised to raise by the issue of shares. Subsequently the company may wish to make changes to the capital clause, probably to enable it to raise more capital by the issue of new shares. Alteration of share capital is controlled by s.121 CA 1985, which sets out the grounds on which an alteration is permitted. A company may:

(i)   increase its share capital, which may be achieved by means of an ordinary resolution to alter the capital clause, if the articles permit it (Table A does). If they do not then a special resolution is needed to alter them. That same resolution can also be used to authorise the increase;

(ii)   consolidate, or sub-divide shares. Consolidation involves converting a number of individual shares into a single share, whereas sub-dividing occurs where a single share of, say, a £1 nominal value is split into four shares of 25p nominal value. Sub-dividing in this way is useful where the market value of individual shares has become very high, and members wish to have more manageable units, perhaps with a view to selling their shares. A successful private company may be operating on the basis of perhaps only 100 shares with a nominal value of £1, which were issued when the company was first established, but which now have a market value measured in thousands of pounds;

(iii)   convert shares into stock, or vice versa. *Stock* is a members holding expressed in money terms. A member may hold £100 worth of stock as an alternative to 100 £1 shares. The stock can be sold in any units the holder wishes, rather than in the case of shares which are fixed units and can only be transferred in that way. Stock is thus more flexible. If articles allow it, fully paid shares can be converted into stock, and stock reconverted into paid up shares of any denomination. Stock cannot be issued directly by a company under English company law, however, so it can only be created through the conversion of shares;

(iv)   cancel unissued shares, thus eliminating the difference between the nominal capital of the company and its issued capital.

An alteration in cases (ii), (iii) and (iv) above is achieved by means of a company resolution. Table A provides than an ordinary resolution is sufficient. Alternatively the unanimous written resolution procedure may be used to achieve any of these alterations.

Capital reduction

It is a basic principle of company law that a company must maintain its share capital. This is essentially to protect the company's creditors, who are entitled to expect that capital will not be returned to the members and that shares will be paid for in full. A creditor may however expect that capital can be lost through business misfortune.

Thus provisions exist:

- to stop capital being watered down as it comes in, through the payment of underwriting commission and the issue of shares at a discount; and

- to stop capital going out of the company by means of various methods whose effect is the dissipation of capital, for instance where the company pays dividends out of capital instead of distributable profits.

The broad aim of the law is to ensure that the financial standing of the company bears some relation to the nominal value of its share capital.

Exceptions to the principle

There are certain particular and general exceptions to the basic principle of capital reduction, where it is lawful for capital to be diminished. Particular exceptions are those under which the court can order a company to purchase its own shares as a remedy for minority shareholders. Thus where there is minority objection to: alteration of articles under s.5 CA 1985; the re-registering of a public company as a private company under s.54; or where the minority have established unfair prejudice under s.459, the court may order the purchase of the shares of the minority by the company.

General exceptions are contained in s.135. This allows a company to reduce the share capital if:

(a)   a special resolution is passed; and

(b)   the articles permit (Table A art 34 does); and

(c)   the court confirms the resolution.

The grounds upon which this statutory power can be exercised are:

- to reduce or extinguish liability on issued shares for unpaid amounts (which is very rare);

- to cancel paid up share capital lost or no longer represented by available assets (i.e. the tidying up of the company books following trading losses/depreciation);

- to pay off paid-up shares in excess of the company's commercial needs (e.g. where it is reducing the scope of its commercial activities).

In *Re: Westburn Sugar Refineries* 1951 it was said that the court should always sanction the reduction unless to do so would be unfair regarding the interests of the creditors, shareholders or the public.

Directors duties on a serious capital loss in a public company

In a public company if its net assets fall to 50% or less of its called up share capital the directors must within 28 days of becoming aware call a meeting of the company to consider the commercial position. There are criminal sanctions for failure to comply.

Purchase by a company of its own shares

Basically such a transaction is unlawful, originally at common law under the *rule in Trevor v. Whitworth* 1887, and now under s.143 CA 1985. If a company buys back its own shares a criminal offence is committed. The company can be fined, and authorising officers may be fined and/or imprisoned. However a purchase is lawful where:

- shares were acquired under a s.135 capital reduction;

- there has been a court order permitting the acquisition by the company under ss.5, 54 or 459;

- shares have been *forfeited* for non payment (i.e. where the company has expropriated them from a member who has defaulted in making payment);

- there has been a *redemptional purchase* of shares (see below).

Redeemable shares

Under s.159 a company limited by shares may issue *redeemable* shares if certain conditions are satisfied. These are that:

(i)   such an issue is permitted by the articles;

(ii)   some shares have been issued which are not redeemable;

(iii)   the redeemable shares are fully paid;

(iv)   the shares are redeemed either from distributable profits, or out of the proceeds of a fresh share issue made for the purpose (s.160).

Redeemable shares are those which are capable of being bought back by the company. Under the terms of the issue they may be definitely redeemable, or be redeemable at the option of either the company or the shareholder. When shares are redeemed they are treated as cancelled. The issued share capital is reduced accordingly, but the authorised share capital remains unaltered. Redeemable shares may be issued as either ordinary or preference shares.

Financial assistance for the purchase of a company's shares

The basic rule, contained in s.151, provides that no financial assistance, direct or indirect, may be provided by a company or its subsidiaries for the purpose of acquiring shares in itself. Direct assistance would include a loan; indirect assistance would occur where the company issued a guarantee to support a loan given by a third party. There are however exceptions to the section, and thus financial assistance can be provided:

- to assist in management buy-out schemes;

- where the loan is made in the ordinary course of the company's business, for example where a finance company lends commercially to X, who uses the loan to purchase shares in the company;

- to assist in employee share schemes, by providing loans to employees (including directors);

- to assist employees (other than directors) in taking up shares in the company in the ordinary way.

Other exceptions include:

- the distribution of assets by way of a lawful dividend, or distribution of profits on a winding-up;

- the issue of *bonus* shares. Bonus shares are shares issued to existing members which they do not have to pay for. Usually the issue of such shares is funded by the company capitalising its profits, i.e. using profits to issue more shares;

- the lawful redemption or purchase of shares;

- arrangements and compositions with creditors made under the Insolvency Act 1986.

Consequences of contravention

If the financial assistance rules are broken:

(i) the company is liable to a fine and defaulting officers to a fine and/or imprisonment;

(ii) the directors will be liable to compensate the company for any losses on the basis of a breach of trust: *Wallersteiner v. Moir* 1974;

(iii) any securities given for providing financial assistance are void: *Selangor United Rubber Co. v. Cradock (No.3)* 1968; and

(iv) any guarantees similarly provided will be unenforceable: *Heald v. O'Connor* 1971.

Under s.155 the rules are relaxed for private companies provided they meet certain conditions, e.g. that the company's net assets are not thereby reduced, or if they are reduced that the financial assistance comes from distributable profits.

Company Borrowing

As a legal person a company can borrow money. The term *loan capital* is applied to the funds the company raises in this way. The level of borrowing, and the procedures to be followed to exercise the power to borrow may be regulated by the memorandum and articles if the company so chooses. If these matters *are* regulated, and the company borrows in breach of them, the lender may still be able to hold the company bound through the application of the internal management rule (the rule in *Turquands Case*) and s.35 Companies Act 1989.

When a company borrows, the lender may require some form of security which the lender can realise in the event of the company defaulting on the loan. This is not a legal requirement, simply commercial common sense. The larger the borrowing, the more likely it is that the lender will demand protection in the event of a default. If security is not taken the lender is an unsecured creditor, and very vulnerable in the event of the company getting into financial difficulties, since secured creditors are able to realise their securities first, often leaving the unsecured creditors with virtually nothing left.

In larger companies there will be plenty of property which can be used as security, such as land and buildings, equipment, stock, together with non tangibles like book debts. In small companies however, with few assets, a lender such as a bank may require individual members to provide personal security. In this way the shareholders/directors of a company in which they are the only members can find that much of the benefit of limited liability is lost to them when they have to put up their homes as a security in relation to their company borrowing.

If a lender to a company takes no security the lender is simply an unsecured creditor, having the capacity to sue the company on the debt (and takes steps to enforce any judgment awarded), or petition as a creditor to have the company wound up if the debt is for £750 or more. A lender who has security is in a much stronger position, since if the company defaults the security can be used to meet the debt.

Debentures

Company borrowing and the term *debenture* are so closely linked it can sometimes be difficult to distinguish between them. The most widely recognised judicial definition of a debenture is that of Chitty J in *Levy v. Abercorris Slate and Slab Co.* 1887 where he said, *"In my opinion a debenture means a document which either creates a debt or acknowledges it and any document which fulfils either of these conditions is a `debenture'. I cannot find any precise legal definition of the term, it is not either in law or commerce a strictly technical term...."* A debenture is thus no more than a written acknowledgement of a debt a company owes. Although debentures are usually secured, they do not have to be. If they are unsecured they are sometimes called *naked* debentures. S.744 Companies Act 1985 does not attempt a definition, but it does allude to the question of security, for it states that a debenture *"includes debenture stock, bonds and any other securities of a company, whether contributing a charge on the assets of the company or not."* A charge involves taking security; the Act indicates that this is not necessary to create a debenture.

Many types of company borrowing arrangements come within the umbrella term debenture. At its simplest it can be merely a written note evidencing a debt, but in its usual commercial sense a debenture is regarded as a document expressing some secured obligation. This security will be in the form of a *charge* on property of the company. This is most important, for a secured debenture holder will normally have the power to appoint a receiver to protect the holders interests if the company defaults in any way, or if the property charged is felt to be in jeopardy.

Debentures are issued in accordance with the articles of the company, and this usually means that their issue will be made following a board resolution. There are three main types of debenture:

- the *single debenture*, where the borrowing is from a single source, such as a merchant bank;

- a *series of debentures*. This occurs for example where the company is raising loan capital from its members. Although each loan is separate usually it is intended that the lenders should rank equally as regards repayment.

- *debenture stock*. This method is used to raise very large sums of money from different lenders at the same time and on the same terms. It is the way public companies raise loan capital on the investment market. The process of issuing debenture stock is not dissimilar to a share issue, however the debenture stock holders are a class of creditors rather than company members. Usually a trust deed is created, under which trustees are appointed to look after the interests of the investors as a class. The trust deed will provide for such matters as meetings of holders of the debenture stock at which votes can be cast, so that their collective views can be ascertained and then represented to the company by the trustees. Usually nowadays all the loans are aggregated into a total fund which is advanced to the company by the trustees. From the company's point of view this is a single loan, but it is made up of loans from different parties and the amount they have contributed determines the amount of debenture stock they hold. The trustees have a contractual relationship with the company. The use of a trust deed is necessary for two reasons. Firstly if the debentures are secured by way of a legal charge, for example where the company has provided land as security, a legal mortgage is created. This is a legal estate in land, and as such cannot be vested in more than four people. Since the company has borrowed from many people the appointment of trustees under the trust deed enables them to hold the land subject to the security as legal owners on behalf of the debenture holders.

Secondly individual lenders may have such a small investment that they would not find it worth their while to take enforcement action if the company defaulted on its obligations, for instance by failing to pay interest. Under the trust deed the entitlements of the individual lenders become the responsibility of the trustees and must be enforced by them. This is a valuable benefit to the lenders.

Although it is not a legal requirement, the company will usually maintain a register of debenture holders. If this is done the debentures so registered are transferable in the way that shares are. Under s.185 a *debenture certificate* must be issued by the company within two months of the allotment or the transfer of debentures or debenture stock.

Charges

A charge is a security interest which the owner of the asset(s), the *chargor* agrees to create in favour of a creditor, the *chargee*. The agreement will provide that the asset charged may be sold by the chargee in the event of default by the chargor. There are two methods used to secure debentures by means of charges, the *fixed charge* and the *floating charge*.

Fixed charges

A fixed or specific charge is like an ordinary mortgage taken out by an individual. It is created by taking out a legal or equitable mortgage on specific property, such as land or equipment. Its advantage is that it attaches to specifically identified assets, and thereafter these assets cannot be disposed of lawfully by the chargor without the chargee's permission. Moreover it should be possible to ascertain the value of the asset at the time the charge is created.

Floating charges

A floating charge also requires the property subject to the charge to be identified, but the charge recognises that the chargor can deal with the property in the ordinary course of business without the permission of chargee. This is referred to sometimes as the *trading power*. A floating charge can only be an equitable charge, but it can apply to company property both present and future.

> In *Re: Yorkshire Woolcombers Association Ltd.* 1903 Romer LJ identified three characteristics of the floating charge. He said *"it is a charge on a class of assets of a company present and future; if that class is one which, in the ordinary course of the business of the company, would be changing from time to time; and if you find that by the charge it is contemplated that, until some future step is taken by or on behalf of those interested in the charge, the company may carry on its business in the ordinary way as far as concerns the particular class of assets...."*

Floating charges are used to charge company property of a fluctuating kind which are constantly in use or being turned over in the course of business. Stock in trade is a common example. The company is free to acquire and sell stock subject to the charge, the trading power, unless the charge *crystallises*. Crystallisation results in the floating charge becoming a fixed charge, an event which will occur on any one of a number of grounds. These are where:

(i)   a receiver is appointed;

(ii)   the company goes into liquidation;

(iii)   the company ceases to trade (*Re: Woodroffes (Musical Instruments) Ltd.* 1986), or sells its business (*Re: Real Meat Co. Ltd.* 1996);

(iv)   the debenture enables the charge holder to convert the floating charge into a fixed charge by notice and the notice is given;

(v)   an event identified in the charge document as giving rise to automatic crystallisation has occurred. An example would be if a company creditor seeks to execute a judgment in his favour against the property charged. This last ground has been the subject of considerable controversy, since the crystallisation can occur without either the company or the charge holder being aware of it.

Once crystallisation takes place the directors can no longer deal with the assets charged. Of course it will not be known what the value of the assets actually is until crystallisation has occurred and the charge fixes to the assets in question. Whether a charge is fixed or floating depends upon the substance of the charge; express words identifying it as one or the other are not regarded as totally conclusive. In *Re: Brightlife Ltd.* 1987 Hoffmann J held that a charge over the book debts of a company, expressed as a fixed charge, was in reality a floating charge.

Registration and preferences

Unlike debentures, which do not require registration under statute, charges do require registration. If they are not registered within 21 days of creation the charge is void, and the holder becomes an unsecured creditor (s.395 CA 1985). A charge is also void if it is regarded as a preference.

A *preference* is something a company does or allows to be done which puts a company creditor in a better position in the event of the company going into insolvent liquidation, than they would otherwise have been in. For example if the directors, anticipating imminent company insolvency but intending they will subsequently set up a new business, grant a charge over company land to its principal creditor and trade supplier in the hope the supplier will continue to supply the new company, the charge is likely to be treated as a preference. The intended effect of the charge is to place the supplier before other company creditors, and the charge will consequently be a void one.

The rules on preferences are contained in the Insolvency Act 1986. A floating charge given as a preference within twelve months of commencement of a winding up (or within two years to a connected person) is void. Any other charge given as a preference within six months of winding up commencing (or within two years to a connected person) is also void. A connected person includes a director or shadow director, or an associate of that person or the company itself. This covers a spouse, and relatives of the individual or the spouse, namely parents, siblings, children, an uncle, aunt, nephew or niece.

Priority of charges

Sometimes a company may create successive charges over the same property. In these circumstances the general rule is that they rank in order of creation. This means second and subsequent chargees have less valuable security than the first chargee, who can satisfy full liability out of the assets subject of the charge. Furthermore the normal rule is that a fixed charge will rank in priority to a floating charge even if the floating charge was created before it. However if the floating charge contained a prohibition against creating a fixed charge over the same property, and the fixed chargee was aware of this prohibition when he took the charge, his charge will rank after the floating charge. Apart from this one exception the fixed chargee is in a far more secured position than the floating chargee, whose interest is further eroded by certain other creditors who take priority over the floating charge. They are:

(i)   statutory preferential creditors, such as the Inland Revenue, (even though they are unsecured);

(ii)   the claims of a judgment creditor who executed judgment on the property subject to the charge before the charge crystallised;

(iii)   the owner of any property subject to the charge who has the protection of a retention of title clause (a *Romalpa* clause). The use of such clauses is discussed in Chapter 11. The essence of a retention of the title clause is that it enables a seller of goods to retain title in them even when they have passed into the possession of the buyer until the buyer has paid for them in full.

Other Forms of Financing

These include short term loans, such as overdraft arrangements. Additionally, through the use of *factoring* a company may raise money by selling its debts.

The acquisition of assets

A limited company is able to acquire property and property rights in the same way as an individual. As well as purchasing property outright, companies frequently take leased property such as vehicles and land under which they acquire limited rights of ownership. They also obtain goods on credit terms, for example by hiring equipment. The legal considerations applying to such arrangements are examined in detail later in the book.

Assignment - "Its limited liability and all that"

Peter Green's company, Wildblood Records Ltd., was in financial difficulties, and the situation was entirely of Peter's making. As its managing director he had become over ambitious. He decided the company should diversify. Ignoring the objects clause which restricts its commercial activities to music promotion, and its articles, which required all contracts over £100,000 to be approved by the company in a general meeting, Peter negotiated a £250,000 loan with the company's bank Gladstone De La Zouche for the purchase of a restaurant.

The restaurant venture was not a success, and within a few months Peter realised that his company was not going to survive. Concerned about the prospect of being left without a business and the income generated from it he acted quickly. He gave instructions to his friend Sarah Parsons, an accountant, to take all the necessary steps to form a new company, and a few weeks later the new company, Phoenix Music Ltd. received its certificate of incorporation. Peter was appointed as its managing director and took 990 of its 1000 £1 ordinary shares. Sarah took the remaining 10. At the first meeting of the new company it was agreed that it would purchase recording equipment belonging to Peter. Peter valued this equipment at £18,000, and this was the price paid for it by Phoenix. In fact the real market value of the equipment was nearer £7,000, and it has subsequently transpired that some of this equipment was not Peters, but belonged to Wildblood Records.

Wildblood Records has now gone into compulsory liquidation. The liquidator, Mohammed Khan, is particularly interested in the extent of Peter Green's personal liability for the misfortunes of Wildblood Records. His initial view is that the company may be able to avoid the borrowing agreement made with the bank on the grounds that it was unconstitutional, that Peter may be in breach of his duty to the company, that he acted unlawfully in selling the company's property to Phoenix Music Ltd., and that Phoenix is merely a sham. During a telephone conversation Mohammed had with Peter to discuss these issues, Peter angrily remarked *"That's business mate! Its limited liability and all that. You can't touch me."*

Task

You work for Mr Khan, and he has asked you to confirm whether his initial ideas concerning the validity of Peter Green's actions are legally sustainable. Coincidentally, you know Sarah Parsons professionally, and over a drink she has asked for your opinion about any possible breach of promoters duties disclosed in the property transaction between Peter and Phoenix Music Ltd.

Provide Mr Khan and Sarah with the information they are seeking.

Chapter 5

Registered Companies: Directors, Shareholders and Auditors

In this chapter we shall be considering the legal position of the major participants in company activities; the directors who manage the company, the shareholders who own it, and auditors who report on its financial condition.

Directors as Business Managers

One of the fundamental differences between a limited company and a partnership is found in the management structure. In a partnership, ownership and management are in the same hands, for all partners are entitled to manage the firm and each is an agent of the firm and of the other partners. By contrast, a company is a separate entity which cannot manage itself, but needs people to fulfil this function for it. These people are its directors, and under company legislation all companies must have at least one director. For a public company there must be at least two directors – usually there will be several – and in private companies there are frequently more than the statutory minimum of one.

The function of company directors is crucial to the affairs of the organisation. It needs to be fully grasped to gain any proper understanding of the law relating to company operations. It may help to bear in mind that even in the smallest company there are three distinct components. These are the company *itself*, its *managers* (the directors), and its *owners* or proprietors (the shareholders). A complex legal relationship exists between the three. In a private company with few shareholders, it is common for each shareholder to act also as a director. In larger companies with many members, such an arrangement is not appropriate and consequently ownership and management will not be in the same hands. Public companies invariably appoint as directors people with proven track-records in the management of large organisations, and with commensurately high salaries. In contrast, directors of small private companies may be people with little if any commercial experience. Such experience, whilst clearly of considerable practical importance, is not a legal pre-requisite of directorship.

The following broad observations can be made concerning the relationship between the company, its directors and its shareholders. The directors have certain legal obligations or duties which they owe to the company. They control the company's business affairs and its assets, and in general meeting they are accountable to the company for the way in which they have exercised this control.

They are not accountable to the shareholders as proprietors other than in general meeting. This meeting, has substantial powers and may, for example, be the forum used to remove directors. It is a meeting open to all the membership of the company. Although directors are not answerable to the shareholders as proprietors, directors must, under statute, provide them with a range of information to enable the shareholders to assess how the company is being, and has been operated.

Whilst shareholders are usually responsible for appointing directors, and can remove them, they are not able to tell them how to exercise their powers. At best they can restrict powers available to the directors under the articles, and in respect of some matters it is now necessary for directors to seek approval to act from the general meeting. What this all amounts to is that directors act essentially as agents, not of the shareholders, but of the company itself.

Statutory references below are references to the Companies Act 1985 unless otherwise stated.

Directorship

Definition of a Director

The term director is applied to anyone entrusted with the management of a company who attends board meetings and takes part in their decision-making activities. There must be at least one director for a private company and two for a public one (s.282), but under the articles it is possible to provide for the appointment of more than the statutory minimum, and there is no statutory upper limit. Table A states that unless otherwise determined by ordinary resolution, the number of directors shall not be subject to any maximum but shall not be less than two.

Although the Act defines the term director to include, *"any person occupying the position of director, by whatever name called"* (s.741(1)), this is clearly not a helpful definition because it says nothing about what the nature of what such a position actually involves. Table A is more helpful however. It provides that subject to the provisions of the Act, and the memorandum and articles, and any directions given under the terms of any special resolution, *"the business of the company shall be managed by the directors who may exercise all the powers of the company"*. Thus the role of a director involves managing the company business, and as a consequence of s.741(1), it does not matter whether a person having such responsibility within the company is given the title of director or not. Furthermore, a director could include someone who has not actually been appointed to the board at all, but is acting as if he were a director; a *de facto* director.

This proposition was expressed judicially by Lord Jessel in *Re Forest of Dean Coal Mining Company* 1878 where he stated *"It does not matter much what you call them, so long as you understand what their true position is which is that they are merely commercial men, managing a trading concern for the benefit of themselves and all other shareholders in it"*.

> In *Secretary of State for Trade and Industry v. Tjolle* 1998 the Secretary of State was seeking disqualification orders against those who could be regarded as directors of a company, Land Travel Ltd. The company had gone into voluntary liquidation with debts of approximately £12.4m. One issue was whether an employee, Mrs Kenning, who used the title 'Sales and Marketing Director' but had never been formally appointed as a director, could be regarded as a director for the purposes of a disqualification order.

> Jacob J concluded that the court should look at all relevant surrounding circumstances, but that the major test should be whether the person was part of the corporate governing structure. On the basis that Mrs Kenning had no access to the company's financial matters she could not properly be regarded as part of the corporate governing structure, was not therefore a de facto director, and a disqualification order could not be made against her.

Under the Act a director is an officer of the company; so too is a manager and the company secretary (s.744).

There is no statutory requirement that a director hold shares in the company he is managing.

Shadow Directors

A *shadow director* is a person who gives directions or instructions to the board which the board customarily acts upon. A person acting as a professional adviser to the board, such as a lawyer or an accountant, will not by reason of that capacity alone be regarded as a shadow director. A shadow director is thus someone who is able to exercise influence over the board, even though not formally appointed to sit on it himself. A shadow director could be a majority shareholder who tells the board members how to manage the affairs of the company, but for lack of time or for the avoidance of publicity chooses not to be a member himself. A person does not become a shadow director merely through the act of attempting to assert control. The board must do his bidding.

Other than in exceptional circumstances, a bank which has lent money to a company to help it overcome financial difficulties, will not be regarded as a shadow director (*Re: Hydrodam (Corby) Ltd.* 1994).

The possibility of shadow directors being associated with a company is important, since s.741 extends a number of the provisions of the 1985 Act which apply to properly appointed directors, to *de facto* and to shadow directors as well. The relevant provisions are:

- long-term service contracts;

- substantial property transactions;

- loans and similar dealings;

- interests in contracts made with the company;

- requirements regarding disclosures to be made in accounts;

- the rules relating to wrongful trading.

A company is also required to keep a copy of any service contract it has with a shadow director. These contracts are usually held at the company's registered office.

The Company Secretary

Every company must have a secretary, and the secretary has the power to bind the company in any contract of an administrative nature.

> In *Panorama Developments (Guildford) Ltd. v. Fidelis Furnishing Fabrics Ltd.* 1971 the defendant's company secretary hired cars on behalf of the company on the understanding that the cars were being used to meet company customers. In fact he was using them for his own purposes. The court held the company to be bound to pay the hire charges. The transactions were of a kind a company secretary has the power to make, falling within the category of general administrative tasks.

Under Table A, directors have the power to appoint the secretary on such terms as they think fit, and they may also remove the secretary. In a private company the directors can appoint anyone they choose. However, in the case of a public company the directors must be satisfied that the secretary meets the criteria laid down under s.286, namely:

- appears to the board to have the requisite knowledge and experience to discharge the functions of secretary; and

- possesses one of the qualifications set out under the section. These range from holding a professional qualification as an accountant or lawyer, to having gained the appropriate experience through a previous position held.

Appointment

There are three methods by which a person may be properly appointed as a director. These are:

(i)   under the statement of first directors sent to the Registrar;

(ii)   by being named in the articles;

(iii)   under the provisions for appointment laid down in the articles.

One of the forms sent to the Registrar prior to incorporation is the statement of the person(s) to be the first director(s) of the company. S.13(5) says that the person(s) so named is or are deemed to have been appointed as the first director(s). They must, however, have given their consent to act. The appointment of these named people is thus automatic on the granting of the certificate of incorporation.

Often there is a provision in the articles which provides for the appointment of the first directors. If the articles are silent on this point it will be the subscribers who make the appointment. The subscribers are the people named in the memorandum as having agreed to take shares in the company on incorporation.

Whichever means are used to appoint the first directors, that is either the subscribers making the appointment or the articles stipulating who shall act in this capacity, thereafter all subsequent appointments, and also terminations from office, are regulated by the articles.

Broadly, under the standard system contained in Table A, the following arrangements apply:

(i)   at the first annual general meeting after incorporation, all directors must retire. They may, of course, be reappointed at the meeting;

(ii)   at all subsequent annual general meetings one-third of the board must retire. This is referred to as retirement by rotation. Again, there is nothing to prevent a retiring director from being re-elected. Which directors are to retire is determined by length of office, but if they were all appointed at the same time, for instance at the first AGM, then the matter is decided by drawing lots;

(iii)   a director retiring by rotation who is not replaced is automatically re-elected, unless it is resolved not to fill the vacancy or a resolution to re-elect the director is lost;

(iv)   any member can by written notice give intention to propose a person for election with that person's written consent;

(v)   *casual vacancies*, those occurring between annual general meetings where a director has died or has resigned during his or her term of office, can be temporarily filled by an appointment made by the existing board. They may also appoint additional directors between AGMs if they wish, for instance to replace a director who cannot attend board meetings through illness. The filling of casual vacancies by the board under the articles saves the need to summon a general meeting to do so. However, anyone appointed in this way must retire at the next annual general meeting of the company enabling the members to vote against such director if they wish to do so;

(vi)   in a public company directors must be individually elected unless a resolution has been passed, with no votes cast against it, proposing to vote back the whole board (s.291);

(vii)   if the articles appoint a director for life such person is not eligible for re-election under the rotation rules, but can still be removed under the statutory removal provisions contained in s.303, by means of an ordinary resolution. The appointment of a director for life under the articles does not give rise to a *personal* contract between that director and the company, a separate contract would be needed for this. In the case of removal from office of a director who has a service contract with the company, a claim for unfair dismissal may be brought by the director;

(viii)   a director may only assign his or her directorship by means of a special resolution (s.308) if the articles permit this;

(ix)   a director may appoint an *alternate director,* that is, someone to act as a temporary replacement. The alternate may be another director or some other person. If he is another director it is only the alternate who needs to give his consent, whereas the appointment of a new director requires the consent of the board. Alternate directors have full powers and are liable for their own acts and defaults. They are not agents of the directors who appoint them, and they are not entitled to remuneration. Their appointment can be made and terminated by notice to the board given by the appointing directors.

Persons who cannot be appointed

Table A contains no restrictions on who may be appointed as a director, although articles may be drafted to include particular restrictions. For instance the company may seek to exclude minors from acting as directors, or perhaps another company.

Under statute, a person cannot be a company's sole director and secretary at the same time, nor its sole director and auditor. In addition statute provides that no person shall be appointed as a director of a public company, or of a private company which is the subsidiary of a public company, if at the time of his appointment he has reached the age of 70. This provision may be varied or excluded altogether under the articles, and in any case such a person may be appointed by the members in general meeting by an ordinary resolution of which special notice (of 28 days) has been given.

Under the Company Directors Disqualification Act 1986 it is an offence for an undischarged bankrupt to act as a director without permission of the court. Articles may provide that anyone who has been bankrupt shall not be appointed as a director, and Table A more specifically states that a directors office becomes vacant on his bankruptcy. The 1986 Act also empowers the court to make a disqualification order against a named person. The person named is then prevented for the duration of the order except by leave of the court from:

- being a director of a company;

- being concerned with, or taking part in, directly or indirectly, the promotion, formation or management of a company (s.1).

Grounds for a disqualification order

Under the 1986 Act a number of grounds are identified under which the court may grant a disqualification order. Breach of an order renders the disqualified person liable to criminal proceedings carrying a maximum penalty of six months imprisonment, and it also renders the offender personally liable for the company's debts. These are formidable penalties. The imposition of personal liability, with its effect of lifting the corporate veil, is seen as an appropriate way to deal with someone who has had a disqualification order made against him because he has shown himself not fit to be a director, yet has continued in breach of the order to manage a company.

The grounds include:

(a) *conviction of an indictable offence (s.2)*

An indictable offence is one which can be tried before a Crown Court, however a s.2 offence may alternatively be dealt with summarily before Magistrates. The Crown Court can on conviction disqualify for up to 15 years, the Magistrates Court up to five years. There is no minimum disqualification period.

One of the most common offences associated with company affairs is fraud. In *R v. Corbin* 1984 the defendant ran a business selling yachts through companies he owned. He was convicted of various fraudulent practices including borrowing from finance companies to buy yachts, falsely stating he had paid a deposit on them. He received two a half years imprisonment and a disqualification order for five years;

(b) *persistent breaches of company law (s.3)*

Under s.3 the breaches in question involve the failure to provide any return account or documents required to be filed with the Registrar of Companies. There is a presumption that a person has been persistently in default if he has been convicted of a default three times in the past five years. The maximum period for disqualification is five years;

(c) *fraud, fraudulent trading or breach of duty revealed in a winding up (s.4)*

The court may make an order following the offence of fraudulent trading under s.458 Companies Act 1985, or where the person has otherwise been guilty of any fraud in relation to the company or breach of duty, in his capacity as an officer, liquidator, receiver or manager. The maximum period for disqualification is fifteen years;

(d) *unfitness (s.6)*

When a company becomes insolvent the person involved in administering the insolvency such as the liquidator or administrative receiver must make a return to the Secretary of State regarding the conduct of the company's directors. On the basis of this information the Secretary of State may apply to the court for a disqualification order against an individual director on the grounds of his unfitness as evidenced in the return. The court must then satisfy itself as to the unfitness before it can make an order. Schedule 1 of the 1986 Act lists the factors to be considered by the court in reaching its decision. In broad terms these factors share a common feature, namely the way the directors have managed the company. The list is a long one, and it includes the following:

(i)   any misfeasance or breach of duty by the director in relation to the company;

(ii)   any misapplication or retention of company money or property by the director;

(iii)   the directors responsibility for the company entering into transactions liable to be set aside in a liquidation;

(iv)   the directors failure to keep proper company records, or prepare or file annual company accounts;

(v)   the directors responsibility for the company becoming insolvent;

(vi)   the directors responsibility for any failure by the company to supply goods or services which have already been paid for;

(vii)   the directors responsibility for failing to call a creditors meeting in a creditors voluntary winding up;

(viii) any failure by the director to produce a statement of affairs as required in any insolvency proceedings concerning the company.

A disqualification order on grounds of unfitness can only be made if the company is insolvent, which in this context means either that an *administration order* has been made against it, or an *administrative receiver* has been appointed, or at the time of the liquidation its assets are insufficient to pay its debts or other liabilities. An order made on grounds of unfitness must be for a minimum of two years, and may be up to a maximum of fifteen years.

In *Re: Continental Assurance Co. of London plc* 1997, the court had to consider whether a disqualification order could be made against a director, who was a corporate financier, on the grounds of his unfitness. The facts were that the company had been making certain payments to its parent company, which amounted to unlawful financial assistance for the purchase of shares in itself under s.151. Despite the fact that the director, who was a non-executive member of the board of both Continental and its parent, was unaware of unlawful payments and that as a result of them Continental's accounts were seriously misleading, the court disqualified him. For a person with his knowledge, and in his position, a plea of ignorance was no defence.

(e)   *matters revealed following a DTI investigation (s.8)*

If the DTI has investigated the affairs of the company and following an inspectors report, or information or documents obtained under powers to require production of documents and enter and search premises (s.447 and s.448 Companies Act 1985 respectively), it appears to the Secretary of State that a disqualification order should be made because a person is unfit to manage or in the public interest, he may apply to the Court. The maximum period for disqualification is fifteen years. This may give rise to a legal challenge against the Secretary of State where the Secretary decides not to proceed with an application. Such was the case in *R v. Secretary of State for Trade and Industry ex parte Lonrho plc* 1992, court proceedings which emerged out of the acrimonious public dispute between Lonrho, under the chairmanship of Tiny Rowland, and the Fayed brothers who had been successful in a take-over bid to acquire Harrods. DTI Inspectors who had criticised the brothers behaviour had not however recommended disqualification, and as a result the Secretary of State decided not to apply to the court for disqualification orders. The challenge against this decision was unsuccessful, the court concluding that it had been arrived at lawfully.

Unfitness under ss6 and 8 relates to management of companies generally rather than unfitness associated with a particular company, even though it will be as a result of specific malpractice that the issue of unfitness will emerge. Consequently disqualification will not be avoided by arguing that a director who is unfit to manage a public company may be fit to manage a private one, a proposition raised, and rejected, in *Re: Poly Peck International plc No.2* 1994. The company had experienced spectacular prosperity under the entrepreneurial direction of Asil Nadir, who held 25% of its shares, but it subsequently suffered an equally spectacular financial collapse. This was allegedly the result of large sums raised by the company from banks and shareholders being passed to subsidiary companies, who did not need it, and who deposited it in banks in the Turkish sector of Cyprus from which it could not be recovered. Facing criminal charges Mr Nadir fled the country. The Secretary of State then sought to commence disqualification proceedings against four remaining directors. This was outside the time limit for an application, which is two years from the date of the insolvency. The court would not waive the time limit. It found the Secretary's case against the remaining directors as *"speculative and very weak"* for they were a minority group on the board, and one of their number, the financial director, had worked hard to secure better financial management.

What should be the duration of a disqualification order?

In *Re: Sevenoaks Stationers (Retail) Ltd.* 1991 Dillon LJ suggested guidelines for determining the appropriate length of a disqualification under the 1986

Act. Periods of between 10 and 15 years should should be for the most serious cases, such as recidivist directors, periods of between 2 to 5 years should cover the least serious cases, and six to ten years should be appropriate for serious cases not meriting the most severe penalties.

In *R v. Millard* 1993, a case brought under s.2, a director whose four years of fraudulent trading resulted in losses of £3/4m, was felt by the court to come within the middle category, and an 8 year disqualification was made.

Remuneration

There is no automatic right to payment for a director, but Table A allows for remuneration by way of an ordinary resolution, and grants the right to receive expenses incurred in the discharge of a director's duties (i.e. without the need for a resolution). Such a payment is treated as a gross taxable sum.

It should be remembered in the context of payments to directors that the nature of the relationship between a director and the company will depend upon a variety of factors, not least of which is the size and type of company involved. In some companies with very few members, it is not uncommon to find that each member of the company is also a director. Under such an arrangement the directors may well be satisfied to receive dividends from the company, which they gain in their capacity as members. Another possibility is that the director is someone contributing his or her time to the management of the company on a part-time basis. For instance a person could be a full-time accountant, who also acts as a company director of a company in which he or she holds no shares but receives fees for the advisory or supervisory work involved. Then there are the full-time executives or managers whose directorships are associated with the existence of a contract of employment between themselves and the company. Such a directors are company employees in receipt of a salary. If a director's remuneration is to be by way of payment of fees, the articles must expressly permit such payment. If they do not, the payment of fees is unlawful, even if the members have agreed to it by passing a resolution in general meeting (*Re George Newman & Co.* 1895).

Where a director works under a contract of service, normal principles of employment law will apply. Thus, if the directorship is terminated by the company (under s.303, Companies Act 1985, any director may be removed by the members in general meeting by means of an ordinary resolution), and if the director was working under a contract of service he may:

- bring a claim for wrongful dismissal if he has not been given the necessary notice, or there is still some part of his fixed-term contract unexpired at the time of its termination;

- bring a claim before an industrial tribunal for unfair dismissal, or redundancy. To be eligible to bring such a claim, the employee director must meet the statutory qualification requirements, such as length of service, which are contained in the Employment Rights Act 1996. It may be that the director was required to waive the right to claim for unfair dismissal or redundancy in the event of the contract being terminated or a fixed-term contract not being renewed. Such a waiver of rights is lawful, and precludes a claim from being brought.

Table A grants the board the power to fix the terms of a contract of service with a *service director* as an employee director is called. A director who is not an employee of the company is usually referred to as someone *"holding an office"*. Mere appointment to a directorship, without more, does not give rise to an employer/employee relationship between the company and the director.

There are two important statutory provisions which apply to contracts of service made between companies and their directors. S.318, Companies Act 1985 requires every company to keep a contract of service it has with any director (or director of a subsidiary company), or a memorandum if the contract is an oral one, at either the registered office, the place where the register of members is held, or its principal place of business. The Registrar must be notified of the location of this information, and it must be available for inspection to the members, without charge, for at least two hours per day. Thus members can ascertain the terms under which their directors are employed, and the probable costs involved in removing them.

Some relief is given from these provisions. For work carried out by a director wholly or mainly outside the UK, the company need only keep a memorandum which names the director and notes the duration of the agreement.

S.319 provides a safeguard against possible abuse by directors of their powers to fix their own terms of employment. Any contract for a director's services, even as a self-employed consultant, requires the approval of the company by means of an ordinary resolution in general meeting, unless the contract is one which the company is free to terminate without suffering any penalty within five years of its creation. Approval of any contract coming under s.319 must be sought in advance. Failure to meet s.319 entitles the company to terminate the contract at any time on serving reasonable notice, a term not defined by the Act.

In *James v. Kent & Co. Ltd.* 1950 the plaintiff director had been appointed at a shareholders meeting *"subject to a three year contract with the company"*, however the company solicitor failed to prepare a service agreement, and two years into the contract the company dismissed the plaintiff. In the absence of a written agreement the court was prepared to imply a service contract, and read into it a requirement that it could only be terminated on reasonable notice, which on the facts would be three months notice.

Both sections 318 and 319 apply to shadow directors.

In addition to these provisions, the Act also contains further provisions designed to provide publicity about directors. Thus:

- every company must maintain a register of directors and secretary at its registered office (s.288);

- the annual return sent to the Registrar each year must reproduce this information (s.363);

- changes to this information must be given to the Registrar within 14 days, and receipt of the change published in London Gazette (s.711);

- the company must maintain a register of directors' interests in shares or debentures in it or any other company in the same group;

- the annual accounts must disclose certain specified information regarding the salaries, fees and other payments made to the directors as a group.

Disclosure by Director

A director who is directly or indirectly interested in a contract of the company is required to declare the nature of the interest to the board at the first opportunity, so that the other directors are made aware of it (s.317). This is sometimes referred to as the *self-dealing rule*. Under Table A he may not vote at the meeting of the directors on any matter in which such an interest is held. The purpose of such provisions is to bring into the open any circumstance in which the director faces or is likely to face a conflict of interest. An example would be a situation where a director is a shareholder of another company which is in the process of negotiating a contract with the company of which he is a director. In effect, s.317 imposes a statutory duty of disclosure upon a director. In *Hely-Hutchinson v. Brayhead Ltd.* 1967 the Court of Appeal held that s.317 renders a contract voidable by the company if a director does not declare his interest.

One issue which emerges from s.317 is whether disclosure obligations apply to companies with a single director. The matter was tested in *Neptune (Vehicle Washing Equipment) Ltd. v. Fitzgerald* 1995. The plaintiff company had a sole director, Mr Fitzgerald. The company was later taken over. The new holding company did not appoint a director itself, but it took an active part in its management, and in due course Mr Fitzgerald decided to retire as his services were no longer needed. He caused the plaintiff company to pass a resolution authorising it to make a payment to him of £100,000 as compensation for the termination of his directorship. He retired, the payment was made, and then a new director was appointed to the plaintiff company, who immediately challenged the validity of the payment arguing there had not been formal disclosures of the personal interest of Mr Fitzgerald at a board meeting (of which he was the sole participating director). On its facts the action failed, however the court made clear that as a point of law s.317 does apply to a company with a sole director, with the result that the ordinary meaning of the word *meeting* which demands at least two participants is in these circumstances displaced.

Under s.324, any person who becomes a director of a company and is interested in shares or debentures of the company, or its subsidiary or holding or other subsidiary company must within five days give written notice to the company of these interests. The number of shares, their class and the amount of debentures must be specified. Similar notification must be given where a s.324 interest ceases. The interest of a spouse or infant child is treated as the interest of the director. Information obtained by the company under s.324 is kept in a register of directors' interests which the company must maintain. Contravention of the section is a criminal offence.

Property transactions involving directors

Further recognition of the powerful position enjoyed by directors over the companies they manage is found in the statutory rules which seek to regulate the transactions of directors by which they might gain personal advantage at the expense of the company. These rules can be considered under two heads; substantial property transactions involving directors and loans to directors.

Substantial property transactions involving directors

S.320 makes it unlawful for a company to enter into an arrangement with a director or connected person for the acquisition of a *non-cash asset of the requisite value,* without the prior approval of the company in general meeting.

The aim of s.320 is to prevent directors purchasing company property at less than its true value, or selling the company their own property at above market value, without the approval of the members. Non-cash assets cover a wide range of property, from the tangible such as land to the non-tangible such as patents and debts.

The meanings of the expressions used in the section require explanation. A *connected person* includes the director's spouse, child or step-child (whilst they are minors); a body corporate with which the director is associated (having at least a 20% holding); a person acting as a partner of the director (or of a partner of someone within the previous categories); and certain types of trustee. The term director includes shadow directors.

A *non-cash asset* does not include a loan, but any other property transaction, for instance, the acquisition by the director from the company of fully paid shares. *Requisite value* means a non-cash asset whose value exceeds £50,000 or 10% or more of the company's net assets taken from the last accounts, subject to a minimum value of £1,000.

Non-compliance renders the agreement avoidable at the option of the company. In other words, it may take steps to end the contract unless:

(a)   restitution is impossible, i.e. because the parties cannot be restored to their pre-contractual positions; or

(b)   the company has been indemnified; or

(c)   third party rights have been acquired; or

(d)   the company affirms the arrangement in general meeting within a reasonable time.

It also renders the director, plus anyone connected with him plus any authorising director, personally liable to account to the company for any direct gain which results, and jointly and severally liable to indemnify the company for any resultant loss.

Liability is, however, avoided where the transaction was with a connected person and the relevant director took all reasonable steps to comply with the section. Relief is also granted to a connected person and the authorising director(s) if they did not know of the contravention at the time of the transaction.

There are certain exceptions from s.320, such as the provision that a transaction of less than £1,000 value need not be disclosed.

Loans to directors

In principle, although there are a number of exceptions, a company may not make loans or enter into similar transactions with or for the benefit of a director of the company or of its holding company: s.320. The provisions are complex, and apply mainly to what are called *relevant* companies; that is, public limited companies and private companies which form part of a group containing a public company. The following provides an outline of the law as it applies to loans.

Under s.330(2) no company, whether a relevant one or not, may make a loan to any of its directors or to any director of its holding company, nor enter into any guarantee or provide any security in relation to a loan made by an outsider to one of its directors.

Ss.330(3) and (4), which apply only to relevant companies, extend this prohibition to quasi-loans and credit transactions involving the director or a connected person. A *quasi-loan* arises where a director incurs personal expenditure but the bill is met by the company and the director repays later. For instance, a company might initially pay for a rail season ticket for the director who later recompenses the company, or the company may issue him with a company credit card, enabling the purchase of personal items for which the company is subsequently reimbursed. A *credit transaction* arises where the company acts as the creditor under an arrangement with a director or connected person involving a hire purchase or conditional sale agreement, or a leasing or hiring arrangement involving periodical payments or a deferred payment arrangement. Thus, it would be a credit transaction where a company transferred video equipment it manufactures to a director on the basis that it should be paid for by instalments, or where a company hires out a company car to a director. A relevant company is also prohibited from entering into a guarantee or providing any security in connection with a credit transaction or quasi-loan made by a third party for a director or connected person.

Certain loans are, however, lawful. Under s.332 a quasi-loan not exceeding £5,000 for which the director must reimburse the company within two months is exempted. So too is a loan made by any company to a director for any purpose, which does not exceed £5,000 (s.334). Under s.335 a company which is in the business of providing finance facilities may enter into a credit transaction with a director where the amount is in excess of £5,000, provided this is done in the ordinary course of business and the terms are not more favourable to the director than those that would be offered to another person. Similar provisions apply to moneylending companies (s.338).

Finally, there are exemptions contained in s.337 for companies providing financial assistance to directors in performance of their duties. The company may do anything to provide directors with funds to meet expenditure they incur for company purposes or in performance of their duties. The financial assistance must be either approved by the company in general meeting in advance, or alternatively at the next Annual General Meeting after the assistance has been provided. For a relevant company the section imposes an upper limit of £10,000 on the amount that may be advanced. There is no limit for any other company. If the members do not give their approval, the sum involved must be repaid within six months.

There are both civil and criminal consequences for breach of the loan provisions. S.341 states that a transaction made in breach is voidable at the instance of the company unless restitution is impossible, or the company has been indemnified, or third party rights have arisen. The director and any convicted person will also be personally liable to account for any gain, and indemnify the company for any loss. By s.342 a director of a relevant company who authorises or permits the making by the company of an agreement which contravenes the rules under s.330 commits an offence. The company also commits an offence.

Disclosure of loan transactions

Any transaction coming under s.330, or under any of the exemption provisions of sections 332-338, must be disclosed in notes to the company accounts, and so too any agreement with the company in which the director has a material interest (see section 317 above). The main terms must be identified in the notes; the parties, the terms and so on. Certain transactions are, however, exempt from disclosure, e.g. those not made during the period to which the accounts relate.

The Powers of Directors

In order to understand the significance of directors' powers we need to reflect on the way in which power is divided within a company. What this reveals is two potential power bases; the board of directors, and the members in general meeting. There are certain things which lawfully can only be done by a company in general meeting, for example, passing an ordinary resolution under s.303 to remove a director from office. Moreover, it is necessary under the Companies Act to secure the passing of a special resolution, requiring 75% support of the voting shareholders, in order to make certain decisions in general meetings; alteration of the articles and the objects clause are both examples.

Many other matters affecting companies are not required to be decided in general meeting, and can be dealt with by the board of directors as part of the ordinary day-to-day running of the business. It will be recalled that Table A gives directors the power to manage the business of the company and exercise all its powers, that is, carry out the activities expressly or impliedly contained in the objects clause, subject to any restrictions under the Act, the memorandum and articles. The members can however control the activities of the board through any directions issued to the board under the terms of any special resolution they pass. This power-sharing arrangement recognises that a balance must be struck which enables the managers to manage effectively, whilst ensuring that ultimate control is vested in the proprietors of the organisation, the shareholders.

There are various reasons why the division between what the board does, and what the company as a whole must do in general meeting, can be seen sometimes as rather artificial. In the case of very small companies measured in terms of membership, the members may all be directors. Ownership and control is thus in the same hands. In companies having a larger membership, where there is not complete coincidence between those who are members and those who are directors, the question of who does what is sometimes rather stretched. For example, in the case of a share issue, it is the company in general meeting which has the power (under s.121) to pass an ordinary resolution to increase the authorised capital for the purposes of ensuring that it is adequate to cover the issue and to ensure the directors have the necessary authority to issue the shares (s.80). However, the actual issuing of the shares is carried out by the directors themselves.

Despite the power sharing structure which applies to registered companies, real power undoubtedly rests in the hands of the board, partly because of Table A which, as we have seen, grants the board wide management powers, but also because in companies with a large membership, the board members are in close and regular contact with each other. The shareholders are unlikely to maintain such contacts amongst themselves, thus reducing their effectiveness as decision-makers in general meeting. Indeed, in larger companies the management is so firmly placed in the hands of the directors that the only occasion when members are likely to hear from them is when they receive notice of the Annual General Meeting. In such companies there is nothing artificial about the division of power; it is an appropriate practical way of conducting business. It also reflects the traditional view that investors in public companies are more interested in profits than in participation.

Members' control over the directors

This is achieved in two ways. Firstly, shareholders have the right in certain circumstances to take action on the company's behalf to prevent wrongdoing carried out by or committed against it. On this see *Foss v. Harbottle* 1843 and the various exceptions to it, and also the remedies under s.459 of the Act available where a member has suffered unfair prejudice which are considered later in the chapter. Secondly, the members have powers which they can exercise in general meeting to control the board. These are:

(a)   passing an ordinary resolution under s.303 to remove a director before his or her term of office expires;

(b)   not voting for the re-election of a director when he or she seeks re-election if the company's articles provide for retirement by rotation;

(c)   passing a special resolution to alter the articles to cut down the powers of the directors; and

(d)   passing a special resolution which gives the directors directions on how they should act in relation in a particular matter; in other words, giving them orders in advance.

Delegation of functions

The larger an organisation is, the more valuable it becomes to have the capacity to delegate functions. This helps to avoid the need to hold frequent meetings involving all the managers in order to arrive at decisions which could more appropriately have been taken simply by one of them. In larger companies with boards having many directors on them, the ability to delegate is particularly useful. However, the general principle contained in both the Companies Act 1985 and Table A is that the board should act as a body, taking collective responsibility for its decisions. Article 72 of Table A does, however, allow for delegation of any of the directors' powers (i) to a committee of any one or more directors, or (ii) to a *managing director* or any other director holding executive office (such as a finance director). In exercising the power to delegate, the directors may impose any conditions they see fit, and may alter or revoke the delegation; thus the board has complete control over the terms of the delegation.

Commonly the boards of companies are headed by a managing director who by virtue of delegated powers is able to carry out executive functions alone, without the need to seek the approval of the board as a whole. The mere assumption of the title managing director, however, does not of itself give rise to an act of delegation by the board to that office holder.

Table A also permits the board to employ professional persons and agents to carry out functions which the board itself may carry out.

Beyond those circumstances where the articles allow for delegation, or the members have given their permission, it is well established that directors cannot delegate their powers or functions to others, for the agency principle – *delegatus non potest delegare* – a delegate cannot delegate, applies to them.

The Duties of Directors

The nature of a director's position

The relationship between a company and its directors is unique. They control the company, but cannot treat it as though it were their own, for they owe duties to it.

In this broad sense, and in the context of specific duties which directors must carry out, the expression *company* means the corporate body, the members, but, as we shall see, it can sometimes be taken to include the employees and the creditors as well. All these parties, shareholders, employees and creditors have interests in the company and it is the responsibility of the directors to take account of the overall interests of the company, rather than particular sections of it.

A director does not have to be employed by a company to act as its director, thus his position is not necessarily that of an employee or servant. Even if the director is employed under a contract of service, his role as a manager, together with his custodianship of the interests of the company, mean that the duties he must discharge are not limited to those owed by an employee to an employer. Depending upon the particular circumstances he will act as the agent of the company and so will owe an agent's duties, however a director does not enjoy all the rights of an agent, and therefore examination of the law of agency does not provide us with a full account of the director's position either.

In some respects directors are in the position of trustees; they control the company's property and must manage it for the company's benefit. They owe the company a *fiduciary duty*, a duty associated with trusteeship, and must account for any breach of this duty. They are not true trustees, however, since they do not own the company's property. A true trustee must exercise considerable caution in managing the trust, but directors are engaged in commercial activities involving speculation and risk-taking and consequently their liability for the negligent management of the company's business is far less stringent than would be the case for a trustee. Thus, the nature of a director's position draws from a number of legally recognised roles, a clear illustration of the breadth and complexity of the post. It is worth recalling here that a person involved with a company does not need to be designated as a director to fall within the s.741 definition (see earlier) and, therefore may owe the company the same duties as those owed by a properly appointed director.

There have been many judicial statements describing the general nature of directors' duties and Lord Cranworth's remarks in *Aberdeen Railway Co. v Blaikie Bros.* 1854 sum them up: *"The directors are a body to whom is delegated the duty of managing the general affairs of the company. A corporate body can only act by agents, and it is, of course, the duty of those agents to act as best to promote the interests of the corporation whose affairs they are conducting. Such agents have duties of a fiduciary nature towards their principal. And it is a rule of universal application, that no one, having such duties to discharge, shall be allowed to enter into engagements in which he has, or can have, a personal interest conflicting, or which possibly may conflict, with the interests of those whom he is bound to protect."*

To whom are the duties owed?

The shareholders

Directors owe their duties to the company as a whole. This is usually taken to mean the shareholders as a single body, and it will include both present and future shareholders: *Abbey Glen Property Corp. v. Stumborg* 1978. This does not prevent directors from considering the interests of particular sections of shareholders, including themselves, when they make decisions. They do not have to see the company as something distinct from its members. Nor do they, however, owe a general duty to individual shareholders.

> In *Percival v. Wright* 1902 the plaintiff, who wished to sell his shares in the company, entered into an agreement to sell them to the members of the board at a valuation he placed on them himself. The transaction went ahead, after which the plaintiff discovered that whilst his negotiations with the board were taking place, a third party was also negotiating a possible take-over of the company. These negotiations were never revealed to the plaintiff by the board, and in the event the take-over negotiations came to nothing. The plaintiff, however, sought to have the sale of his shares to the board set aside on the grounds of non-disclosure. The court held that the sale was binding. The directors were not trustees for individual shareholders who wished to sell their shares to them. They had not dealt unfairly with the plaintiff, since he had approached them and had named his price. Moreover, were the plaintiff to succeed, it would mean that the board should have disclosed to him prematurely the negotiations for the sale of the company which had been taking place, and this might well have damaged the company's interests. Under the Criminal Justice Act 1993, similar conduct on the part of a board could now give rise to criminal liability, although its provisions do not apply to private dealings in shares, and since in *Percival v Wright* the transaction was a private one, it would seem that even today no criminal liability would result.

If directors give advice to shareholders regarding a take-over bid for their company, an injunction may lie to prevent the bid going ahead if there is evidence that the directors have not been honest, as for example, by concealing the information that professional advisers have recommended rejection: *Gething v. Kilner* 1972.

No duty is owed to *individual* shareholders for any loss they have suffered through a fall in the value of their shares resulting from negligent mismanagement, since the loss is the company's. Minority shareholders may however seek relief in such circumstances under s.459, a provision designed to protect minority interests, and which is considered later. The basic rights of shareholders to participate in the company's affairs by taking part in company meetings are not affected by fluctuations in share values: *Prudential v. Newman Industries (No.2)* 1982.

Exceptionally, a fiduciary duty may be owed to an individual shareholder on the particular facts of a case, such as those in *Coleman v. Myers* 1977 where the minority shareholders in a small family firm sold their shares to the managing director after he had made misrepresentations to them.

The employees

Under s.309 directors are required to take account of the interests of company employees in general, as well as the interests of the company, in the performance of their functions. Presumably, therefore, it would come within this duty for the directors to adopt a strategy avoiding redundancies, as long as such a strategy also served the interests of the company. The problem for employees lies in their capacity to enforce the section, since it states that the duty is enforceable in the same way as any other fiduciary duty owed to a company by its directors, in other words, by shareholders bringing a claim on behalf of the company within one of the *Foss v Harbottle* exceptions. It would have to be shown that the company had suffered damage to obtain any more than a declaration that the directors had failed to consider the employees' interests, and in any case the employees could only bring such an action if they were also shareholders.

Furthermore the Act deems a company to have the power to provide for its own or a subsidiary's employees or former employees when the company or its subsidiary either ceases to carry on its business or transfers the whole or any part of it. Such power does not need to be exercised in the best interests of the company. This reverses the decision in *Parke v. Daily News Ltd.* 1962 where redundancy payments which the defendant company proposed to pay its staff following the sale of most of its business, were held to be unlawful since, at that time, the law did not require such payments to redundant staff. In consequence, the payments were purely gratuitous, and did not therefore benefit the company.

The creditors

In a solvent company, the duty owed by the directors is a duty owed to the shareholders as a body. They are not responsible to the creditors. In the words of Lord Templeman in *Kuwait Asia Bank v. National Mutual Life* 1991: *"A director does not by reason only of his position as director owe any duty to creditors or trustees for creditors of the company."* If however the company becomes insolvent the interests of the creditors arise. They control the company's assets by means of insolvency procedures and these assets, from a practical position, now belong to them rather than the shareholders.

In *Liquidator of West Mercia Safetywear Ltd. v. Dodd* 1988 the defendant was a director of two companies, West Mercia and A.J. Dodd. Both companies became insolvent. The liquidator of West Mercia brought a claim against the defendant on the basis of his breach of duty to the West Mercia creditors. The liquidator had instructed the directors not to operate the bank account of either company, but despite this instruction the defendant paid £4,000 from West Mercia's account into the other company's account to discharge a debt West Mercia owed it. This benefited the defendant personally, since it reduced his liability on a personal guarantee on the other company's overdraft. The Court of Appeal ordered him personally to repay the West Mercia liquidator.

Specific duties owed

In broad terms, the duties of a director are:

- *fiduciary duties*, arising as a result of the equitable view of directors as quasi-trustees;

- *duties of care and skill*, arising under the common law through the operation of the tort of negligence; and

- *statutory duties*, arising out of the provisions contained in the Companies Act 1985. Since these have already been considered, it is only necessary here to summarise them before examining the non-statutory duties owed.

Statutory duties

These are:

(a)   to notify the company of his or her interest in its shares or debentures or those of an associated company: s.324;

(b)   to disclose for approval at a general meeting any substantial non-cash transaction with the company: ss.320-322;

(c)   to have regard to the interests of the employees: s.309; and

(d)   to disclose personal interests in contracts of the company: s.317.

Fiduciary duties

The fiduciary duties owed by directors can be treated as coming under two headings; firstly the obligation to exercise powers bona fide and for the benefit of the company, and secondly, the obligation to avoid any conflict between their personal interests and those of the company, or as it is sometimes expressed, the duty not to make a *secret profit*. Case law illustrates the application of these duties in practice.

> In *Hogg v. Cramphorn Ltd.* 1967 the question of fiduciary duty arose in relation to the issue of shares by the company directors. The share issue was made to trustees to be held for the benefit of company employees. The aim of the board was to fight off a take-over bid. The company made an interest-free loan to the trustees to assist them in the purchase. It was held that the directors were in breach of their fiduciary duty to the company. However, the company members could ratify the decision by simple majority in a general meeting, so long as the new shareholders did not vote. The issue was subsequently ratified.

> In *Howard Smith Ltd. v. Ampol Petroleum Ltd.* 1974 directors, acting honestly and within their powers, allotted shares to a company which wanted to make a take-over bid. By doing so, they aimed to prevent two shareholders who between them held 55% of the shares and had indicated they would reject any take-over bid, from being able to do so. It was held that the board had acted improperly. The issue of the shares would be set aside. The proper reason for the issue of shares is the raising of capital, and, *"it must be unconstitutional for directors to use their fiduciary powers over the shares in the company purely for the purpose of destroying an existing majority, or creating a new majority which did not previously exist"*.

Breach of the duty to act bona fide and in the interests of the company will also occur where the directors:

- *issue new shares to themselves, not because the company needs more capital but merely to increase their voting power;*

  > In *Piercy v. S. Mills & Co. Ltd.* 1920 the directors used their powers to issue new voting shares to themselves, solely to acquire majority voting power. The court held that the directors had abused their powers and the allotment was declared void.

- *approve a transfer of their own partly-paid shares to escape liability for a call they intend to make;*

  > In *Alexander v. Automatic Telephone Co.* 1900 the directors used their position to require all shareholders to pay 3s 6d on each share excluding themselves. The court held that his was a clear abuse of power and the directors were required to pay to the company the same amounts.

- *negotiate a new service agreement between the company and its managing director simply in order to confer additional benefits on him or his dependents;*

  In *Re W and M Roith* 1967 it was held that a new service contract negotiated between a managing director and his company was unlawful as it was solely to make a pension provision for his widow and that no regard had been taken as to whether this was for the benefit of the company.

- *abdicate responsibility for the running of the company and appoint a manager with full powers who is not under the control of the board of directors, or obey the majority shareholder without exercising their own judgment or discretion.*

The following cases illustrate the position regarding the making of a secret profit. In a company law context the term "secret" is somewhat misleading, for a profit remains secret even if it has been disclosed by the director. The profit must be *approved* by the company in general meeting before it becomes lawful.

It is not surprising that a secret profit will arise when a director takes a bribe: *Boston Deep Sea Fishing Co. v. Ansell* 1888. However, a director will also be liable to account for a secret profit even though he could not have profited personally, or even though the company would have suffered no loss.

In *Regal (Hastings) Ltd. v. Gulliver* 1942 Regal owned one cinema, but wished to purchase two others so that it could sell all three together. The company had insufficient capital to buy the two cinemas itself, so it formed a subsidiary, and its directors took sufficient shares in the subsidiary to provide it with the capital to make the purchase. The shares in Regal and the subsidiary were later sold at a profit. The new owners of the Regal company then claimed the profit made by the directors from the sale of their shares in the subsidiary, bringing an action against them in the company name. The House of Lords held that the directors were liable to account, on the grounds that it was through their position as directors of the Regal that they gained the knowledge and opportunity to obtain the shares and make the profit. The decision appears to be rather harsh and to impose a high level of accountability on the directors. It was their money which they put into the subsidiary. They had acted in good faith, and believed they had acted lawfully, and their actions could have been ratified by the company in general meeting. In the later case of *Boardman v. Phipps* 1967 the House of Lords, however, followed its earlier decision in *Regal*.

In *Industrial Development Consultants v. Cooley* 1972 the court arrived at a similar decision on a different set of facts. Here the defendant acted as the managing director of a design company and in this capacity he tried to obtain some work for the company from the Eastern Gas Board. The Board indicated to the defendant that they were not prepared to give his company the work. Realising that he might secure the work for himself, the defendant managed to leave his company on the pretence that he was close to a nervous breakdown. He set up his own company and secured the Gas Board contract. It was held that he must account to his former company for the profit he had made, despite the fact that it was most unlikely the company would ever have obtained the work for itself. Thus it seems a director will remain accountable even where the company has not sustained a loss.

There will be a clear breach of duty where directors negotiate a contract in the company's name, but then take the contract for themselves.

This occurred in *Cook v. Deeks* 1916 where the directors of a company negotiated a construction contract which they took in their names, following which they called a company meeting where they were able to use their 75% shareholding in the company to pass a resolution that the company had no interest in the contract. This was held to constitute a fraud on the minority. It was of no effect, and the directors had to account to the company for the profit they made.

Breach may also occur where a director places himself in a conflict of interest situation.

The case of *Guinness plc v. Saunders* 1990 provides an interesting example. In order to implement its objective of launching a take-over-bid for the Distillers company, the Guinness board appointed a committee comprising of three directors *"with full power and authority"* to settle the terms for the Distillers offer. The three directors were Mr Saunders, Mr Roux and Mr Ward. The committee made an agreement with Mr Ward that Guinness would pay him a sum amounting 0.2% of the ultimate value of a successful bid, for his advice and services. A successful bid was made, and an invoice for £5.2m representing the sum payable to Mr Ward was presented to the committee, and paid by them on behalf of Guinness. When however the full board discovered the payment the company sought to recover the money from Mr Ward. The House of Lords held it was entitled to do so. Under the articles a committee of the board had no power to make such an agreement; only the board could authorise special remuneration to a director. It was a void contract for want of authority. No quantum meruit claim could be based upon an implied contract since the agreement itself was void. Nor was equitable relief available to grant Ward an allowance for his services because he had acted in breach of his fiduciary duty by putting himself in a position where his duty to the company and his personal interests conflicted irreconcilably. In Lord Templemans words the agreement prevented him *"from giving independent and impartial advice to Guinness."* However, in the absence of a firm contract, he was not in breach of the disclosure requirements under s.317.

Duties of care and skill

As we saw earlier, there are common law duties applying to directors, which arise from the obligation of a director not to act negligently in managing the company's affairs. The question is essentially one of identifying the standard of care and skill owed by the particular director towards his or her company.

> The leading case is that of *Re City Equitable Fire Insurance Co.* 1925. Here the company directors had delegated almost all responsibilities of management to the managing director. As a result, the directors failed to recognise a loss of over £1,200,000 from the company's funds, which was caused by the deliberate fraud of the managing director, described by the judge as, *"a daring and unprincipled scoundrel"*. The loss was discovered in the course of the winding-up of the company, and the liquidator successfully sought to make all the other directors liable for their negligence. Romer J. stated the following general propositions of law:

(i)   a director need not show a greater degree of skill than may reasonably be expected of a person with his knowledge and experience;

(ii)   a director need not give continuous attention to the affairs of the company. He is not bound to attend all meetings of the board, although he ought to attend whenever he is reasonably able to do so;

(iii)   a director may delegate duties to other officials in the company and trust them to be performed properly so long as there is no reason to doubt or mistrust them.

The judge commented *"It is indeed possible to describe the duties of directors in general terms ... The position of a director of a company carrying on a small retail business is very different from that of a director of a railway company. The duties of a bank director may differ widely from those of an insurance director, and the duties of a director of one insurance company may differ from those of a director of another."*

It is clear, therefore, that the duties of care and skill owed to a company by its directors are of a variable kind. Much higher standards of expertise will be expected of directors who are employed in a professional capacity in executive posts, for example, finance and engineering directors, than of directors who have nor claim to have such professional expertise. Yet even non-executive directors who have experience or qualifications in a field of relevance to the company's affairs may find that high objective standards appropriate to their specialist fields will be expected of them in law, despite their non-executive roles.

This point emerged in the case of *Dorchester Finance Co. Ltd. v. Stebbing* 1989 where the company lost money as a result of the gross negligence of the actions of the company's one executive director. He failed to take out adequate securities on loans made by the company and the company found itself unable to recover the loans made. The two non-executive directors, who had little to do with the company, had signed cheques in blank at the request of the executive director. All three directors had considerable financial experience. The court held the two non-executive directors equally liable with the executive director in damages to the company.

The effect of breach of duty

A director who is in breach of duty is jointly and severally liable with other directors who are similarly liable to make good the loss. He must account for any secret profit made, and in such cases the company is usually able to avoid a contract made with him. In appropriate circumstances the court may grant an injunction.

Relief from breach of duty may occur in the following ways:

- where the company by ordinary resolution waives the breach;

- if the company has indemnified and insured directors against liability for breach, using of any powers available to do so contained in the Companies Acts 1985 and 1989. S.310 of the 1985 Act renders void any provisions in the articles of a company or in any contract it makes which exempts or indemnifies an officer for negligence, breach of duty, breach of trust or default. It is however lawful for articles or a contract term to indemnify a director against liability in defending civil or criminal proceedings against him, where judgment is in his favour or he is acquitted, i.e. meeting any costs incurred by him. S.137 Companies Act 1989 enables a company to insure its directors against liability for their wrongdoing. If it does so there must be disclosure in the directors report;

- if the court has granted relief under the powers available to it under s.727 of the 1985 Act. Relief is available where the director has acted honestly and reasonably and ought in all the circumstances to be excused. The section applies to proceedings brought against a director alleging negligence, default, breach of duty or breach of trust.

In *Re Duomatic* 1969 the court had to consider what would constitute reasonable conduct by a director to obtain relief. The directors in question, without seeking legal advice, had authorised payment of compensation of £4,000 out of company funds to another director who they were unhappy with. He could have been removed by a board vote, but they anticipated he would cause the company trouble if this were done, so offered him the money instead if he would leave. He did. S.312 of the 1985 Act requires such a payment to be disclosed to the members in general meeting and approved by them. These things had not been done. Subsequently the company went into liquidation. The liquidator's claim against the two authorising directors to recover the £4,000 was successful. Moreover, the director in receipt of the payment held it on trust for the company and could be required to repay it. Making a decision like this, *"without a proper exploration of the considerations which contribute, or ought to contribute, to a decision as to what should be done on the company's behalf,"* could not be said to be acting reasonably, said the trial judge, Buckley J.

Auditors

Having looked at the position of directors in some depth we can now consider the role of auditors. The auditing of company accounts is a process by which the company auditors carry out an annual investigation into the financial affairs of the company, so that they can confirm, primarily for the shareholders benefit, that the companies books reflect the actual position of the company's finances.

The relationship between the auditors, shareholders and directors of a company was summarised by Bingham L.J. in *Caparo Industries v. Dickman* 1990:

"The members, or shareholders, of the company are its owners. But they are too numerous, and in most cases too unskilled, to undertake the day-to-day management of that which they own. So responsibility for day-to-day management of the company is delegated to directors, The shareholders, despite their overall powers of control, are in most companies for most of the time investors and little more. But it would, of course, be unsatisfactory and open to abuse if the shareholders received no report on the financial stewardship of their investment save from those to who the stewardship had been entrusted. So provision is made for the company in general meeting to appoint an auditor (Companies Act 1985, s.384) whose duty is to investigate and form an opinion on the adequacy of the company's accounting records and returns and the correspondence between the company's accounting

records and returns and its accounts (s.237). The auditor has then to report to the company's members (among other things) whether in his opinion the company's accounts give a true and fair view of the company's financial position (s.236). In carrying out his investigation and in forming his opinion the auditor necessarily works very closely with the directors and officers of the company. He receives his remuneration from the company. He naturally, and rightly, regards the company as his client. But he is employed by the company to exercise his professional skills and judgment for the purpose of giving the shareholders an independent report on the reliability of the company's accounts and thus on their investment."

All registered companies must appoint auditors, unless the company is a dormant one, that is a *"small"* company which has had no *"significant accounting transaction"* since the end of the previous financial year. Appointment is made at each general meeting at which accounts in respect of an accounting reference period are laid. It is thus the members who make the appointment. The first auditors may be appointed by the directors, and casual vacancies may be filled either by the directors, or by the company in general meeting. A private company may now, by means of an elective resolution, opt out of annual appointment arrangements, so that the appointed auditors will continue in office until either side choose to terminate the appointment.

It is clearly important that auditors be both independent from the company, and suitably qualified to perform their functions. Only a registered auditor can carry out company auditing work, and a registered auditor is someone who is regarded as qualified by the Chartered Institutes of Accountants, or the Chartered Association of Certified Accountants, or the Department of Trade and Industry as having the appropriate overseas or other professional qualifications. Education, training and other matters affecting the work of auditors has now been brought under general statutory control. Certain persons are not permitted to act as auditors. These include an officer or servant of the company, a person employed by them, officers and servants of the company's holding or subsidiary companies or persons who have a *connection* with the company. A body corporate may act as an auditor.

A company may remove an auditor by means of an ordinary resolution under s.391. The provisions relating to such a removal are identical to those contained in s.303 for the removal of directors. An auditor may also resign from office, by depositing a notice to that effect at the company's registered office. The resignation is ineffective unless it either states that there are no circumstances connected with the resignation that should be brought to the attention of the members or creditors or alternatively it contains a statement outlining what those circumstances are. If such a statement is made a copy of it must be sent within fourteen days to all members, debenture holders, and every person entitled to receive notices of general meetings of the company. In such cases the auditor may also require the directors to convene an extraordinary general meeting of the company for the purpose of considering the resignation, a very powerful if rarely used threat.

Payment of auditors is determined by the company in general meeting.

Liability of auditors

In *Caparo Industries plc v. Dickman* 1990 the House of Lords was required to consider the extent of an auditor's liability for negligently audited accounts. The auditors in question had verified accounts which showed a pre-tax profit of £1.2m, when the company had in fact sustained a loss of over £400,000. Caparo Industries, who already held shares in the audited company, took more of its shares and later made a take-over bid for it on the strength of the inaccurate accounts. Caparo sued the auditors when the true position was discovered. The action was unsuccessful. The court took the view that auditors of a public limited company owe no duty of care either to a potential investor or to an existing member who takes more shares in the company. To allow otherwise would be to create an unlimited liability on the part of auditors. On the facts there was not a sufficient relationship of proximity between the parties. The audited accounts went into general circulation and might foreseeably have been relied on by strangers for many different purposes. The duty of the auditors was a statutory duty owed to the company as a whole, to enable the members as a body to exercise proper control over it. A duty of care can however arise in cases when auditors have provided accounts with the intention or knowledge that they would be supplied by the company to a particular person or class of people, for example a specific bank, or banks generally, even though the precise purpose for which the accounts will be used is not known by the auditors.

The Shareholders in a Company

Becoming a shareholder

There are two ways in which a person can become a company member (the words member and shareholder are for all practical purposes interchangeable). These are by subscribing to the company's memorandum, which involves the members name appearing in the subscription clause of the memorandum against the number of shares they agreed to take, or by their name being entered on the register of members under s.22 Companies Act 1985. This is of course the most common method.

The maintenance of this register is a statutory requirement. The register is kept either at the registered office or some other office used for this purpose and it must be available for public inspection. The Act prohibits trusts being entered on the register, so it is only the legal owner of the shares whose name appears. Normally a persons name is included on the register either because they have successfully applied to the company for shares in it, or because an existing shareholder has transferred ownership to them by selling them the shares.

The question of who may become a member is regulated by a combination of the general law and the articles. The articles may wish to exclude certain people from acquiring membership. The shareholders who make up the membership of public and private companies include both individual investors and institutional investors. The latter include organisations such as pension funds. Investors will usually be seeking a return on their investment in the form of dividend payments from the company to them. They will also be looking for the market value of their shares to increase. As we have seen directors manage companies for the benefit of the shareholders whilst auditors advise the shareholders of the financial health of their company. Whilst the principal obligation of shareholders is to pay for their shares, the rights they enjoy and general position they hold within the company is more complex, and we shall now examine it. To begin with it will be useful to consider what holding a share actually means.

Transferring shares

Shares are the shareholders property. They can be transferred at any time to anyone the shareholder chooses. If a number of shares are held some can be transferred and some retained. The articles may however restrict this general right of transfer. The two most common ways in which this will be achieved are by granting the directors power to refuse to register a transfer, and by granting the members pre-emption rights.

When a member wishes to transfer shares the executed *transfer form* together with the share certificate must be sent to the company. On receipt the directors have two months within which to register the transfer and issue the transferee with a share certificate, or notify the transferee that the transfer is refused (s.183). Once the two month deadline has passed a transfer cannot be refused.

If the articles grant the board of directors the discretionary power to refuse a transfer, the fiduciary duty they owe to the company means they must exercise the power in good faith and in what they regard as the company's best interests. Although the courts presume good faith has been present in the decision making (*Tett v. Phoenix Property & Investment Co. Ltd.* 1986), if there is evidence to the contrary the court can order the registration of the transfer to go ahead.

In *Re: Smith and Fawcett Ltd.* 1942 a company article granted the directors the uncontrolled and absolute discretion to refuse to register any transfer of shares. Smith and Fawcett were the only members of the company. They were also its directors. They held 4001 shares each. Following Fawcetts death, Smith and a co-opted director refused to register the transfer of Fawcett's shares to his son, who was acting as his fathers executor. However Smith offered instead to register 2001 of the shares, and purchase the remaining 2000 shares at a valuation fixed by himself. The sons challenge against the refusal to register all the shares failed. The court could find no evidence of bad faith and was not therefore prepared to intervene. Lord Greene MR observed that small private companies are both commercially and at a personal level closer to partnerships than to public companies, and *"it is to be expected that in the articles of such a company the control of the directors over the membership may be very strict indeed"*.

If the power granted is not an absolute one, but permits refusal on specified grounds, then in the absence of anything to the contrary in the articles the court will compel the directors to specify the ground upon which their refusal is based (*Berry v. Tottenham Hotspur Ltd.* 1935).

Pre-emption rights

If a company issues new shares the interests of existing members may be adversely affected in two ways. Firstly, the balance of power will shift if the shares carry voting rights and they are taken up by new members. Secondly, if the new shares are issued at a price below their real market value, the value of the existing shares will be diluted. S.89 Companies Act 1985 provides protection for existing shareholders by requiring that new equity shares be first offered to existing members so that their proportionate holding in the company can be maintained. This is known as a *rights issue*. There are however a range of exceptions to the statutory obligation. It does not apply for example to shares allotted for a non cash consideration. Moreover shareholders may waive the requirement using a special resolution, and in the case of a private company the right of pre-emption may be excluded by a suitable provision in the company's constitution.

A different form of pre-emption arrangement sometimes found in the articles of a private company is the requirement that if a shareholder wishes to sell his shares they must first be offered to the existing members at a fair value. This has the same effect as a rights issue for it grants the existing members a right of first refusal in respect of company shares which have become available and can be used to prevent the introduction of new members into the company. In very small private companies with perhaps three or four members it can be of great value to retain all the control of the company in the hands of the remaining shareholders when one of their number sells his or her interest. Case-law examples of this form of pre-emption right can be found elsewhere in the chapter.

Shareholders as company controllers

Shareholders collectively own the undertaking of the company. In effect the company is their agent. This agency role is performed by directors appointed by shareholders in company meetings. Directors are accountable to the company for the management of its activities (see Figure 5.1).

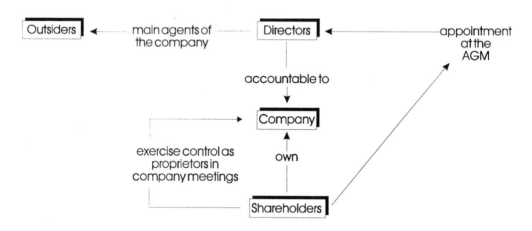

Figure 5.1   *Shareholders as company controllers*

Share certificates

A *share certificate* is a document issued by a company with provides evidence of title to the shares of the person named on it. It does not have to be issued under the companies seal, but can be issued under the signature of the secretary and a director. S.186 Companies Act 1985 provides that the share certificate is *prima facie* evidence of the title the shareholder has to the shares. This means it is not necessarily conclusive evidence, however the onus is on the person challenging the certificate to prove a defective title.

The share certificate is treated as a representation by the company issuing it that the person named in it was the true owner of the shares at the date the certificate was issued. The company may therefore find itself liable to anyone relying on the information the certificate contains if that information turns out to be untrue.

The application of this principle is well illustrated in the *Re: Bahia & San Francisco Railway Co.* 1868 case. Brokers of a company member, Miss Tritten, transferred her shares to themselves by forging her signature on a share transfer form. They sent the form together with the share certificate they held for her to the company, and it duly issued a new share certificate in their names. They then sold the shares to two innocent parties, whose names were entered on the register of shareholders. Subsequently Miss Tritten discovered the forgery. The company was obliged to restore her name to the register, and remove the names of the innocent parties from it. They then sued the company. The court held that although the signature on the transfer was a forgery so that the transfer was of no effect, the company was still bound by the representations contained in the new share certificate which erroneously showed the brokers to be the owners of the shares. It was liable to pay the innocent parties damages equal to the value of shares at the time their names were removed from the register.

The effect of forgery needs to be carefully noted. In the *San Francisco Railway* case it was the share transfer which was forged. If someone forges a *share certificate* then the certificate is not issued with the authority of the company and the company is not liable for it. The only exception would be if the forgery has been done by a director of the company, since a director is someone having the authority of the company to issue share certificates.

The Statutory Contract

An important provision for shareholders is s.14 of the Companies Act 1985 which provides that the articles and the memorandum of a company constitute a binding contract between the company and its members. The section has caused some difficulty for the courts in the past, for it has not been clear precisely what the effects of the section are. It states that the company and its members are bound to each other as though each shareholder has covenanted to observe the provisions of the memorandum and articles, the *statutory contract*. It also provides that any money owed by a member to the company is a speciality debt. This means the company has twelve years in which to recover the debt. In the case of debts arising from a simple contract the period would otherwise be six years.

The effect of the articles on shareholders can be summarised as follows:

* *The company is bound to the members in their capacity as members, and they are bound to it in the same way.*

An illustration of this principle is provided by *Salmon v. Quin & Axtens Ltd.* 1909. Here the articles gave directors full management powers, but prevented the directors from purchasing or letting any premises if the managing director dissented. The directors however resolved to deal in premises, despite the dissent of the managing director, and an extraordinary meeting of shareholders affirmed this action by a simple majority. The managing director sought an order from the court that the resolutions were invalid. The Court of

Appeal agreed. The resolutions conflicted with the articles, and the company was bound by the articles. It could be restrained from its proposed action.

In *Hickman v. Kent or Romney Marsh Sheepbreeders Association* 1915 the articles of the association stipulated that disputes between itself and its members should be referred to arbitration. The plaintiff, a member, brought court action against the association in relation to a number of matters. It was held that in accordance with the articles these matters must be referred to arbitration.

- *The members are contractually bound to each other, under the terms of the articles.*

Generally it is not possible for an individual member to enforce the contract in his own name against another member, although exceptionally this may be possible if the articles grant him a personal right.

The position is illustrated in the case of *Rayfield v. Hands* 1960. A clause in the articles of a private company stated, *"Every member who intends to transfer shares shall inform the directors who will take the said shares equally between them at a fair value."* The plaintiff notified the defendant directors of his intention to transfer his shares, however they denied any liability to take and pay for them. The court held they were obliged to do so, firstly because of their binding obligation indicated by the word "will" and secondly because the clause was a term of the contractual relationship between the plaintiff and the directors as company members.

- *The company is only bound to the members in their capacity as members.*

This proposition of law emerges from the following case.

In *Eley v. Positive Life Assurance Co Ltd.*, 1876, a provision in the articles of the company stated that the plaintiff should be the company's solicitor for life. He took up shares in the company. Sometime later the company removed him as its solicitor, and he sued the company for breach of contract. The action failed. The court said the statutory contract only granted him rights as a member, and what he was complaining of was breach of an article giving him rights as a legal advisor. Doubts have however been expressed about this decision, for it adds a rider to s.14 which the section does not contain, the phrase, *"in their capacity as members"*.

There is however no problem in using provisions contained in the articles as evidence of the contents of a separate service contract.

In *Re New British Iron Co Ltd.*, 1898, the articles provided that the directors, all of whom were members, were entitled to remuneration of £1000 p.a.. Their company went into liquidation, and they sought to recover from the liquidator the payment the company owed them for their services. The court held that the article was sufficient evidence of the terms of their contract as to payment, and they were able on this basis to recover the money owing to them.

A further important effect of s.14 results from its assertion that shareholders have entered into *covenants* with the company, for it means that they are bound to the company as if they had made a deed with it. The consequences of this arrangement can be seen in Figure 5.2. As well as resulting in the members being bound to each other, an idea already examined above, the company is bound to people who have become members by purchasing shares from existing shareholders rather than the company itself. Thus legal relationships are created which extend beyond the common law contractual relationship which only exists between the company and those members who have taken shares directly from it. In the figure, Z can enforce his rights as a shareholder against the company, for instance to secure his voting rights, whilst X and Z are bound to each other to the extent that they can enforce personal provisions in the articles. *Rayfield v. Hands* provides an example.

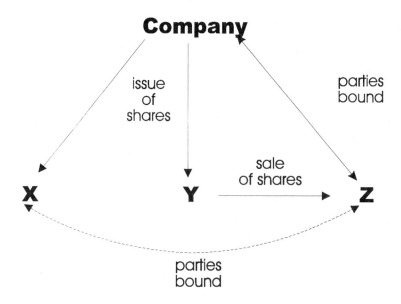

Figure 5.2   *The effect of the statutory contract*

Alteration of the Articles

Although the constitutional documents of a company make up the terms of the contract between itself and its members, the memorandum and articles are not tablets of stone. The company does have the opportunity to amend them provided it does so lawfully. In the case of the articles they may be altered or added to by means of a special resolution which requires a 75% majority of the members voting in favour of it. No such resolution is necessary if there is unanimous agreement of the members to the proposed alteration. Alterations must however be made *bona fide,* that is in good faith, and for the benefit of the company as a whole. This is an important aspect of the law regulating companies, for as we have just seen articles constitute a contract between the company and its members and identify members' rights, such as the right to vote. Clearly the ability of the company to change the terms of this contract at some future time may have the effect of placing individual members who might be harmed by such changes, in a disadvantageous position. Thus the courts reserve the power to refuse an alteration to the articles which has such an effect, unless there is a benefit to the company as a whole and the alteration has been made in good faith. This principle is best appreciated by looking at some of the caselaw on the subject.

> In the leading case, *Allen v. Gold Reefs of West Africa* 1900 the articles of the company which already granted it a *lien* on partly paid shares to cover any liabilities owed to it by a member, were altered by extending the lien to holders of fully paid shares as well. A lien is simply a charge on shares, enabling the company to sell the shares in order to meet the debts owed to it by the members. Here a shareholder who at the time of his death held both fully and partly paid shares in the company and owed the company money for the partly paid shares, was also the only holder of fully paid shares. His executors challenged the alteration on the grounds of bad faith, but the court upheld the alteration. There was no evidence that the company was attempting to discriminate against the deceased personally; it was simply chance that he was the only holder of fully paid shares. In the words of Lord Lindley, *"The altered articles applied to all holders of fully paid shares and made no distinction between them."*

It seems that the test which should be applied is whether the proposal is in the honest opinion of those voting for it, for the benefit of the members. An alteration may be challenged if it is, *"so oppressive as to cast suspicion on the honesty of the persons responsible for it, or so extravagant that no reasonable men could really consider it for the benefit of the company."* (Bankes L.J. in *Shuttleworth v. Cox Bros. & Co. (Maidenhead) Ltd.* 1927). If it can be established that the alteration has the effect of discriminating between members, granting advantages to the majority which are denied to the minority then a challenge will normally be successful, although an alteration may be upheld as bona fide even though the members voting for it are improving their own personal prospects.

In *Greenhalgh v. Arderne Cinemas Ltd.* 1951 the articles of company, which prohibited the transfer of shares to a non member as long as an existing member was willing to pay a fair price for them, were altered to enable a transfer of shares to anyone by means of an ordinary resolution passed in a general meeting. The alteration was made because the majority shareholder wished to transfer his shares to a non member. This was held to be a valid alteration.

The courts will also uphold alterations which cause direct prejudice to individual members, as long as they are shown to be alterations made in good faith, and in the company's interest.

In *Sidebottom v. Kershaw Leese & Co.* 1920 an alteration was made enabling the directors, who were the majority shareholders, to request the transfer to their nominees at a fair value the shares of any member competing with the company's business. The court found this to be a valid and proper alteration for, in the words of Lord Sterndale M R, *"it is for the benefit of the company that they should not be obliged to have amongst them as members, persons who are competing with them in business and who may get knowledge from their membership which would enable them to compete better."*

By way of contrast in *Brown v. British Abrasive Wheel Co.* 1919 a majority of the shareholders (98%) were willing to provide the company with much needed extra capital if they could buy the 2% minority interest. As the minority were unwilling to sell, the majority proposed to alter the articles so as to enable nine-tenths of the shareholders to buy out any other shareholders. The plaintiff, representing the minority, brought an action to restrain the majority. It was held by the court that the alteration would be restrained as it was not for the benefit of the company as a whole but rather for the benefit of the majority shareholding, and was in any case too wide a power and was therefore unlawful as constituting a potential fraud on the members.

In addition the following common law and statutory conditions apply to an alteration:

- *it must be lawful,* that is not be in conflict with the Act or with the general law;

In *Russell v. Northern Bank Development Corp Ltd.* 1992 an agreement made between the company and its shareholders provided that the capital of the company could not be increased without the consent of all the parties to the agreement. The agreement was expressed to take preference over any conflicting provision in the articles of association. The court held the agreement to be an improper fetter on the powers of a company to increase its share capital, a matter regulated by s.121, and not binding as between the company and its shareholders. In arriving at this conclusion the decision in *Bushell v. Faith* 1969 was cited, in which Russell LJ had observed that a company could not legitimately either by *"its articles or otherwise"* restrict its ability to alter its articles. In the present case the agreement made by the company fell within the expression *or otherwise*.

- it must not create a conflict between the memorandum and the articles. If this does occur the provisions of the memorandum will prevail for it is the superior document;

- *it will require the leave of the court in certain circumstances*. These are where a minority of members have applied to the court for the cancellation of an alteration to the objects clause (s.5), where there has been an application for the cancellation of a resolution of a public company to re-register as a private company (s.54), or where a petition has been presented to the court on the ground that the affairs of the company are being conducted in a manner unfairly prejudicial to some part of the membership (s.461);

- *if it involves an increase in a member's liability it will only be valid if the member has given a written consent (s.16);*

- *if it affects the rights attached to a particular class of shareholders*. If it does it is subject to the capacity of those disagreeing with the change, who may apply to the court for a cancellation, not exercising this power successfully. This power is available to 15% or more of the holders of the shares who did not give their consent, and it must be exercised within 21 days.

Controlling the company – the powers of the members

A company has two principal sources of control over its affairs. These are the shareholders in general meeting and the directors. The most important matters affecting the company, for example changes in its constitution, rest with the shareholders in general meeting. Decisions reached at such meetings are arrived at through the putting of resolutions, which are then voted on. Generally a simple majority vote is sufficient to carry them, although some matters of special significance require a 75% majority. Since voting power plays such an important role in company matters the type of shares the company has issued is of considerable significance. Some shares, for example ordinary shares, usually carry full voting rights.

However other classes of share, such as preference shares, may carry no voting rights at all and therefore exclude shareholders of that class from effectively influencing the company in its decision making.

Since companies generally consist of numerous members it is impractical to operate the company on a daily basis by means of general meetings. The articles will therefore provide for directors to be responsible for the daily running of the company and usually grant them the right to exercise all the powers of the company. They will remain answerable to the members in a general meeting although acts carried out by the directors within the powers delegated to them under the articles cannot be affected by decisions of a general meeting. So, if the directors have acted contrary to the wishes of the members, the ultimate sanction is to dismiss them or to change the articles and so bring in provisions that restrict the powers of the directors. In small companies the directors will often be the principal or only shareholders, so that such considerations will not be relevant.

Meetings

The fundamental principle of accountability of the directors to the members necessarily involves strict regulation of the company's operation. The Companies Act 1985 provides therefore that every company must, in each year, hold an *annual general meeting* and that every member is entitled to notice of this meeting. In addition, the holders of one-tenth or more of paid-up shares with voting rights may at any time compel the directors to call an extra-ordinary general meeting. The articles usually regulate the procedures to be adopted at these meetings, but in any case the minutes of all meetings must be strictly recorded.

Decisions at general meetings are usually taken by ordinary resolution, that is a simple majority of voting members present. For some types of business, usually related to the company's constitution such as the alteration of the articles or objects of the company, a special resolution is necessary which requires a three-quarter majority of voting members. The position is summarised in figure 5.3

Types	Business	When called	Notice
Annual General Meeting *(AGM)*	Declaring dividends Directors' and Auditors' reports, Appointment of Directors	Within 18 months of incorporation then once a year with no more than 15 months between each	At least 21 days Items of ordinary business need not be mentioned in notice
Extraordinary General Meeting *(EGM)*	All business is 'special' e.g. alteration of memorandum and articles, removal of directors	If demanded by holders of one tenth or more of paid up shares	At least 14 days. If called by members they must state why they want it

Figure 5.3   *Company meetings*

Shareholders' rights – majority rule, minority protection

As we have seen the rights enjoyed by a member of a company are primarily contractual, arising from the class of shares acquired and the rights attached to them as specified in the articles. Unlike a partner, who will usually possess the right to take part in the management of the firm, a shareholder will not always be involved in the daily management of the company, unless the organisation has a very small membership and its shareholders are also its directors. Companies' articles usually confer power on directors to operate the business, which they will perform on behalf of the members. The effect of such an arrangement is that ownership and management are separated. Nevertheless, ultimate control of the business is in the hands of the shareholders by the exercise of voting power in the general meeting. Where appropriate they can vote to remove a director.

In any vote which does not produce a unanimous outcome there will be two groups, the majority shareholders and the minority shareholders. In effect it is the majority that make the company decisions. Those who hold 75% or more of the voting shares are the ultimate company controllers. Under company legilsation a three-quarter majority to secure changes to the constitution of the company itself. Thus the majority group can run the company almost as if it were their own. If the minority have a grievance, legally there is little they can do to redress it. The courts have been reluctant to assist minority shareholders who are claiming they have been oppressed or have had their interests prejudiced by the majority. Since it is the majority who rule the company it is not for the court to thwart their actions. If the minority are arguing that the majority have acted in breach of the memorandum or the articles, then it is a wrong which has been done to the company. The proper plaintiff is the company itself, not the minority shareholders. Of course they will find it impossible to pass a resolution that the company sue the majority, for the voting strength of the majority will be sufficient to block such a move. This leaves the minority in a very vulnerable position.

The case of *Foss v. Harbottle* 1843 laid down as a general principle that the courts will not interfere in the internal management of a company at the insistence of the minority shareholders. Here an action had been brought by the minority alleging that the directors were responsible for losses that had occurred when they sold some of their own land to the company, at what was alleged to be an over valuation. The court held that the action must fail as the proper plaintiff in such circumstances was the company itself. As the action to which the minority shareholders objected could have been ratified by the majority then it was the majority shareholders who should decide whether an action should be brought in the company name. The court saw no merit in interfering in the internal management of a company by passing judgment on its commercial decisions.

In *Pavlides v. Jenson and others* 1956, a company sold an asbestos mine for £182,000 when its real value was close to £1,000,000. A minority shareholder brought an action for damages against three directors who were responsible for the sale and against the company, alleging gross negligence. The court held that the action could not be brought by a minority shareholder because it was the company itself which should decide whether to redress the wrong that had been committed.

Thus the process of incorporation, having invested a company with a separate legal personality, dictates that the company and individual members are separate. If a wrong is committed against the company it is the company, by virtue of a decision made by the board of directors, that should seek redress for it.

The rule in *Foss v. Harbottle* does not however apply to every type of action taken by the majority. In certain situations the court will hear a claim brought by minority shareholders, even though the majority do not wish it. Thus:

• proposed *ultra vires* activities can be restrained, even by a member holding a single share;

• where directors attempt to do something requiring a special resolution which they do not obtain, their action cannot be ratified by an ordinary resolution. Were this to be otherwise, the protection for minorities granted in circumstances where a three-quarters majority is needed would be avoided;

• where a wrong is suffered to a member in his personal capacity, through the action of the directors.

For instance in *Pender v. Lushington* 1877 the company chairman wrongfully refused to accept the votes cast by certain shareholders. The resolution they opposed was in consequence able to be carried. The court held that the company could be restrained from carrying out the proposed resolution;

• when a fraud has been committed against the minority. This does not mean fraud in the criminal sense, rather conduct which is grossly unfair.

An example is provided by *Daniels v. Daniels* 1978.

The company was managed by Mr and Mrs Daniels. They were also the controlling shareholders. In 1970 they agreed to sell land belonging to the company to Mrs Daniels, at a price of £4250. In 1974 she resold the land for £120,000 and minority shareholders brought an action claiming that damages should be payable to the company. The court held that despite no allegation of fraud the action by the individual shareholders should be allowed to proceed. The trial judge, Templeman J, distinguished *Pavlides v. Jensen* on the grounds that the directors there had not benefited from their negligence. He stated *"to put up with foolish directors is one thing; to put up with directors who are so foolish that they make a profit of £115,000 odd at the expense of the company is something entirely different ... a minority shareholder who has no other remedy may sue where directors use their powers, intentionally or unintentionally, fraudulently or negligently, in a manner which benefits them at the expense of the company".*

In addition to the common law, the Companies Act 1985 confers certain statutory rights on minority shareholders.

An important example of this is s.459 which gives a member the right to apply to the court for an order on the ground that the affairs of the company are being or have been conducted in a manner which is unfairly prejudicial to some members (including at least himself), or that any actual or proposed act or omission of the company is or would be prejudicial.

If the case is proved the court may issue an order to:

- regulate the company's affairs for the future;

- require the company to act or refrain from acting in a particular way;

- authorise civil proceedings in the name and on behalf of the company by a person; or

- require the purchase of any member's shares by the company or by other members.

In *Scottish CWS v. Meyer,* 1958, Meyer was a minority shareholder in a manufacturing company which was a subsidiary of the Scottish CWS. The CWS, as holding company, decided to close down the subsidiary, and took steps to cause it to cease trading. As a result Meyer's shares, which had been worth £3.75 each whilst the subsidiary was trading, fell in value to £1. The court ordered the holding company to purchase the shares of the minority members at their original value.

An example of a court order regulating a company's future affairs is seen in *Re H R Harmer Limited* 1959. The company was run by an elderly father acting as chairman and his two sons as directors. The father had voting control. He largely ignored the wishes of the board of directors and ran the business as his own. On an application by the sons as minority shareholders, alleging oppression, the court held that relief should be granted. The father was appointed life president of the company without rights, duties or powers and was ordered not to interfere with the company's affairs.

In *Re Elgindata Ltd.* 1991 the court held that in exceptional cases, serious mismanagement of a company could amount to unfairly prejudicial conduct under s. 459. Generally however the court should be reluctant to arrive at such a finding bearing in mind managerial decision making is matter of commercial judgment and that taking shares in a company carries the risk of their value being tied to the competence of the board of directors.

In *Re a Company, ex p Burr* 1992 Vinelott J discussed the possibility of a s.459 action where the directors continue to run the company despite it operating at a loss and it having no realistic chance of becoming profitable in the future. He said: *"There can be no doubt that if the directors of a company continue to trade when the company is making losses and when it should have been apparent that there was no real prospect that the company would return to profitability, the court may draw the inference that the directors' decision was improperly influenced by their desire to continue in office and in control of the company and to draw remuneration and other benefits for themselves and others connected with them ... if that inference is drawn, the court may conclude that the affairs of the company are being conducted in a way which is unfairly prejudicial to the members or the members other than the directors and those who obtain such benefit."*

Non payment of dividends can amount to unfairly prejudicial conduct under s.459.

In *Re: Sam Weller & Sons Ltd.* 1990 the petitioners, who between them held 42.5% of the shares in their family business, complained that the company had not increased its dividend for 37 years, despite its profitability. In 1985 its net profit had been £36,000, but only £2,520 was paid out in dividends. The company was controlled by the petitioner's uncle, Sam Weller, who, together with his sons, continued to receive directors fees and remuneration. Peter Gibson J commented of the petitioners position, *"As their only income from the company is by way of dividend, their interests may be not only prejudiced by the policy of low dividend payments, but unfairly prejudiced."*

In *O'Neill v. Phillips* 1999 the House of Lords was required, for the first time, to consider the scope of the relief available under s.459. Phillips, who held all the shares in a construction company, and was its sole director, had become so impressed by O'Neill, a manual employee of the company, that he promoted him to the board, and gave him 25% of his shares. The company traded very successfully, and Phillips withdrew from the board. The result was that O'Neill had effectively become managing director. By this time he was also receiving 50% of the annual profits of the company. In outline discussions Phillips indicated that he would be willing to increase O'Neill's shareholding to 50% if the company continued to grow, and its net value reached £500,000, but no formal agreement was drawn up. The fortunes of the company then changed. General problems in the construction industry caused its profits to fall. Phillips, as majority shareholder, now removed O'Neill from his position as Managing Director, and advised him that in future he would receive only his salary, and dividends on his 25% shareholding.

O'Neill petitioned under s.459 that, by these actions, and the effective withdrawal of the promise to increase his shareholding, Phillips had forced him out of the company.

The House of Lords did not agree. Even though in a quasi partnership company like this there might be expectations on the part of the members going beyond what might be found in a larger company, this should not enable a shareholder to force the remaining shareholders to buy him out at a fair price on the basis of an alleged breakdown of trust and confidence, The only basis upon which O'Neill might succeed would be showing unfairness. This would occur either from infringement of his rights under the articles, or from unfair use of power. On its facts no unfairness had been shown in this case. The discussions regarding the increase in O'Neill's shareholding had never gone beyond negotiation.

In the certain circumstances the remedy under s. 459 will not be available. It cannot be used where:

- the petitioner's complaint is not being made in his capacity as a member.

In *Elder v. Elder & Watson* 1952 the remedy was sought by the applicants for their removal from office as directors and from their loss of employment as company secretary and manager respectively. Their claims failed because the wrong had been done to them in their capacity as officers and employees rather than as members.

- the petitioner is the cause of the harm complained of.

This occurred in *Re R A Noble (Clothing) Ltd.,* 1983. The petitioner's complaint was that he had been excluded from important decision making concerning the company's affairs by his co-director, but his action failed because he had left management in the hands of the co-director and had taken no interest in the business.

The s.459 remedy is often referred to as the *alternative remedy*, since it is an alternative to the more drastic step that minority shareholders can take of bringing the company to an end by petitioning the court to have it compulsorily wound up on just and equitable grounds under s.122 Insolvency Act 1986.

The Law Commissions Report on Shareholders Remedies in 1997 has suggested that the court should have power to dismiss any s.459 claim which, in its opinion has no reasonable prospect of success at full trial. In this way the kind of situation noted by Sir Richard Scott V-C in *Re: a Company* 1997 might be overcome, when he said *"There has been a tendency in some past s.459 cases for the litigation to become a Chancery version of a bitterly contested divorce with grievances from the history of the marriage dredged up and hurled about the court in an attempt to blacken the opposing party"*.

When an action is brought by a minority shareholder it may be in one of two forms. It will be a *derivative* action if the shareholder is suing in the name of the company. If the action is successful the remedy being sought will be awarded to the company. *Daniels v. Daniels* is an example. It will be a representative action if it is brought by a member to enforce a personal right, for instance as in *Pender v. Lushington*.

The law considered above in relation to the protection available to aggrieved minority shareholders relies ultimately upon litigation, or the threat of litigation to obtain a remedy. Such action is only likely where unhappy shareholders have found that their 'voice', that is the control they are able to exercise over corporate decision-making through their voting power, is inadequate to achieve what they are seeking. There is of course an alternative remedy available to such shareholders, the control that is sometimes referred to as 'exit'. If there is an active market in the shares of their company they can sell as a way of expressing dissatisfaction with the way the board is running the company. If dissatisfaction is general, widespread selling will cause the shareprice to drop, and the result may be that the company will become the target of a takeover bid. Control of this kind is only appropriate in large companies with a substantial number of scattered investors.

The exercise of control through the mechanisms, in particular s.459, which we have examined in this final section of the chapter, are relevant to smaller companies, where the shareholders are involved in company management, or are connected through friendship or family relationship to each other. In such companies the exit method of control is simply not available.

Assignment - A Family Affair

West Riding Woollens Ltd. is a long established and well regarded company which manufactures high quality woollen garments from its two mills in West Yorkshire. The company was founded in 1913 by John Grisethwaite, and is still controlled by members of the founders family. At present its shares, all of which are ordinary shares carrying voting rights and of which there are 1000 in total, are held by the following shareholders: George Grisethwaite, the founder's son, who is 84 and acts as chairman and managing director, holds 49%; his two sons Ralph and Peter hold 10% each, and so does his daughter Elizabeth. The remaining shares are held by a local businessman Lawrence Stott (8%), a relative of the family by marriage, Grace Clarke (8%), and Walter Thompson, the son of the company's former accountant (5%). The board of directors comprises the Grisethwaite family members.

In the past the business had flourished, but three years ago, at a lively general meeting, the company members voted to alter the objects clause, enabling it to diversify into property development. It was a majority decision, the board members voting in favour, the remaining shareholders against. Since then the value of the company's assets has diminished significantly, largely the non board members feel because of the incompetence of the board in its property development transactions. Last year the company lost £3/4m on the purchase and subsequent resale of a development site which the board had been advised by its accountants to be a potentially high risk commercial property.

Seeing the company's profitability sliding, and aware of the impact on the value of their shares, the minority members criticised the business judgment of the board at the last AGM, held a month ago. They see the chairman, whose style is highly autocratic and who cannot accept criticism, as the author of the company's misfortunes. They understand that he commonly makes decisions without consulting the board, and recently made himself a large profit by selling the company a piece of land which he owned personally. Last week, at a general meeting, the company voted to alter its articles. The alteration provides that the company can, by means of an ordinary resolution, request the sale to the company at a fair market value, the shares of any member holding less than 10% of the ordinary shares of the company, if *"it is in the business interests of the company"* to do so.

You are working at present in a large law firm Leeds whilst deciding whether to train to become a solicitor. The partner you are attached to, Jeremy Lake, specialises in company law matters. Walter Thompson is a client of his, and has arranged an interview with Jeremy as a matter of urgency, to discuss the problems at West Riding Woollens.

Task

Investigate the legal implications of the way in which the board has been running the company and what action, if any, Mr. Thompson can take. Provide a summary of your advice, which should explore all aspects of the company's affairs, for the attention of Mr. Lake.

Assignment - Trouble at Mills

In 1993 Mark Mills, together with his cousin Bryan and an accountant called Peter Marshall, decided to form a company to deal in personal insurance services. The company received its certificate of incorporation at the end of 1993. It was called Mills & Co. (Insurance Services) Ltd. and its premises were in Leeds. Mark and Bryan took up 35% of the shares each, Peter took the remainder. The company objects stated that it could carry on the business of providing *"personal insurance of any kind"*. In 1996 Peter was anxious that his wife should join the company, and each of the existing shareholders agreed to transfer some of their shares to her. As a result she obtained a 25% stake, Mark, Bryan and Peter's shareholding being reduced to 25% each.

Mark was happy with the company structure, since Peter's wife brought to the business considerable commercial expertise, and he received a large sum for the shares he transferred to her. Within a year however, the relationship between the shareholders had deteriorated. In particular Mark felt increasingly isolated. He was anxious that the company expand its insurance business. The other shareholders however were of the view that the company, which was suffering a reduced level of profit, should diversify, and move into the lucrative field of marketing, the area in which Peter's wife had previously worked.

By 1999 Mark had decided to form a separate business to offer a complete range of insurance facilities. He formed a partnership with James Blake-Smith, an old schoolfriend, to carry on the additional business. He did not reveal the existence of this business to his fellow shareholders in Mills & Co. Ltd., assuming that since it was based in Barnsley, a town twenty miles away from the company's place of business in Leeds, it had nothing to do with them. No partnership articles were drawn up. The other members of Mills & Co. Ltd. recently discovered the existence of Mark's new firm. They responded by calling a company meeting, at which, during very stormy business they resolved to alter the company articles to enable it to pursue marketing work, to sell off the company's present business undertaking at a figure well below what Mark believes to be its true value, and to remove him as a director. In addition they are threatening to take away his voting rights. Mark's problems have been compounded by problems in the partnership. He has discovered that James Blake-Smith has been in financial difficulties, and that bankruptcy proceedings have been commenced against him this week. He has also purchased, in a firm's name, an expensive computer system, despite a recent partnership meeting at which it was agreed to defer the expenditure until the next financial year.

In an effort to clarify the legal position in relation to these business difficulties Mark has sought your help., Prior to meeting Mark in a couple of days time, you have decided to analyse the legal position he has found himself in, in order to fully advise him as to the extent of his rights and liabilities.

Task

Draft an outline report which you can give to Mark at your meeting with him, that expresses your considered legal opinion on his present business problems.

Chapter 6

The Dissolution of Business Organisations

Introduction

The life of a business organisation can come to an end for many reasons. It may have achieved what its members required of it, so that it no longer has any useful value. It is not, for instance, unknown for a group of people to form a limited company for the purpose of carrying out a specific business venture, and insert a provision in the company's articles of association making it clear that the business is to last for a fixed period, or that it will expire on the happening of a certain event. A group of businessmen may contribute capital to a company they have formed, with the aim that the company will purchase, renovate and then sell certain industrial premises, or buy and then resell some other substantial asset. The company will end when the sale takes place if its sole purpose was the making of the sale.

A business may also come to an end because the commercial foundations upon which it was based have ceased to exist, or it has become no longer commercially viable to continue. If this occurs there is nothing to prevent the organisation from diversifying if this is acceptable to the members, thus prolonging the life of the business.

An interesting illustration of this process, and the legal consequences which can attach to it, is provided by *Prudential Assurance Co. v. Chatterley-Whitfield Collieries Ltd.* 1949. The colliery company's main business interest was in coal mining, although it had other business interests as well. Following the nationalisation of the coal industry in 1946, the company, in common with other colliery companies, received a large payment by way of compensation. It decided to continue to operate its other business activities, but had more capital than it needed for these, and so it passed a special resolution to repay all its preference shareholders. Under the articles they had the right to priority of repayment of capital in the event of the company being brought to an end. The preference shareholders objected, claiming they would lose the opportunity to share in future profit.

Company legislation strictly controls the power of a company to reduce its capital, in order to protect creditors, shareholders and the public. The court must sanction the reductions, which it will not do if the reduction is not fair and equitable as between different classes of shareholders. The House of Lords nevertheless held that this reduction was fair and equitable on the basis that surplus capital should first be returned to the class of shareholders having priority to repayment in the event of the company being brought to an end.

Most businesses which are terminated however, do not end their own lives out of choice, but because such action has been forced on them by their creditors. This occurs when the creditors lose confidence in the capacity of the organisation to repay them. It is a common feature of commercial life that when a business develops financial ill-health, its creditors will seek to reduce their losses by dissolving the business whilst there are still assets remaining in it.

Thus in considering the law as it affects the dissolution of businesses it is helpful to bear in mind the health of the organisation at the time it is being dissolved. The law, quite understandably, exerts far greater control over businesses which are terminated in circumstances of financial failure, than in cases where they are brought to an end fit and healthy, and nobody will lose money. Dissolution is important to the members of the business, who will be concerned as to what share of the assets they are entitled to, and for much the same reason it will be of concern to the creditors; they will want to know what the assets of the business are, and how they are to be distributed.

The process of dissolution

The process laid down for terminating or dissolving a business depends upon two factors:

- what the type of business is; and

- what its financial condition is.

We have previously seen that business organisations can be classified according to their legal status. Some are corporate bodies, some are unincorporated associations, whilst others are simple one man businesses. By now it should be clear that there are significant differences between these alternative business forms. This is reflected in the procedures for dissolving them. In the case of a limited company the procedure by which it is dissolved is referred to as a *winding-up*. *Bankruptcy* is the term used to describe the process by which an insolvent individual's assets are collected in, converted into money and distributed between his creditors. There is no technical term to describe the process for terminating a partnership. It is simply referred to as dissolution.

Dissolution of a Partnership

When the commercial activity of a partnership ceases so does the business itself, for it is no longer being *"carried on"* as required under the Partnership Act 1890. In such circumstances the partnership will be dissolved, and its assets disposed of to those legally entitled to them. Alternatively, a partnership which is still in operation may be dissolved on any one of a number of different grounds.

Dissolution can occur either with or without the intervention of the court. Under the Partnership Act 1890 a partnership is dissolved *without* the intervention of the court,

- if it was entered into for a fixed term, which has now expired, or was entered into for a single venture, which has been completed;

- if entered into for an undefined time, by any partner giving notice to the other or others of an intention to dissolve the partnership. If such a notice is served then the partnership is dissolved from the date mentioned in the notice as the date of dissolution. If no date has been given, dissolution operates from the time the notice was received, subject to the partnership articles providing for some other date;

- by the death or bankruptcy of any partner. Partnership articles will often provide that in such an event the partnership will continue to be run by the remaining partners;

- if a partner's share of the business is charged to secure a separate judgment debt, the other partners may dissolve the business;

- if it becomes unlawful for the business of the firm to be carried on, or for the members of the firm to carry it on in partnership. This may occur, for example, where there is a partnership between a British partner and a foreign partner, the business is carried on in the United Kingdom, and war breaks out between the countries of the respective partners.

Dissolution can be granted by *the court* on an application to dissolve, made by a partner, in any of the following cases:

- where a partner is suffering from a mental disorder;

- where a partner other than the partner petitioning:

  (i)   becomes in any way permanently incapable of performing their part of the partnership contract, e.g. through physical illness, or

(ii)   has been guilty of misconduct in business or private life, as in the opinion of the court, bearing in mind the nature of the partnership business, is calculated to be prejudicial to the carrying on of the business, or

(iii)   wilfully or persistently commits a breach of the partnership agreement, or otherwise behaves in a way in matters relating to the partnership business making it impractical for the other partners to carry on in business with that partner.

Cases on dissolution on these grounds have included a refusal to meet for discussions on business matters, the keeping of erroneous accounts, persistent disagreement between the parties, and in *Anderson v. Anderson* 1857 where a father and son were in partnership together, by the opening by the father of all his son's correspondence;

- where the business of the partnership can only be carried on at a loss;

- if circumstances have arisen which, in the opinion of the court, render it just and equitable that the partnership be dissolved.

In *Re: Yenidje Tobacco Co. Ltd.* 1916 although the company was trading profitably the court held that it was just and equitable to wind it up, on the basis that its two directors had become so hostile towards each other that they would only communicate by means of messages passed to each other via the Secretary, and that this amounted to a position of deadlock. It was pointed out that a private limited company is similar to a partnership, and that had the directors been partners in a partnership, there would have been sufficient grounds for dissolution. Lord Justice Warrington stated *"... I am prepared to say that in a case like the present, where there are only two persons interested, and there are no shareholders other than those two, where there are no means of over-ruling by the action of a general meeting of shareholders the trouble which is occasioned by the quarrels of the two directors and shareholders, the company ought to be wound up if there exists such a ground as would be sufficient for the dissolution of a private partnership at the suit of one of the partners against the other. Such grounds exist in the present case."*

The partnership and bankruptcy

Two distinct insolvency situations may arise which affect the partnership:

- one of the partners is declared personally bankrupt, whilst the remaining partners are personally solvent. This automatically brings the partnership to an end, although a new one may well be formed, without the bankrupt partner. The reason the firm automatically dissolves in such circumstances is because the bankrupt party's share passes to his trustee in bankruptcy, and thus in effect he is withdrawing his contribution and his stake in the business;

- the partnership itself is insolvent. If this is so, all the partners will normally have bankruptcy proceedings brought against them. It should be remembered that since a partnership does not grant limited liability to its members, they become personally liable for the debts which cannot be met by the assets of the firm.

The administration and distribution of assets

If the partnership is dissolved its property is gathered in, and used to pay all debts and liabilities. If after this is done a surplus is left, it is distributed between the partners. What they receive will depend upon what their partnership agreement says. If it makes no provision for such a situation, the position is regulated by the 1890 Act. It recognises two situations, (a) where the firm has no losses, and (b) where the firm has sustained a loss.

(a)   If there is no loss suffered by the firm, the surplus is used firstly to repay the capital contribution of the partners, and then to the partners in equal shares. Thus if the firm has three partners, A, B, and C, whose respective capital contributions were £2,000, £1,000 and £500, and on dissolution the firm has debts of £3,000 and assets of £8,000, the distribution to the partners will be as follows:

		£
Assets available for distribution		**8,000**
Firm's debts		**3,000**
Surplus assets available for distribution		**5,000**
Repayment of capital contributions	A	**2,000**
	B	**1,000**
	C	**500**
		3,500
Remaining surplus to be equally distributed		**1,500**

The share of net assets taken by each partner will be:
A **£2,500** B **£1,500** C **£1,000**

(b) If there are losses these are met in the following order:

(i)   out of *profits*

(ii)   out of *capital*

(iii)   by the partners individually according to the proportions by which they shared profits.

Using the example of A, B and C above, if the partnership assets on dissolution were £5,000 and the debts £3,000, then assuming profits were shared equally, the distribution to each partner would be as follows:

	£
Assets available for distribution	**5,000**
Firm's debts	**3,000**
Surplus assets available for distribution	**2,000**
Repayment of capital contributions	**3,500**
Shortfall	**1,500**
Lossess shared equally	**500**
	3,500

A receives	£2,000 -	£500	=	£1,500
B receives	£1,000 -	£500	=	£500
C receives	£ 500 -	£500	=	£0

Where there has been a bankruptcy situation with either a partner or the firm itself being adjudicated bankrupt, there will be two groups of creditors; those of the partners personally, and those of the firm itself. It is important therefore that the personal debts and property of the partners can be kept separate from those of the partnership itself.

Members of a partnership may be persuaded that, to protect themselves from liability for their firm's debts, it is desirable to convert the firm into a limited liability company, and many firms do so convert. At the end of the next chapter is a summary of the legal and commercial advantages and disadvantages of operating a business either as a partnership or a registered company.

Dissolution of a Registered Company

We have already seen that the process by which a registered company can be brought to an end is known as a winding up or a liquidation. The process is a detailed and complex one. It is regulated by the Insolvency Act 1986, a statute based upon the report of Sir Kenneth Cork. Shortly before the Royal Assent was granted, the Insolvency Bill as it then was, came back to the House of Lords for approval, where Lord Denning remarked, *"In 1977 Sir Kenneth Cork and his committee entered upon a review of the insolvency law. They sat for five years and heard the most expert evidence. It is the most technical subject you can imagine. Both lawyers and accountants hate it. Most of them know nothing about it."*

The main aspects of it will be examined shortly, but before doing so two points need to be made regarding dissolution. The first is that there are other methods by which a company can be dissolved that do not involve winding up procedures. The second is that where the threat of dissolution is based upon company insolvency, alternatives to the drastic step of terminating the company by winding it up and realising its assets are available to creditors. A creditors composition may be entered into, or an administration order may be made by the court. These points are considered below.

Methods of dissolution

A company is created by incorporation through registration. It can therefore only come to an end when the registration is discharged. Once this happens the contractual relationship between the company and its members, based upon the memorandum and articles of the company, also comes to an end.

A company can be dissolved:

(a)   by proceedings brought by the Attorney-General for cancellation of the registration, on the grounds that the company's objects are illegal.

In *Attorney-General v. Lindi St. Claire (Personal Services) Ltd.* 1980 a lady, Miss St. Claire, formed the defendant company for the purposes of prostitution. The Registrar had granted it a certificate of incorporation, after refusing to register it under various names submitted by Miss St. Claire, including Hookers Ltd., Prostitutes Ltd. and even Lindi St. Claire French Lessons Ltd. The court however granted the cancellation on the grounds that the objects of the company were illegal;

(b)   by an order of the court where the company is transferring its undertaking to another company under a scheme of reconstruction or reorganisation;

(c)   by the Registrar, who under s.652 Companies Act 1985, may strike off the register a company that is defunct. A *defunct* company is one which is no longer carrying on business. The section lays down a procedure to be followed by the Registrar before he can validly exercise the power to remove the company from the register. This has become a very common method of dissolution, for it is cheap and easy;

(d)   by being wound-up, which may be either voluntary or compulsory. The legal provisions relating to company liquidations are contained in the Insolvency Act 1986. The title of this statute is perhaps rather misleading, since it contains provisions which regulate not only companies which are being dissolved on the basis of their insolvency, but also companies which, for a variety of reasons, are being wound up fully able to meet their liabilities.

The process of winding up

Like a partnership, a limited company can be wound up as mentioned above either *voluntarily*, or *compulsorily* by order of the court. The grounds for winding up, whether on a voluntary or compulsory basis, are set out in the Insolvency Act 1986. They recognise that winding up is a step which may become necessary not only in cases of financial instability, but also because the company, which is of course a creature of statute, has failed to comply with the statutory provisions which bind it, or simply because the members no longer wish to trade together. When examining the operation of the limited company it is common to draw an analogy with natural persons. Thus the company is said to be born when its certificate of incorporation is granted, and henceforth its brain, the board of directors, guides its actions and formulates its decisions, which are executed through those it employs. Following this analogy through to its conclusion the process of winding up is akin to the process of administering the estate of a deceased person. Assets are collected and used to satisfy debts owing, after which any property remaining can be distributed to those lawfully entitled to them. In the case of a company this will be to its members. However the process of administering the estate of a deceased person commences with death, whereas winding up is a process which culminates in the dissolution of the company, the administration being completed before the life of the company ends. Statutory references below are to the Insolvency Act 1986 unless stated otherwise.

Terminology

A number of technical expressions are used in liquidation and it is helpful to briefly identify and describe them before proceeding further.

A *petition* is an application to the court requesting the court to exercise its jurisdiction over company liquidations. A petition is presented where the liquidation is compulsory. In such cases the court has a major role to play. This is not so however in voluntary liquidations, where the liquidation is under the control of either the members or the creditors of the company.

A *contributory* is a person liable to contribute to the assets of a company if it is wound up. Existing members whose shares have not been fully paid fall within the definition of a contributory, and so do similarly placed past members, whose shareholding ceased within the year preceding the winding up. However a past member is not liable in respect of any debt contracted after his membership ceased. Nor is he required to make a contribution if the existing members are able to satisfy the contributions required of them.

A *liquidator* is a person appointed to take control of the company, collect its assets, pay its debts, and distribute any surplus to the members according to their rights as shareholders. The liquidator therefore holds a position of great responsibility, and it is important to ensure that only individuals of integrity are qualified to hold such a post. In recent years some disquiet has been felt as a result of company liquidations in which the liquidator has been found to be conducting the winding up for the benefit of directors, rather than the company's creditors. The Insolvency Act 1986 copes with this by requiring that only an *insolvency practitioner*, a term covering liquidators, can act in a winding up. He must be authorised to do so by his own professional body (these include accountancy bodies and the Law Society), or by the Department of Trade and Industry. Certain people are completely excluded. An applicant must be shown to be a fit and proper person, and must provide security, to become an insolvency practitioner.

Liquidators need to be distinguished from receivers. *Receivers* are appointed by the holders of secured debentures, under the terms of the debenture, when the company defaults in making a repayment or commits some other breach. Three types of receiver can be identified; *ordinary receivers* who literally do receive on behalf of the debenture holders, by for example receiving rent from property subject to charge; *receivers and managers*, who are appointed under a floating charge which covers only a part of the company's undertaking and who manage the business of the company to the extent of the assets subject to the charge; and *administrative receivers*. An *administrative receiver* is a receiver appointed under a floating charge which extends to *"the whole or substantially the whole of the company's property"* (s.529). Since floating charges generally do so extend, most appointments are of administrative receivers. Although a company may go into liquidation following the appointment of a receiver this is not an automatic consequence.

The *Official Receiver* is appointed by the Department of Trade, and is concerned both with personal insolvency and with corporate insolvency. Official receivers are attached to courts with insolvency jurisdiction, and they act in the capacity of liquidators in the case of compulsory liquidations, being appointed automatically when a *winding up order* is made, that is when the court issues an order that the company be wound up. The Official Receiver (OR) remains in this office until another liquidator is appointed.

Finally the *London Gazette* is an official publication used to satisfy the requirement of providing public notice of certain legal events, for example, in the case of a liquidation notice of a creditors' meeting.

The Basic Aspects of a Company Liquidation

We have seen that when the process of winding-up has been completed the company will be struck off the register of companies and will cease to exist. Of course no further claims can then be made against it. Consequently for anyone who is connected with the company, whether as an investor, creditor or employee, winding-up is of great significance.

Although statutory winding up provisions are detailed, and sometimes complex, there are basically three aspects to a liquidation:

- who has the ability to institute and control the winding up, and on what grounds;

- what are the legal provisions to be fulfilled during the procedure; and

- in what order are claims made against the company for payment met?

Methods of Winding Up

Under s.73 two methods of winding up are recognised. These are:

(a) a *voluntary* winding up, which according to s.90 may be either:

(i)   a members' voluntary winding up, or

(ii) a creditors' voluntary winding up, and

(b) a winding up by the court, usually referred to as a *compulsory* winding up.

Voluntary winding up is more common than compulsory liquidation. It is a less formal procedure, and is therefore quicker and cheaper.

Voluntary winding up

Shareholders can at any time resolve to end the company. They initiate the procedure by passing a resolution to wind up, either a special resolution if the company is solvent, or, in the case of insolvency, an extraordinary resolution that it cannot continue in business by reason of its liabilities. An ordinary resolution is sufficient where the time period fixed in the articles for the life of the company has passed, or an event stipulated in the articles as giving rise to dissolution has taken place.

Under s.86 when the resolution is passed the liquidation procedure begins. The consequences are that:

- the company ceases to carry on business, other than to enable it to wind up;

- the company's corporate status remains intact until dissolution;

- transfers of shares, and changes in members' rights are void unless sanctioned by the liquidator;

- the directors' powers cease when the liquidator is appointed, although he, or in a creditors' voluntary winding up, they themselves, may permit the directors to continue; and

- if the liquidation is due to insolvency, company employees, who may include directors, will be dismissed. The liquidator may however employ them under a new contract.

Notice of the resolution must be advertised in the *London Gazette* within fourteen days of it being passed. If a majority of the directors within five weeks of the passing of the resolution make a statutory declaration that the company is solvent, then the company members manage the winding up. This includes the appointment of their own liquidator. This is a valuable power for the person appointed will be under their control, rather than the control of the creditors or the court. The court can nevertheless remove a liquidator on the basis of unfitness for office. The declaration of solvency states that the directors have examined the company's affairs and formed the opinion that within a stated period (up to a maximum of twelve months) the company will be able to pay its debts in full. If a declaration of solvency is not made, the winding up is creditors' winding up. A creditors' meeting must be summoned by the company. Details of this meeting must be posted to creditors and members giving them at least seven days notice, and be advertised in the London Gazette and two local newspapers.

The business of the creditors' meeting is to receive from the directors a full statement of the company's affairs, to draw up a list of creditors with estimates of their claims, to appoint a liquidator who will insert a notice in the *London Gazette* notifying other creditors to send in claims and if considered necessary, appoint a liquidation committee.

The liquidation committee cannot consist of more than five people. They will be creditors of company. It is designed to work in conjunction with the liquidator, overseeing the liquidators work, and receiving reports from the liquidator on any matters of concern.

The liquidators' powers in a voluntary winding up

The liquidator has wide powers to act for and in the name of the company, without the need to consult anyone or obtain the sanction of the court.

The liquidator can:

(i)   bring or defend legal proceedings on behalf of the company;

(ii)   continue to operate the company's business to the extent necessary to wind it up beneficially;

(iii)   issue company documents and use the company seal;

(iv)   claim in insolvency proceedings brought by the company against an insolvent estate in which the company has an interest;

(v)   deal with any negotiable instrument issued by or received by the company;

(vi)   raise money needed by the company on security of its assets;

(vii)   collect in monies due from contributories;

(viii) appoint an agent to carry out work on behalf of the liquidator.

In addition to these powers the liquidator may, in a members' voluntary winding up with the sanction of an extraordinary resolution of the company, or in a creditors' voluntary winding up with the sanction of the court, the liquidation committee or the creditors:

• pay off in full any class of creditors;

- enter into any compromise or arrangement with creditors.

It is possible for a voluntary winding up to be converted into a compulsory winding up, on a petition to the court by a creditor or contributory. This will only be successful if the court is satisfied that it is inappropriate for the winding up to proceed as a voluntary one, for instance where the liquidator is found to have some personal interest in the company he is winding up.

Fraudulent and Wrongful Trading

The concept of *fraudulent trading* is a well known one in company law. It is a crime under the Companies Act 1985, and gives rise to civil liability under the Insolvency Act 1986. Civil liability can only occur when the company is being wound up. If in the course of the liquidation it appears to the liquidator that the company's business has been carried on with intent to defraud creditors or for any fraudulent purpose, the liquidator may apply to the court for an order that any person who has knowingly been a party to such conduct be liable to contribute to the assets of the company. The court can order such a contribution as it thinks proper in the circumstances. In this way the creditors as a whole are compensated in the winding up for any serious wrongdoing committed by the directors, or any other party, in their management of or dealings with the company. The expression *fraudulent* is not defined by statute, however the courts have provided some indication of what must be established.

> In *Re William C. Leitch Brass Ltd.* 1932 it was said that a company will be acting fraudulently by incurring debts either knowing it will be unable to meet them when they fall due, or reckless as to whether it will be able to pay them at such time. An important qualification to liability was given in *Re Patrick & Lyon Ltd.* 1933 where it was said that the behaviour of the directors had to demonstrate real moral blame, and it is this feature of fraudulent trading which presents the major limitation upon its effectiveness as a civil remedy. So long as the directors can satisfy the court that, even when the company was in an insolvent situation, they genuinely and honestly believed that the company would be able to meet its debts when they fell due, then it is unlikely that they will be held personally accountable. Clearly the less business competence and experience they possess the easier it will be for them to avoid liability.

It was because of this difficulty in establishing fraudulent trading that the Cork Committee, in the course of examining the reform of the insolvency laws in the early 1980s, recommended the introduction of an additional head of civil liability, which could be established by proving negligence. This recommendation was implemented by the *wrongful trading* provisions contained in s.214 Insolvency Act

1986. Only a director can incur liability for wrongful trading, and as with s.213 action can only be taken by the liquidator of the company. The liquidator needs to establish that the person was at the time a director, that the company had gone into insolvent liquidation, and that at some time before the proceedings to wind up commenced, the person against whom they were being brought knew or ought to have concluded that there was no reasonable prospect that the company would avoid going into insolvent liquidation. If these criteria are met the court may declare the person concerned liable to contribute to the assets of the company. The section is particularly demanding on directors in a number of aspects. Insolvent liquidation means, in the context of s.214, that the assets as realised in the liquidation are insufficient to meet not only the company's debts and other liabilities, but also the costs of the winding up itself, which are generally substantial. The standard of skill expected of the director is based upon two sets of criteria, that is not only the general knowledge, skill and experience which that particular director holds, but also the skill and experience that can be reasonably expected from a reasonably diligent director. The test is an objective rather than a subjective one. Even the defence available under the section operates in a rigorous fashion towards directors. It provides that no order may be made by the court if it is satisfied that the person in question took every step with a view to minimising the potential loss to the company's creditors as he ought to have taken. The expression *every step* is clearly very stringent.

> The wrongful trading provisions were applied in *Re Produce Marketing Consortium Ltd.* 1989 where two directors had continued to trade when the accounts showed their company to be insolvent, in the honest but unrealistically optimistic belief that the company's fortunes would change. They were ordered by the court to contribute £75,000 plus interest to the assets of the company.

> In *Re Purpoint Ltd.* 1991 the liquidator brought action against a director under both ss212 and 214, to compel contribution from him to the assets of the company. S.212 enables a liquidator, a creditor or a member to petition the court to order repayment or restoration of property obtained by a promoter or director in breach of duty. It is useful because s.214 can only be used when there was a likelihood the company would go into insolvent liquidation, whereas such a requirement does not apply under s.212. Also s.214 is concerned with loss suffered by creditors. S.212 deals with losses caused to the *company*. The court found the director guilty of misfeasance and liable to make a contribution under both sections. The court said his contribution under s.214 should be an amount representing the aggregation of unpaid debts for the period to which the liability under the s.214 order applied.

It seems that s.214 is a more potent weapon in the hands of liquidators than s.213. Establishing fraud is more difficult than establishing negligence, and this together with the rigorous standards demanded by s.214 suggests that wrongful trading is likely to be regarded increasingly by liquidators as a more attractive remedy than fraudulent trading. Even so there may still be reasons why a claim under s.213 may be brought by a liquidator. Orders made under s.213 can be punitive, for example, but perhaps the most significant reason is where a contribution is being sought from someone other than a director, for unlike s.214, s.213 catches anyone 'knowingly' a party to the fraud.

In *Re Gerald Cooper Chemicals Ltd.* 1978 the court held that a creditor who accepts money from the company knowing it has been procured by carrying on business with the intent to defraud other creditors by the act of paying him, will be liable under s.213. Templeman, J. stated *"A man who warms himself with the fire of fraud cannot complain if he is singed"*.

Compulsory winding up

A compulsory winding up is carried out by the court. This is either the High Court or, if the company's paid up share capital does not exceed £120,000, the County Court in whose district the company has its registered office. Not all County Courts however, possess the necessary insolvency jurisdiction.

Proceedings are commenced by a person presenting a petition to the appropriate court. The petitioner may be the company itself, by resolution, the Secretary of State following an investigation or, in most cases, a creditor.

In *Re Othery Construction Ltd.* 1966 Lord Buckley stated that if a fully paid up shareholder is to successfully petition to wind up:

"... he must show either that there will be a surplus available for distribution amongst the shareholders or that the affairs of the company require investigation in respects which are likely to produce such a surplus".

Under s.122 a company may be wound up by the court if:

(a)   the company has passed a special resolution requesting it; or

(b)   in the case of a company registered as a public company, the company has been registered for more than a year, but as yet no certificate of ability to commence business has been issued. This certificate, which is issued by the Registrar, can only be obtained when certain financial details have been given to him. The company cannot commence business until the certificate, which is required under s.117 Companies Act 1985, has been issued. Private companies do not require such a certificate and can commence business immediately on incorporation; or

(c)   the company does not commence business in the first year of its incorporation, or suspends business at any time for a whole year. An order will only be granted on this ground if the company has no intention of carrying on business again.

In *Re Middlesbrough Assembly Rooms Co.* 1880 a shareholder petitioned for winding up where the company had suspended trading for over three years, because of a trade depression. The majority shareholders opposed the petition on the basis that the company intended to recommence trading when the economic situation improved. It was held that in the circumstances the petition should be dismissed;

(d)   in the case of a public company if the membership has fallen below two; or

(e)   if the company is unable to pay its debts. This is the ground most commonly relied upon. The company is deemed to be unable to pay its debts if a creditor who is owed a sum exceeding £750 by the company has left a statutory demand for it at the company's registered office, and the demand has remained unpaid for a period of three clear weeks. The £750 figure can be made up by aggregating the debts of different creditors. The company is not however regarded as neglecting the debt if it disputes the payment of it. In such circumstances the petitioner would not be regarded as a creditor. It is also well established law that winding up proceedings are not to be used as a system for debt collection. In *Re a Company ex. p Fin Soft Holding SA* 1991 Harman J regarded the correct test in such cases to be *"is there a substantial dispute as to the debt upon which the petition is allegedly founded?"*. It follows that absence of good faith on the part of the company in disputing payment is irrelevant.

Alternatively the company is deemed unable to pay its debts if:

(i)   execution has been issued on a judgment in favour of a creditor which is returned either wholly or partially unsatisfied; or

(ii)   it is proved to the satisfaction of the court that the company is unable to pay its debts as they fall due.

In *Re a Company* 1986 it was held that a company can be regarded as unable to pay its debts under this ground, where it has funds but persistently fails or neglects to pay its debts unless it is forced to do so. Many companies have a deliberate policy of holding back payment for as long as possible, and for some this may be their means of survival; or

(iii)   where the court is satisfied that taking into account the company's present and future liabilities, the value of its assets is less than the amount of its liabilities; or

(f)   the court is of the opinion that it is just and equitable that the company should be wound up. This ground covers a number of situations. For instance it covers cases where the substratum of the company has been destroyed.

In *Re German Date Coffee Co*. 1882 the company was wound up on the basis that it had become impossible to carry out the main object in the memorandum of association, namely the acquisition and working of a German patent to make coffee from dates, because the patent could not be obtained.

It also extends to circumstances in which the company has been formed for a fraudulent purpose; where the company is a sham, having no business or property; or where the rights of members are being flouted.

In *Loch v. John Blackwood Ltd*. 1924 a director with voting control refused to hold meetings, produce accounts or pay dividends. The court held that the company could be wound up.

In *Ebrahami v. Westbourne Galleries* 1972 two individuals E and N had operated successfully in partnership together for many years. Later they converted the business to a company, with themselves as sole shareholders and directors, and after a time N's son was allowed into the business. This was granted as a favour by the plaintiff, who transferred some of his shares to the son. Unfortunately his generosity was met by N and his son combining their interests to force the plaintiff out of the business. The court granted the plaintiff's application to wind up. Commenting on the expression *"just and equitable"* Lord Wilberforce said:

"The words are a recognition of the fact that a limited company is more than a mere legal entity, with a personality in law of its own; that there is room in company law for the recognition of the fact that behind it, or amongst it, there are individuals, with rights, expectations and obligations ... which are not necessarily submerged in the company structure".

The petition to wind up is presented to the district judge of the court who fixes a time and place for the hearing. The petition must be advertised in the *London Gazette* at least seven clear days (excluding Saturday and Sunday) before the hearing. Rules of Court set out the form in which this advertised information must be provided; if they are not complied with the petitioner may have to meet all the court costs. The aim of the advertisement is to invite interested parties, the company's creditors and contributories, to oppose or support the petition. A person intending to appear at the hearing must give notice of this to the petitioner. After presentation of the petition a provisional liquidator may be appointed who is generally the Official Receiver. In any event when the hearing takes place, and the court makes a winding-up order, the Official Receiver becomes provisional liquidator by statute, and continues as liquidator unless the meeting of the creditors and contributories agree to the appointment of some other liquidator. This person must be an insolvency practitioner. The 1986 Act sets out the liquidator's powers. Essentially his task is to collect and realise the company's assets, including unpaid sums due to the company from contributories for their shares, to settle the lists of creditors and contributories, pay the company's debts in a fixed order, and finally to adjust the rights of the contributories distributing any surplus assets among them. At meetings of creditors and contributories it may be decided to apply to the court to form a committee of inspection. Having fulfilled these responsibilities the liquidator applies to the court for an order that the company be dissolved, and is then released from his or her role. The court has a complete and unfettered discretion as to whether to make an order for winding up. It may as an alternative conditionally or unconditionally adjourn the hearing, make an interim order, or dismiss the petition altogether.

The order of priorities

On dissolution there are likely to be many claims against the assets of the company. Provided the company is solvent this does not create any problems, but if it is insolvent the question which arises is how the shortfall is dealt with. Do all the company's creditors absorb the loss according to the proportion of credit they have provided, or do some creditors rank before others, so that whilst those at the top of the list may be repaid in full, those at the bottom could find themselves with nothing?

The answer is that the Insolvency Act 1986 lays down an order of priorities for the distribution of assets. The relevant provisions are contained in ss.175 and 176, which lays down the following order:

(a)   the costs of winding up (for example the liquidator's fees);

(b)   preferential debts. These include: income tax deducted from the pay of company employees under the PAYE system over the past year; VAT payments owed by the company that have accrued over the past six months; wages and salaries of employees outstanding for the previous four months, up to a present maximum figure of £800 per employee. A director may be a salaried employee, and thus qualify under this head, however a director's fee rather than a salary will not rank as a preferential debt. If assets are sufficient, preferential debts are paid in full. If not, the available assets are distributed rateably between the preferential creditors, and in these circumstances property subject to a floating charge must be applied first in the payment of preferential debts, the holder being entitled only to the balance. Creditors who have the security of a fixed charge over assets of the company are, of course, able to realise the assets charged to meet the company's liability towards them;

(c) ordinary unsecured debts, such as sums owing to trade creditors. If these cannot be paid in full they are paid rateably amongst the creditors;

(d) the members according to their rights under the memorandum and articles. It may be that one class of shareholders is entitled to repayment of a certain amount of the surplus before the others, thus preference shareholders may receive repayment of their paid up capital in priority to ordinary shareholders.

Advantages and disadvantages of compulsory winding up

The main advantages of a compulsory winding up over a voluntary winding up are:

(a) Under s.129 Insolvency Act 1986 a compulsory winding up is deemed to commence when the petition is presented, whilst in a voluntary winding up it commences when the resolution is passed (s.86). The effect is that a compulsory winding up will commence earlier. This can be important since as part of the task of collecting in assets the liquidator can apply to the court to recover assets disposed of by the company within a fixed period before the insolvency, and can seek to have certain transactions set aside where these transactions occurred within a certain date of the insolvency. Going back further into the recent past of the company may mean the recovery of a larger quantity of assets. Examples include:

(i) the setting aside of a transaction made by the company at undervalue within the two years before the winding up has commenced. A transaction at undervalue would cover a gift made by the company at a time it was unable to pay its debts;

(ii) the setting aside of a preference made by the company to a connected person (e.g. a director) within two years of the winding up commencing, or to any other person (e.g. a trade creditor) within six months of the winding up commencing. Again this must have occurred at a time when the company was unable to pay its debts. A preference would occur where the directors, in the knowledge that the company is completely insolvent, settle the debts of just one of the company's creditors, in the expectation that if they subsequently set up a new company the trade creditor will continue to supply them;

(iii)   the avoidance of floating charges created by the company within the two years prior to the insolvency if the chargee is a connected person, and one year if the chargee is anyone else.

(b)   Wider powers of investigation into the management of the company's affairs, for example where the directors have been acting wrongfully.

The main disadvantages are that a compulsory liquidation will be slower and more expensive. The company will always be the respondent under a compulsory winding up order, and as the 'loser' in the action it will meet both sides' costs, thus reducing the money available for the creditors when the realised assets are finally distributed.

Alternatives to Winding Up

Whilst as we have seen, a company may be dissolved for reasons other than financial difficulty, most dissolutions are the result of a financial crisis. Directors faced with this situation may have the future affairs of the company taken out of their hands in a compulsory or creditors' liquidation, the result of which will be that the life of the company will come to an end, and some creditors at least will be left with their debts unsatisfied. One of the aims of the Insolvency Act 1986 was to provide alternatives to this drastic outcome, which would act as financial rescue packages for companies in difficulty.

(a)   Corporate voluntary arrangements - compositions with creditors

These are provided for by ss1–7 Insolvency Act 1986. They enable a company which is insolvent or partially insolvent to follow a procedure which will result in a legally binding arrangement with its creditors. In outline the following stages have to be followed. The directors, or the liquidator if a winding up is in progress, choose an insolvency practitioner to act as a *nominee*, and help them produce proposals to put to the creditors. These may be a composition or a scheme of arrangement for the company i.e. the revision of its financial affairs in some way, such as alterations to class rights, or the extension of time for payment given by debenture notices.

The proposals are reported to the court and a meeting of creditors and shareholders is called both of which must approve them. The outcome is reported to the court. If approved, the proposals bind all the creditors and shareholders having notice of them, under s.5.

(b) Administration orders

One of the problems with a voluntary arrangement is of course the difficulty of obtaining the agreement of large creditors, such as banks. They will want greater control over the organisation of the company's affairs. In such circumstances an administration order may be a useful device. Such an order can be made by the court once it is satisfied that the company is, or is likely to become, unable to pay its debts, and that an administration order would be likely to achieve:

(i)   the survival of the company, and the whole or any part of its undertaking as a going concern; or

(ii)   the approval of a voluntary arrangement (i.e. because of the appointment of an administrator); or

(iii) a more advantageous realisation of the company's assets than in a winding up.

The company itself, its directors, a creditor or creditors may petition the court for such an order: individual members cannot petition however, in contrast with their power to do so under s.122 to have the company wound-up on just and equitable grounds and under s.459 CA 1985, which enables them to seek relief on the ground of unfair prejudice. If the order is granted the court will appoint an administrator who will be responsible for the management of the affairs, business and property of the company for the duration of the order. This can include the calling of meetings and the appointment and removal of directors. Any winding up petition previously presented must be dismissed on the grant of an administration order. The administrator is empowered to carry on the business of the company generally, including dealing with and disposing of its assets, borrowing, employing agents and so on. He can establish subsidiary companies and transfer the whole or some part of the existing business to them. He can remove directors, and appoint new directors, and call meetings of the members and the creditors. His duties are to control and manage the company's assets and business operations, initially in accordance with directions from the court given in the order, and subsequently in accordance with the proposals he has put forward as to how the purposes stated in the order are to be achieved. The administrator's proposals must be sent to the Registrar of Companies and all the creditors within three months of the administration order being made. A creditors' meeting must then be held to approve the proposals before they can be implemented.

It remains to be seen how much use will be made of the administration order as an alternative to liquidation, however a useful illustration of an order in operation occurred in *Re Consumer & Industrial Press* 1987. The company involved, a small printing and publishing organisation, had only one major asset when it became insolvent, a magazine which it published. An application was made for the appointment of an administrator, so that he could exercise the statutory power to borrow in the company's name in order to continue publishing the magazine. In this way it could be sold as a going concern, rather than it going out of publication and having far less value. The court held that in the interests of the creditors the order should be granted.

Individual Insolvency

Personal insolvency occurs when an individual finds himself in serious financial difficulties and is unable to pay his creditors when debts fall due. If the creditors are unwilling or unable to wait for payment, the debtor may face bankruptcy proceedings under the Insolvency Act 1986. Broadly the purpose of bankruptcy is to ensure a fair distribution of assets to creditors and to allow the debtor to make a fresh start after his discharge.

The law relating to individual insolvency has undergone substantial change in recent years. The procedures under the Bankruptcy Act 1914 have been abolished and replaced with simpler procedures first introduced by the Insolvency Act 1985 and now contained in the Insolvency Act 1986. The new legislation was introduced with two main aims:

(a)   to encourage voluntary arrangements between debtors and creditors; and

(b)   to simplify and update bankruptcy procedures and bring them into line with the procedures applicable to company liquidations.

Under the 1986 Act there are two possible outcomes of individual insolvency: a *voluntary arrangement* or a *bankruptcy order*.

Voluntary arrangements

Where an individual is facing insolvency, he may try to avoid a bankruptcy order by proposing a voluntary arrangement with his creditors. The advantages from the debtor's point of view of such an arrangement are that he avoids the stigma, loss of status and adverse publicity associated with a bankruptcy order, and avoids the disabilities to which an undischarged bankrupt is subject. The benefit of a voluntary arrangement for the creditor is that it should be less expensive, leaving more assets available for payment to him; and it will usually be quicker than bankruptcy procedure, which means that he will be paid sooner. The disadvantage from the creditors point of view is that the supervisor of a voluntary arrangement will not have as many powers as a trustee in bankruptcy, for example to set aside transactions at an undervalue or preferences.

Bankruptcy Orders

A petition for a bankruptcy order may be presented by a creditor, the debtor himself, the supervisor, or a creditor bound by a voluntary arrangement where the debtor has defaulted under the arrangement.

Petition by a creditor

A petition by a creditor must be based on an unpaid debt or debts owed to him by the debtor. The amount owing must be at least £750. In order to commence bankruptcy proceedings, a creditor either must obtain a judgment debt for at least £750 and be unable to enforce it; or he must serve on the debtor a *statutory demand* for payment of the debt. Where a statutory demand is served and the debtor fails to pay within three weeks, the creditor can petition the court for a bankruptcy order. The court can dismiss the creditor's petition if it is satisfied that the debtor is able to pay all of his debts or that he has made an offer to provide security for the payment of the debt or to enter into a voluntary arrangement and the creditor has unreasonably refused to accept his offer.

The trustee in bankruptcy

The function of the trustee in bankruptcy is to collect in the assets of the bankrupt and distribute them in accordance with the rules in the Insolvency Act. The order of priority for repayment of debts is similar to that described for the winding-up of companies. All of the bankrupt's property vests in the trustee in bankruptcy, with the exception of tools, vehicles and equipment for use by the bankrupt in his employment or business; and such clothing, bedding, furniture and household equipment as are necessary to satisfy the basic domestic needs of the bankrupt and his family.

Duration of bankruptcy

The bankruptcy continues until an individual is discharged from it. If a person is bankrupt for the first time, he will be discharged automatically after three years from the date of the Bankruptcy Order. In a summary administration, as we have seen, discharge will occur after two years. In either case, the period can be extended by the court if the bankrupt has failed to comply with any of his obligations under the Insolvency Act 1986. If the bankrupt has previously been an undischarged bankrupt during the previous fifteen years, he will not automatically be discharged. He must apply to the court for discharge after five years from the making of the bankruptcy order. Where such an application is made, the court may refuse to discharge the bankrupt. It may grant a discharge, either unconditionally or upon condition that he, for example, makes further payments to his creditors.

An undischarged bankrupt is subject to certain legal disabilities. He cannot obtain credit; or become a member of Parliament, a justice of the peace or a councillor.

Discharge from bankruptcy releases the bankrupt from the debts which existed at the commencement of his bankruptcy. A discharge from bankruptcy, however, does not affect his liability for fines imposed by a court for any criminal offence, or the enforcement of any security by a secured creditor.

Assignment - The Rise and Fall of John Russell

At the beginning of 1998 the further success of John Russell Ltd as a commercial enterprise seemed assured. The company had been incorporated at the beginning of 1997 out of an existing partnership business, for the purposes, to quote its objects clause of *"carrying on the business of motor vehicle dealers and ancillary activities"*.

The new company quickly established a name for itself, and by the winter of 1998 it felt itself in a strong enough commercial position to proceed with arrangements for the design and construction of expensive and prestigious new sales and office premises on the outskirts of Birmingham. Architects Van Mildert, Clarke, Foster were contracted to carry out the design work, the builders appointed were Western Construction plc, and the office equipment and the computer system was purchased from Zenith Office Supplies Ltd.

The downfall of the company was if anything more dramatic than its rapid growth. It came with the loss of the most lucrative business, fleet car sales. During the first five months of 1999 its three principal fleet customers failed to place new orders as a result of recessionary pressures. John Russell Ltd's three directors, Paul O'Grady, Jim Morgan, and John Russell himself, the managing director, struggled to keep the company afloat.

Still owing large sums on the new premises and advised by their accountants that the business *"would be unlikely to survive beyond the end of the year"* they decided to keep trading in the hope the fleet market would return. In the meantime, with insufficient funds to pay all the creditors, the directors decided to pay their architects charges of £75,000 in full, and to ask the architects to use their influence with the builders, Western Construction, to allow Russells more time to pay the final instalment of the building work, a sum of £400,000, now four months overdue.

The strategy did not work. The builders lost patience and petitioned the court at the end of July 1999 to have the company compulsorily wound up. The petition was granted and Simon Scott was subsequently appointed as liquidator.

You have recently joined the firm of accountants, in which Simon Scott is a partner, as an administrative assistant. In order to give you some experience of company liquidations, and also because he has a heavy workload at present, Simon Scott has asked you to consider a number of aspects of the John Russell liquidation. In particular he would like you to report back to him on the following matters.

1. Whether the payment made to the architects can be recovered for the company's creditors.

2.   If any form of personal liability is likely to have been incurred by the directors in their conduct of the operations of John Russell Ltd.

3.   Whether the contract the company made to purchase the computer system from Zenith Office Supplies can be avoided. The system purchased is more sophisticated than John Russell Ltd needs, and perhaps falls outside its objects clause. It has been established that Paul O'Grady is also a director of Zenith, although he has never disclosed the fact to the John Russell board.

Task

Advise Simon Scott in writing as to the legal position on the three points referred to above.

Chapter 7

Tortious Liability in Business

The concept of legal liability is the major theme throughout the book. This is hardly surprising for legal liability is one of the most fundamental of all legal concepts and in relation to business is usually contractual or tortious in origin. Chapters 8 to 11 in the book are devoted to contractual liability arising in the course of supplying goods and services. This chapter is concerned with business liability which may arise outside the law of contract and under the law of tort. A tort is simply a civil wrong and tortious liability in business is the subject of this chapter.

A legal liability arises when someone is under a legal obligation to do or refrain from doing something, and is answerable if they act in breach of such an obligation. Businesses are subject to an extensive range of actual and potential legal liabilities resulting from the performance of their business operations. There are different ways these liabilities can be categorised. If we look at them from the standpoint of the purposes they are designed to meet we come across one of the most well known of all legal categorisations, the division of the law into civil and criminal branches. The distinction between civil and criminal law was discussed in Chapter 1. Essentially, civil law is concerned with private rights and obligations and the remedying of private grievances whereas the criminal law is concerned with the welfare of society generally. Civil law is concerned with compensating victims, criminal law with, amongst other things, the punishment of offenders. Both civil liability and criminal liability arise from the existence of legal rules. In civil law the legal rules which have the greatest impact upon business operations are those involved with contractual and tortious liability.

Criminal Liability in Business

We have previously seen how business organisations can incur criminal liabilities arising from the way in which they conduct their activities. An unincorporated association cannot be held criminally liable, for the body in question is not a person. Thus in an organisation like a partnership it will be the partners themselves, rather than their firm, who may be found to be criminally liable. The case of *Parsons v. Barnes* 1973 in Chapter 3 illustrates the point.

The position regarding corporate bodies such as registered companies and local authorities is quite different however. Because a corporation is a *person* in law, it follows that it can be held criminally liable. There are in fact two ways in which such liability can be imposed:

Directly

Liability is incurred directly where those in control of the company commit an offence in the course of its business, and the company is treated as committing the offence itself on the basis that the state of mind of its controllers constitutes its own state of mind.

> One of the first cases establishing this principle was *R v. ICR Haulage* 1944 in which the company was convicted of the offence of conspiring to defraud, the mens rea of the offence - the mental element of it, being provided by the state of mind of its managing director.

There appear to be two limitations placed upon the direct, or primary criminal liability of a corporation. Firstly it will only be liable for the acts or omissions of those at the top of the organisational hierarchy, the officers of the company who in the words of Lord Pearson in *Tesco Supermarkets v. Natrass* 1972 *may "be identified with it, as being or having its directing mind and will ..."*. Secondly it seems that a company will only be liable for the acts of an individual manager or director with whom it is identified, making it impossible to aggregate the acts of more than one directing mind to create a corporate offence. The position however is not entirely clear. It does seem though that on the basis of direct or primary liability a corporation could be charged with any offence except those which carry a mandatory prison sentence on a conviction, such as murder.

There are numerous examples of companies and individual directors being prosecuted for health and safety at work offences and even corporate manslaughter when someone in the workplace is killed due to gross negligence. A contemporary example of health and safety prosecution and the imposition of a fine is provided by the following case.

> *R v. Rollco Screw and Rivet Co. Ltd*. 1999. is a health and safety case concerning the inadequate precautions taken when carrying out shipping of asbestos. Factory staff and the public were put in danger when work was carried out without proper precautions. A prosecution was brought against the company and its two directors who had contracted out the work to a firm and who had in turn sub contracted the work. A severe fine was imposed on the company and its directors. On appeal it was argued that the sum the company was ordered to pay was grossly excessive amounting to over seventy thousand

pounds payable over six years. The period of repayment was excessive and was reduced by a year and sum payable for the costs element was reduced by £10,000.

In *Dexter v. Tenby Electrical Accessories Ltd.* 1991 contractors were employed by the defendants to install fresh air fans at their factory premises and for this purpose an employee of the contractor was required to work for a period on the factory roof. Despite the fact that the defendants were unaware that the employee was working on the roof they were nevertheless liable as occupiers of the factory when he suffered injuries after falling through it. The Health and Safety Executive charged the defendant with a contravention of s29(1) of the Factories Act 1961 which provides *"there shall, so far as is reasonably practicable, be provided and maintained safe means of access to every place which any person has at anytime to work, and every such place shall, so far as is reasonably practicable, be made and kept safe for any person working there"*. While the Magistrates accepted the argument that the defendants had no control over the employee's place of work and so there was no case to answer, this was rejected in an appeal by the prosecution to the Queen's Bench Divisional Court. The appeal court held that lack of knowledge was no defence and if a person is ordered by his employer, a contractor, to work on a factory roof, the occupier of the factory is liable under the Act if the roof is in an unsafe condition.

Vicariously

Liability is vicarious where the company is held liable for the criminal acts of its employees and agents committed within the course of their employment. Usually liability of this kind only occurs where the offence is one of strict liability - that is where no mens rea is required. In the ICR case mentioned above the company could not have been vicariously liable for the act of another in a crime like conspiracy to defraud.

In *James and Son Ltd. v. Smee* 1955 a driver employed by the company was sent out with a lorry and trailer on a round. During the round he had to disconnect the brakes to the trailer and forgot to reconnect them. It was an offence for anyone to use or cause or permit to be used a vehicle or trailer without an efficient braking system. On appeal by the company against a conviction that it had permitted the trailer to be used Parker J in the Divisional Court said *"before the company can be held guilty of permitting ... it must be proved that some person for whose acts the company is responsible permitted as opposed to committed the offence. There was no such evidence in the present case"*. The mens rea of the offence, the permitting, had to be shown to be present in the employee if the company was to be held vicariously liable for what he had done. He had used the vehicle, but not permitted its use.

It seems that there are two circumstances in which a corporation many be criminally vicariously liable under statute. Firstly the statute may make express reference to such liability arising. Examples can be found in the Licensing Act 1964. For instance s.59 of the Act provides that " ... *no person shall, except during the permitted hours ... himself or by his servant or agent sell or supply to any person in licensed premises ... any intoxicating liquor, whether to be consumed on or off the premises"*. Secondly liability may arise where a statutory duty supported by criminal sanctions is delegated to an employee. In such circumstances the conduct of the employee will be imputed to the employer.

Vicarious liability in tort is considered in some depth later in the chapter.

Fault and strict liability

At common law the basis upon which criminal liability was founded required that the offender not only committed the facts constituting the prohibited conduct, referred to as the *actus reus* of the offence, but also demonstrated an accompanying state of mind suggesting moral culpability or fault. The criminal law has many examples of terms connoting degrees of fault or blameworthiness, words such as *deliberately, recklessly, negligently, wilfully, knowingly, dishonestly, fraudulently* and so on. Such terms are referred to as the mens rea of the offence, the guilty mind.

Parliament has seen fit however to introduce many offences under statute, which dispense with the need to prove that the offender was at fault. Usually such offences, which are referred to as *strict* or *absolute* offences, seek to impose liability without fault because it is socially or practically expedient to do so. Many of the minor offences associated with road traffic law are strict liability offences, such as speeding. There are also plentiful examples in the field of consumer protection. For example the Children and Young Persons Act 1937 creates a strict liability offence in relation to the sale of tobacco to children.

> In *St Helens MBC v. Hill* 1991 a shop owner was held liable for the sale of tobacco to a young child even though he was absent from the shop when the sale was made. The court held that the sale must be regarded in the eyes of the law as having been made by the shop owner, and therefore he was liable as though he had sold the cigarettes himself.

As we have seen there is nothing to prevent a business organisation incurring liability for offences where liability is either strict or fault based, although it is more common to find liability arising in relation to the former. Examples of criminal liability which commonly effect business organisations and which are considered elsewhere in the text are those in fields of consumer protection and company law.

Tortious Liability in Business

A tort is a civil wrong, and a person or organisation committing a tort is someone who incurs tortious liability. Unlike a contract, where liability depends upon the making of an agreement, in tort liability arises without the need for any agreement between the parties but simply through the operation of the general law.

The civil law recognises a number of distinct areas of tortious liability, each of them resulting from the development of specific torts. Torts are designed to protect people from certain recognised kinds of harm, and to grant them legal remedies if they actually sustain harm as a consequence of a tort being committed against them. Tortious harm covers such areas as:

- the protection of business and personal reputations – *the tort of defamation*;

- the unlawful interference with another's land or personal property – *the tort of trespass*; and

- the unlawful interference with a person's use and enjoyment of land – *the tort of private nuisance*.

The basis upon which liability arises depends upon the specific rules governing each tort. Some torts, for instance, require no proof of fault on the part of the wrongdoer. The tort of *trespass to land* is an example. Another is the tort *of Rylands v. Fletcher*, where strict liability is imposed upon a landowner in respect of any damage caused by the escape of non-natural things brought onto the land. Relying on this tort, strict liability has been imposed for damage caused by escaping water, gas, electricity, germs and even people.

Tortious liability however is normally associated with fault, which involves establishing that the defendant failed to act as a reasonable person would have acted in a particular set of circumstances. Thus in the tort of negligence, a defendant who is not shown to be at fault will not incur liability.

In *Dixon v. London Fire and Civil Defence* 1993 water had leaked from a fire appliance onto the floor of the fire station. The court heard that such leaks were endemic in the fire service and appeared to be insoluble. As a consequence the court held that the fire authority was not in breach of the legal duty of care that it owed to a fire officer who had slipped and fallen as a result of the wet floor.

The tort of negligence is generally regarded as the most important of all the torts, and its impact upon business operations is potentially so significant that we need to look at it in some detail.

Negligence

The nature of liability in negligence

Liability in the tort of negligence arises where foreseeable damage to the plaintiff is caused by the defendant's breach of a legal duty to take care. The tort has wide application and includes liability for losses or injuries suffered at work, on the roads, in dangerous premises, or as a result of medical accidents, professional malpractice or defective products.

A central feature of liability in negligence is that liability is fault-based. A defendant will be liable only if the court is satisfied that he failed to take reasonable care. Negligence provides a mechanism for loss distribution and the apportionment of the risks inherent in activities likely to result in loss or injury. It can be argued that a fault-based system is far from ideal as a means of ensuring fair treatment and proper financial assistance to those who are injured or disabled through no fault of their own. Indeed it has often been said that the law of negligence is like a lottery in which a few successful litigants are handsomely rewarded. Many other claimants are unable to obtain compensation due to lack of evidence of fault, lack of a substantial defendant to pursue or the refusal of the court to impose liability in the circumstances of the case.

One alternative to a system of fault-based liability is the introduction of strict liability for injuries sustained either generally or in particular categories of situation. Under a system of strict liability the injured party should find it much easier to obtain compensation because he will not need to prove a failure to take care on the part of the defendant. Such a system could be financed centrally through taxation, for example an additional tax on petrol to finance a scheme for road accidents. Alternatively it could be funded by compulsory insurance for those who would be exposed to liability, for example medical practitioners in respect of medical accidents. A further alternative is to have a combination of both methods of funding. However the likelihood of the widespread introduction of strict liability for these and other categories of personal injuries in the foreseeable future is remote.

A notable exception is the introduction of strict liability for injuries caused by defective products to the customer in the Consumer Protection Act 1987. The effect of the 1987 Act has been to increase substantially the number of successful claims against manufacturers of defective products. The Act, however, does not impose an obligation on those affected to insure against the liability it creates, nor does it provide an independent source of funds to compensate claimants. It falls upon the individual businessman to make sure that his own insurance arrangements are adequate to cover the additional liability which he is likely to face. The Consumer Protection Act is explored in Chapter 12 on Consumer Protection Law

The significance of negligence liability for the businessman

A business is exposed to potential claims in negligence from a number of diverse sources. It is especially vulnerable because, under the rules of vicarious liability examined later, it is liable as an employer for wrongful acts committed by its employees in the course of their work. The prudent business will wish to take steps to minimise the liabilities to which it would otherwise be exposed. There are two things which it can do. First it can try to ensure that the business practices and the systems under which the employees operate are tightly structured and controlled so as to reduce the risk of injury and thereby prevent claims arising. Second it would be well advised to maintain an appropriate range of insurance policies to cover those risks which are most likely to affect the particular type of business it operates.

Types of insurance cover available

Insurance companies usually offer a wide range of policies and will arrange cover to meet the requirements of the individual business. Some types of cover are compulsory and therefore all businesses affected must have them; whilst others, although not compulsory, are such that no prudent businessman would consider it worthwhile to operate without them. Most businesses would be covered by all or most of the following types of policy:

(a)   *employers liability* – elsewhere we shall be considering the duty of care owed by the employer at common law to provide a safe system of work, safe equipment and premises and safe fellow employees; and examine the employer's liability in negligence for injury to an employee caused by a breach of any of these duties. Under the Employers Liability (Compulsory Insurance) Act 1969 all employers other than local authorities and nationalised industries are required to insure against the risk of personal injury to their employees. The insurance must be contained in an approved policy which has prescribed contents. The policy must be issued by an authorised insurer.

(b)   *motor vehicles* – under the Road Traffic Act 1988 the driver of a motor vehicle is required to be insured against third party personal injury and property risks. Most businesses running motor vehicles, and indeed most other motorists, obtain insurance cover well beyond the minimum laid down by the Act. Additional cover beyond the statutory minimum could include the risks of fire, theft of the vehicle, or full comprehensive cover which would include losses of the insured person's vehicle or property caused by his own fault.

(c)   *product liability* – a policy of this type is designed to cover liability for injury or losses caused by defective products manufactured or supplied by the insured in the course of his business. It should cover liabilities arising in contract, negligence or under the Consumer Protection Act 1987.

(d)   *public liability* – product liability cover is often included in this type of policy. The policy generally includes loss or injury sustained by a member of the public as a result of the activities of the business, for example liability under the Occupiers Liability Act 1957 for injury to a customer caused by the unsafe state of the business premises, or the organisation's liability in negligence resulting from an accident caused by an employee in failing safely to carry out his duties.

(e)   *premises and stock* – this provides insurance against loss of or damage to business property caused by fire, theft or negligence.

(f)   *professional indemnity* – a policy of this type covers the insured for claims made against him in respect of professional negligence, for example a claim against an architect for miscalculating the depth of the foundations of a multistorey building or specifying inadequate reinforcements for the structure. In some professions, for example, solicitors, professional indemnity insurance is in effect compulsory because the professional body will refuse to issue a *practising certificate* without evidence of premium payment on an appropriate policy.

(g)   *legal expenses insurance* – this is a relative newcomer to the UK insurance market and provides the insured with a full indemnity for legal costs incurred in engaging in legal action in the civil or criminal courts.

Having identified some of the major types of insurance cover available to protect the business from losses which could otherwise be incurred by the business, it is worth pointing out that the levels of cover, in terms of the financial limits on the claims that the insurer would satisfy, are a matter of commercial judgment which will depend on the nature of the business concerned.

Additionally, a business entering into a contract of insurance must disclose all material facts which could affect the insurer's assessment of the risk. It would also be well advised to examine carefully the detailed wording of the policy in order to be certain that it is actually getting the cover which it wants.

Because of the universal use of insurance by businesses, many of the commercial cases litigated before the courts are in reality disputes between insurance companies standing in the shoes of the named plaintiffs and defendants who have often already been paid out by the insurance companies.

Essential Elements of Liability in Negligence

In order to succeed in a claim in negligence the plaintiff will have to prove three things:

(a)   that the defendant owed him a legal duty of care,

(b)   that *the duty was broken*, and

(c)   that the defendant's breach of duty resulted in *foreseeable loss or damage* to the plaintiff.

Once the plaintiff has established these elements there are a number of defences available to the defendant. He may try to establish:

- that the plaintiff contributed to his injury by his own negligence - the defence of *contributory negligence*.

- that the plaintiff had voluntarily assumed the risk of injury - a defence based on consent known technically as a *volenti non fit injuria*, or

- that the plaintiff's claim is out of time and therefore *statute-barred* under the Limitation Act 1980 (as amended).

We shall now examine in more detail the elements of liability and the defences available in a negligence claim.

The Duty of Care

The tort of negligence is an area of legal liability which has been developed by the common law through the decisions of judges in individual cases over the centuries. The process is a continuing one and significant developments have taken place in recent years particularly in relation to the question of when a duty of care is owed by a defendant to the plaintiff.

The major milestone in the evolution of the law of negligence was the decision of the House of Lords in *Donoghue v. Stevenson* 1932 in which Lord Atkin laid down general principles which could be applied to any situation in order to determine whether a duty of care is owed. Prior to 1932 there were no legal principles of general application which defined the circumstances in which a person could be liable for loss or injury caused by his carelessness to another.

> The facts of *Donoghue v. Stevenson* 1932 are that the plaintiff's friend bought her a bottle of ginger beer in a cafe. The ginger beer was in an opaque bottle and, after pouring some of it and drinking from her glass, the remainder was poured from the bottle into the glass. This was found to contain the remains of a decomposed snail, the sight of which caused the plaintiff to suffer shock and become ill. As the drink was a gift from her friend, the plaintiff had no contract with the seller. She therefore sued the manufacturer claiming that he owed a duty of care to her to ensure that his product was not contaminated during the process of manufacture. The defendant argued that he owed no legal duty to the plaintiff because there was no contract between them and the case fell outside the existing recognised categories of duty. The House of Lords rejected the defendant's arguments and, by a slim majority of three judges to two, found for the plaintiff.

This case is important for two reasons. First, in the field of product liability, because Lord Atkin's judgment defines the duty of a manufacturer of a product towards a person injured by a defect in the product.

Second, in the context of the development of the law of negligence as a whole, because Lord Atkin in formulating the neighbour principle, laid down a unifying principle of liability for harm caused unintentionally by the defendant. For this reason the decision in *Donoghue* is often regarded as marking the birth of negligence as a tort. In the celebrated passage from his judgment Lord Atkin said *"The rule that you are to love your neighbour becomes in law, you must not injure your neighbour; and the lawyers question, Who is my neighbour? receives a restricted reply. You must take reasonable care to avoid acts or omissions which you can reasonably foresee would be likely to injure your neighbour. Who, then, in law is my neighbour? The answer seems to be - persons who are so closely and directly affected by my act that I ought reasonably to have them in contemplation as being so affected when I am directing my mind to the acts or omissions which are called in question"*

The defendant's duty is a duty to take reasonable care to avoid causing foreseeable harm and it is owed to anyone closely and directly affected by the defendant's conduct. The close relationship necessary between the defendant and plaintiff in order for a duty to exist is often referred to as a *relationship of proximity* between the parties.

The status of the neighbour principle as a rule of general applicability was underlined by the House of Lords in *Home Office v. Dorset Yacht Co.* 1970. Here the plaintiff's yacht was damaged by borstal trainees who had escaped while on a training exercise on an island. They had been carelessly left unsupervised by their guards. Applying the neighbour principle, it was held that the defendant owed a duty of care to the plaintiff whose yacht had been moored between the island and the mainland, as it was reasonably foreseeable that the trainees might use the yacht as a means of escape. The defendant was vicariously liable for the failure of its employees to supervise the trainees. This breach of duty caused the plaintiff's loss for which the Home Office was liable.In a leading judgment, Lord Reid stated *"Donoghue v. Stevenson may be regarded as a milestone, and the well known passage in Lord Atkin's speech should I think be regarded as a statement of principle. It is not to be treated as if it were a statutory definition. It will require qualification in new circumstances. But I think that the time has come when we can and should say that it ought to apply unless there is some justification or valid explanation for its exclusion."*

Lord Reid's statement implies that there may be cases in which a straight application of the neighbour principle will suggest the existence of a duty of care, but nevertheless the court would refuse to recognise a duty because there are valid justifications for failing to impose liability. The justifications which are used in these circumstances are often referred to as considerations of public policy. We can interpret this expression as meaning reasons based on judicial perceptions of what may or may not be in the best interests of the community at large. It is inevitable that policy issues arise in the course of deciding cases in negligence. This is because Parliament has rarely intervened to influence the direction of legal developments in this field by passing legislation. The judges have, therefore, found it necessary to make decisions on policy issues as part of the process of deciding cases and developing an acceptable coherent and workable body of legal rules.

It should be appreciated that in the majority of claims for personal injuries or damage to property, for example in the field of product liability, there will not be any policy considerations restricting the application of the neighbour principle in order to establish that a duty of care exists. It is in relation to claims for financial loss, for example in the area of professional negligence, that policy considerations - such as the fear of creating open-ended liability - may be taken in to account.

The views expressed by Lord Reid in *Home Office v. Dorset Yacht Co.* 1970 about the significance of the neighbour principle were supported by the House of Lords in *Anns v. London Borough of Merton* 1977. Lord Wilberforce explained the approach which a court should take in determining whether a duty of care exists in any given case *"... the position has now been reached that in order to establish that a duty of care arises in a particular situation, it is not necessary to bring the facts of that situation within those of previous situations in which a duty of care has been held to exist. Rather the question has to be approached in two stages. First, one has to ask whether, as between the alleged wrongdoer and the person who has suffered damage there is a sufficient relationship of proximity or neighbourhood such that, in the reasonable contemplation of the former carelessness on his part may be likely to cause damage to the latter, in which case a prima facie duty of care arises. Secondly, if the first question is answered affirmatively, it is necessary to consider whether there are any considerations which ought to negative, or to reduce or limit the scope of the duty or the class of person to whom it is owed or the damages to which a breach of it may give rise."*

The introduction of Lord Wilberforce's *two-stage* test led to a reassessment of the existence and scope of the duty of care in some situations. Some judges believed that it relieved them of the obligation to follow restrictive pre-1977 precedents and allowed them re-assess those situations having regard only to the two-stage test.

In a number of cases in the 1980's the House of Lords emphasised that the two stage approach to establishing a duty of care laid down in *Anns* was to be applied only to new situations not already the subject of precedent.

One of the first was the decision *in Leigh & Sillavan Ltd. v. Aliakmon Shipping Co. Ltd, The Aliakmon* 1986 where Lord Brandon, delivering a judgment with which the other presiding Law Lords were in complete agreement, expressed the view that the test applied only to novel types of factual situation and that the test was not to be applied where the situation was already covered by pre-1977 precedents. Referring to the two-stage test, Lord Brandon stated that it *"... does not provide, and cannot in my view have been intended by Lord Wilberforce to provide, a universally applicable test of the existence and scope of a duty of care in the law of negligence.."*

The process was taken further in *Curran v. Northern Ireland Co-ownership Housing Association Ltd.* 1987 when Lord Bridge, delivering the single judgment of the House of Lords, stated that the approach adopted in *Anns "may be said to represent the high water mark of a trend in the development of the law of negligence by your Lordship's House towards the elevation of the 'neighbourhood' principle ... into one of general application from which a duty of care may always be derived unless there are clear counterveiling considerations to exclude it."*

It is clear that the tide of judicial creativity which rose on the strength of the two-stage test in Anns, reached, for a relatively brief period, a high water mark from which it has steadily retreated as a result of a number of decisions both of the House of Lords and the Privy Council over recent years. The present position can perhaps best be summed up by quoting from the judgment of Lord Bridge in *Caparo Industries plc v. Dickman* 1990: *"What emerges is that, in addition to the foreseeability of damage, necessary ingredients in any situation giving rise to a duty of care are that there should exist between the party owing the duty and the party to whom it is owed a relationship characterised by the law as one of 'proximity' or 'neighbourhood' and that the situation should be one in which the court considers it fair, just and reasonable that the law should impose a duty of a given scope on the one party for the benefit of the other"..."*

The *Caparo* three stage approach to establishing a duty of care requires a positive response to three questions:

- was the harm caused reasonably foreseeable?

- was there a relationship of proximity between the defendant and the plaintiff?

- in all the circumstances is it just, fair and reasonable to impose a duty of care?

This approach has since been upheld by the Court of Appeal *in Marc Rich & Co. and others v. Bishop Rock Marine Co. Ltd. and others, The Nicholas H* 1994. Here the Court of Appeal held that the three stage approach to establishing a duty of care laid down in *Caparo* should be applied in every case where negligence is alleged. This universal test should be applied to all negligence cases whether the harm alleged is nervous shock, physical harm or purely financial loss. While such a consistant approach to establishing a duty of care is superficially attractive it should be appreciated that there will still be different factors to take account of in determining foreseeability, for example, in relation to physical harm as opposed to psychiatric illness. On a given set of facts one type of harm may be foreseeable, whilst another type may not.

In *Spring v. Guardian Assurance plc* 1994 the Court of Appeal decided that despite the fact that the giver of a reference which was factually incorrect had been negligent, there could be no liability, because a referee owes no duty of care to the subject of the reference. The House of Lords however disagreed. The Law Lords held that an employer can be liable in negligence for failure to take reasonable care in providing a reference for an employee or an ex-employee. This is because there is a proximate relationship between them and it is fair, just and reasonable that the employer should be under such a duty. A further justification for recognising this a duty is that the employer assumes responsibility for the reference and the employee relies on the employer to take reasonable care. It seems that the majority of the judges thought that as references are crucial in the recruitment process it is vital that they are written with reasonable care. It is in the public interest that the referee owes a legal duty of care to the subject of the reference.

Further guidance in relation to the extent of the duty of care was provided in *Kidd v. Axa Equity & Law Life Assurance Society plc* 2000. Here the High Court considered the extent of the duty of care owed by an employer when giving a reference. It was held that to impose an obligation on the employer to give a full frank and comprehensive reference was not in the public interest or even in the interest of employees since such a reference would have to include the bad as well as the good. Mr Justice Burton said that *"the duty owed by the giver of the reference to the subject of that reference, whether arising in tort or from contract, is a duty to take reasonable care not to give misleading information about him, whether as a result of the unfairly selective provision of information, or by the inclusion of facts and opinions in such a manner as to give rise to a false or mistaken inference in the mind of a reasonable recipient. The giver of a reference owes no additional duty to the subject to take reasonable care to give a full and comprehensive reference, or to include in a reference all material facts"*

The important decision of the House of Lords *in White and another v. Jones and others* 1995 considered the potential liability of defendant solicitors who caused the plaintiff's financial loss as a result of a negligent *omission*. The plaintiffs had originally been cut out of their father's (the testator) will but then reinstated on the testator's instructions to the defendant solicitors. The solicitors had delayed for over six weeks in carrying out the instructions to change the will and unfortunately, in the meanwhile, the testator died. As there was no contractual relationship between the plaintiffs and the defendants the action for financial loss could only be based on the tort of negligence. The central issue in the dispute was whether a solicitor in drafting a will owes a legal duty of care in the tort of negligence to a potential beneficiary. The High Court thought not. This decision was reversed on appeal and the solicitors then made a final appeal to the House of Lords. By a three to two majority decision their Lordships held that the potential loss to the plaintiffs in these circumstances was reasonably foreseeable and the relationship of a solicitor, called upon to draft a will, and the potential beneficiary, should be brought within the established categories of relationship under which a duty of care arises. This duty of care had been broken by the solicitor's negligence causing financial loss for which the defendants were liable.

The approach to establishing a legal duty of care where the damage is psychiatric harm was considered by the House of Lords in a number of cases which arose out of the tragic Hillsborough disaster in 1989. Claims were brought by the relatives of the 96 people who died and the 400 who were injured due to the negligence of South Yorkshire Police but rejected by the House of Lords in *Alcock v. Chief Constable of South Yorkshire Police* 1992 .

In *White v. Chief Constable of South Yorkshire Police* 1999 a claim for damages in the tort of negligence was brought by police officers who suffered post traumatic stress disorder as a result of tendering the dead and injured. They claimed that their employer owed them a duty of care as employees/rescuers to avoid exposing them to increasing risk of physical or psychiatric injury. Claims by police officers who had actually dragged dead and injured spectators from the scene and risked injury themselves had earlier been conceded and settled by their employers. By a majority the Court of Appeal held that a duty of care was owed to those officers at the ground who suffered psychiatric harm as rescuers and the primary victims of their employer's negligence. On further appeal to the House of Lords the decision was reversed by a majority and the door seems to be closed on further expansion of potential liability for psychiatric loss. The police officers could not be classified as primary victims of the defendants negligence for it does not follow that a duty to avoid causing physical harm extends to psychiatric injury except in stress related cases such as *Walker v. Northumberland County Council 1995* (see later in the chapter). Here the harm resulted from a traumatic experience as a secondary victim and as the police officers lacked the close ties of love and affection with the victims a duty of care could not extend to them. Also to qualify as rescuers their psychiatric harm must result from a fear of foreseeable physical injury and this was held not to be the case here.

Breach of Duty

Once it has been established that the defendant in a given situation owes a duty of care to avoid injury to the plaintiff, the next question which falls to be decided is whether the defendant was in breach of that duty. It should be stressed that these are two separate issues and only after the court is satisfied that a duty exists will it go on to consider the question of breach. A breach of duty is a failure to take reasonable care. This involves a finding of fault on the part of the defendant. In the words of *Alderson B. in Blyth v. Birmingham Waterworks Co.* 1856:

> *"Negligence (in the sense of a breach of duty) is the omission to do something which a reasonable man, guided upon those considerations which ordinarily regulate the conduct of human affairs, would do, or something which a reasonable and prudent man would not do."*

The duty of care is broken when a person fails to do what a reasonable man would do in the same circumstances. The standard of care required of the defendant in a particular case will vary according to the circumstances of the case and the skills which the defendant holds himself out as possessing. Thus a surgeon carrying out out an operation is required to demonstrate the skills and knowledge of a reasonably competent surgeon. On the other hand the degree of care expected of a hospital porter is not so exacting. Whilst the standard of care required of a skilled defendant such as a professional person will be high, the reverse cannot be said to be true. An inexperienced or unskilled defendant will not be able to argue that the standard of care which he is required to demonstrate is correspondingly low.

Thus in *Nettleship v. Weston* 1971 the Court of Appeal held that a learner driver was in breach of her duty of care to the plaintiff, a passenger, for failing to demonstrate the driving skills of a reasonably competent qualified driver, and was liable for the injuries sustained by the plaintiff as a result.

The same principle was applied by the Court of Appeal in *Wilsher v. Essex Area Health Authority* 1986 when it held, by a majority of two judges to one, that inexperience was no defence to an action in negligence against a junior doctor, who would be in breach of his duty of care if he failed to demonstrate the skill of a reasonably competent qualified doctor. On the facts of the case, however, the junior doctor had discharged his duty by asking a more senior colleague to check his work.

In determining whether a duty of care has been broken the court must assess the conduct of the defendant and decide whether he acted reasonably or unreasonably. This assessment allows the judge a large measure of discretion in an individual case, although it could be argued that it also produces some uncertainty in the law. The main factors which the court will take into account in deciding whether there has been a breach of the duty of care are:

- the extent of the risk created by the defendant's conduct - whether the risk was serious or obvious;

- the nature of the harm which is likely to be caused to the plaintiff;

- the practicability and expense of taking steps to minimise the risk;

- the particular circumstances of the case.

A good example of the way in which the courts attempt to balance these factors is provided by the case of *Bolton v. Stone* 1951.

In *Bolton v. Stone* 1951 the plaintiff was standing on the highway outside her home and was struck by a cricket ball hit by a visiting batsman off the pitch of the local cricket club. She sued the members and committee of the cricket club. The ground had been used for cricket since 1864, well before the surrounding houses were built. Balls were rarely hit out of the ground and onto the highway, perhaps only six times in the previous thirty years, and there was no record of any previous accident. The ball in question had travelled seventy-eight yards before passing over the fence and about twenty-five yards further before hitting the plaintiff. The top of the fence was seven feet about the highway and seventeen feet above the pitch. The House of Lords held that the defendants were not liable because they had taken reasonable care. The chances of such an accident were so slim that the reasonable man would have done no more than the defendants had done to prevent it from happening. In the course of his judgment, Lord Ratcliffe stated *"A breach of duty has taken place if the defendants are guilty of a failure to take reasonable care to prevent the accident. One may phrase it as reasonable care or ordinary care or proper care - all these phrases are to be found in decisions of authority - but the fact remains that, unless there has been something which a reasonable man would blame as falling beneath the standard of conduct that he would set for himself and require of his neighbour, there has been no breach of legal duty. It seems to me in this case that a reasonable man, taking account of the chances against an accident happening, would not have felt himself called upon either to abandon the use of the ground for cricket or to increase the height of his surrounding fences."*

Under the common law an employer owes a legal duty of care to ensure the health and safety of his employees. An employer is required to take reasonable care with regard to the safety of his employees by providing a safe system of work. The provision of a safe system of work involves an obligation to provide:

* safe fellow employees;

* safe plant and equipment;

* safe working methods;

* safe working premises.

It should be stressed that in civil proceedings it is often the case that a claim is based upon both the breach of a common law duty and for breach of statutory duty if relevant.

In *Smith v. Vange Scaffolding & Engineering Company Ltd. and Another* 1970 the plaintiff scaffolder suffered injury when he fell over a welding cable when walking back from his place of work. The High Court held that the employee's immediate employers were liable for breach of their common law duty of care because they were aware of the dangerous state of the site where their employees worked. In addition the employers were in breach of their statutory duty imposed, by regulation 6 of the Construction (working places) Regulations 1966, to provide a suitable and sufficient access to an egress from the plaintiff's place of work.

Certainly there is no intention that statutory regulation is designed to supersede the common law so that even if an employer has complied with a regulation, for instance to supply his workers with safety equipment, an employee is still entitled to pursue a claim under the common law if he is injured due to a failure to wear it.

In *Bux v. Slough Metals* 1973 the plaintiff lost the sight of one eye as a result of a splash from molten metal when he was pouring it into a die. While safety goggles had been supplied, the plaintiff refused to wear them because they misted up, and no attempt was made to persuade him otherwise. The Court of Appeal held that while the employer had provided suitable goggles for the purpose of safety regulations, they were nevertheless negligent under the common law. The evidence suggested that the plaintiff would have followed clear instructions to wear the goggles, and that the question whether or not an employer's common law duty of care extended to instructing, persuading or insisting on the use of protective equipment depended on the facts. By failing to make use of the goggles the plaintiff was guilty of contributory fault and damages were reduced by forty percent.

As far as safety equipment is concerned, the contemporary view seems to be that the common law duty to make it available and ensure that employees are aware of it does not necessarily carry with it any further obligation to inspect it or insist that it is worn. Obviously there is some obligation on the employee to take some responsibility for his own safety by ensuring that safety equipment is renewed when necessary.

In *Smith v. Scott Bowyers Ltd.* 1986 the plaintiff, who was just twenty years of age, and employed by the company for nineteen months, suffered injury when he slipped on the greasy factory floor. To help minimise the risk the employer provided the workers with wellington boots with diamond ridge soles and they were renewed on request. Having already replaced one pair of boots the accident was due to the plaintiff's failure to renew the replacement pair which had also worn out and were a danger. In an action for damages for breach of the employer's duty of care, the High Court found that the failure of the employers to emphasise the danger and carry out checks of the safety equipment made them in breach of the legal duty of care they owed to the plaintiff. Damages were to be reduced by one third however, due to the plaintiff's contributory fault. On appeal however, the Court of Appeal reversed the decision and held that there was no breach of the employer's duty to take reasonable care. The failure of the employee to renew the boots was due to his own lack of care and could not be taken as the fault of the employer. *"The employer's duty to provide employees with properly designed Wellington boots would not be filled out with any further obligation to instruct them to wear them or to inspect the condition of the soles from time to time."*

In *Pape v. Cumbria County Council* 1991 the plaintiff had been employed as a cleaner by the council for many years and her job involved the use of chemical cleaning materials and detergents. While rubber gloves were supplied they were rarely used the employer failing to point out the dangers of frequent contact of the skin with cleaners or encouraging the use of gloves. In 1982 the plaintiff was diagnosed as suffering from dermatitis and told by a consultant to protect her skin at work. This she did but her medical condition deteriorated so that all her skin became infected and in 1989 she gave up her job as a result. Mrs Pape claimed damages against her employer for negligence in that her dermatitis resulted from exposure to chemicals in the course of her employment and the employer was in breach of a clear duty to warn of the dangers and persuade staff to take preventative measures. The High Court awarded her £58,000 in damages stating that *"there is a duty on an employer to warn cleaners of the dangers of handling chemical cleaning materials with unprotected hands and to instruct them as to the need to wear gloves all the time. The argument on behalf of the defendant that an employer's duty to his office cleaners is fully discharged when he provides them with gloves could not be accepted."* The risk of dermatitis was not an obvious risk to the cleaners but should be appreciated by a reasonable employer.

The common law duty encompasses an obligation to provide safe plant and appliances. If an employer was aware that machinery or tools are not reasonably safe, and an employee is injured as a result, the employer will be in breach of his duty under the common law.

In *Bradford v. Robinson Rentals* 1967 the employer provided an unheated van for the employee, a 57 year old, to make a 400 mile journey during the winter, which would involve him in at least 20 hours driving. The court held that the employer was liable for the employee's frost bite, which was the type of injury that was reasonably foreseeable from prolonged exposure to severe cold and fatigue. The court also confirmed that even if the plaintiff had been abnormally susceptible to frost bite he would still be entitled to succeed under the rule that the defendant must take his victim as he finds him.

In the past an employer could satisfy his duty to provide safe equipment by showing that he purchased the equipment from a reputable supplier and that he had no knowledge of any defect. Under the Employers Liability (Defective Equipment) Act 1969, injury occurring to an employee under those circumstances may be attributed to the deemed negligence of the employer. If damages are awarded against the employer then it is up to him to seek a remedy from the supplier of the defective equipment.

In *Knowles v. Liverpool City Council* 1993 a council *"flagger"* was injured when a flagstone he was handling broke because it had not been properly cured by the supplier. He relied on the Employer's Liability (Defective Equipment) Act 1969 to impose liability on his employer who is deemed to be negligent if injury occurs as a result of equipment provided from a supplier. The main issue before the court was whether equipment defined as plant and machinery vehicles, aircraft and clothing, would cover a flagstone which seems to fall in the category of work materials. The Court of Appeal and subsequently the House of Lords agreed with the county court and held that the term equipment should be interpreted broadly to include *the "materials which an employee is given by his employer to use to do his job. Such a broad approach reflects the general purpose of the legislation and is consistent with the ordinary meaning of the word in the context of an employee carrying out his job"*. As a consequence the employer was liable under the 1969 Act for the injuries sustained by the plaintiff by the defective equipment used in the course of employment.

The obligation to provide a safe system of work also encompasses a requirement to provide safe fellow employees. If there are untrained or unskilled people employed at the workplace then a higher standard of care is owed by the employer to ensure their safety and the safety of those who work with them.

In *Hawkins v. Ross Castings Ltd.* 1970 the plaintiff was injured following a spillage of molten metal, due partly to the employer's failure to comply with safety regulations in relation to the maintenance of a safe pouring systems. An additional contributing factor was the fact that the plaintiff was working closely with a seventeen year old untrained Indian who spoke little English and yet was required to carry and pour molten metal with the plaintiff. This factor contributed to the employer's liability.

The conduct of fellow employees of contributing to an unhealthy working environment by smoking could be the responsibility of the employer in relation to an employee who suffers damage to health through passive smoking.

The duty to provide safe fellow employees exists irrespective of any issue of the employer's vicarious liability for the actions of his employees. Vicarious liability is considered later in the chapter. If an employee is injured through the negligence of some third party then the court must decide in the circumstances whether this constitutes a breach of the employer's duty of care and so imposing liability.

In *Reid v. Rush & Tompkins Group* 1989 the plaintiff driver claimed that his employer was in breach of their duty of care in failing to insure him or advising him to obtain insurance cover when driving abroad. The plaintiff had suffered severe injuries as a result of an accident which occurred in Ethiopia resulting from the negligence of another driver. Both the High Court and the Court of Appeal were reluctant to impose liability on the employer for the loss sustained by the employee. *"It was impossible to imply into the plaintiff's contract of service any term a breach of which would entitle him to recover damages from the defendants for the loss he sustained. There was no basis on the facts as pleaded for holding that the defendants gave an implied undertaking to insure his plaintiff against the risk of uncompensated injury caused to him, while acting in the course of his employment in Ethiopia, by third party drivers."*

The employer's common law duty also imposes an obligation to provide safe working methods and safe working premises. To determine whether an employer is providing safe working methods, it is necessary to consider a number of factors including:

- the layout of the work place;

- training and supervision;

- warnings; and

- whether protective equipment is provided.

It should be stressed that the common law duty on an employer is to take reasonable care, and if he gives proper instructions which the employee fails to observe then the employer will not be liable if the employee is then injured.

In *Charlton v. Forrest Printing Ink Company Ltd.* 1980 the employer gave proper instructions to an employee who was given the job of collecting the firm's wages. The instructions required the employee to vary his collecting arrangements to prevent robbery. The employee failed to do this and suffered severe injury when he was robbed. The Court of Appeal held that the employer was not liable as he had taken reasonable steps to cut down the risk. The normal industrial practice of firms of that size in that area was to make their own payroll collection rather than employ a security firm. The employers *"did what was reasonable in the circumstances to eliminate the risk and no more could have been expected of them. They could not be held liable for the injuries incurred by the employee"*.

It should be stressed that the common law duty is not one of strict liability but rather a duty to take reasonable care in the circumstances.

In *Latimer v. AEC* 1953 after a factory was flooded, the employer asked his workforce to return, warning them of the dangerous state of the factory floor.

Sawdust had been used to cover most of the damp areas but not enough was available, and the plaintiff slipped, and was injured. To determine whether the employer had broken the common law duty of care he owed his employees the court weighed the cost of avoiding the injury against the risk of injury and held that the employer had acted reasonably in the circumstances.

More recently in *Dixon v. London Fire and Civil Defence* 1993 the fire authority was held not to be in breach of its common law duty of care to an officer who slipped and fell as a result of a wet floor. The fact that water had leaked on to the floor of the fire station from an appliance did not constitute negligence for such an occurrence was endemic in the fire service and appeared to be insoluble.

If the plaintiff is a trained professional it may be reasonable to allow the employer to rely on the plaintiff's expertise without the need for warnings or instruction.

In *Woolgar v. West Surrey and Hampshire Health Authority* 1993 the Court of Appeal held that the defendant was not in breach of duty when it failed to warn a nurse against the use of a method of lifting a patient which caused the nurse back injury. The nurse should have realised the likely consequences of her action and used her own reasonable skill and judgement.

The courts have recognised that to require an employee to work long hours, which is related to health problems, could put an employer in breach of his common law duty.

In *Johnstone v. Bloomsbury Health Authority* 1991 the plaintiff, a senior house officer, was required to work forty hours by his contract with an additional average of forty eight hours per week on call. He alleged that some weeks he had been required to work for one hundred hours with inadequate sleep and as a consequence he suffered from stress, depression, diminished appetite, exhaustion and suicidal feelings. It was claimed that the employers were in breach of the legal duty to take reasonable care for the safety and well being of their employee by requiring him to work intolerable hours with deprivation of sleep. The majority of the Court of Appeal held that an employer's express contractual rights had to be exercised in the light of their duty to take care of the employee's safety and if the employer knew that they were exposing an employee to the risk of injury to health by requiring him to work such long hours, then they should not require him to work more hours than he safely could have done.

Although only a majority decision, the Court of Appeal by this judgment is recognising that the implied objective of health and safety in an employment contract may override a clear express contractual right in relation to the hours of work.

There is an increased recognition that individual employees may suffer stress as a direct result of their work. If an employer has reason to believe that this is the case and takes no steps to alleviate the problem there is now authority to suggest he could be in breach of duty.

In *Walker v. Northumberland CC* 1995 the High Court held that a local authority was in breach of duty if care to a senior social worker who was required to cope with an increased workload despite the fact the employer was aware of his susceptibility to mental breakdown. Mr Justice Coleman said that *"An employer owes a duty to his employees not to cause them psychiatric damage by the volume or character of the work which they are required to perform. Although the law on the extent of the duty on an employer to provide an employee with a safe system of work and to take reasonable steps to protect him from risks which are reasonably foreseeable has developed almost exclusively in cases involving physical injury to the employee, there is no logical reason why risk of injury to an employee's mental health should be excluded from the scope of the employer's duty. The standard of care required for performance of that duty must be measured against the yardstick of reasonable conduct on the part of a person in the employer's position. What is reasonable depends on the nature of the relationship, the magnitude of the risk of injury which was reasonably foreseeable, the seriousness of the consequences for the person to whom the duty is owed of the risk eventuating, and the cost and practicability of preventing the risk. The practicability of remedial measures must take into account the resources and facilities at the disposal of the person or body who owes the duty of care, and purpose of the activity which has given rise to the risk of injury".*

It should be noted that a material fact in deciding liability in the Walker case was that the plaintiff complained of his employers breach of duty in relation to a second nervous breakdown which was reasonably forseeable. Previously Mr Walker had suffered a breakdown due to the stress caused by his heavy workload which was not reasonably foreseeable and for which there would have been no breach of duty. By allowing Mr Walker to be exposed to the same workload as before however the employer should have appreciated that he was as a result of the first breakdown more vulnerable to psychiatric damage.

Employers should be aware of the case of stress and can obtain that stress by carrying out a full assessment of

- factors that could lead to stress including the stress levels of particular job functions

- training requirements for staff, particularly those changing job functions

- individual needs and the requirement to record individual progress

- potential signs of deterioration due to work loads.

In *Lancaster v. Birmingham City Council* 1999 the employee had been moved from a technical environment to a customer contact role in the housing department. Unfortunately no adequate training had been provided to deal with the particular stresses that the job entailed. When she suffered mental illness as a result of the change the court found that the employers had taken no obvious steps to deal with the problem. An award of £67,000 in damages was made against her employer.

In *Pickford v. Imperial Chemical Industries* 1998 a secretary who suffered *repetitive strain injury* due to her secretarial duties claimed that her employer had been negligent in failing to instruct her about the need for rest breaks and work organisation to alleviate the need for long periods of typing. By a majority decision the Court of Appeal reversed the decision of the High Court and found that the employer was in breach of the duty of care he owed to his employee. A majority of the House of Lords however reversed the court Appeal and confirmed the decision of the High Court and dismissed the claim. They felt that Ms Pickford as a general secretary had a number of duties other than typing and would have organised her own rest periods from the word processor. In addition they thought that the medical evidence was insufficient to prove that her condition was caused by repetitive movements while typing.

The standard of care owed by an employer will vary with regard to each individual employee. A young apprentice should be provided with effective supervision while this may not be required for an experienced employee.

In *Paris v. Stepney BC* 1951 the plaintiff, a one-eyed motor mechanic, lost the sight of his good eye while working at chipping rust from under a bus. Despite there being no usual practice to provide mechanics with safety goggles, the court decided that they should have been provided to the plaintiff. The defendants were liable as they could foresee serious consequences for the plaintiff if he suffered eye injury. *"The special risk of injury is a relevant consideration in determining the precautions which the employer should take in the fulfilment of the duty of care which he owes to the workman."*

If an employer is in breach of the implied common law duty that he owes to an employee this could lead to a claim for unfair constructive dismissal.

Proof of the defendant's breach of duty

The normal rule in a civil case is that the plaintiff must adduce evidence to prove his case on balance of probabilities. It will therefore be the plaintiff's job, in a negligence case, to show that the defendant did not act in a reasonable way. If he is unable to do this his claim will fail.

> In *Wakelin v. London and South Western Railway Co.* 1886 the body of the plaintiff's husband was found near a level crossing on a railway. He had been hit by a train but there was no evidence to suggest what had happened. The accident could have been his own fault or it could have been attributable to the fault of the defendant. As the plaintiff was unable to prove that the defendant acted in an unreasonable manner, her claim failed.

The difficulty involved in proving that a defendant is in breach of the duty of care is illustrated by the legal claims arising from the injuries caused to unborn children by the drug Thalidomide. Although legal proceedings were issued in the UK, none of the claims were ever brought before the courts. There were two main legal reasons for this. Firstly because it was not certain that a duty of care could be owed to an unborn child (this has since been established by legislation under the Congenital Disabilities (Civil Liability) Act 1976). Secondly because the plaintiffs would probably have been unable to prove that the defendants had failed to take reasonable care. The drug had undergone extensive testing before it was released onto the market. Although it had not been tested on pregnant women, it is not clear that a reasonable drug manufacturer would have tested a drug of that type - a tranquilliser - for its effect upon the developing child within the womb of the pregnant woman, given the state of scientific knowledge within the pharmaceutical industry at that time. After protracted negotiations an out of court settlement was reached between the parties on terms dictated by the defendants. The levels of agreed compensation were widely regarded as being well below those which might have been awarded at the conclusion of a successful trial. Some observers believe that the defendants would not even have agreed to settle the claims on those terms had it not been for the considerable pressure of public opinion and the efforts of a well organised group of the defendant company's own shareholders on the plaintiffs' behalf.

Res ipsa loquitur

In some cases the plaintiff may be relieved of the burden of proving negligence if the court accepts a plea of *res ipsa loquitur* (the thing speaks for itself). This is a rule of evidence which applies where the plaintiff's injury is one that would not in the ordinary course of events have happened without negligence and there is no satisfactory alternative explanation for the injury other than negligence by the defendant.

The effect of the rule is that the court will infer negligence on the part of the defendant without the need for the plaintiff to pinpoint the cause of the injury or explain how the defendant failed to take reasonable care. The defendant will be liable unless he furnishes evidence to show that his negligence did not cause the plaintiff's loss.

The rule will be of great assistance to the plaintiff where it seems to be obvious that the defendant was negligent but the plaintiff is unable to pinpoint the exact nature of the defendant's breach of duty.

In *Scott v. London and St. Catherine Docks Co.* 1865 a customs officer was injured when six sacks of sugar fell on him as he was passing the defendant's warehouse. The court held that the res ipsa loquitur rule applied and inferred negligence on the part of the defendant which it was unable to disprove. During the course of his judgment, Erle, C.J. stated: *"Where the thing is shown to be under the management of the defendant, or his servants, and the accident is such as, in the ordinary course of things, does not happen if those who have the management use proper care, it affords reasonable evidence, in the absence of explanation by the defendant, that the accident arose from want of care."*

In *Cassidy v. Ministry of Health* 1951, the plaintiff was injured in a surgical operation on his hand. Denning, L.J. asserted that the res ipsa loquitur rule enabled the plaintiff to say, in effect: *"... I went into hospital to be cured of two stiff fingers. I have come out with four stiff fingers, and my hand is useless. That should not have happened if due care had been used. Explain it, if you can."* The defendant was held liable as he was unable to explain how such a result was consistent with the use of reasonable care.

In *Ward v. Tesco Stores* 1976 the plaintiff was injured when she slipped on a pool of yoghurt which had previously been spilled onto the floor of the defendant's supermarket and had not been cleaned up. The Court of Appeal applied the *res ipsa loquitur* rule and the defendant was held liable as it was unable to show that it had taken reasonable care.

Resulting Damage

The third essential element of liability in negligence is that the defendant's breach of duty resulted in foreseeable loss or damage to the plaintiff. In reality this involves two separate issues - the issues of *causation* and *remoteness* of damage.

Causation of damage

The causation issue is concerned with the question of cause and effect: was the defendant's breach of duty the operative cause of the plaintiff's loss. The plaintiff's claim will fail if he is unable to prove this link. He must show that but for the defendant's negligence his loss would not have occurred.

> In *Barnett v. Chelsea and Kensington Hospital Management Committee* 1969 the plaintiff's husband was a night watchman, who called at the defendant's hospital in the early hours of the morning complaining of vomiting. He was sent home without being examined and was told to contact his own doctor later that day. He was suffering from arsenic poisoning and died a few hours later. The court held that the defendants were in breach of their duty of care, but the claim failed because the negligence of the hospital had not caused the death. The court accepted on the evidence that even if he had been examined immediately, the plaintiff's husband would still have died from arsenic poisoning.

Remoteness of damage

Where the plaintiff proves that his injuries were caused by the defendant's breach of duty, he can recover damages provided that his injuries were not too remote a consequence of the breach. The law does not necessarily impose liability for all of the consequences of a negligent act. Some damage may be too remote. Only damage which was reasonably foreseeable at the time of the negligent act can be recovered by the plaintiff.

> In *The Wagon Mound* 1961 a large quantity of fuel oil was carelessly spilled by the defendant's employees while a ship was taking on fuel in Sydney Harbour. Some of the oil spread to the plaintiff's wharf where welding operations were taking place. The plaintiff stopped welding temporarily, but recommenced after receiving expert opinion that fuel oil would not ignite when spread on water. Two days later the oil ignited when a drop of molten metal fell onto a piece of waste floating in the oil, causing extensive damage to the plaintiff's wharf. The court found as a fact that it was not reasonably foreseeable that the oil would ignite in these circumstances. It was held that the damage to the wharf was too remote, and the plaintiff's claim failed.

Once it has been established that the type of injury the plaintiff has suffered is foreseeable, then the defendant is potentially liable for all the injury of that type which occurs.

> The common law rule that a defendant must *"take the plaintiff as he finds him"* was illustrated in *Page v. Smith* 1995. Here the plaintiff was the victim

of a road accident caused by negligent driving. He was physically unhurt but had suffered psychiatric injury from the accident. The plaintiff had suffered from the illness myalgic encephalomyelitis (ME) sporadically for many years and the accident had caused it to become chronic. The Court of Appeal held that even though the plaintiff was directly involved in the accident, nervous shock had to be reasonably foreseeable to establish a duty of care, and in the circumstances of this accident such an injury could not have been foreseen. By a majority however, the House of Lords disagreed. They held that in negligent driving cases, to establish a duty of care it is necessary to show that personal injury of *some kind* was reasonably foreseeable, whether physical or psychiatric. In this case therefore the fact that no physical injury, but rather nervous shock resulted from the accident, did not prevent a legal duty of care being established. The defendant was liable for the full extent of the psychiatric injury on the principle that since the duty of care was established he had to take his victim as he found him.

The plaintiff's damage may be held to be too remote where an unforeseen new independent act, outside the defendant's control, intervenes to break the chain of causation. If the plaintiff's damage is caused by such a *novus actus interveniens* the defendant will not be liable for it. For example an employer's liability for injury suffered by an employee at work will not extend to further injuries received in the course of negligent medical treatment in hospital.

In *Cobb v. Great Western Railway* 1894 the defendant allowed a railway carriage to become overcrowded. As a result the plaintiff's pocket was picked and he lost nearly £100. It was held that the act of the thief was a novus actus interveniens and therefore that the plaintiff's loss was too remote.

Liability for Financial Loss

In the business world it is often the case that the negligent act or statement of an individual or organisation results in anothers financial loss. If the advice is given in the context of a contract the victim will have a potential remedy for breach. If however the innocent victim is a third party then the only cause of action is a claim in the tort of negligence. The basis and scope of a duty of care will depend whether the claim is based upon:

- financial loss caused by negligent statements

- financial loss caused by negligent acts.

Financial loss caused by negligent statements

Prior to the decision of the House of Lords in *Hedley Byrne v. Heller* 1964 it was well settled law that there could be no liability in tort for financial loss caused by negligently made statements. In *Candler v. Crane, Christmas & Co.* 1951, for example, the Court of Appeal by a majority held that a false statement, carelessly made, was not actionable in the tort of negligence. Lord Denning dissented and was prepared to recognise the existence of a duty of care where the defendant had some special knowledge or skill upon which the plaintiff relied. He stated *"From early times it has been held that persons who engage in a calling which requires special knowledge and skill owe a duty of care to those who are closely and directly affected by their work, apart altogether from any contract or undertaking in that behalf."*

The judgment of Lord Denning was approved by the house of Lords in *Hedley Byrne v. Heller*, and the decision of the majority in the Candler case was overruled.

> In *Hedley Byrne & Co. v. Heller and Partners Ltd.* 1964 the plaintiffs were advertising agents whose clients, Easipower Ltd, were customers of the defendant merchant bank. The plaintiffs had been instructed to buy advertising space for Easipower's products on television and in the newspapers. This involved them in the expenditure of large sums of money. Never having dealt with Easipower before, the plaintiffs sought a reference as to their credit worthiness to the extent of £100,000 from the defendant. The reference was given `without responsibility on the part of the bank' and stated with reference to Easipower: *"Respectably constituted company, considered good for its ordinary business engagements. Your figures are larger than we are accustomed to see"*. In fact Easipower had an overdraft with the bank, which ought to have known that the company would have difficulty meeting payments to the plaintiff. Within one week of giving the reference the bank was pressing Easipower to reduce its overdraft. Relying on the reference the plaintiffs incurred personal liability by placing advertising contracts. Easipower then went into liquidation due to insolvency and as a result the plaintiffs lost over £17,500. The actual decision in the case was that the defendant was not liable as the disclaimer of responsibility was effective to prevent the bank from assuming a duty of care.

The principal importance of the decision, however, is that the House of Lords recognised the existence, in certain circumstances, of a duty of care in relation to financial loss caused by negligently made statements. Lord Morris stated:

> *"if someone possessed of a special skill undertakes, quite irrespective of contract, to apply that skill for the assistance of another person who relies upon such skill, a duty of care will arise."*

Lord Pearce expressed the view that the duty would only arise in relation to a statement about *"a business or professional transaction whose nature makes clear the gravity of the inquiry and the importance and influence attached to the answer"*.

For reasons of public policy, the scope of the duty and the class of persons to whom it is owed was restricted by the House of Lords. The main policy reason for this was a reluctance to create open ended liability by exposing a defendant to claims by numerous plaintiffs for a single instance of negligence. In Lord Reid's view the danger of 'opening the floodgates' in this way was particularly acute for a number of reasons: *"I would think that the law must treat negligent words differently from negligent acts... Quite careful people often express definite opinions on social or informal occasions even when they see that others are likely to be influenced by them; and they often do so without taking that care which they would take if asked for their opinion professionally or in a business connection... But it is at least unusual casually to put into circulation negligently made articles which are dangerous... Another obvious difference is that a negligently made article will only cause one accident and so it is not very difficult to find the necessary degree of proximity or neighbourhood between the negligent manufacturer and the person injured. But words can be broadcast with or without the consent or the foresight of the speaker or writer. It would be one thing to say that the speaker owes a duty to a limited class, but it would be going very far to say that he owes a duty to every ultimate 'consumer' who acts on those words to his detriment."*

For these reasons the House of Lords held that in order for a duty to arise there must be a special relationship of reliance between the parties. It was characterised by Lord Devlin as a relationship equivalent to a contract (albeit lacking the essential ingredient of consideration). A useful definition of the special relationship of reliance was given by Lord Reid who said that it included: *"... all those relationships where it is plain that the party seeking information or advice was trusting the other to exercise such a degree of care as the circumstances required, where it is reasonable for him to do that, and where the other gave the information or advice when he knew or ought to have known that the inquirer was relying on him."*

Clearly there would be no special relationship of reliance in respect of casual remarks in the course of conversation on a social or informal occasion. In any event the person who is asked for information or an opinion could refuse to give it; make clear that it was given without careful consideration, or, as happened in the Hedley Byrne case, disclaim responsibility for it. In Lord Reid's opinion: *"A reasonable man, knowing that he was being trusted or that his skill and judgment were being relied on, would, I think, have three courses open to him. He could keep silent or decline to give the information or advice sought: or he could give an answer with a clear qualification that he accepted no responsibility for it or that it was given without that reflection or inquiry which a careful answer would require: or he could simply answer without any such qualification. If he chooses to adopt the last course he must, I think, be held to have accepted some responsibility for his answer being given carefully, or to have accepted a relationship with the inquirer which requires him to exercise such care as the circumstances require."*

Where the person making the statement excludes liability for it or states that it is given without responsibility, the Unfair Contract Terms Act 1977 applies with the result that the disclaimer will be invalid unless the person who made the statement proves that it is fair and reasonable in the circumstances to allow reliance on the disclaimer. It may be then that a case with similar facts to those of *Hedley Byrne v. Heller* would be decided differently if it came before the courts today.

The test for determining whether a duty of care exists outside a contract in relation to careless statements causing financial loss is whether a special relationship of reliance exists between the parties. This is narrower in its scope than the neighbour principle and under it the duty will be established if the plaintiff can prove:

- that the defendant possessed special skill or knowledge,

- that the plaintiff relied on the defendant to exercise care,

- that the defendant knew or ought to have know that the plaintiff was relying on him, and

- that reliance by the plaintiff was reasonable in the circumstances.

Financial loss caused by negligent acts

It has been a long-standing principle of law of negligence that pure financial loss caused by a negligent act rather than a statement is not recoverable.

> Thus for example in *Weller Co. v. Foot & Mouth Disease Research Institute* 1965 the defendants carried out research into foot and mouth disease, a highly infectious disease affecting cattle. The virus escaped from their premises and affected cattle in the surrounding area. As a result restrictions on the movement of cattle were introduced and two cattle markets belonging to the plaintiff auctioneers had to be closed. The plaintiffs sued for loss caused to their business. It was held that, because the loss was purely financial and not connected with any physical harm caused to the plaintiffs or their property, no duty of care was owed by the defendants to the plaintiffs, and the claim failed.

The major policy reason for refusing to recognise a duty of care for pure financial loss is that it could lead to open ended liability. In the *Weller* case, for example, the closure of the markets would have affected the businesses of all those who transported cattle to and from the markets; of the shops, cafes and public houses in the vicinity of the markets; of the banks which would have handled the money in the sale and purchase of cattle; and the destruction of cattle caused by the escape of the virus could have adversely affected the economic interests of cattle feed suppliers, agricultural workers and milkmen, with substantial knock-on effects throughout the local economy. If the defendants were not to be liable for all of these consequences, the line of legal liability has to be drawn restrictively. Thus claims can be brought for injury to the person and damage to property, and for financial losses which are closely associated with such injury or damage. However, with one exception discussed below, claims for pure financial loss caused by the defendant's negligent act are not allowed. The extent of a plaintiff's financial loss may not readily be foreseen by the defendant before the negligent act occurs and the plaintiff will be in the best position to assess the extent and insure against the risk of financial loss.

Financial loss directly associated with physical injury may be referred to as consequential rather than pure financial loss. Here the defendant may owe a duty to the plaintiff under the neighbour principle. An example of the distinction between these types of financial loss can be seen in the following case:.

In *Spartan Steel & Alloys Ltd. v. Martin & Co. (Contractors) Ltd.* 1972 the defendant's employee, while digging up a road with a mechanical excavator, carelessly damaged an electricity supply cable and cut off the power to the plaintiff's factory. In order to prevent damage to a furnace, the molten metal in it had to be poured off before it solidified. The melt was damaged to the value of £368, and the plaintiffs lost the profit of £400 which they would have made had the process been completed. The electricity supply was cut off for 14 hours during which four additional melts could have been processed. The profit on the additional melts would have been £1,767. The Court of Appeal held that the first two items claimed were recoverable - these were damage to property and consequential financial loss. The loss of profits on additional melts, however, was a pure financial loss not sufficiently connected with the physical damage and therefore not recoverable.

A 1982 decision of the House of Lords has created an exception to the rule that no duty can be owed in respect of pure financial loss unassociated with physical damage.

In *Junior Books Ltd. v. Veitchi Co. Ltd.* 1982 the plaintiff engaged a main contractor to build a new factory. The main contractor, at the request of the plaintiff, engaged the defendant to lay the floor of the building. The defendant was therefore a nominated sub-contractor and had no contractual relationship with the plaintiff. Due to the defendant's failure to mix and lay the floor with reasonable care, the floor began to crack up leaving the plaintiff with an unserviceable building bearing high maintenance costs. The plaintiff ceased production, had the floor relaid and sued the defendant for all the costs and losses incurred by him. The defendant denied that he owed a duty to the plaintiff in respect of that part of the claim which represented pure financial loss. The House of Lords, by a majority, held the defendant liable for the full claim, including the element of pure financial loss. The duty of care was thus extended beyond one of preventing physical harm being done by faulty work to a duty to avoid the presence of defects in the work itself and to avoid the resultant financial losses. Lord Fraser, in his judgment, stressed that he was deciding the case *"strictly on its own facts. I rely particularly on the very close proximity between the parties."* After discussing the floodgates argument Lord Fraser continued: *"The proximity between the parties is extremely close, falling only just short of a direct contractual relationship. The injury to the plaintiff was a direct and foreseeable result of negligence by the defendants. The plaintiffs nominated the defendants as specialist sub-contractors and they must therefore have relied on their skill and knowledge."*

The *Junior Books* case has been treated in subsequent cases as laying down a narrow exception to a general principle, rather than as a springboard for the extension of liability. Thus in *Muirhead v. Industrial Tank Specialities* 1985, discussed in the context of product liability, the Court of Appeal refused to extend the duty to a manufacturer of defective electric motors which caused financial loss to the ultimate consumer. The decision was made on the grounds that there was not a sufficient degree of close proximity between the plaintiff and the defendant to give rise to a duty of care to avoid causing financial loss.

In *D & F Estates Ltd. v. Church Commissioners for England* 1988 the third defendants, who were builders, had been employed to erect flats on land owned by the Church Commissioners. The plaintiff, a tenant of one of the flats, found that the plaster on the wall of its flat was loose, and sued the builders for the cost of replastering the flat. The basis of the claim was that the plastering was defective in quality. There was no allegation that it had caused damage to other property of the plaintiff or that it had caused personal injury. The claim was therefore to recover damages for pure economic loss in the tort of negligence. The House of Lords held that the builders were not liable as such losses are irrecoverable. The decision in *Junior Books v. Veitchi* was treated as *"not laying down any principle of general application"*, and as being dependent upon the finding of a *"unique, albeit non-contractual relationship"* and the ratio of Junior Books was effectively confined to its own particular facts.

In any case in which a plaintiff claims damages for economic loss resulting from damage to property caused by a negligent act, it should be noted that the plaintiff cannot succeed unless he has a proprietary or possessory interest in the property at the time the damage occurs.

In *Leigh & Sillavan Ltd. v. Aliakmon Shipping Co. Ltd. The Aliakmon* 1986 the House of Lords held that the buyer under an export contract, to whom the ownership of the goods had not passed, but to whom the risk of accidental destruction had been transferred by the terms of the contract, could not sue the shipowner in negligence for pure financial loss caused to him by the fact that the goods were damaged whilst in transit on board ship, as he had no proprietary or possessory interest in the goods at the time they were damaged.

The law relating to potential negligence liability for the supply of goods and services, including professional services, is explored in Chapter 12 on Consumer Protection Law.

Defences to a Negligence Action

Contributory negligence

Where the plaintiff has successfully established all of the elements of a negligence action, but has in some way contributed to his injuries by his own negligence, the defendant may raise the defence of contributory negligence.

Section 1(1) of the Law Reform (Contributory Negligence) Act 1945 provides:

> "*Where any person suffers damage as the result partly of his own fault and partly of the fault of any other person or persons, a claim in respect of that damage shall not be defeated by reason of the fault of the person suffering the damage, but the damages recoverable in respect thereof shall be reduced to such extent as the court thinks just and equitable having regard to the claimant's share in the responsibility for the damage.*"

The effect of this provision is simply that the plaintiff's damages will be reduced in direct proportion to the extent to which he is to blame for his injuries.

In *Davies v. Swan Motor Co. (Swansea) Ltd. (third party James)* 1949 the plaintiff's damages were reduced by 20% when he was held to be contributorily negligent. He was riding on the back of a dust lorry contrary to his employer's instructions and was injured when the dust lorry was in collision with a bus.

In *Stapley v. Gypsum Mines* 1953 the plaintiffs were miners who, contrary to specific instructions by their employer, worked under a dangerous roof. They were injured when the roof collapsed and fell in on them. Their damages were reduced by 80% for contributory negligence.

In *Froome v. Butcher* 1976 it was held that the failure to wear a seat belt was contributory negligence and that the appropriate reduction in damages was 25% if the seat belt would have prevented the injury altogether, or 15% if it would merely have reduced the extent of the injury.

In *Sayers v. Harlow* UDC 1958 the plaintiff became locked inside a public lavatory because of the defendant's negligence in failing to maintain the door lock. After failing to attract attention or assistance, she attempted to climb out over the top of the door. In doing so she fell and was injured. It was held that the defendant was liable in negligence, but the plaintiff's damages were reduced by 25% for contributory negligence.

Voluntary assumption of risk (volenti non fit injuria)

This defence, which is universally referred to by its latin name *volenti non fit injuria*, is available to the defendant where the plaintiff freely and voluntarily accepts a risk of which he has full knowledge. In modern times the courts have been reluctant to apply the defence, which has the effect of completely defeating the plaintiff's claim, other than in exceptional circumstances. The reason for this is that the type of behaviour which would come within the defence would also usually amount to contributory negligence. The courts probably take the view that a more just outcome can be achieved by applying the rules of contributory negligence.

In *Smith v. Charles Baker & Sons* 1891 the plaintiff was employed in the excavation of a railway cutting. He was injured by a stone which fell from an overhead crane. He had known that there was an element of risk in working beneath the crane but had not objected to his employer. As a defence to his action for compensation, the employer argued that the plaintiff had voluntarily undertaken the risk of injury. The House of Lords held that the employer was liable. The defence failed because mere knowledge of the risk was not the same as consent to the danger. Lord Herschell stated the volenti rule in the following terms: *"One who has invited or assented to an act being done towards him cannot, when he suffers from it, complain of it as a wrong ... if then, the employer thus fails in his duty towards the employed, I do not think that because (the employee) does not straightaway refuse to continue his service, it is true to say that he is willing that his employer should act thus towards him. I believe it would be contrary to the facts to assert that the plaintiff in this case either invited or assented to the employer's negligence."*

In *Bowater v. Rowley Regis Corporation* 1944 the plaintiff was employed as a carter, and was ordered to take out a particular horse to pull his cart. He protested because the horse was known to be vicious but his protests were in vain. He was injured by the horse and in an action for damages the defendant raised the defence of *volenti non fit injuria*. It was held that the defence was inapplicable because the plaintiff had not genuinely consented to run the risk. In reality he had little choice but to take out the horse.

The defence of *volenti non fit injuria* will not usually be available where the plaintiff has been injured while attempting to rescue someone from a peril created by the defendant's negligence. In these circumstances the rescuer cannot normally be regarded as having freely consented to the risk of injury.

> In *Haynes v. Harwood* 1935 for example, a policeman was injured while stopping a runaway horse and cart which endangered the safety of members of the public, including children, in a busy street. It was held that, in the circumstances, he had at least a moral duty to intervene, and his claim for damages succeeded.

By way of contrast in *Cutler v. United Dairies Ltd.* 1933 the plaintiff intervened to stop a runaway horse within a field. It posed no risk of injury to anyone. The plaintiff was unable to recover damages for the injuries which he sustained as the court held that he had voluntarily assumed the risk of injury.

Exclusion of liability for negligence

Under the rules of common law it used to be possible for a defendant to exclude his liability for negligence, either by including an appropriately worded term in a contract, or by displaying a notice to that effect.

> In *White v. Blakemore* 1972, for example, the plaintiff's husband, a member of a racing club, stood next to the ropes near a stake watching a race. The wheel of a racing car caught on the rope pulling the stake out of the ground. The stake killed the plaintiff's husband. Notices had been displayed by the defendant in prominent positions excluding all liability for accidents howsoever caused. It was held that the notices were effective to protect the defendant from liability.

Since the introduction of the Unfair Contract Terms Act 1977, however, the scope of the common rules have been considerably cut down. Under s.2 of the 1977 Act liability for death or personal injury caused by negligence cannot be excluded, but that it may be possible to exclude liability for other types of damage or loss. Such an exclusion will only be effective however if the defendant can prove that it is fair and reasonable to allow reliance on it in the circumstances of the case.

Time limits for claims in negligence

The Limitation Act 1980, as amended by the Latent Damage Act 1986, provides that no legal action may be taken in respect of certain types of claim unless proceedings are issued within the limitation period. After this time the claim is said to be statute barred and the court will refuse to entertain it. The limitation period varies according to the legal basis of the claim and the type of injury or damage suffered by the plaintiff.

(a)   Personal injuries or death

Personal injury claims in negligence and in contract are subject to a limitation period of three years. Time starts to run either on the date on which the right to sue first arises, or, if later, on the date on which the plaintiff is aware:

- that he has suffered significant injury,

- that this is attributable to the defendant's negligence or breach of contract, and

- of the identity of the defendant.

Where this formula applies there is no final long term cut off date after which the plaintiff's claim cannot be brought. The plaintiff will usually use this formula when he is suing for injuries which did not manifest themselves at the time of the negligent act. This could apply if, for example, the plaintiff contracted a lung disease through exposure to industrial dust from asbestos or coal, and the disease did not become apparent for a number of years.

(b)   Claims other than personal injury

In the case of a claim which does not involve personal injury, for example for property damage or financial loss, the limitation period both in negligence and in contract is six years from the date on which the right to sue first arises. In the case of a negligence claim for this type of loss the Latent Damage Act 1986 enables the plaintiff to commence legal proceedings outside the six year period the 1986 Act does not apply to a contract claim. Under the Act the claim must be made within three years of the date on which the plaintiff became aware:

- that the damage was significant,

- that it was attributable to the negligence of the defendant, and

- of the identity of the defendant.

Under the 1986 Act, however, the limitation period cannot be extended beyond 15 years of the date of the event which constituted the defendant's breach of duty. As we noted above there is no such *long stop* date beyond which the period for bringing a personal injuries claim cannot be extended.

One of the principal reasons for the introduction of the Latent Damages Act 1986 was to provide an effective remedy for a person in the situation of the plaintiff in the case of *Pirelli v. Oscar Faber*.

> In *Pirelli General Cable Works Ltd. v. Oscar Faber & Partners* 1983 the defendants were consulting engineers who advised the plaintiffs on the design and erection of a large chimney for the boiler at their factory. The design was defective and expert evidence showed that internal cracks had occurred within the chimney before April 1970. The damage was not discovered, however, until 1977 and the plaintiff did not commence legal proceedings until 1978. The House of Lords held that the six year limitation period began to run as soon as the damage occurred and therefore the claim was statute barred. The limitation period had expired even before the plaintiffs knew that they had suffered any damage.

Under the provisions of the 1986 Act the issue of limitation would have been decided in the plaintiff's favour on the facts of the *Pirelli* case. The Act is designed to eliminate this type of injustice.

Business Premises and Liability

Occupiers of business premises whether freeholders or business tenants have duties placed upon them to ensure the safety of all lawful entrants by virtue of the Occupiers Liability Act 1957 and in some cases an obligation to take reasonable care extends to uninvited visitors under the Occupiers Liability Act 1984.

Under the Occupiers Liability Act 1957 an occupier of business premises owes the common duty of care to all his lawful visitors and that is to take such care as in all the circumstances is reasonable to provide for their safety. Notice that the duty is owed by the occupier, the person in control of the premises and he would certainly include the owner in possession or a business tenant or licensee.

> In *Ferguson v. Welsh and others* 1988 an employee, Mr. Ferguson, sustained serious injuries when engaged on demolition work on a site owned by the district council. Having invited and accepted a tender to do the demolition work from Mr. Spence, an approved contractor of the council, the council were unaware that the work had been subcontracted to Mr. Ferguson's employers, the Welsh brothers. This was despite the fact that the original

invitation to tender expressly prohibited subcontracting without the council's approval. Mr. Ferguson's claim for damages against his employers, the Welsh brothers, for breach of statutory duty was upheld in the High Court. Whether the council as occupier of the premises owed Mr. Ferguson a duty of care under the 1957 Act was only finally resolved in the House of Lords. Their Lordships held that despite the express prohibition on subcontracts, Mr. Ferguson was nevertheless a lawful visitor of the council. *"The contractor engaged by the council was placed in control of the site for demolition purposes and to one who had no knowledge of the council's policy of prohibiting subcontracts, that would indicate that he was entitled to invite whomsoever he pleased onto the site for the purposes of carrying out the demolition. Moreover having put the contractor into occupation of the premises and thus into a position to invite the subcontractors and their employees onto them for the purpose of demolishing the building, the council must be taken to have invited the appellant in for that purpose so as to create a duty of care."* The House of Lords therefore confirmed that for the purposes of liability there may be different occupiers of the premises. In this case however the council although occupiers were not in breach of the common duty of care when the injury occurred as a result of the unsafe system of work adopted by subcontractors.

The business landlord is regarded as the occupier in relation to parts of the premises which remain under his control, e.g. entrance hall, lifts, forecourt or other common parts. Also if the landlord is under an obligation to repair, he may under s.4 Defective Premises Act 1972 be made liable for injuries that occur as a result of his failure to fulfil a repair obligation. Where the premises are let therefore, both the landlord and the tenant may be regarded as occupier of the premises for different purposes under the Act.

The obligation of the occupier in these circumstances is to take reasonable care in entrusting the work to an independent contractor and to take such steps as he reasonably ought in order to satisfy himself that the contractor was competent and that the work had been done properly. The occupier will have acted reasonably if he selected a reputable organisation to do work on the premises rather than a local handyman.

In *O'Connor v. Swan & Edgar* 1963 the plaintiff was injured by a fall of plaster when she worked as a demonstrator on the first defendant's premises. The fall of plaster was due to the faulty workmanship of the second defendants who had been engaged as contractors to work on the premises. The court held that as the first defendants had acted reasonably in entrusting the work to a reputable contractor then as an occupier he had satisfied the duty of care which was owed. The second defendants however were held liable in the tort of negligence for faulty workmanship.

Following the Unfair Contract Terms Act 1977 it is no longer possible for an occupier of business premises to exclude the common duty of care in relation to his visitors. To fulfil the duty owed it is necessary to ensure that premises are indeed reasonably safe or alternatively ensure that visitors are safe by giving adequate warning of any dangers. The 1957 Act mentions two categories of visitor in particular, children and independent contractors. It says that in relation to child visitors an occupier must be prepared for them to be less careful than adults. This suggests that for instance that an occupier of retail premises to which the public have access will owe a higher standard of care towards children than adults. The requirement of parental control however is a significant factor in establishing liability for injury caused to child visitors.

> In *Simkiss v. Rhondda B. C.* 1983 a seven year old suffered injury when she fell 30 or 40 feet after sliding on a blanket down a steep slope owned by the council. The High Court found the council liable for breach of the common duty of care in failing to either ensure that the mountainside was safe for children to play on or alternatively fencing it off. The Court of Appeal took a different view of the matter however and pointing out that adults would have realised that the mountainside must have been an obvious danger, the council was entitled to assume that parents would have warned their children of the danger. In reversing the decision of the High Court, the Court of Appeal stressed that the council's duty of care was not broken by failing to fence the mountain. To require a local authority to fence every natural hazard under its control would impose too onerous a burden.

Not only children but independent contractors are also singled out for mention in the Act. Such persons engaged to carry out specialist work should be aware of the risks inherent in their own trades.

> This is reflected in *Roles v. Nathan* 1963 where, despite being warned of the danger, two chimney sweeps carried on working on a boiler and were killed by carbon monoxide poisoning entering from the ventilation system. The employer/occupier was held in the circumstances not to be liable. Lord Denning MR stated that *"when a householder calls in a specialist to deal with a defective installation on his premises he can reasonably expect the specialist to appreciate and guard against the dangers arising from the defect"*.

> In *Rae (Geoffrey) v. Mars (UK)* 1990 an experienced surveyor was instructed to survey business premises and given the assistance of a graduate trainee by the defendant to show him round. The surveyor fell and suffered severe injuries when entering a printing ink store, the floor of which was three feet below the level of the door. No warning of the danger had been given by the trainee. In an action for damages under the Occupiers Liability Act 1957 the court held that notwithstanding his specialist expertise the surveyor, like all

visitors should have been given a warning of the exceptional nature of the hazard and the occupiers were accordingly in breach of their duty. By failing to switch on his torch however, while entering the store room, the surveyor was also at fault and the damages awarded were reduced by one third to reflect his contributory negligence.

In relation to uninvited visitors it was not until 1972 that the courts finally recognised that in some circumstances an occupier of business premises could be found liable in damages for injuries caused to a child trespasser.

In *British Railways Board v. Herrington* 1972 British Rail had negligently failed to maintain fencing which ran between their railway track and a park frequently used by children. A six-year old climbed through the fence, wandered onto the track, and suffered severe injury on the electrified rail. The House of Lords held the Board liable in negligence to the child trespasser. The Court stated that, "... *if the presence of the trespasser is known or ought reasonably to be anticipated by the occupier then the occupier has a duty to treat the trespasser with ordinary humanity.*"

It should be noted that the duty owed to a trespasser is a restricted duty and much less than the standard of care owed to a lawful visitor. In addition, the court pointed to the economic resources of the occupier as a factor to determine whether he had acted reasonably. The rule in *British Railways Board v. Herrington* has been applied in later cases.

In *Pannett v. McGuinness Ltd.* 1972 a demolition contractor was made liable for injuries caused to a five-year old trespasser by an unguarded fire. This was despite the fact that the contractor, aware of the danger, had posted workmen to guard the fire. The fact that the workmen were absent when the injury occurred meant, as far as the injured child was concerned, nothing was done to safeguard him.

In an attempt to clarify the rules relating to the liability of an occupier towards non-visitors, usually trespassers, the Occupiers Liability Act 1984 was passed. The Act replaces the common law, which includes the rules laid down by the House of Lords in *Herrington's* case, 1972. Surprisingly not all non-visitors are trespassers and in *McGeown v. Northern Ireland Housing Executive* 1994 the House of Lords confirmed that users of a right of way, whether public or private, are not "visitors" and as uninvited entrants are only entitled to the protection given by the Occupiers Liability Act 1984.

Under the 1984 Act the occupier will owe a duty to trespassers if:

(a)   he is aware or ought to be of danger; and

(b)   knows or has reasonable grounds to believe that the trespasser is or may be in the vicinity of danger; and

(c)   may reasonably be expected in all the circumstances to offer some protection to the trespasser against the danger.

Having established the existence of a duty the Act goes on to provide that the duty extends to taking such care as in all the circumstances is reasonable to see that the trespasser does not suffer injury by reason of the danger concerned. It is also provided that the duty may in an appropriate case be discharged by warning.

The existence of a duty of care still demands a consideration *of "all the circumstances"* to determine whether the trespasser deserves protection. This may well involve a consideration of the circumstances identified in *Herrington's* case such as the resources of the occupier, the extent of likely harm, the frequency of trespass etc. In addition the 1984 Act has confined itself to personal injury and so the common law is still relevant if the claim involves damage to the property of the trespasser.

Since the Act was passed in 1984 there have been very few cases involving the application of the occupier's duty of care towards trespassers.

In *Adams v. Southern Electricity Board* 1993 the Court of Appeal held that the board owed a duty of care to a fifteen year old boy who suffered severe injuries when he climbed up a pole-mounted high voltage electrical installation. The board had fitted an anti-climbing device, as required by statute, but at the time of the accident it was in a defective state and the plaintiff had simply climbed over it. While deciding that the board was in breach of its duty of care, as the plaintiff was old enough to appreciate the stupidity of his actions, the amount of damages was reduced by two-thirds to reflect his substantial contributory negligence.

In *Revill v. Newbery* 1996 the issue of liability was considered in the widely publicised case of a 76 year old defendant who caused injury to a 21 year old burglar when he fired his shotgun through a hole in his allotment shed door. The defendant was in the process of protecting property stored in his shed and had been awoken at night by the plaintiff attempting to break in. Subsequently the plaintiff was convicted of criminal offences and the defendant acquitted, and this case was a civil action for damages for personal injuries caused to the plaintiff trespasser. The claim was based upon common law negligence, the Occupiers Liability Act 1984 and trespass to person. The Court of Appeal confirmed the decision of the High Court that the plaintiff was not barred from succeeding in his claim by the fact that he was a trespasser and engaged in committing a crime at the time he was injured, however his damages should be reduced by two-thirds to reflect his contributory negligence.

Vicarious Liability

There are some situations where the law is prepared to impose *vicarious* (substituted) liability on an individual who is not at fault for the commission of the wrongful (tortious) act of another. The best known example of this situation is the common law rule which imposes vicarious liability on employers in respect of torts committed by their employees during the course of their employment. Accordingly, if one employee (Jones) by his negligent act causes harm to a fellow employee Smith then in addition to the possibility of (Smith) pursuing a legal action against Jones he may have the further option of suing his employer who will have become vicariously liable if the negligent act occurred during the course of Jones's employment. The same principle applies equally where the injuries are caused by an employee to some third party. However, while employers have a choice as to whether they insure against the risk of injury to third parties, under the Employer's Liability (Compulsory Insurance) Act 1969, an employer is required to insure himself in respect of injuries caused by his employees to their colleagues.

The imposition of vicarious liability does not require proof of any fault on the employer's part, or any express or implied authorisation to commit the wrongful act. All that must be proved for the purpose of vicarious liability is:

1.   an actionable wrong committed by the worker;

2.   that the worker is an employee;

3.   that the wrongful act occurred during the course of his employment.

What then is the *theoretical* basis for imposing liability in these circumstances? A number of reasons have emerged, such as he who creates and benefits from a situation should assume the risk of liability arising from it. There is also the idea that if an organisation embarks on an enterprise and as a result harm is caused by one member of the organisation, it should be the responsibility of the organisation to compensate for the harm. It is after all the employer who selects and controls the employees who work for him. The employer has the responsibility of training staff and can of course dismiss those whose work is performed incompetently. The practical reason for vicarious liability is of course that if the employee were solely liable he would have to insure himself, and the cost of this would be indirectly borne by the employer in the form of higher wages. Under the present system insurance costs are borne directly by the employer who, as a principle of sound business practice, will normally carry adequate insurance.

To determine an employer's liability it is first necessary to establish the employment status of the worker who is alleged to have committed the wrongful act. This is because the legal position differs dramatically depending on whether the worker is employed as an employee under a contract of service rather than as a self employed contractor under a contract for services. Usually this issue may be settled without argument but in the small proportion of cases where there is doubt the courts are left with the task of identifying the true contractual status of the worker. Obviously the express terms of the contract will be a strong indicator of the parties status but in some cases it is only by examining the substance of the relationship that the true position can be determined.

Course of Employment

As a general principle an employer is vicariously liable for the tortious acts of his employees committed during the *course of their employment*. The phrase course of employment has produced numerous interpretations in the courts, but essentially it concerns the question of whether the employee was doing his job at the time of the tortious act. It should be emphasised that an employee will have both express and implied authority to perform work for his employer and while he will normally have no authority to commit torts, he may nevertheless be guilty of a tortious act in the performance of his authorised duties.

> In *Century Insurance Ltd. v. Northern Ireland Road Transport Board* 1942 a tanker driver while delivering petrol at a garage, lit a cigarette and carelessly threw away the lighted match which caused an explosion and considerable damage. His employer was held to be vicariously liable for his negligence as the employee had acted within the course of his employment. By supervising the unloading, the employee was doing his job, but by smoking he was doing it in a grossly negligent manner.

Even if an employee is carrying out an act outside the basic obligation of his contract of employment, his employer may nevertheless be made vicariously liable if the act is carried out for the benefit of the employer.

> In *Kay v. ITW* 1968 the employee injured a colleague when he negligently drove a five ton diesel lorry which was blocking his way. Despite the fact that he was contractually authorised to drive only small vans and trucks, his employer was held to be vicariously liable for his action.

If an employee is doing something of purely personal benefit at the time of the negligent act then he may be regarded, to quote from the colourful language of the Victorian era as *"off on a frolic of his own"*, and his employer will not be responsible.

In *Hilton v. Thomas Burton (Rhodes) Ltd.* 1961 the plaintiff's husband was a demolition worker who was killed through the negligent driving of one of his colleagues. The defendant employer denied vicarious liability as, at the time of the accident, the van was being driven from a cafe on an unauthorised break. The court held that although the van had been driven with the permission of the employer, at the time of the incident the driver was not doing that which he was employed to do. Accordingly the employer was not liable for the negligent driving.

The extent to which an express prohibition by the employer will prevent vicarious liability will depend upon the nature of the prohibition. If it merely attempts to instruct the employee how he is to do his job, the employee may still be within the course of his employment for the purposes of vicarious liability.

In *Rose v. Plenty* 1976 a milkman, contrary to an express prohibition, engaged a thirteen year old boy to help him deliver the milk. The boy was subsequently injured by the milkman's negligent driving and sued both the milkman and his employer. The Court of Appeal held that despite the prohibition of the employer, he remained vicariously liable as the milkman had acted within the course of his employment. Scarman L J having considered the prohibition stated that *"There was nothing in the prohibition which defined or limited the sphere of his employment, the sphere of his employment remained precisely the same as before the prohibition was brought to his notice. The sphere was as a roundsman to go the rounds delivering milk, collecting empties and obtaining payment. Contrary to instructions the roundsman chose to do what he was employed to do in an improper way. But the sphere of his employment was in no way affected by his express instructions".*

It seems therefore that only an express prohibition which effectively cuts down the *sphere of employment'* will prevent the establishment of vicarious liability. The fact that contemporary courts seem to favour the idea of a very wide sphere of employment in individual cases, severely limits the opportunity of employers to restrict liability by express instruction. It is only by deciding the authorised parameters of an individual's job, and deciding that the act complained of fell outside these parameters that vicarious liability can be successfully denied.

Two recent decisions of the Court of Appeal confront the issue of course of employment and the potential common law liability of an employer for the abuse of children by school masters responsible for their care. In *ST v. North Yorkshire County Council* 1999 the county court had found the local authority employer vicariously liable for an alleged indecent assault by a deputy headmaster on the claimant, a mentally handicapped pupil in his care. Deciding that what occurred could not be described as a mode, authorised or not, of carrying out his work, the headmaster had stepped outside the course of employment when he committed the act so that the employer was not liable. The court also stressed that while this was the common law position different principles governed potential statutory liability.

The second case *L and Others v. Hesley Hall Ltd.* 1999 involved a similar issue of abuse by a housemaster of vulnerable boys in his care in a residential home. While accepting that there could be no vicarious liability for the acts of abuse the argument was advanced that the employer should be liable for the failure of the housemaster to report the fact that children had been traumatised and arrange treatment and protection. This argument was rejected however the court deciding that the failure to take remedial action was also part of a wrongful and unauthorised course of conduct outside the course of employment of the housemaster so the employer could not be made vicariously liable for it.

If the act is done on the employer's premises with the employer's interest in mind, the employer may be made liable provided the act has a close connection with the employee's job.

> In *Compton v. McClure* 1975 the employer was held to be vicariously liable for the negligence of an employee who, when late for work, caused an accident when driving negligently on the factory road.

While it may be reasonable for an employee to use a degree of force in protection of his employer's property, or to keep order, an employee who commits an assault which has no connection with his work will be solely liable for his conduct.

So in *Warren v. Henleys Ltd.* 1948 the employer was held not to be vicariously liable for a physical attack by a petrol pump attendant on one of his customers. The claim that the attendant was acting within the scope of his employment was rejected, for while the attack developed out of an argument over payment for petrol, it was in reality motivated by an act of private vengeance.

Statutory Torts

An employer can be vicariously liable for the statutory torts of sex, race or disability discrimination committed by employees during the course of employment unless he can show that he took such steps as were reasonably practicable to prevent the employee from committing the act of discrimination. A contentious issue is the extent to which an employee can be regarded as acting within the course of employment when committing an act of racial or sexual harassment.

> In *Irving & Irving v. Post Office* 1987 the complaint of race discrimination was based on the conduct of an employee of the post office who when sorting

the mail had written a racially insulting comment on a letter addressed to his neighbours who were of Jamaican origin. The issue before the Court of Appeal was whether the employee was acting in the course of his employment so that the Post Office could be made vicariously liable for the discriminatory act. The employee's act of writing on the mail was clearly unauthorised so the question was whether the act was an unauthorised mode of doing an authorised act. Here the misconduct formed no part of the postman's duties and could not be regarded as an unauthorised way of performing his work. *"An employer is not to be held liable merely because the opportunity to commit the wrongful act had been created by the employee's employment, or because the act in question had been committed during the period of that particular employment".*

In *Bracebridge Engineering v. Derby* 1990 the complainant was the victim of serious sexual harassment by her supervisor which constituted unlawful discrimination. The employer was vicariously liable for the misconduct as at the time the act of sexual harassment took place the perpetrators were supposedly engaged in exercising their disciplinary and supervisory functions and were in the course of their employment. Here the court applied a liberal interpretation of course of employment.

In *Jones v. Tower Boot Co Ltd.* 1997 the EAT held that racial taunts of fellow workers were not an unauthorised wrongful act connected with employment so as to make the employer vicariously liable. *"The phrase in the course of employment has a well established meaning in law. The nub of the test is whether the unauthorised wrongful act of the servant is so connected with that which he was employed to do as to be a mode of doing it. That has to be judged by reference to all the circumstances of the case. Applying that test to the facts of the present case, the acts complained of, including the deliberate branding with a hot screwdriver and whipping, could not be described by any stretch of the imagination, as an improper mode of performing authorised tasks."* Adopting a sensible pragmatic approach to this type of case, the Court of Appeal, in giving emphasis to the object of the legislation gave the phrase *"course of employment"* different interpretation from that applied when potential vicarious liability is determined in relation to common law tort. For the purposes of statutory torts, such as race discrimination the court held that course of employment should be given an everyday meaning so that if an employee commits an act of race discrimination at the workplace his employer would be held liable.

This novel approach to the liability of employers for the statutory torts of their employees was further tested in *Chief Constable of the Lincolnshire Police v. Stubbs* 1999. Here the EAT upheld the tribunal's decision that a police officer was acting the course of his employment when he subjected a fellow officer to sexual harassment contrary to the Sex Discrimination Act 1975. The EAT found the employer vicariously liable despite the fact that the conduct complained of occurred at social events outside the police station. The tribunal had decided that such gatherings were extensions of the working day and so within the course of employment for the purposes of liability.

While there is no doubt that this interpretation of *'course of employment'* represents a dramatic but sensible change of the law of vicarious liability in relation to statutory torts it should be stressed that there is a possible defence to a statutory claim. The employer can avoid responsibility if he can prove that he had taken such steps as were reasonably practicable to prevent the employee from committing the unlawful act.

Contractors

The increasing practice of employers contracting out areas of work to contractors and sub contractors has important implications when determining liability for injuries caused due to negligence at the workplace.

In *Sime v. Sutcliffe Catering Scotland Ltd.* 1990 an employee brought a claim alleging negligence by the above catering company when, carrying out her work as a canteen assistant she slipped on some food dropped by a fellow worker and suffered injury. The case was complicated by the fact that the employee was not directly employed by the catering company but by a paper manufacturer, Tullis Russell and Company. Previously the paper manufacturer had contracted out the management of the canteen to the above company, but following pressure from the trade union, had agreed to retain existing canteen staff, including the employee. It was never established whether the worker who had dropped the food was an employee of the catering company or not. The issue therefore was whether the catering company could be held liable vicariously to a worker for the possible negligent act of a worker who they did not employ. The Scottish Court of Session held that responsibility should be with the employer in control. Although not directly employed by the catering company, whether the employer relationship is *"such as to render the company liable for the negligence depends upon whether the substitute employer has sufficient power of control and supervision purely to be regarded as the effective employer at the critical time"*. As the *"whole day to day management of the catering operation and staff was undertaken by the catering company and the canteen manager had complete control over the way in which all the canteen workers did their job"*...and *"since one of the employed persons caused the accident by being negligent in dropping food stuff onto the floor and failing to clean it up the company had to accept responsibility for that negligence"*. The fault of the injured employee was also recognised and damages were reduced by twenty five percent to reflect her contributory negligence. *"Where a person is working in or near a kitchen where a number of people are working with food or dirty dishes and where it is quite predictable that food might be spilt it is reasonably necessary that a look out be kept for any wet or slippery patches on the floor."*

Generally vicarious liability has been confined to the employer/employee relationship and where contractors are employed, responsibility for their wrongful acts is solely their own. The justification for not extending vicarious liability to employers of contractors, other than in exceptional cases, stems from the fact that the contractor is not subjected to his employer's control in the same way as an employee.

There are then certain legal duties that cannot be delegated, and if the wrongful act of a contractor constitutes a breach of such a duty, owed by an employer to a third party, then the contractor's employer may be made vicariously liable for the default.

In *Rogers v. Nightriders* 1983 a mini cab firm undertook to provide a hire car to the plaintiff for a journey and did so by engaging a contractor driver. The plaintiff was injured in an accident caused by the negligent maintenance of the mini cab by the contractor. In an action against the mini cab firm the court held that they were not liable as an employer could not be made vicariously liable for their contractor's default. On appeal however, it was held that as the employer had undertaken to provide a vehicle to carry the plaintiff, and since they ought to have foreseen harm to the plaintiff if the vehicle *was defective, they owed a duty of care to the plaintiff to ensure that the vehicle was reasonably fit. Such a duty could not be delegated to a contractor and accordingly the employers were liable for breach of the primary duty that they owed to her.*

This case is a further example of the distinction that must be drawn between vicarious and direct or primary liability previously considered. By providing a negligent contractor, the employer in *Rogers v. Nightriders* had failed to fulfil a direct duty of care he owed to those he could reasonably foresee being affected.

Defamation

The tort of defamation is a civil wrong providing redress for an individual or organisation which has suffered damage to its reputation due to the defamatory statements of another. To the extent that it provides for the protection of business reputation it can be regarded as a *business tort*. As we have seen reputation is the goodwill of a business, an important element of business property. Any business is entitled therefore to seek a remedy to protect this property if defamatory statements are made about it by another. While there are many examples of litigants recovering substantial damages in defamation actions, particularly when compared with victims of serious personal injuries, a prospective plaintiff should commence proceedings with caution, for defamation is not legally aided and costs are likely to be substantial. Defamation lawyers tend to be highly paid specialists and the costs of the trial have the added burden of the costs of a jury.

Libel and slander

As you are probably aware there are two forms of defamation, *libel* and *slander*. An action is based upon libel where the defamation is contained in a medium which has a degree of *permanence* such as writing, recordings, paintings, films etc. The less serious form of defamation and more difficult to prove is slander which is usually an oral statement alleged to be defamatory. By statute oral statements broadcast on the radio or television or on the stage fall into the category of libel. Unlike slander, libel may also constitute a crime, but prosecutions for *criminal* libel are extremely rare. Also libel is actionable *per se* (that is without proof of damage) while in an action for slander the plaintiff must prove actual loss resulting from the slanderous statement. For serious forms of slander this is not the case and for our purposes the relevant exception is defamatory statements about an individual's *office, profession, calling, trade or business*.

Defamatory statements

The essence of the tort of defamation is lies in establishing that the defendant has made a defamatory statement about the plaintiff. An untrue statement is not necessarily defamatory and neither is a mere insult or a derogatory comment. What must be established is a loss of reputation which necessarily involves a publication of the statement to some third party. The courts still rely on the test devised by Lord Atkin in *Sim v. Stretch* 1936. He said that *"the conventional phrase exposing the plaintiff to hatred, ridicule and contempt is probably too narrow. The question is complicated by having to consider the person or class of persons whose reaction to the publication is the test of the wrongful character of the words used…. I propose in the present case the test: would the words tend to lower the plaintiff in the estimation of right-thinking members of society generally?"*

It is crucial to consider the words used in the context in which they appear. To say that an Australian rugby player is too fat as in *Boyd v. Mirror Newspapers* 1980 could constitute an attack on professional competence of a professional player. Similarly to remark of a company during the course of the first World War that it was a German company could also be treated as defamatory; *Slazengers Ltd. v. Gibbs & Co.* 1919.

The intention of the defendant is irrelevant in deciding whether a statement is defamatory. What is significant is the effect it has on those to whom it is published. An unintended innuendo could therefore be defamatory.

> In *Tolley v. Fry* 1931 a prominent amateur golfer was depicted in a caricature advertising chocolate. The House of Lords held that the advertisement was capable of defamatory meaning by innuendo for it suggested that the golfer had accepted money for the advertisement and so offended his amateur status.

> In defamation cases it is for the court to determine as a matter of law whether the words used are capable of being defamatory but then it is a matter for the jury to decide whether in fact they are. In *Mitchell v. Faber & Faber* 1994 Hurst LJ said that *"it is well settled that the question whether the words which are complained of are capable of conveying a defamatory meaning is a question of law and therefore one calling for decision by the court. If the words are so capable then it is a question for the jury to decide whether the words do in fact convey a defamatory meaning"*.

In the highly competitive travel industry there have been a number of recent examples of airlines and tour operators describing their competitor's products in a manner which is capable of being defamatory. Certainly if representatives of a tour operator tell travel agents and hoteliers that a particular competitor is *"going bust"* or will be *"bankrupt in a few days"* such words are clearly defamatory.

> The Court of Appeal in *Aspro Travel Ltd. v. Owners Abroad* 1995 thought that such words were also capable of meaning that a travel company was insolvent and the directors continued to trade, knowing of the insolvency. The fact that a company is insolvent could be due to market forces some misfortune or the actions of third parties and all these reasons would have no impact on the reputation of the director and so would not be defamatory. However *"to say of a director of a family company that he permitted the company to trade knowing that it was insolvent, without making .... extra comments, could be defamatory in the sense that the director standing in the community could be injured because even a fair minded member of the community might .... hold it against the director that he permitted an insolvent company to continue trading"*.

A shameful practice occasionally adopted by the tabloid press is to represent public figures in unusual situations in the guise of so-called news. If a full story is factually correct it is nevertheless defamatory when it is obvious that a large number of readers will have only read part of the material which is capable of being defamatory.

In *Charleston and another v. News Group Newspapers* 1995 the defendant newspaper published images of a computer game in which the plaintiff's faces were superimposed onto the bodies of pornographic film action engaged in sexual activity. An accompanying headline made it appear that the images were of the plaintiffs, actors in the television soap Neighbours, but the rest of the article made it clear that the material had been produced without the plaintiff's consent. The House of Lords had to decide whether an action for defamation could succeed because a number of readers would only read the part capable of a defamatory meaning. Their Lordships upheld the traditional view that the meaning to be given to an article must be gathered by considering the article as a whole. Despite the fact therefore that many readers would not have read the full article and merely glanced at the headline and the photograph the article was not capable of conveying a defamatory meaning to the reasonable and fair minded reader.

The tort of defamation is concerned with the loss of reputation of an individual or organisation in the minds of third parties. A crucial element of the tort is that the statement has been brought to the attention of a third party referred to in legal terms as being published. Usually there is no question that a statement has been published because it is included in a newspaper story or a book and in such circumstances every organisation involved in the publication process is a potential defendant. However a defamatory statement made face to face and not in the presence of a third party is not actionable and neither is a letter containing defamatory material sent to the potential plaintiff. Also for the purposes of publication a husband and wife are regarded as one.

Beyond these limited exceptions prima facie liability in defamation is established if the plaintiff proves that the defendant has published a defamatory statement which refers to him, subject to the defendant establishing one of the many defences to the tort.

Defences

The primary defence to an action in defamation is to establish that the statement made is true or substantially true. This defence is called *justification* and while there is at present a continuing debate about the right to privacy, for the purposes of defamation even a *malicious publication* is not actionable if it is proved to be true. While it is the task of the plaintiff to show that a statement is defamatory it is for the defendant to establish, on the *balance of probabilities*, that the statement is true or substantially so. It may be that the defendant fails to establish the truth of every one of a number of allegations. In such circumstances s.5 of the Defamation Act 1952 provides that he may still rely on the defence of justification.

Absolute privilege attaches to defamatory statements that are made by a judge in the course of legal proceedings, in Parliament by an MP or between husband and wife. Even if such statements are made with a malicious motive absolute privilege provides a complete defence. Of more relevance to business is the defence of *qualified privilege* which attaches to statements made in the performance of a legal or moral duty. Not only must the maker of the statement have a duty in publishing it, the recipient must have a corresponding interest in receiving it.

Qualified privilege can be destroyed as a defence if the plaintiff establishes that the defendant made the defamatory statement with a *malicious motive*. In business qualified privilege could apply to such matters as external and internal communications within business organisations, employee references and professional advice.

The defence of *fair comment* embodies the notion that in a democratic society everyone including broadcasters and the press, has the right to make outspoken comment on matters of public interest. What then constitutes *public interest* is a dilemma often faced by the courts and in *London Artists Ltd. v. Littler* 1969 Lord Denning expressed the view that *"whenever a matter is such as to affect people at large so that they may be legitimately interested in, or concerned at, what is going on; or what may happen to them or to others; then it is a matter of public interest on which everyone is entitled to make fair comment."*

Whereas the defence of justification is concerned with establishing that a defamatory statement is factually true, fair comment is concerned with statements of opinion, for example that a particular tour operator, firm of accountants, manufacturer, retail outlet, or business entrepreneur is not reliable. Once again the defence of fair comment may be destroyed by *malice* so the crux of the defence is that the opinion expressed is one that is honestly held. Once again Lord Denning has provided some guidance when he said in *Slim v. Daily Telegraph* 1968 that *"the important thing is to determine whether or not the writer was activated by malice. If he was an honest man expressing his genuine opinion on a subject of public interest, then no matter that his words conveyed derogatory imputations: no matter that his opinion was wrong or exaggerated or prejudiced; and no matter that it was badly expressed so that other people read all sorts of innuendoes into it; nevertheless he has a good defence of fair comment"*.

If there is a case of unintentional defamation the Defamation Act 1952 provides that the publishers can make an *offer of amends* which is an offer to publish a suitable correction with a suitable apology. Usually the publisher will also have to pay the plaintiff's costs. If such an offer is made but not accepted it may nevertheless provide the publisher with a defence.

Remedies

If the plaintiff can establish a prima facie case of libel he will be entitled to an injunction to prevent further publication. If in the face of an *injunction* the publication goes ahead then this will constitute contempt of court. The main remedy for defamation is of course an award of damages, and for a number of successful litigants in the past quite often a substantial sum awarded by the jury. A sum should be awarded to reflect the extent to which the defamatory statement has an impact on the plaintiff's good name. In rare cases the sum is a *nominal* amount or the damages awarded are contemptuous. More usually however the defendant, perhaps a large media corporation, has acted so badly that the damages awarded have a punitive element and *exemplary* damages are added to compensatory damages awarded.

Under s.8 of the Court of Legal Services Act 1990 the Court of Appeal is empowered where the damages awarded are excessive, in place of ordering a new trial, to substitute for the sum awarded by the jury such sum as appears to the court to be reasonable. In *Rantzen v. Mirror Group Newspapers (1988) Ltd.* 1993 the Court of Appeal held that the appellate court should ask *"whether a reasonable jury could have thought that this award was necessary to compensate the plaintiff and to re-establish his reputation"*.

Assignment - The Wandering Child

Fiona Berry and John Cheng are business partners who run a number of travel agency related outlets in Lancashire. One such agency Fiesta Travel is situated in premises in Bolton held on a 21 year lease from North Western Properties Ltd. The lease has now run for six years and despite repeated requests by Fiona, the landlords seem reluctant to fulfil their clear repairing obligation in relation to the plaster work on the ceiling of the main office which is in a dangerous state of disrepair. A further cause for anxiety is the condition of the electrical wiring in the building, which again falls within the landlords responsibility.

Concerned at the time it takes for the landlord to respond to requests to repair, Fiona decided to hire Gerry, a local odd job man, to carry out wiring work in the premises. Coincidently, at the same time, North Western Properties finally responded to the request for repairs to the ceiling by hiring Joplings, a well known building contractor to carry out the work. Because of pressure of work, Joplings decide to sub contract the work to Tom and Jim, a couple of lads who are "quick and cheap and can manage small jobs".

The events of the last two weeks have driven Fiona to despair! The replastering work, while completed in good time, has not been a success. Firstly Jim, in carrying out the replastering work, sustained a violent electric shock when he touched exposed electric cables to a light fitting which Gerry had not properly insulated. Secondly the plaster did not bond properly to the ceiling, and fell on to Sheila, a prospective customer, whilst she was glancing at travel brochures. The plaster fall has caused Sheila head injuries requiring hospital treatment and a period of convalescence.

The icing on the cake was an incident yesterday. Wayne, a six year old on the premises with his parents there to book a holiday, wandered through a door marked *private* apparently in search of toilets. He fell down the steps inside the door leading to the cellar and suffered a broken arm. The stairs were not lit.

Fiona and John feel that they may face potential legal claims for these incidents and fix an appointment with Masters & Milburn a local firm of solicitors to seek legal advice. Despite their problems they don't wish to leave the Bolton Premises.

Task

You are working for Masters and Milburn as part of a work experience programme and have been asked to interview Fiona and John and to follow up the interview with a written report to one of the senior partners Janet Stephenson. You need to include in the report your assessment of the legal position in relation to liability. Your task is to produce the report for Ms Stephenson. The report should clearly state the legal arguments both for and against the likelihood of Fiona and John incurring liability for the injuries to Sheila and Wayne.

Chapter 8

The Principles of Contract Law: Establishing Contracts

Introduction

The next three chapters explore the principles of the law of contract. Chapter 8 begins with an examination of the background to contract making, then goes on to consider how a contract is set up. Chapter 9 looks at the main legal principles which apply to contracts once they have been created, in particular how a contract may be broken or declared invalid. Chapter 10 deals with the various ways that the parties to a contract can discharge their obligations under it and the redress available in the event of a contractual breach.

The Idea of the Contract

Why a law of contract?

The idea of the contract owes its existence to a concept which is central to economics, that of the market. Market activity, the interaction of buyers and sellers of goods and services, has origins going back to the early civilisations and the emergence of the first forms of trading activity within and between societies. One of the conditions necessary for trade to function effectively is the existence within the market place of a code of trading behaviour which provides a framework of rules within which trading parties can transact and to which they are willing to adhere. Without such a framework trading anarchy would prevail, and such a condition would be too uncertain and unstable a climate for individuals and businesses to make investment decisions and financial commitments. In a market free for all where no remedy is obtainable to repair a broken bargain few would have the confidence to trade. The contract has developed as a legal mechanism to provide a formalised set of rules of trading. Modern contract law has increasingly reflected a significant social dimension also. Examples we shall come across later include the limitations placed upon excluding certain types of contractual liability, and the rights of consumers injured as a result of defective manufactured goods, but there are many others. The objectives of social justice can also be seen reflected in the various rights granted to employees within the contract of employment.

The law of contract may thus be regarded in broad terms as a set of rules and principles which:

- provide a legal framework offering a measure of trading security to anyone engaging in the process of buying and selling;

- seek to achieve a measure of social justice by restricting activities which are seen as unfair or harmful;

- identify and control economic practices which are regarded as contrary to the public interest;

- establish the technical means by which parties who wish to make legally enforceable transactions can do so.

A Definition of Contract

A contract is simply a legally enforceable agreement. As it stands this is not a definition which takes us very far, for it raises further questions. We need to establish what the components are of an agreement, and what conditions have to be satisfied in order that an agreement can become legally recognised. Making an agreement does not automatically result in the making of a contract, for there are many other factors that are taken into account before a contract can materialise. For instance the parties to the agreement must have the legal *capacity* to contract, and there must be evidence that they intend their transaction to be legally binding.

An agreement which does not achieve contractual status will, in consequence, contain undertakings which the parties have exchanged with each other that do not bind them in a legal sense. Non-contractual agreements of this kind may still be honoured by the parties making them out of a sense of moral or social obligation. The observance of rules and principles is frequently based upon a sense of duty or responsibility and does not always have to be underpinned by legal sanctions to be carried out. When friends agree to meet in town in the evening for a drink it is unlikely the law would see the arrangement as legally binding. We would nevertheless expect them to honour their arrangement because they will not want to let each other down, and break their promises.

Contractual Liability

Whenever a contract is made it produces contractual liabilities. The content of such liabilities depends upon the substance of the contract in question, but all contractual liabilities are based upon a simple common element. They involve people entering into agreements consisting of legally enforceable promises exchanged between them. Such promises may be simple or complex; they may be single promises or sets of promises. But in whatever form they emerge contractual promises give rise to contractual liabilities. The result is that if a promise of this kind is not carried out, or is carried out improperly, a legal obligation has been broken and the injured party may choose to seek a remedy from the contract breaker before the courts.

The Concept of Freedom of Contract

Contracting parties have never enjoyed unlimited freedom to make whatever deal they choose. No court, for example has ever been prepared to enforce a contract whose purpose is unlawful, such as an agreement to commit a criminal offence. But how interventionist should the law be?

Eighteenth and nineteenth century capitalist philosophy advocated a *laissez-faire* economic approach, leaving the markets for goods and services, as far as reasonably practicable, to regulate themselves. The idea of a free market, left to control itself unhindered by the interventions of the courts or Parliament, found its legal expression in the concept of *freedom of contract*. The advocates of freedom of contract considered that as few restrictions as possible should be placed upon the liberty of individuals to make agreements. The Master of the Rolls, Sir George Jessel, expressed it in the following way in 1875: *"If there is one thing which more than any other public policy requires it is that men of full age and understanding shall have the utmost liberty of contracting and their contracts when entered into freely and voluntarily shall be held sacred and shall be enforced by the courts of justice."*

There are compelling reasons for allowing a wide measure of contractual freedom, for example:

* *market needs:*

    in the interests of healthy markets the participants in market activity should be allowed to trade unhindered. The able will survive and the weak will flounder. External intervention in this process will tend to weaken rather than strengthen economic performance by the artificial distortion of the bargaining process;

- *personal liberty:*

    interference in contract making is an infringement of individual liberty. In the same way that a person chooses when to marry, or for whom to vote, they should be free to negotiate their own bargains. The contract is a private, not a public event;

- *knowledge:*

    it should be assumed that contracting parties act in a rational manner so that the contract they make is the contract they want. Nobody else is better placed to identify contractual wants and needs than the parties themselves.

Closer analysis, however, suggests these factors reflect more a theoretical ideal than the reality of modern contract making. This is most strikingly apparent when we look at the role of *consent* in contract making.

The Role of Consent in Contract Making

In a sense we enjoy complete contractual freedom, for individuals and organisations alike are free to choose whether or not to enter into a contractual relationship. It cannot be forced on them for consent is a precondition of the relationship. But what precisely does consent mean? To answer this question we need to examine how the courts discriminate between those situations where consent is regarded as genuine, and those in which the consent is in reality artificial. Where the consent given to an agreement is not genuine consent there is said to be no *consensus ad idem,* or meeting of the minds of the parties. Circumstances in which the courts will be prepared to consider a claim that the consent is unreal are in cases of misrepresentation, mistake, fraud, duress and undue influence. They are referred to technically as *vitiating elements*. Once established they have the effect of either invalidating the contract in its entirety, in which case the contract is said to be *void,* or of entitling the injured party to escape from the contract if he or she wishes to do so. In such circumstances the contract is said to be *voidable* in the injured parties favour. To vitiate literally means to make invalid or ineffectual.

The presence of a vitiating factor in an agreement can defeat the entire contract. By granting relief where consent is a sham because a person has been misled, tricked, coerced or mistaken, the courts are demonstrating that they will look at what the parties believed they were agreeing to when the contract was made. Equally of course, the notion of freedom carries with it responsibility. It is not the role of the courts to repair bad bargains made through lack of prudence. The balance between intervening in an attempt to right legitimate wrongs, whilst leaving the parties to learn from their trading mistakes is not easily achieved. The point is that the courts are prepared in appropriate cases to untie the bond that has been made, thereby protecting parties in a limited way from the consequences that complete freedom of contract would otherwise produce.

Bargaining Inequality

That the freedom of contract is largely a myth can be seen when we consider the issue of bargaining strength. True consensus is only possible where parties meet as bargaining equals. In practice such equality is generally elusive; the commercial reality is an inequality of bargaining power where one party is able to dominate the other. The result is that far from arriving at agreement through a process of negotiation, the contract is a one sided arrangement in which the dominant party presents terms to the weaker party on a take-it-or-leave it basis. Commonly the dominant party will only be prepared to do business on the basis of standard terms designed to provide it with a high level of commercial protection. If the dominant party is a monopoly supplier, like a railway company, the consumer is unable to shop around for a better deal or a different set of terms. Even in a reasonably competitive market, suppliers of goods or services trade invariably on the same or very similar terms, for instance by using a contract designed by the trade association of which they are a member. Contracts arising in this way are sometimes referred to as contracts of *adhesion*, for the weaker party is required to adhere all the terms imposed by the stronger party.

Legal Intervention in the Market Place

To help overcome market place imbalances Parliament and the courts have been prepared to intervene in appropriate circumstances, to produce a kind of externally manipulated commercial justice. Parliament has for example legislated to strengthen the rights of *consumers*, business consumers as well as individuals. The range of legislative measures which seek to create a more level playing field for contracting parties is now very extensive. They are considered later in the book, but the most notable examples are the Consumer Credit Act 1974, the Unfair Contract Terms Act 1977, and Sale of Goods Act 1979, the Supply of Goods and Services Act 1982 and the Consumer Protection Act 1987. Parliament has also sought to protect the interests of *employees*. The major statutory employment rights are found in the Employment Rights Act 1996.

In addition the courts have been prepared to intervene in circumstances of exceptional exploitation, drawing on an equitable principle known as *undue influence*.

This is well illustrated by the decision of the Court of Appeal in *Lloyds Bank Ltd. v. Bundy* 1975. Here an elderly farmer, who was ill and had little business knowledge, agreed with the bank to guarantee the account of his son's company. The company was in difficulties, and over a period of time the father increased the size of the guarantee, which was secured by a mortgage on his house, so that eventually the mortgage on the property was for more than the property was worth. This arrangement had been made by the father in consultation with the bank manager, upon whom he implicitly relied. The company's debts remained outstanding, and the bank sought to sell the father's house in order to realise the guarantee. The Court of Appeal unanimously set aside the agreement between the father and the bank, Lord Denning MR observing that: *"no bargain will be upset which is the result of the ordinary interplay of forces. There are many hard cases which are caught by this rule ... yet there are exceptions to this general rule ... in which the courts will set aside a contract, when the parties have not met on equal terms, when the one is so strong in bargaining power and the other so weak that, as a matter of common fairness, it is not right that the strong should be allowed to push the weak to the wall .... English law gives relief to one who, without independent advice, enters into a contract on terms which are very unfair..."*

However the mere fact that one party is weaker than the other is not enough, in itself, to escape the contract. The agreement must be unconscionable to obtain equitable relief. In *Barclays Bank plc v. Schwarz* 1995 the defendant, the principal director of a number of property companies, argued before the Court of Appeal that he was not liable to make good debts of over £1/2 m which his companies owed the bank. He had signed personal guarantees in favour of the bank regarding these debts. His defence was his poor understanding of English, something the bank was aware of, and that the bank should have explained to him the nature of the documents he was signing. The court rejected these arguments, finding that his weakness in the English language was not a sufficient ground to set aside the guarantees. Illiteracy was not a defence. Simon Brown LJ was not convinced that a man with a number of property companies could argue that *"his understanding of the ... English language, and the nuts and bolts of ordinary commercial life, was so deficient that he could thereby escape the consequences of signing routine legal instruments."*

There are many other examples of market interventions which parliament and courts have introduced and which are not included here. What is certainly clear is that the practice of responding to perceived market inadequacies or injustices by judicial or legislative activity is not a process that is yet complete. New examples continue to emerge. A recent illustration is the Late Payment of Commercial Debts (Interest)

Act 1998, a measure introduced to give effect to the Governments desire to grant a statutory right for businesses to interest on late payment of debts. The Act grants the rights to interest payments on certain commercial debts, without the need to establish that a contract term provides for this, and without the need to have brought legal proceedings in respect of such debts.

The Form of the Contract

At common law no restriction is placed upon the way in which a contract can be expressed. The parties are free to make the contract orally, or in writing, or if they wish by using a combination of these methods. In appropriate cases a contract can even be inferred from the conduct of the parties. The term *simple* contract, suggesting a transaction that does not have to meet special technicalities of form, is therefore used to describe such arrangements.

It is a commonly held view, although an entirely erroneous one, that written evidence of the transaction is essential if a contract is to be valid. In fact the only circumstances in which writing is a legal requirement occur where Parliament demands it. Allowing oral contracts is based upon practicalities. For most transactions written agreements would be cumbersome, time consuming, and most unnecessary. However there are good reasons for expressing a contract in writing. In particular:

(a) the writing will stand as evidence of the transaction, should anyone challenge its existence, and

(b) the task of reducing the agreement into writing is likely to help the parties focus more precisely on what each is promising the other, in other words the terms or obligations that have been agreed between them. Most of the simple contracts we make regularly as individual consumers are oral agreements; buying food, petrol, a record or tape, clothes and so on. The existence of a contract may also be *inferred* when the facts support it.

In *Martin-Smith v. Williams* 1998 it was alleged that an oral agreement between the manager and the band 'Take That', made in the presence of solicitors, to extend the term of the management agreement indefinitely was made subject to contract and so not legally binding. The High Court decided however that as there was no direct evidence that the agreement was intended to be made subject to a written contract it was in fact legally binding, An oral contract to extend the term indefinitely subject to six month's notice and reduce the manager's commission by 5% was enforceable.

There is however a type of contract which is expressed in very formal terms. This is the *deed*, sometimes referred to as a speciality contract. Under the Law of Property (Miscellaneous Provisions) Act 1989 a deed must be contained in writing, and be signed by the parties making it, with their signatures being witnessed.

There are relatively few circumstances in which the law demands a deed to give effect to a contract. Under the Law of Property Act 1925 a deed is required to transfer legal ownership in land from one party to another, and to create a lease of more than three years duration.

Contracts where writing is necessary

Certain contracts are required by statute to be made in writing. In some cases, the objective is to protect the consumer by requiring a clear statement of rights and responsibilities under the contract to be contained in the written agreement. In others it is required to oblige parties involved in technical transactions, particularly those involving non-tangible property such as shares and copyright, to formally record the making and content of the transaction.

The most important examples include:

(a)   hire purchase and conditional sale agreements. Under s.65(1) of the Consumer Credit Act 1974 such agreements cannot been enforced unless they are properly executed. This occurs when a legible document containing all the express terms of the agreement and in the prescribed form is signed by the parties;

(b)   the transfer of shares in a registered company, a requirement under s.183 Companies Act 1985, which states that a *"proper instrument of transfer"* must be delivered to the company. The company cannot register the transfer until this is done;

(c)   an assignment of copyright, under s.90 Copyright Designs and Patents Act 1988;

(d)   cheques, bills of exchange and promissory notes, under the Bills of Exchange Act 1882; and

(e)   contracts for the sale or other disposition of land under the Law of Property (Miscellaneous Provisions) Act 1989.   s2(1) of the Act provides that, *"a contract for the sale or other disposition of an interest in land can only be made in writing and only by incorporating all the terms which the parties have expressly agreed in the document or, where contracts are exchanged, in each." S2(3) provides that, "the document incorporating the terms... must be signed by or on behalf of each party to the contract."*

The Court of Appeal applied s.2 in *Firstpost Homes Ltd v. Johnson* 1995 Here an oral agreement for the sale of land was supported by a letter prepared by the purchaser with the vendors name on it which both parties were expected to sign. In fact the vendor did not sign the letter but merely the enclosed plan of the land she agreed to sell. The purchaser signed both the letter and the plan. The court concluded that the requirements of s.2 had not been complied with for the typing of a name could not amount to a signature and while one document could incorporate another, here the plan was not the principal document for that purpose.

Failure to comply with the any of these statutory requirements renders the contract *invalid*.

Other than for merchant seaman and apprentices, there is no legal requirement that a *contract of employment* be in writing. Given the fluid nature of a contract of employment there is no guarantee that a requirement to reduce the original contract to writing would solve all the problems of interpreting its content.

Under s.1 of the Employment Rights Act 1996 there is however a statutory requirement on employers to provide their employees within eight weeks of the commencement of employment with a written statement of the main terms and conditions of employment.

Making a Contract

We have seen that a contract is a legally enforceable agreement. But what exactly is an agreement, and what is needed for an agreement to become legally enforceable?

Agreement

A contract cannot occur without an agreement, and so the idea of agreement is central to an understanding of the law of contract. Agreements are undertakings to do, or sometimes refrain from doing, specific things.

Perhaps most people can rely on instinct or common sense to assess whether they have an agreement or not, but for legal purposes it is not sufficient to rely upon subjective judgments to decide events of such significance. If a disputed agreement comes before a court, obviously the court cannot get inside the minds of the parties to discover their actual intentions. At best it can look at the way they have conducted themselves, examining what they have said and what they have done, in order to decide the matter on the basis of what a reasonable person would assume their intentions to be.

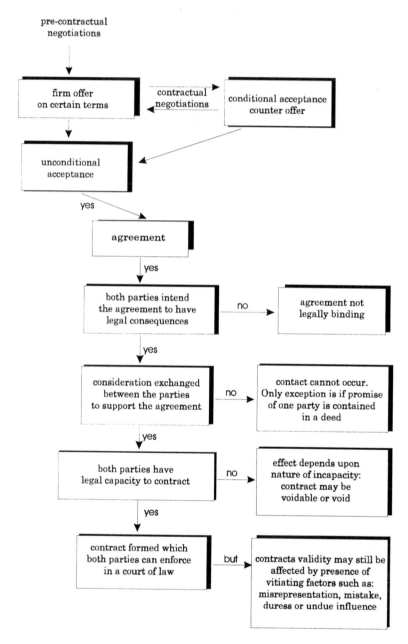

Figure 8.1   *Elements in the formation of contract*

An agreement contains two elements:

(i)   an *offer*, made by one party to the other; and

(ii)   an *acceptance* by the other of the terms contained in the offer.

If a court cannot identify the presence of these two components in a transaction, a simple contract cannot arise.

The process of negotiation

The person making an offer is referred to as the *offeror*, and the person to whom it is addressed the *offeree*. In business the parties usually reach agreement following a period of negotiation. Negotiations will focus the details of the proposed transaction, and include such matters as price, specifications concerning the subject matter of the agreement, and the time and place for performing it. Often during these negotiations offers will be made by one party to the other which are rejected, or met by a fresh offer. Either of the parties to the transaction is able to make an offer, not just the one who wishes to sell the goods or services in question or who is the owner or supplier of them.

Examining the negotiating process is important for many reasons. For instance it enables us to identify which party made the final offer, and thus the terms upon which the offer was based and hence which make up the terms of the; in addition during negotiations false statements may sometimes made by one of the parties which induce the other to enter into the contract. These are referred to as *misrepresentations*, and are actionable.

Characteristics of a Valid Offer

To be legally effective an offer must satisfy the following general requirements:

* it must be firmly made;

* it must be communicated;

* its terms must be certain; and

* it must not have terminated.

Firm offer or invitation to treat

The offeror must intend the offer to be unequivocal, so that when acceptance occurs he will be bound. It is sometimes difficult to distinguish firm offers from statements which do not carry the full legal status of offers. What appears to be a firm offer may merely be an incentive or encouragement designed by the person making it to encourage the making of offers to him and not intended to be legally binding. A statement of this kind is known as an *invitation to treat*. It is an indication that the person is willing to do business with anyone who is interested.

In *Pharmaceutical Society of Great Britain v. Boots Cash Chemists (Southern) Ltd.* 1953 one of the shops in the company's chain had been converted into a self-service supermarket. Some of the shelves carried poisons which by statute were required to be sold in the presence of a qualified chemist. The chemist was in attendance at the checkout. The Pharmaceutical Society, which had a duty to enforce the statutory provisions, claimed that the company was in breach of them. The Society argued that the contract was made at the shelves where there was no pharmacist in attendance. The court however held that the goods displayed on the shelves were merely invitations to treat. The contract was made at the checkout. The customers made the offer when presenting the goods for payment and the offer was accepted by the cashier passing them through the checkout.

Advertisements are also generally regarded as constituting invitations to treat. In *Partridge v. Crittenden* 1968 the Divisional Court of the Queens Bench Division was asked to determine whether an advertisement in a magazine which read, *"Bramblefinch cocks,bramblefinch hens 25/- each"*, constituted the offence of offering to sell wild birds contrary to the Protection of Birds Act 1954. The court quashed the conviction against the defendant which had been issued in the Magistrates Court. The advertisement was simply an encouragement to stimulate the market into making offers. Members of the public responding to the advert made the offers, but of course they could not commit an offence since they were offering to buy, not to sell. The defendant should have been charged with the separate offence contained in the Act of selling wild birds.

In *British Car Auctions Ltd. v. Wright* 1972, an unroadworthy car had been sold at auction. The auctioneers were convicted in the Magistrates Court of offering to sell an unroadworthy vehicle, contrary to the Road Traffic Act 1972. In quashing the conviction Widgery LCJ stated: *"The auctioneer when he stands on his rostrum does not make an offer to sell the goods on behalf of the vendor; he stands there making an invitation to those present at the auction themselves to make offers to buy"*.

Further examples of the invitation to treat are advertisements inviting suppliers of goods and services to submit tenders, and prospectuses issued by limited companies inviting members of the public to subscribe for shares.

Tenders

The use of tenders is a common commercial practice. Indeed local authorities are required by the Local Government Act 1972 to contract in this way. Under the tendering process a tender is an offer and an invitation to tender is an invitation to treat. It is merely an invitation by an individual or organisation wishing to purchase goods or services to request suppliers to submit a contractual offer in the form of a tender.

In appropriate circumstances an invitation to tender can give rise to a binding contractual obligation. If there is clear evidence from what the parties have said and done that a contractual obligation to consider a particular tender in conjunction with all other tenders meeting the tendering requirements was intended, the court will enforce it.

> In *Blackpool and Fylde Aero Club v. Blackpool Borough Council* 1990 the local authority owned and managed an airport. The plaintiff flying club had for some years operated pleasure flights from the airport. When the grant of the club's concession came up for renewal the council prepared invitations to tender. These were then sent to the club and six other parties. The forms sent out stated that the council did not bind itself, *"to accept all or any part of any tender"*. The form added, *"No tender which is received after the last date and time specified shall be admitted for consideration."*

The plaintiffs delivered their tender to the council offices before the deadline, however because council staff failed to empty the council letter box when they should have done the council received the tender too late to be considered, and accepted a tender from another tenderer lower in value than the plaintiff's tender. The club sued for damages alleging breach of contract and negligence. The court held that although contracts in such circumstances should not be freely implied, the evidence here was of a clear intention that the council was contractually obliged to consider the plaintiff's tender with the other tenders, or at least that it would be considered if all the others were. The claim for breach of contract was successful.

An invitation to treat is not however devoid of legal effect. It can give rise to legal liability in the following ways:

- as a statement it can amount to an actionable misrepresentation (see later); and

- it may also give rise to criminal liability under the Trade Descriptions Act 1968, if it constitutes a false trade description, or under the Consumer Protection Act 1987 if it gives a false or misleading indication as to the price of goods or services.

Communicating the offer

The party to whom an offer is directed must be aware of it. Although an offer will normally be made to a single individual or organisation, there is nothing to prevent an offer being directed to a specific group of individuals, anyone or more of whom may choose to accept it. For instance a private limited company that is going public may offer some of its shares at favourable rates to the members of its workforce.

It is possible to make an offer to the public generally, without at the time being able to identify who all the possible recipients may be. One of the most celebrated instances of an offer made to the public at large, occurred in *Carlill v. Carbolic Smokeball Co.* 1893 which is considered below.

What constitutes communication is a question of fact for the court. Letters, telephone calls, voice mail messages, faxes and emails are all recognised methods of communication.

Certainty of terms

If the parties disagree about the meaning of a term it will ultimately fall to the court to decide the question. The courts always endeavour to find certainty but a term which is obscure or meaningless will fail. This will not prove fatal to the contract if the term constitutes only a minor part of the overall obligations, but an uncertain term that is central to the functioning of the contract, will inevitably defeat the contract as a whole.

In *Loftus v. Roberts* 1902 an agreement provided for the appointment of an actress by another person at a *"West End salary to be mutually agreed between us."* Subsequently the parties were unable to arrive at a salary which satisfied them both. The court held that the contract must fail. Even if it were possible to assess a suitable salary by reference to West End rates of pay, the court could not impose such a figure since the parties had already stated that it had to be mutually agreed, something they had been unable to achieve. What they had was an agreement to agree at a further date. The contract failed.

In *Scammel v. Ouston* 1941 an agreement for the sale of a van where the balance of the price was to be met *"on hire purchase terms over a period of two years"* also failed. Since there was no previous course of dealing between the parties to enable the court to identify what these "hire purchase" terms might be, the only alternative would have been to treat the terms as standard hire purchase terms. Unfortunately, as the court observed, hire purchase terms are not standardised and identical, but vary from agreement to agreement, for example by charging different rates of interest.

A meaningless term can however often be ignored.

In *Nicolene Ltd. v. Simmonds* 1953 a contract was made for the sale of 3000 tons of steel bars. The seller later broke the contract. When the buyer sued for damages the seller argued there was no contract between them, relying on a statement in one of the contractual documents that, *"we are in agreement that the usual conditions of acceptance apply"*. The court, whilst recognising that there are no *"usual conditions of acceptance"*, found that the contract was in every other respect clear as to the obligations of the parties. The meaningless term could be cut out from the rest of the contract. In the course of his judgment Lord Denning MR commented that, *"A clause which is meaningless can often be ignored . . .; whereas a clause which has yet to be agreed may mean there is no contract at all."*

Some issues of uncertainty are overcome by statutory mechanisms. S.8 Sale of Goods Act 1979 is an example. It provides that if a contract for goods the parties have not agreed a price, the buyer is bound to pay a *reasonable* price (usually the going market price).

Sometimes the contract will have a mechanism which can be used to fix the price, or indeed resolve any other aspect of uncertainty.

In *Sykes (F & G) Wessex v. Fine Fare* 1967 a supplier of chickens undertook to supply a supermarket chain with between 30,000 and 80,000 birds each week over a period of one year. The agreement also provided that for a further four years the supplier would provide chickens in quantities *"as might be agreed"*. The meaning of this expression subsequently led to a dispute between the parties. The court held that since the contract provided for arbitration to settle disagreements, the contract was not void on the basis of the uncertainty of the term as to quantity.

The offer must not have terminated

If the offer has come to an end in some way before the offeree accepts it, the acceptance is ineffective for there is no longer an offer to accept. An offer will be regarded as terminated where:

(a)   the offeror has *revoked* the offer; or

(b)   it has *lapsed*; or

(c)   it has been *accepted* or met with *a counter offer.*

Where the offeror has revoked the offer

Revoking, or withdrawing, the offer is permissible at any time before the offeree has accepted it, and the revocation can be effective even if it is not communicated directly by the offeror, provided it is communicated through some reliable channel. However, like an offer, a revocation is only effective when it is actually communicated by being brought to the attention of the offeree. The following case illustrate the point.

> In *Byrne & Co. v. Leon Van Tienhoven & Co.* 1880 an offer to sell tin plate was received by the offeree on 11 October, and immediately accepted by telegram. The offeror however had posted a revocation which the offeree received on 20 October. It was held the revocation was only effective when actually received, and was therefore too late.

Does actual receipt mean physical delivery to the business premises of the offeree or must it in addition be opened and read? In *Eagleshill Ltd. v. J Needham (Builders)Ltd.* 1972 the House of Lords suggested that it will be effective even if it has not been opened, provided that it would have been opened, *"if the ordinary course of business was followed".*

Where the offer has lapsed

When an offer is made it will not remain open indefinitely, but will lapse. This occurs automatically in certain circumstances, for example

- after a stated time limit for which the offer was to be held open has passed; or if there is no such time limit, after a reasonable time;

In *Ramsgate Victoria Hotel Co. Ltd. v. Montefiore* 1866 the defendant offered by letter on 8 June to buy shares in the company, and was allotted the shares on 23 November. It was held that the defendant was entitle to refuse the shares on the grounds that his offer had lapsed before the company had made the allotment. Clearly the market value of shares can fluctuate widely over a period of six months;

- if the situation on which it was based has fundamentally changed, for instance if the property which has been offered for sale has been destroyed by fire or has been stolen, before acceptance occurs;

An offeror is not obliged to keep the offer open for any particular length of time, unless a separate contract is made by the parties to achieve this. So if A is interested in buying goods from B, and B promises to hold open the offer to sell A the goods at a particular price for a fixed period of time, the promise is only binding if A has given a valuable promise in return – probably by agreeing to pay B for the benefit of the offer being kept open.

Characteristics of a Valid Acceptance

Acceptance is defined as the unconditional assent to all the terms of the offer. It must be unequivocal.

The following points indicate how the courts determine whether an acceptance will be regarded as valid.

It must be unconditional

Often people believe they have accepted the offer, when in fact they have made a fresh offer themselves by introducing new conditions.

An acceptance which is qualified by containing new terms constitutes a *counter offer,* and a continuation of the negotiating process. A counter offer both rejects and extinguishes an original offer.

In *Hyde v. Wrench* 1840 the defendant offered his farm to the plaintiff for £1,000. The plaintiff replied offering £950. The defendant subsequently rejected this, so the plaintiff purported to accept the original £1,000 offer. It was held that there was no contract since the original offer had been extinguished by the counter offer. Although expressed as an acceptance, it was in fact a fresh offer.

If the offer is made subject to a condition there can be no acceptance until that condition is fulfilled. Quite often an offer of employment is made *conditional*, for instance, "*subject to the receipt of satisfactory written references*" or the " *passing of a medical examination*".

> In *Wishart v. National Association of Citizens Advice Bureaux Ltd.* 1990 The Court of Appeal considered a case where the plaintiff had been offered the post of information officer "subject to satisfactory references" and then when the employer discovered his past attendance record withdrew the job offer. The issue before the Court of Appeal was whether the employer's decision to treat the references as unsatisfactory could be viewed objectively and tested by the standard of the reasonable person in the position of the employer. In fact the court decided that unlike medical opinion as to the employee's fitness which could be tested objectively, there was no obligation in law on the employer other than to decide in good faith whether the references were satisfactory. "*The natural reading of a communication, the purpose of which is to tell the prospective employee that part of the decision on whether he is firmly offered the post has yet to be made, is that the employer is reserving the right to make up his own mind when the references have been received and studied.*"

Any alteration to the terms of the offer will render the acceptance invalid, and in commercial negotiations between parties, each trading on their standard terms, the terms which apply to the contract will often be those belonging to the party who fired the last shot. This situation has become known as the *battle of the forms*.

> In *Butler Machine Tool Co. v. Ex-Cell-O Corporation (England)Ltd.* 1979 the plaintiffs offered to sell a machine tool to the defendants in a quotation. The quotation contained a price variation clause, which by means of a specific formula enabled the plaintiffs to raise the quoted price between contract and delivery if their own costs rose. The defendants ordered the goods but on their own standard terms which did not include a price variation clause. The plaintiffs, on receipt of the order form, signed and returned an acknowledgement slip contained on the order form. The plaintiff's costs rose considerably between contract and delivery and they sought to apply the price variation clause. The defendants disputed that it was part of the contract. The Court of Appeal treated the defendant's order as a counter offer, and the return of the acknowledgement slip as the plaintiff's acceptance, consequently the contract between them did not contain the price variation clause.

Communicating the acceptance

The offeror is free to stipulate the method by which acceptance may be made. If no stipulation is given, anything that achieves communication will suffice; words, writing or conduct. Where it is clear that the offeror demands a particular method of acceptance then no other method will be effective. In most cases however, the offeror is likely to do little more than to give a general indication of the form of acceptance to be used. Where this occurs but the offeree adopts a different method of acceptance which is as quick or quicker than the specified method, the acceptance will be effective, since the offeror will have suffered no disadvantage.

> Consequently the Court of Appeal in *Yates Building Co. v. R J Pulleyn & Son (York)* 1976 held that an acceptance by means of ordinary post was effective, despite the offeror directing that registered post or recorded delivery should be used.

Since contractual communications require positive action silence can never amount to an effective acceptance of the offer. This holds true even if the parties have, in advance, agreed such an arrangement. For instance, if following an interview, an employer says to the interviewee that the job is his or hers if they hear nothing from the employer in the next seven days, the interviewee agrees this arrangement, and the seven days elapse without word from the employer, a binding contract will not have come into existence. What the law requires is some positive act.

> In *Felthouse v. Bindley* 1862 an uncle wrote to his nephew offering to buy the nephew's horse for £30.15s. and stating *"If I hear no more about him I shall consider the horse mine at that price"*. The nephew gave instructions to the defendant, an auctioneer, not to sell the horse as he intended it for his uncle. The defendant inadvertently sold the horse, and the uncle sued him in the tort of conversion. The court held that action must fail. Ownership in the horse had not passed from the nephew to the uncle for there was not a contract between them. Actual communication of acceptance never occurred.

There are two circumstances in which acceptance can operate without communication occurring at the same time, firstly in cases where the post is used to create the contract and secondly where the nature of the offer makes formal notification of acceptance unrealistic.

Transactions using the post

Transactions effected by means of correspondence in the form of letters, fax's, email, invoices, quotations and share applications are obviously very common forms of commercial activity. Business organisations need to keep records of their commercial activities, and the use of written correspondence is an effective way of achieving this.

Where the post is used there is of course the period whilst the letter is in transit when the person to whom it is addressed is unaware of its contents. Whereas an offer or revocation of an offer made by post is effective only when it is received by the party to whom it is sent, in the case of an *acceptance* by post the courts have laid down a rule that the letter is effective at the time and place of posting, provided it was correctly addressed and pre-paid. This remarkable rule, which is completely at odds with he normal requirements regarding communication, applies even if the letter of acceptance is lost or destroyed in the post.

The parties are free to vary these rules if they wish to do so, and it may be prudent for an offeror to stipulate that an acceptance in writing which is posted to him shall not be effective until it is actually received. It is common to find terms in standard form business contracts to this effect, and the courts seem willing to infer a variation of the post rules whenever possible.

> The post rules can produce some surprising results. In *Household Fire Insurance Co. v. Grant* 1879 the defendant applied for 100 shares in the plaintiff company. The company received his application form, and the company secretary completed and posted a letter of allotment to the defendant, and entered his name on the register of shareholders. The letter never arrived. The company later went into liquidation, and the liquidator claimed the payment outstanding on the shares from the defendant. By a majority the Court of Appeal held that the defendant was liable to pay. The shares became his when the letter of allotment was posted, even though he never received it and was therefore unaware that he had become a shareholder.

Formal acceptance unrealistic

Sometimes the circumstances of an offer are such that the courts will regard conduct which occurs without the knowledge of the offeror as a sufficient method of acceptance. Where an offer has been made to the public at large the courts may take the view that the offeror could not possibly have expected to receive an acceptance from every person who has decided to take up the offer. This would be a commercial nonsense.

> In *Carlill v. Carbolic Smokeball Co.* 1893 the defendant company advertised a medical preparation they manufactured, and claimed in the advertisement that they would pay £100 reward to anybody who contracted *"the increasing*

epidemic of influenza" after purchasing and using the product as directed. The advertisement added that £1000 was deposited with the Alliance Bank *"showing our sincerity in the matter"* The plaintiff purchased the product, used it as directed, then caught influenza. She sued for her £100 reward. The court held that the advertisement constituted a firm offer intended to be legally binding since the bank deposit indicated an intention to meet claims, the offer could be made to the public at large, and acceptance of the offer in such circumstances could be implied by the conduct of those like the plaintiff, who performed the stated conditions. In consequence the company were held liable.

In *Percy Trentham Ltd. v. Archital Luxfer Ltd.* 1993 the Court of Appeal found itself having to review the whole question of contractual agreements. The plaintiffs were the main contractors engaged in a building contract, and they had negotiated with the defendants a sub-contract under which the defendants were to supply and fit architectural furniture, such as doors and windows. The sub-contract was satisfactorily performed, but a dispute arose when the plaintiffs, who were obliged to make a penalty payment under the main contract, sought a contribution from the defendants. The defendant's response was that no contract had ever been concluded between the parties. Telephone calls had been made and letters exchanged but no discernible offer and acceptance could be identified. As a result it was not possible to determine whose standard terms of trading applied to the agreement.

The Court of Appeal held that a contract had been made between the parties. In carrying out the work the defendants had agreed to an offer from the plaintiffs. Steyn LJ took the view that the test to determine whether a contract has been formed is an objective one, and in this case one should look to *"the reasonable expectations of sensible businessmen"* rather than the *"subjective and unexpressed mental reservations of the parties."* Although the usual mechanism of contractual formation is offer and acceptance in some circumstances this is not necessary. The instant case was an example, which concerned *"a contract alleged to have come into existence during and as a result of performance."* The contract was an executed one (i.e. had been carried out) making it very difficult to argue either lack of intention to create legal relations, or invalidly based upon uncertainty of terms. *"If a contract comes into existence during and as a result of performance of the transaction,"* said his Lordship, *"it will frequently be possible to hold that the contract impliedly and retrospectively covers pre-contractual performance."*

Consideration

Under English law the simple contract has always been seen as a bargain struck between the parties. The bargain is arrived at by negotiations and concluded when a definite and certain offer has been made which has been met with an unequivocal acceptance. Millions of transactions of this kind are made each day.

Making an agreement, as we have seen, involves giving undertakings or promises. The offeror makes a promise, and indicates what the offeree must do in return. The idea of a contract as an exchange of promises is fundamental to an understanding of the simple contract.

Lawyers refer to the promises exchanged under a contract as the consideration each party is providing the other. A number of important principles of consideration exist, and which we need to examine. Of these the most fundamental is that consideration is needed to support all simple contracts, and so in any case where valid consideration has not passed between the parties the general rule is the agreement they have made will be of no legal effect.

Consideration need not be adequate but must have some value

The word *adequate* in this context means equal to the promise given. The principle of adequacy of consideration has developed to cope with contractual disputes in which one of the parties is arguing that the contract is bad because the value of the consideration provided by the other party is not the economic equivalent of the value of the promise given in return.

The courts are not prepared to defeat an agreement merely on the grounds that one of the parties has, in effect, made a bad bargain. Bad bargains are a fact of commercial life. A deal that is struck where one of the parties has entered it in haste, or without proper enquiry, or has been swayed by convincing salesmanship, may be bitterly regretted subsequently, but it is certainly not possible in such circumstances to escape liability on the grounds that *"I gave more than I got"*. Consequently there is no relief for the business or the individual who is at the receiving end of a hard bargain.

> In *Mountford v. Scott* 1975 the defendant made an agreement with the plaintiff, granting the plaintiff an option to purchase the defendant's house for £10,000 within six months. The plaintiff paid £1 for the option, and later sought to exercise it. The value of the defendant's property had risen by this time and he refused to sell. The court was prepared to grant an order for specific performance, compelling the defendant to transfer the property for the

agreed price. It was for the defendant to fix the value of the option. Some consideration was provided and this was enough. The trial judge commented: *"It is only necessary, as I see it, that the option should have been validly created"*.

However apparently insignificant the consideration may be, as long as it has some discernible value it will be valid.

In *Chappell and Co. Ltd. v. Nestlé. Ltd* 1960 the defendants, as part of a sales promotion, offered a record at a reduced price if their chocolate bar wrappers accompanied the payment. The plaintiffs held the copyright in the record, and argued that the royalties they were entitled to should be assessed on the price of the record plus the value of the wrappers, which the defendants in fact simply threw away when they had been received. The House of Lords agreed with the plaintiffs, seeing the subsequent disposal of the wrappers as irrelevant, since each wrapper in reality represented the profit on the sale of a bar of chocolate, and was therefore part of the consideration.

Adequacy is not determined solely by economic criteria. It is enough that the promise is a promise to refrain from doing something which the promisor is legally entitled to do. It may be a promise not to take legal proceedings, or not to exercise a legal right such as a right of way. Even where the promise is related to a positive act the act may have little to do with anything capable of economic valuation, yet still be good consideration in the eyes of the law. A parent may undertake to pay a sum of money to a son or daughter in the event of them marrying, or graduating, and the marriage or graduation will be valid consideration in these circumstances.

The question of whether a forbearance will operate as adequate consideration may sometimes concern those engaged in business and commercial activity. Suppose the owner of the only retail travel agency in a small town is approached by a larger company, with a number of agencies in the area. The owner is told that in consideration of the payment of £30,000 by him to the company, it will not set up a competing business in the town. Would this be a valid agreement? In *Thorne v. Motor Trade Association* 1937 Lord Atkin, commented, *"it appears to me that if a man may lawfully, in the furtherance of business interests, do acts which will seriously injure another in his business he may also lawfully, if he is still acting in the furtherance of his business interests, invite that other to pay him a sum of money as an alternative to doing the injurious acts"*.

Consideration must be sufficient

Consideration is treated as insufficient, and therefore incapable of supporting a contract, when it involves the promisor undertaking to do something he is already obliged to do legally. The rationale is that since the promisor is bound to carry out the promise anyway, there can be no true bargain in using performance of this promise to support another contract. Consideration is insufficient therefore in the two circumstances. The first is where the promisor has an existing contractual obligation to carry out the promise offered as consideration.

In *Stilk v. Myrick* 1809 a promise by a ships captain to pay sailors an additional sum for working the ship on the return voyage as unenforceable, even though they had to work harder due to the desertion of two crew members. The court found that their existing contracts bound them to work the ship home in such circumstances, thus they had provided no new consideration to support the promise of extra wages.

In dramatically changed circumstances it may be possible to show a fresh contract has been negotiated.

In *Hartley v. Ponsonby* 1857, a ships crew was so depleted that the ship was dangerous to work. In these circumstances the promise of the captain to pay extra wages was held to be enforceable.

In *Williams v. Roffey Bros. & Nicholls (Contractors) Ltd.* 1990 the defendants had a contract with a housing association for the refurbishment of a number of flats. They subcontracted the joinery work to the plaintiff. After performing most of his obligations under the contract the plaintiff found himself in financial difficulties, for the agreed price of £20,000 was too low. The defendants were anxious for their contract with the housing association to be completed by the agreed date, since under a penalty clause they would suffer financially for late completion. The defendants met the plaintiff and agreed to pay him an additional £10,300 for completion of the joinery work. He then carried out most of the remaining work, but refused to finish it when the defendants indicated that they would not pay him the additional agreed sum. They argued that he was under a contractual obligation to carry out the work arising from the original contract. He had given no new consideration for the promise of extra payment.

The Court of Appeal held that the new agreement was binding on the defendants. By promising the extra money they had received a benefit, namely the avoidance of a penalty payment, or alternatively the need to employ another sub-contractor. This benefit was consideration to support the new agreement even though the plaintiff was not required to any more work than he had originally undertaken. The court approved the decision in *Stilk v. Myrick* , however on its facts the Williams case seems to suggest that the courts are now prepared to take a more liberal approach in their willingness to recognise a fresh contract and what can be properly regarded as good consideration.

Of further relevance to the question of how to assess sufficiency is the old common law principle that payment of a lesser amount to a creditor than the full debt cannot discharge the debtor from liability for the full amount even though the creditor agrees it, and accepts the lesser amount. This is known as the rule in *Pinnel's Case* 1602, a rule subsequently confirmed by the House of Lords in *Foakes v. Beer* 1884. It is based upon the view that there can be no real bargain in a person agreeing to accept a lesser sum than they are legally entitled to. But if the varied agreement contains an additional element, such a promise to pay the reduced sum earlier than the date on which the full debt is due, then provided the creditor agrees it, this will be binding. It may be of considerable commercial advantage to receive a smaller amount immediately than have to wait for the full sum, where, for example, the creditor is experiencing cash flow problems.

In addition to early payment of a reduced amount if agreed by the creditor, there are certain other exceptions to the rule in Pinnel's case. They include:

- Substituted performance. This arises where the creditor accepts some other form of consideration instead of money, such as the delivery of goods. Alternatively payment of a lesser sum together with an additional element, such as a promise to repair the creditor's car, would suffice.

- Payment of a lesser sum where the debtor is disputing the value of the work that has been performed, and the creditor accepts the reduced amount. The reason why the creditor is bound by such an arrangement is that if the dispute were to be resolved by court action, the court might determine the value of the work performed as worth even less than the debtor has offered to pay. Accepting the reduced sum may be seen as a new bargain.

- When the equitable doctrine of promissory estoppel applies (see later).

The second example of insufficiency is where the promisor has a public obligation to carry out the act.

Performance of a public duty as a means of providing consideration is insufficient to support the contract. However if the promisor performs some act beyond the public duty, this will operate as valid consideration.

> In *Harris v. Sheffield United F C* 1987 the football club challenged its contractual liability to pay for the policing of its football ground during home matches. It was held however that the contract between itself and the police authority was valid. The number of officers provided was in excess of those who would have been provided had the police simply been fulfilling their public obligation to keep the peace and prevent disorder.

Consideration must not be past

A party to contract cannot use a past act as a basis for consideration. Therefore, if one party performs an act for another, and only receives a promise of payment after the act is complete, the past act would be past consideration. What is required is that the promise of one of the parties to the alleged contract is given in response to the promise of the other. If an act is carried out with no promise of reward having been made, it will be treated as purely gratuitous.

> In *Roscorla v. Thomas* 1842 the seller of a horse, after the buyer had purchased it, promised the buyer that it was sound and free from vice. It was not, and the buyer sued the seller on the promise. The action failed. The promise was supported by no new consideration.

There are exceptions to the past consideration rule, for example where the work has been performed in circumstances which carry an implication of a promise to pay.

> In *Re Casey's Patents, Stewart v. Casey* 1892 the joint owners of a patent agreed with Casey that he should manage and publicise their invention. Two years later they promised him a third share in the patent, as *"consideration of your services as manager"*.The court rejected the view that this promise was supported by past consideration from Casey. The request to him to render his services carried an implied promise to pay for them. The promise of a third share was simply the fixing of the price.

Only the parties to the agreement who have provided each other with consideration can sue on the contract. A person who has provided no consideration does not have the right to sue on the contract, for that person is not a party to it. This principle, known as *privity of contract*, has been subject to much criticism in recent years, and the position is now largely regulated by the Contract (Third Party Rights) Act 1999.

Intention to Create Legal Relations

A valid agreement supported by consideration may still fail as a contract unless it is able to satisfy a further legal test, namely that the parties intended their agreement to have legal consequences. In many agreements it is obvious from the context the parties did not intend a legal relationship. A court distinguishes between those arrangements where the parties did intend their agreement to be legally enforceable, and those where this was not the intention, by looking at all the available evidence, and in particular whether the parties have expressly indicated their intention. For instance a written agreement may suggest a more formal type of relationship.

Common law presumptions regarding intention

At common law certain presumptions regarding intention are applied by the courts. In an agreement of a *social* or *domestic* kind, the courts will presume there was no intention to create a contract. This does not mean, for example, that it is impossible for members of the same family to contract each with the other. They may well be participants in joint business ventures such as partnerships which are founded on a contractual relationship. Rather it is simply a requirement of the common law that there is clear evidence of such an intention. This must be sufficient to overcome the presumption that the parties did not intend a contract.

In *commercial* transactions the courts will presume an intention that they are intended to be legally binding. Indeed whenever there is a business dimension to the agreement the only way to prevent the judicial presumption from operating is to indicate clearly that the agreement is *not* intended to be a contract. The inclusion of the phrase *"binding in honour"* on a football coupon was held by the court in *Jones v. Vernons Pools Ltd.* 1938 to amount to clear evidence that there was no intention to create a contract.

> In *Rose and Frank Co. v. Crompton Bros* 1923 a written agreement entered into by two commercial organisations included the following clause *"This arrangement is not entered into, nor is this memorandum written, as a formal or legal agreement... but... is only a definite expression and record of the purpose and intention of the ... parties concerned, to which they each honourably pledge themselves"*. This clause, the court held, was sufficient evidence to overturn the presumption that the commercial agreement was intended to be legally binding.

Since *honour clauses* have the effect of making an otherwise legally enforceable agreement unenforceable by means of court action, they need to be treated with some care.

A particular commercial practice which can sometimes give rise to questions of contractual intention is the use of the so called *letter of comfort*. These are letters which are designed to provide commercial reassurance, and their use is illustrated in the following case.

> In *Kleinwort Benson Ltd. v. Malaysia Mining Corporation Bhd* 1989 the plaintiff bank agreed to make loan facilities of up to £10M available to a subsidiary company owned by the defendants. The defendants were not prepared to give the bank a formal guarantee to cover the loan facility to the subsidiary, MMC Metals Ltd., however they wrote to the bank stating, *"It is our policy to ensure that the business (of MMC Metals) is at all times in a position to meet its liabilities to you...,"* and, *"We confirm that we will not reduce our current financial interest in MMC Metals Ltd.".*
>
> Subsequently MMC Metals, a tin dealer, went into liquidation following the collapse of the world tin market. The bank looked to the defendants to make good the loss suffered by it on the loans it had made to MMC. The Court of Appeal held that on the facts the defendants letter did not give rise to a binding contract, for on a proper construction of it, it showed no intention to create a legal relationship. In particular the use of the expression "policy" indicated that the defendants were making it clear they were not to be legally bound. Companies are free to change their policies, and often do. The parties were trading equals, and the bank ought to have been aware of the implications of being offered a letter of comfort rather than a letter of guarantee.

Clauses ousting the courts jurisdiction and arbitration clauses

A term contained in an agreement which attempts entirely to exclude the court's jurisdiction will be void on the grounds that its effect would be to prevent a court from even determining the preliminary issue of the nature of the agreement itself. It is quite legitimate to insert an arbitration clause into the contract. Arbitration clauses are a common feature of business agreements providing a dispute solving mechanism which is generally cheaper, quicker and more private than court proceedings. The rights of consumers under agreements they have made which contain arbitration clauses are now protected under the Consumer Arbitration Agreements Act 1988. The Act is designed to deal with contracts where an arbitration clause is being used by a business as a mechanism for preventing a dispute from being heard before the courts, so that the consumer is bound to follow arbitration arrangements which may well be weighted against him. The Act provides that where a consumer has entered into a contract which provides for future differences between the parties to be referred to arbitration, the arbitration arrangements cannot be enforced against him unless, under s.1:

(a)   he has consented in writing after the difference has occurred to the use of the arbitration; or

(b)   he has submitted to the arbitration; or

(c)   the court has made an order under s.4. This enables the court to determine that the consumer will not suffer a detriment to his interests by having the difference determined by the arbitration arrangements rather than by court proceedings.

The court must consider all relevant matters, including the availability of legal aid.

For the purposes of the Act, a consumer is someone who enters into the contract without either making the contract in the course of a business or holding himself out as doing so. The other party must have made the contract in the course of a business, and if the contract is a sale of goods transaction the goods must be of a type ordinarily supplied for private use or consumption.

Collective agreements

Contractual intention is also of significance in relation to collective agreements, A *collective agreement* is one between trade unions and employers' organisations by which an agreement or arrangement is made about matters such as terms and conditions of employment. It is estimated that as many as 14 million employees within the United Kingdom are employed under contracts which are regulated in part by collective agreements. The Trade Union and Labour Relations (Consolidation) Act 1992 provides that a collective agreement is presumed not to have been intended by the parties to be a legally enforceable contract unless the agreement is in writing and contains a statement that the parties intend it to be legally enforceable.

While collective agreements are not legally binding they usually contain provisions which are expressly or impliedly incorporated into individual contracts of employment and so become legally enforceable. Provisions which deal with employee's working time, hours, holidays are obvious examples of terms which may become legally binding.

In *Anderson v. Pringle of Scotland* 1998 it was held that an employer was obliged to comply with the terms of a redundancy procedure which had become expressly incorporated from a collective agreement into individual contracts of employment. The "last in and first out" criterion for selection was contractual and enforceable in a redundancy situation.

Capacity to contract

Capacity is an expression that describes a person's ability to do something. In legal terms it covers the ability to make contracts, commit torts and commit crimes.

The general rule under English law is that anyone can bind themselves by a contract, as long as it is not illegal, or void for public policy. There are however exceptions to the rule. The most significant are contracts made by corporations and contracts made by minors.

Corporations

The nature of corporate bodies was dealt with in Chapter 4. Corporations are regarded as legal persons in their own right, thus enabling then to make contracts, commit torts (and some crimes), and hold land. Since they enjoy legal rights and are subject to legal obligations they can sue, and be sued, in respect of these rights and obligations.

Minors (Children)

The law has always sought to protect minors (Children) from the consequences of making transactions detrimental to themselves. The aim has been to provide them with some protection from their lack of commercial experience, whilst at the same time recognising circumstances where it is appropriate that they should be fully accountable for the agreements they make. The result is a mixture of common law and statutory rules which seek to achieve a balance between these conflicting objectives. The expression *minor* refers to anyone under the age of eighteen, this being the age of majority under the Family Law Reform Act 1969. Categories of contracts a minor can make include beneficial contracts of employment, and contracts for necessaries. A beneficial contract of employment is one which is substantially for the minor's benefit. Benefit is invariably taken to mean that the contract must include some element of training or education, although this can usually be easily established. The court will set aside a contract of employment which viewed overall is not beneficial.

In *Roberts v. Gray* 1913 the defendant, a minor, with a view to becoming a professional billiards player, had entered an agreement with the plaintiff, himself a leading professional, to accompany the plaintiff on a world tour. The plaintiff spent time and money organising the tour, but following a dispute the defendant refused to go. The plaintiff sought damages of £6000 for breach of contract. The Court of Appeal held that the contract was for the defendant's benefit, being in the nature of a course of instruction in the game of billiards. The plaintiff was awarded £1500 damages.

Necessaries are defined in s.3 Sale of Goods Act 1979 as *"goods suitable to the condition in life of the minor ... and to his actual requirements at the time of sale and delivery."* This is a subjective test of the minors needs, found by reference to his economic and social status.

Some contracts made by minors are said to be voidable. They bind the minor until he repudiates them. Repudiation is the expression used to describe the act of rejecting a contract. Repudiation must occur before reaching majority or within a reasonable time thereafter. If a repudiation has not taken place after this time the contract becomes valid. Contracts falling within this category are those of a long term nature, such as non-beneficial contracts of employment, contracts for a lease, contracts to take shares in a company, and partnership agreements.

Assignment - Rock Relics

Rock Relics Limited is a mail order record company located in the north of England primarily engaged in the supply of specialist recorded material direct to the public. Recordings from the 1960 and 1970s are made available on CD at competitive prices. The company's products are marketed mainly through its catalogue direct to the public and the company is anxious to increase the membership base. It is a long term strategy of Rock Relics to increase its market share by expanding its operation.

At a senior management meeting last month the Commercial Director, Alan Keppie arranged to meet Malcolm Lewis, the Managing Director of Frizzels Limited an advertising agency. At that meeting Malcolm and Alan agreed that Frizzels Limited should produce a thirty second advertisement relating to Rock Relics which was suitable for broadcasting on local radio. Malcolm agreed that the advertisement should be subject to Alan's final approval. While no specific agreement was reached as to overall cost, Malcolm convinced Alan that Frizzel's rates are highly competitive and would be unlikely to exceed Alan's budget. The meeting was not formally minuted but notes were taken by Julie, Malcolm's personal assistant.

Two weeks later Alan and his colleagues were given a presentation of the proposed advertisement by a team from Frizzels. The unanimous view of Alan and his colleagues at a subsequent meeting is that the advertisement is entirely unsuitable for Rock Relics image. At that meeting it is resolved that Frizzels should be "dropped" and the radio station, Heart of the North FM should be asked to produce the advertisement.

Alan's contact with Heart of the North FM involved discussions concerning advertising costs and the size and composition of the radio station's audience. It's sales manager Peter Forbes, indicated the figures showed the station to be "the fastest growing radio station in the region, with an average audience of 250,000". Following these discussions Alan agreed with Peter for the station to produce a suitable advertisement for Rock Relics. The agreement was made by exchange of faxes. The sequence of events was as follows. Rock Relics faxed Heart of the North stating "Please go ahead with the arrangements for the advertising campaign as discussed with your Mr Forbes. We confirm the price of £10,500 inclusive of VAT as referred to by you as acceptable to us, and that the arrangement is for you to transmit the advertisement eight times a day for a fortnight, such transmissions to be at peak timings".

Heart of the North then faxed the following reply, "We confirm acceptance of your fax, and look forward to a long and satisfactory relationship with you. Please note that our terms of business provide that the quoted price is subject to a discretionary increase we may levy which is not to exceed 5% and is to cover unforeseen costs we may incur". Rock Relics responded, "Thank you for your last fax. Please note that we are unable to exceed the figure of £10,500 which is the limit of our budget allocation.

Alan Keppie has received an invoice from Frizzels Communications Limited for £4,750 relating to their fee for the production of the advertisement and the subsequent presentation to Alan and his colleagues.

Two weeks ago Heart of the North began the broadcasts, but the advertising campaign was not a success. It only lasted for two weeks but four of the eight slots each day were in the early hours of the morning. Alan then discovered that Heart of the North had been the fastest growing radio station in 1998 but that it's market share was dropped in 1999 and its audience of 250,000 was a projected figure for 2000, which has not materialised. The finishing touch came when Heart of the North informed Alan that is was exercising its contractual ability to raise the contract price by 5% and invoiced Rock Relics for £11,250.

Task

Alan needs to establish the potential liability of Rock Relics to both Frizzel Advertising and Heart of the North Radio. In the role of Rock Relics legal advisor your task is to prepare an informal report in which you advise Alan on the legal position in relation to both companies paying particular attention to a number of issues he wishes you to address:

- the fact that no contract was ever signed with Frizzels and Alan denies any intention to create legal relations with the company;

- the fact that Frizzel's work was subject to Alan's approval and Rock Relics received no benefit from it. Are Frizzels entitled to payment or part payment of their invoice?

- was a contract entered into between Heart of the North and Rock Relics and what is the effect of the statement regarding growth and audience figures?

- are Heart of the North entitled to raise the contract price and should Rock Relics meet any of the payment?

Assignment - Are we Agreed?

You work as a legal assistant in the legal department of Anglo-Swedish Metal Industries plc. On returning from your summer holiday you find two files in your in-tray, accompanied by a memorandum from your superior, Jane West, one of the company's lawyers, which states, "Please respond to the letters contained in the attached files. See me if you have any difficulties."

The first file contains the following letter from a solicitor:

> I represent Miss Sally Goldwell. I understand from my client that she was interviewed for a clerical post with your company. Following the interview she was asked if she would be willing to accept the post, and she indicated that she would. A week later, on 10th September 199X, she received a formal offer of the post from your company's Personnel Officer. She was asked to reply in writing within five days. She was ill at the time and arranged for a friend to notify you of her acceptance by phone. Her friend telephoned sometime after 7 pm on 13th September 199X. This was a Friday, and her friend had to leave a message on the Personnel Department's answerphone. I gather that the Personnel Department closes from 4.30pm on Friday, until 8.30 the following Monday, and that the message only reached the Personnel Officer at midday on Monday 16th September. He had that morning telephoned another interviewee to offer her the job, which she accepted. My client subsequently heard from you that the post was no longer available for her.
>
> I am of the opinion that a contract exists between my client and yourselves, in respect of which you are in breach. I look forward to your prompt response.
>
> Yours faithfully,
>
>
>
> Roger Major

The second file contained the following letter from one of the company's suppliers, Humberside Steels Ltd.:

We refer to our offer to supply you with 40 tonnes reinforced steel bars, to which you responded with an order (68747/5/NX) for the goods to be delivered to you on 1st May. We replied immediately informing you that due to circumstances beyond our control delivery would be on the 24th May. We heard from you, and delivered the goods on 24th May, only to find that you rejected them on the basis that they had not been ordered. We are at a loss to understand your action, particularly as we have often varied the delivery date with you in this way in the past, without complaint by you.

We should be grateful therefore to receive your remittance in due course.

Yours faithfully

James Leach pp
Humberside Steels Ltd.

Tasks

1.   In the form of a memorandum to your superior, Jane West, indicate any weaknesses you have been able to identify regarding the company's legal position in respect of the two claims.

2.   Draft replies to each of the letters, in which you state the legal basis upon which the company challenges the contractual claims they make.

Chapter 9

The Principles of Contract Law: Issues of Validity

In Chapter 8 we concentrated on how a contract is made. It might be supposed that no further contractual issues are likely to emerge. The parties to the agreement, having met the basic legal requirements and formed their contract. They then carry out their respective responsibilities to their mutual satisfaction and performance will have been completed. This is indeed what usually happens. The contract is made and performed. Each side is satisfied and transaction is completed.

But contracts do not always run so smoothly. They can go wrong, sometimes for technical reasons and sometimes for practical reasons. Among the more common claims that are asserted are that:

- the contract is not binding because there was not true consent given to it. It may be alleged that the contract was induced by the making of false statements, or that one or even both parties were mistaken in reaching their agreement. A further possibility is an allegation that one side exerted unfair influence over the other, or perhaps even made threats against the other;

- the contract is invalid because its purpose is something contrary to the public interest, for instance because it imposes an unreasonable restraint upon trading freedom;

- some event has occurred which has brought the contract to an end, without performance having been completed.

- the obligations arising under the contract have not been performed either partially or in total, so that there has been a breach of contract;

Of these various possibilities the most frequent are claims of breach of contract. Whatever the nature of the claim may be, however, it will always involve the innocent party seeking some remedy; perhaps financial compensation in the form of damages, or a court order to prevent a threatened breach of contract or enforcing the performance of the contract.

Sometimes what appears to be a properly constituted contract, proves on closer examination to be one containing a defect which was present when the agreement was made. Certain defects of this kind the law recognises as sufficiently serious to invalidate the contract either partially or wholly. Such defects are referred to as *vitiating* factors, and they occur in circumstances of misrepresentation, mistake, duress and undue influence. To vitiate means to invalidate.

Misrepresentation

Before reaching contractual agreement the parties will often be involved in a process of negotiation. Negotiations can range over any issues which the parties think are relevant to the protection of their interests, but are likely to cover questions of payment, when and how the contract is to be performed, and what terms will be attached to it. The aim of negotiating is both to obtain information and to drive a good bargain, and negotiating skills are a valuable commodity in most areas of commercial and industrial life. Not all contracts are preceded by negotiations however, and as a general rule the more marked the imbalance in trading strength between the parties the less likely will be serious negotiation of terms and conditions. Thus transactions between large organisations on one side, and small organisations or private consumers on the other tend to be characterised by the dominant party presenting the weaker party with a set of terms which are not open to discussion but have to be accepted in their entirety if a contract is to be made.

The nature of representations

Statements made during the bargaining process may become a part of the contract itself, that is, they may become *terms* of the contract and give rise to an action for breach of contract if they prove untrue. But in many cases there will be no intention by the maker of the statement that the statement should be absorbed into the contract at all. It will be made merely to induce the other party to make the contract. Statements of this sort are known as *representations*. If a representation is untrue for any reason it may constitute a *misrepresentation*, and as such it will be actionable. The injured party (*the misrepresentee*) will base a claim not on breach of contract, but on the law applicable to misrepresentation.

A representation is a statement or assertion of fact made by one party to the other before or at a time of the contract, which has the effect of inducing the other to enter into a contract. The statement can be in any form. It can be in writing, such as a company prospectus containing details of the company's trading activities, or it can be spoken, or be implied from conduct. The definition enables us to distinguish a number of statements whose form or content excludes them from being treated as representations.

Statements of opinion

Often during negotiations statements are made which are based purely upon the opinion of the person making them. Since a representation must be a statement of fact, a statement expressed as an opinion cannot become a representation. It can be a difficult task to discriminate between what is, or can be fairly regarded as an issue of fact rather than opinion.

> In *Esso Petroleum Co. Ltd. v. Mardon.* 1976 Mardon took a tenancy of a filling station owned by Esso, having been given a forecast by an experienced Esso sales representative of the quantity of petrol the station could be expected to sell annually. This quantity was never reached during the four years Mardon remained as tenant, and the business ran at a loss. The Court of Appeal decided that the company had made a misrepresentation, since the sales representative's knowledge of such matters made the forecast a statement of fact rather than opinion, and the sales representative was acting in the capacity of an agent of the company. Mardon's claim for damages was successful. The misrepresentation was regarded as a negligent one, and the court also took the view that the representation amounted to a contractual warranty, that is a contractual promise. In his leading judgment Lord Denning MR commented: *"it was a forecast made by a party, Esso who had special knowledge and skill. It was the yardstick by which they measured the worth of a filling station. They knew the facts. They knew the traffic in the town. They knew the throughput of a comparable station. They had much experience and expertise at their disposal. They were in a much better position than Mr. Mardon to make a forecast. It seems to me that if such a person makes a forecast – intending that the other should act on it and he does act on it – it can well be interpreted as a warranty that the forecast is sound and reliable in this sense that they made it with reasonable care and skill. That warranty was broken. Most negligently Esso made a fatal error in the forecast they stated to Mr. Mardon, and on which he took the tenancy. For this they are made liable in damages".*

Clearly it is not possible to avoid liability for a statement which is expressed as, or is subsequently claimed to be an opinion, when the knowledge and experience of the representor in the matter is far greater than that of the representee.

Advertising and sales boasts

Much advertising and sales patter falls outside the rules on misrepresentation because the statements made are not capable of substantial verification. They do not attract any legal consequences. Examples include the holiday tour company's, *holiday of a lifetime,* and the carpet company's *We cannot be equalled for price and quality.* However to advertise that *interest free credit is available on all items bought this month,* or that a motor vehicle has returned *31 m.p.g. at a constant 75 m.p.h* are clearly statements of fact. If untrue they give rise to a criminal offence under the Trade Descriptions Act 1968 as well as amounting to misrepresentations. In respect of descriptions applied to *properties* the Property Misdescription Act 1991 has introduced stringent controls over the language that may be used in their sale.

Statements of law

A false statement of law cannot constitute a misrepresentation. This principle is based upon the general legal proposition that ignorance of the law does not excuse an otherwise unlawful act. The assumption is that the representee knows the law, and cannot therefore rely upon a plea that he relied upon inaccurate statements of law. Of course it would be quite different if these statements were being made by his legal adviser, upon whom he is placing reliance.

Distinguishing statements of law from statements of fact can in some cases be a difficult task. A single statement may be one of mixed law and fact.

> In *Smith v. Land and House Property Corporation* 1884 in a contract for the sale of an hotel the seller stated that it was leased to *"a most desirable tenant".* In fact the tenant was far from desirable and the purchaser attempted to terminate the contract on the grounds of misrepresentation. The court held that the statement was not one of law, for its principal observation was not the evidence of the person being a tenant, but rather that the tenant was a person who had qualities of value to the purchaser.

Silence

Although generally a non-disclosure cannot amount to a representation, there are some important exceptions to this rule. In contracts *uberrimae fidei* (of the utmost good faith) duties of full disclosure are imposed. In general these are contracts where one party alone has full knowledge of all material facts. Insurance contracts and contracts for the sale of shares through the issue of a prospectus are examples of contracts *uberrimae fidei.* If full disclosure is not made in such cases the injured party can rescind the contract. Thus before entering into an insurance agreement the party seeking cover must disclose all facts which are material to the nature of the risk which is to be insured.

In contracts for the sale of land the vendor is under an obligation to disclose any defects in his title, that is in his *ownership* of the property, although the obligation does not apply to defects in the property *itself*, for instance dry rot or damp.

In relation to a contract of employment there is no duty on a job applicatant to volunteer information which is not requested during the recruitment process, including the completion of an application form.

> In *Walton v. TAC Construction Materials Ltd.* 1981 the complainant was dismissed after working for thirteen and a half months when the employer discovered that he was a heroin addict. During a medical inspection prior to employment the employee had answered *"none"* when asked to give details of serious illnesses, and failed to reveal that he was injecting himself with heroin. While the tribunal decided that it was fair to dismiss him because of the deception *"it could not be said that there is any duty on the employee in the ordinary case, though there may be exceptions, to volunteer information about himself otherwise than in response to a direct question"*.

If a statement is true when made but becomes untrue before the contract is concluded, the representor will be under a duty to disclose this alteration to the other party.

Inducement

The representation must induce the person to enter into the contract. There can be no inducement where the other party is unaware of the representation or does not believe the statement, or has relied on his own skill and judgement. In such cases no action will lie in misrepresentation.

> In *Attwood v. Small* 1838 during the course of negotiations for the sale of a mine, the vendor made exaggerated statements of its capacity. The buyers subsequently appointed their own experts to investigate the mine, and the agents reported back to the buyers that the vendor's statements were true. As a result the buyers purchased the mine, only to discover that the statements were inaccurate. It was held that the buyers had no remedy in misrepresentation. They placed reliance upon their own independent investigation.

No test of reasonableness is applied to an inducement so a claim is not prevented by evidence that a reasonable person would not have been induced by the statement, provided the belief in the statement is genuine.

Types of misrepresentation

Actions for breach of contract and for misrepresentation differ in an important respect. If a term of a contract is broken the state of mind of the contract breaker is irrelevant in establishing the existence and extent of liability. If however a mere representation has proved to be untrue and has become a misrepresentation, the effect this has on the liability of the misrepresentor depends on the state of mind accompanying it. A misrepresentation may be made *innocently*, *negligently* or *fraudulently*.

It is *innocent* if the person making it had reasonable grounds for believing it to be true, and negligent where there was a lack of reasonable care taken to determine the accuracy of the statement. In contrast, a *fraudulent* misrepresentation is a representation which a person makes knowing it to be untrue, or believing it to be false, or which is made recklessly where the person making it does not care whether it is true or false. Thus it is a representation which is not honestly believed by the person making it, or where there has been complete disregard for the truth.

> At common law it has been possible since 1964 to claim damages in the tort of negligence for a *negligent* misrepresentation under the principle laid down in *Hedley Byrne v. Heller* 1964. *Hedley Byrne* provides that where there is a special relationship between the person making a statement and the recipient of it, a duty of reasonable care is owed in making it. If the duty is broken damages can be claimed, representing the loss suffered. The special relationship concept is central to the decision. The quality of this relationship was referred to by Lord Morris when he stated: *"Where in a sphere in which a person is so placed that others could reasonably rely on his judgment or his skill or on his ability to make careful inquiry, a person takes it on himself to give information or advice to, or allows his information or advice to be passed on to another, who, as he knows or should know, will place reliance on it then a duty of care will arise"*. (See Chapter 7)

The reliance placed on the statement by the recipient of it must be reasonable. In *Hedley Byrne* itself, a disclaimer of liability was enough to prevent reliance on a financial reference that had been given by a bank to a third party being reasonable.

Remedies available for misrepresentation

A variety of remedies are available. They include common law and equitable remedies, and under the Misrepresentation Act 1967. At common law, as we have seen, damages are available in the tort of deceit for fraudulent misrepresentation, and in the tort of negligence for negligent misrepresentation. In equity *rescission* is available in any case of misrepresentation. It is a remedy which seeks to put the parties back to their pre-contractual position. If this cannot be achieved, for instance where the subject matter of the contract has been altered, lost, or sold to a third party, rescission is not available. Nor can it be claimed if it would be inequitable to grant it. Thus if a person knowing of the misrepresentation *affirms* the contract, so indicating that that he intends to continue, the right to rescind will be lost. Affirmation can occur through delay in bringing an action.

> In *Leaf v. International Galleries* 1959 the plaintiff bought from the defendants a picture described as a Constable, but was unable to rescind the contract some five years later when he discovered on trying to re-sell it that it was not a Constable after all. The plaintiff also argued, unsuccessfully, that the contract was affected by mistake. It can be of advantage to a plaintiff to plead alternative legal arguments in this way, for if one proposition fails the other might succeed, and clearly a plaintiff would not choose to bring two separate actions, or even more, if the matter can be dealt with in one trial.

Unlike the common law remedy of damages, which are available as of right once liability has been established, rescission, being an equitable remedy, is discretionary. The court exercises this discretion in accordance with certain principles, referred to as *equitable maxims*. Essentially these principles are concerned with ensuring that in awarding equitable relief the court should be satisfied not only that the plaintiff has acted fairly, but also that the defendant will not be unfairly treated if the remedy sought by the plaintiff is granted. This is the justification for the restrictions on the granting of rescission which have previously been referred to.

> The appropriate measure of damages in a misrepresentation case is illustrated. In *Smith New Court Securities Ltd. v. Scrimgeour Vickers (Asset Management) Ltd.* 1994. The plaintiffs made a successful bid for shares in the company called FIS Ltd. They paid 82.5 pence per share. There were two factors regarding price which they were unaware of when they made their bid. Firstly a fraudulent misrepresentation had been made to them on behalf of the defendants, that other parties were putting in competing bids. This was a fabrication. Had the plaintiffs known the truth the real market value of the shares would have been 78 pence. Secondly FIS Ltd. had suffered a massive fraud committed against it by another person party which at the time of the bid had not become common knowledge. If the market had been aware of the

fraud it would have reduced the share price to 44 pence The question for the Court of Appeal was the measure of damages available to the plaintiffs. The court concluded that damages should be assessed by reference to the general knowledge of the market at the time the transaction occurred. The unrelated fraud was not common knowledge when the bid was made consequently the price the plaintiffs would have paid if the defendants had not made their misrepresentation was 78 pence instead of 82.5 pence per share. They were awarded £1,176,010 damages. This was a major blow to them for the trial judge had treated the measure of damages as the difference between 82.5 pence and 44 pence a share, and awarded them £10,764,005 damages.

Damages are available under the Misrepresentation Act 1967 in respect of negligent and innocent misrepresentation. Under s.2(1) damages are available for negligent misrepresentation. It is a defence for the maker of the statement to show that up to the time of the contract he believed that the statement was true and that there was reasonable cause to believe this. Obviously such a belief will depend upon the steps taken by representor to verify the statement.Under s.2(2), damages are also claimable for an innocent misrepresentation; however, the section requires that the party seeking relief must ask the court to rescind the contract. If the court is satisfied that grounds for rescission exist it may award damages instead, if it is of the opinion that it would be equitable to do so.

	Fraudulent misrepresentation	Negligent misrepresentation	Innocent misrepresentation
At Common Law	Damages in the tort of deceit	Damages in the tort of negligence under the rule in *Hedley Byrne v Heller* (1964), if a special relationship exists	
In Equity	Rescission (and damages). If the contract is executory the fraud is a defence if the misrepresentor brings action for specific performance	Rescission	Rescission
Under the Misrepresentation Act 1967		In addition to rescission, or, at the court's discretion instead of rescission, damages under s.2(1) if the misrepresentee has suffered loss. If the defendant can prove that up to the time of the contract he believed, with reasonable cause, that his statements were true, this will be a defence.	If the grounds for rescission exist, the court, in its discretion, may award damages instead under s.2(2)

Remedies for misrepresentation

A person cannot exclude liability in respect of claims brought under the Act, unless the court, in its discretion, considers that use of the exclusion is fair and reasonable in the circumstances of the case. The section applies a test of reasonableness to such an exclusion clause.

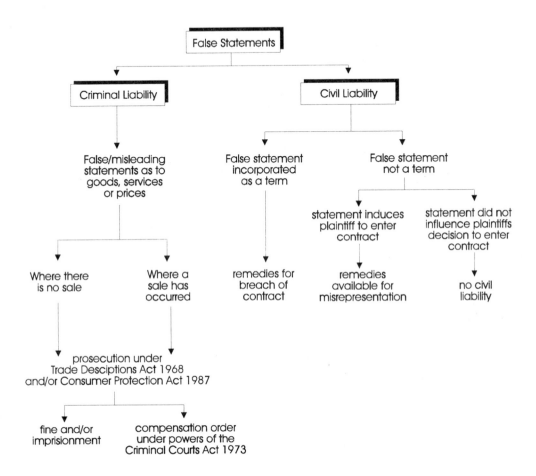

Figure 9.1   *Liability for False Statement*

Mistake

The courts have always been reticent about treating mistake as a ground for the avoidance of contractual liabilities. Previously we have seen that a contract will remain valid despite its proving to be economically disadvantageous to one of the parties because of what is, in effect, a mistake as to the value or quality of the subject matter. Provided the parties have made their deal openly and voluntarily the courts will enforce it. In contracts for goods the common law traditionally has taken the view it is the buyers responsibility to ensure the transaction is worth making. This is summed up in the expression *caveat emptor* (let the buyer beware). Modern consumer legislation, notably the Sale of Goods Act 1979 (as amended) readjusts this responsibility by imposing obligations on sellers regarding the quality, suitability and description of the products they sell. However these obligations attach only to business sellers, for the legislation is designed to prevent business from sheltering behind the *caveat emptor* rule. In private sales, where it is assumed the parties can bargain as equals, caveat emptor still applies. They must live with errors of judgment they make about the transaction they make. Of course if their error was engineered by the seller making false statements the situation is different, for in these circumstances a misrepresentation claim will lie. It can sometimes be difficult to distinguish between mistake and misrepresentation, and they often overlap, but they do involve different principles of liability. Part of the confusion lies in the terminology itself. A misrepresentation involves mistaken belief, because the representee has gone ahead with the contract believing certain statements to be true when they are not true. The essence of misrepresentation is that the false statement simply induces the transaction, but it does not become a part of it. Where however a person is seeking a remedy on the grounds of contractual mistake, the argument being put forward is that the substance of the contract itself is tainted by the mistake, and the remedy is a contractual one.

Some types of mistake do not effect the validity of a contract; notably:

- a mistake of law;

- an error of judgment about the value of the subject matter of the contract, unless a misrepresentation was made;

- a mistake about the meaning of a trade term. In *Harrison & Jones Ltd. v. Bunten & Lancaster Ltd.* 1953 a buyer purchased 100 bales of *Sree brand* kapok from the seller. Both parties believed that this type of kapok was pure, but when the buyer discovered that Sree brand was a mixture of different types of kapok he claimed that the contract was void for mistake. The court, however, held that the contract was valid, being unaffected by the mistake; and

- a mistake about ability to perform the contract within a certain time, e.g. in a building contract.

Other, however, are regarded as so fundamental to the transaction that the courts will take account of them. Such mistakes are known as *operative* mistakes, and they render the contract void. The following is an outline of the types of operative mistakes which are recognised.

Mistake about the nature of a signed document

The law does not permit a person to escape liability from a document they have signed simply because they have not read it, or have read but not understood it. A defence, known as *non est factum* (not my deed), is however available if all the following conditions can be satisfied:

(i) that the document signed is fundamentally or radically different from the one the signatory believed it to be;

(ii) that the signatory exercised reasonable care in signing the document;

(iii) that fraud was used to induce the signature.

Collectively these factors are very demanding, and the defence is thus rarely successful.

> In *Saunders v. Anglia Building Society* 1974 the House of Lords indicated the narrow limits of the defence of non est factum. The facts were that a 78 year old widow had signed a document which a Mr. Lee had told her was a deed of gift of her house to her nephew. She did not read the document as her glasses were broken when she signed it. The document in fact transferred her property to Lee, who subsequently mortgaged the property to a building society. The widow now sought to recover the deeds, pleading non est factum. The action failed. The document had been signed with carelessness, and furthermore it was not substantially different from the one she believed she was signing: they were both assignments of property.

There will sometimes be grounds other than mistake on which a person who has signed a contractual document can rely to avoid the contract. For example, in the case of consumer credit agreements such as hire-purchase agreements, the Consumer Credit Act 1974 grants a five-day period after the agreement is made within which the debtor can cancel the agreement, provided it was signed somewhere other than on the creditor's premises. Signing a contract which is void at law, such as an illegal contract, will incur no contractual liability at all.

Mistake as to the identity of the other party

Mistake of this kind is usually *unilateral*, where only one of the parties is mistaken about the identity of the other party to the contract. When this occurs the contract will be void only if the mistaken party can show that the question of identity was material to the making of the contract, and that the other part knew or ought to have known of the mistake. The majority of cases in which this type of mistake occur involve fraud, so the requirement of knowledge of the mistake will have been satisfied, leaving the mistaken party with the difficult task of trying to show that he would not have made the contract if the true identity of the other party had been known.

> An example of the limited extent to which a unilateral mistake may affect the validity of a contract is provided by *Centrovincial Estates plc v. Merchant Investors Assurance Co. Ltd.* 1983 a case involving a business tenancy between the plaintiffs, the landlords, and the defendants who were the tenants. The issue concerned the fixing of a new rent, under a rent review clause in the lease. The mistake in question was made by solicitors acting for the plaintiffs who wrote to the defendants on June 22 1982 asking them to agree to a new rent of £65,000 per annum to operate from the rent review date. The defendants were happy to agree to the new rent by letter the following day, for the figure suggested was a reduction of over £3,000 per annum on the current rent. The plaintiff's solicitors, when they discovered the error a few days later attempted to persuade the defendants to accept the true figure of £126,000 per annum. The plaintiffs claimed the mistake had prevented any *consensus ad idem* between the parties. The Court of Appeal, applying strict contract law, held that acceptance of an unambiguous offer resulted in a contract. The mere assertion of a mistake, of which the offeree was unaware, did not affect the contract's validity.

Bilateral mistakes

The instances of mistake considered so far have concerned mistakes made by just one of the parties, unilateral mistakes. In cases of bilateral mistake however both the parties are mistaken, either about the same thing, *common* mistake, or about something different, *mutual* mistake.

Where a mutual mistake occurs the parties are at cross purposes, and in cases of fundamental error arguably there can be no contract in existence anyway, on grounds of the uncertainty of their agreement. Thus if one company agrees to sell a machine to another, and the description of it is so vague that the seller believes he is selling an entirely different machine to the one the buyer believes he is buying, there is no effective agreement within the process of offer and acceptance.

An example of a common mistake occurred in *Couturier v. Hastie* 1856. A contract was made for the sale of some wheat which at the time was being carried on board a ship. Unknown to both parties, when they made the agreement the wheat had already been sold by the ship's captain because during the voyage it had started to overheat. The court held the contract to be void, since it was a contract of impossibility.

There are some significant exceptions to this type of claim. At common law relief from a contract affected by a common mistake will not be available where the mistake:

(a)   occurs after the contract is made. In *Amalgamated Investment & Property Co. Ltd. v. John Walker & Sons Ltd.* 1976 the defendants sold the plaintiffs a warehouse for £1.7m. The defendants knew the plaintiffs intended to redevelop the site, and both knew planning permission would be necessary. Contracts were exchanged on 25 September. On 26 September the defendants were informed by the Department of the Environment that the building had become 'listed'. This made development consent most unlikely, and without it the property was worth £200,000. The plaintiffs sought to rescind the contract. The Court of Appeal rejected the claim. There was no mistake in the minds of the parties when the contracts were exchanged sufficient to set the contract aside;

(b)   is as to quality. An example of a mistake about quality occurred in *Leaf v. International Galleries* 1950 (see earlier).

The doctrine of common mistake was reviewed by the court in *Associated Japanese Bank (International) Ltd. v. Credit Du Nord SA* 1988. The facts of the case were that an individual, Bennett, purported to sell specified items of machinery to the plaintiff bank, which the bank then leased back to him. Under the transaction Bennett received approximately £1 million. The plaintiff bank required Bennett to provide a guarantee from another bank, and this he obtained from the defendants. The machinery was non-existent. Bennett disappeared with the money, and the plaintiffs claimed under the guarantee against the defendants. The defendants argued that (a) the guarantee was subject to an express or implied condition that the machinery existed, or alternatively (b) that the guarantee was void from the outset on the grounds of the mistaken belief of both parties that the machinery existed. The plaintiff's claim failed. On the facts the judge, Steyn J took the view that the guarantee agreement included an express condition that the machinery existed. Even if it had not, he was of the view that it would contain an implied term to this effect for a reasonable man would regard this as so obvious as hardly to require saying. The guarantee was also void from the outset for the mistake, at common law. The judge summarised the common law approach to mistake as follows:

(i)   the courts should seek to uphold rather than defeat apparent contracts;

(ii)   the rules regarding mistake are designed to deal with the effect of exceptional circumstances upon apparent contracts;

(iii)   the mistake must concern existing facts at the time of the contract, and both sides must substantially share the mistake;

(iv)   the mistake must render the subject matter of the contract essentially and radically different from what was in the minds of the parties; and

(v)   there must be reasonable grounds for the belief of both parties.

Remedies

At common law

The effect of an operative mistake at common law is to render the contract void *ab initio* - from the outset. The true owner is thus entitled to the return of goods, or damages, from whoever is in wrongful possession.

In equity

The position in equity is different however, for equity recognises certain types of operative mistake which the common law does not grant relief for, in particular in cases involving mistake as to quality. The following cases illustrate the position.

In *Magee v. Pennine Insurance Co. Ltd.* 1969 a proposal for insurance of a motor car had been incorrectly completed without the insured's knowledge. Following a crash, a claim was made and the insurance company agreed to pay £385 which the insured was willing to accept. On discovery of the material inaccuracy in the policy however, the company withdrew their offer of payment and the insured sued them to obtain it. The Court of Appeal held that under the common law the common mistaken belief that the policy was valid was inoperative and the contract of the insurance was valid. In equity however the agreement to pay £385 would be set aside as there had been a fundamental misapprehension, and the party seeking to rescind was not at fault.

Duress and Undue Influence

At common law coercing a person into making a contract by means of actual or threatened violence to them is referred to as *duress,* and if it can be proved the contract is treated, not surprisingly, as void. Because of its narrow limits the plea of duress is an extremely unusual one.

Equity however goes much further than the common law. The doctrine of *undue influence* which it has developed recognises more subtle forms of improper pressure that are sometimes relied on to create agreements. Where undue influence is shown to have occurred equity will allow the innocent party the opportunity to rescind the contract. In certain relationships a presumption of undue influence arises, for example in fiduciary relationships, and in those where one person is in a position of dominance over the other. Parent and child, solicitor and client, doctor and patient, and trustee and beneficiary are classic illustrations. The courts are still prepared to recognise new relationships where the doctrine can be applied, for example an influential secretary companion and his elderly employee in *Re Craig* 1971, and a banker who sought to obtain a benefit from his customer in *Lloyds Bank v. Bundy* 1975. The dominant party who attempts to uphold a transaction entered into in such a relationship must rebut the presumption of undue influence by showing that he has not abused his position in any way. Evidence that the innocent party has taken independent advice will go a long way to achieving this and saving the contract.

In *Barclays Bank plc v. O'Brien* 1993 Mr. O'Brien, who was a shareholder in a manufacturing company, wanted to increase the overdraft available to the company from its bank, Barclays. The bank agreed to an overdraft facility of £135,000. The O'Brien's matrimonial home, jointly owned by Mr. & Mrs. O'Brien, was used as security for the loan, and the O'Briens executed a legal charge in favour of the bank. The bank did not advise Mrs. O'Brien as to the effect of the charge; nor did she read the documents she signed. Her husband had told her merely that the charge was to secure £60,000, and would last for only a short time. The company's debts increased, and the bank sought to enforce its security. The House of Lords unanimously held that Mrs. O'Brien was entitled to set aside the legal charge on the matrimonial home. The court restated the law applying in surety cases involving marriage partners and cohabitees. In a case such as this, where the spouse placed trust and confidence in the principal debtor (the husband) and acted as surety on the basis of a misrepresentation or through undue influence, the legal position would be as follows. If the surrounding circumstances were such as to put the creditor on inquiry, for instance where on the face of it the transaction was not to the wife's benefit, then the creditor should take reasonable steps to establish that her consent had been properly obtained. This could be done by discussing the matter with her privately, warning her of the risks, and suggesting she take independent legal advice. A creditor put on inquiry, who failed to take such reasonable steps would take the security subject to the equitable rights of the wife to have it set aside, for the creditor would have constructive notice of those rights.

There have been a number of subsequent cases which have explored the implications of the *O'Brien* decision. Essentially they have all involved questions of what the duty of a bank is taking into account its knowledge or its potential knowledge of misrepresentation or undue influence occurring between the parties to the relationship.

In modern times the courts have demonstrated an increased willingness to see the principles underlying duress and undue influence as elements in a broader principle of law which Lord Denning referred to in *Lloyds Bank v. Bundy* 1975 as *inequality of bargaining power*.

> In *Clifford Davies Management Ltd. v. WEA Records Ltd.* 1975 this inequality approach was clearly demonstrated. Two composer members of a pop group (Fleetwood Mac) had entered into an agreement with their manager to assign the copyright in all their work to him for a period of ten years. In return they received a very small financial consideration and his promise to use his best endeavours to publish the work they composed. The Court of Appeal found that on the basis of bargaining inequality the contract could be set aside at the option of the composers. The factors cited by the court that pointed to the inequality were: the overall unfairness of a ten year tie, supported by vague consideration offered in return by the manager; the conflict of interest arising from the manager acting as the business adviser to the composers, whilst at the same time representing his own company's interests in negotiating with them; and the absence of any independent advice available to the composers, and their reliance upon the manager, who exerted undue influence over them.

In these cases a crucial question will be whether the agreement has been signed after taking independent specialist advice. If it has a court will be far less likely to declare the agreement invalid. Such was the position in *Panayoitou v. Sony Music Entertainment (UK) Ltd.* 1994 where George Michael unsuccessfully sought to extricate himself from a 15 year deal with Sony. His original contract with the company gave him the opportunity to renegotiate it, and he had used this option to secure superior terms for himself. These terms were renegotiated for him by specialist lawyers. A clause in the renegotiated contract said, *"I am not a minor and I have taken legal advice in relation to this agreement prior to entering into the same."* This evidence, the court felt, supported the view that the contract should be upheld.

Further development of this approach has lead to the recognition of *economic duress*. Economic duress is a plea based upon a claim that the weaker party gave their consent to the agreement as a result of improper commercial influence or pressure put on them. The following cases illustrate situations in which the courts have been prepared to recognise economic duress as a ground for contractual relief.

> In *Atlas Express v. Kafco (Importers and Distributors)* 1989 the defendants were a small company involved in the import and distribution of basketware. They sold a quantity of their goods to Woolworths, and agreed with the plaintiffs, a national road carrier, for deliveries to be made by the plaintiffs. The plaintiffs depot manager quoted a price for deliveries based upon his guess as to how many cartons of goods would be carried on each load. In the event he overestimated this figure and refused to proceed with the contract unless the defendants agreed to a minimum payment for each load of £440, in substitution for the original arrangement of £1.10 per carton. Anxious to ensure the goods were delivered on time, and unable in the circumstances to find an alternative carrier, the defendants agreed to the new arrangement, but later refused to pay. The plaintiff's claim for breach of contract failed. The court took the view that the plaintiff's threat to break the contract together with their knowledge of the defendants dependency on them represented a clear example of economic duress.

Contract Terms

The terms of a contract are the promises which the parties make to each other. These promises, sometimes referred to as legal obligations, are of course legally enforceable.

All contracts contain terms, sometimes complex and detailed sets of undertakings, more often simple comprehendable statements of what each side to the transactions is promising the other. These undertakings may be oral, or contained in a written document. Businesses generally regard a written contract as an essential safeguard against subsequent disagreements over what has actually been agreed. In practice in the commercial world the vast majority of suppliers of goods and services rely on their own standard terms for the purposes of contracting. An example of a standard form contract is included at the end of Chapter 11.

By inserting a range of terms into the contract the parties will seek to clarify their mutual obligations. In a well constructed contract they will anticipate all eventualities, so that no issue can emerge later which cannot be resolved by reference to the contract itself. Different types of contract obviously reflect different sets of terms appropriate to the nature and purpose of the agreement, but whatever the objective is always to ensure that the terms cover all the issues associated with the performance of the contract.

The terms of a contract constitute a kind of index of the parties responsibilities. It is an important index because it is the means by which performance of the contract is measured. If a term has not been carried out properly, or not carried out at all, a breach of contract has occurred giving rise to a potential claim by the injured party, probably for financial compensation. If you take any contract and examine it, it becomes possible to list out all its terms, and so identify which of the parties has to do what to fulfill their side of the bargain.

The classification of terms

The terms of a contract vary in importance. Sometimes the contract itself will say how much importance is attached to a certain term, while in other cases it may be left to the court to decide because the parties to the contract have not made it clear themselves. The value that is attached to each term is of great significance because it determines what the consequences will be if the particular term is broken.

Major terms are called *conditions*. A condition is a term which is said to go to the root of the contract, and whose performance is therefore essential to the contract. Because a condition is so important, if it is broken the innocent party has the right to treat the contract as repudiated and to refuse to perform their obligations under it. In addition the injured party may sue for damages. (See Chapter 11)

Minor terms are called *warranties*. They are terms which are said to be collateral to the main purpose of the contract. In consequence, if a warranty is broken the contract still stands, and the innocent party does not have the right to treat the contract as being at an end, merely the right to damages. (See Chapter 11)

Where breach of a condition occurs the injured party is not bound to repudiate the contract. As an alternative the injured party can elect to treat the contract as continuing, treating the breach of condition as if it were a warranty. The obligation that has been broken is then referred to as an *ex post facto* warranty, and only damages will be available. Sound commercial reasons may justify treating a breach of condition as one of warranty, and letting the contract stand. The innocent party may realise that if the contract is repudiated it will be difficult to obtain an alternative supplier of the goods and services in question, or undue delay and inconvenience will be caused if the goods have to be disassembled, removed from the premises and returned to the supplier.

Sometimes it is impossible to say whether a term is a condition or a warranty when it is first created because it has been so broadly framed that it could be broken in a major respect or a minor respect, in such cases therefore it is only possible to say after the event what effect the particular breach should have on the contract. Such terms are referred to as *innominate*, meaning intermediate, terms.

> The position is illustrated in *Hong Kong Fir Shipping Co. Ltd. v. Kawasaki Kaisen Kaisha Ltd.* 1962. Here a ship was chartered on terms that stated what it would be *"in every way fitted for ordinary cargo service"*. Inefficient engine-room staff and old engines contributed to a number of breakdowns so that during the first seven months of the charter the ship was only able to be at sea for eight and a half weeks. The charterers repudiated the contract. The Court of Appeal decided that this particular breach did not entitle the charterers to repudiate. Diplock J stated that the terms in the contract were not really either a condition or a warranty but rather *"an undertaking, one breach of which may give rise to an event which relieves the charterer of further performance ... if he so elects and another breach of which may not give rise to such an event but entitle him only ... to damages."*

A further illustration is provided by the case of *Cehave NV v. Bremer Handelsgesellschaft, mbh, The Hansa Nord* 1975. A term in a contract under which the defendants agreed to sell citrus pulp pellets to the plaintiffs stipulated *"shipment to be made in good condition"*. Delivery was by consignments. On delivery of one of the consignments, of the 3293 tons supplied 1260 tons were found to be damaged. The market price for such goods had now fallen, and the buyers used the damaged goods as an opportunity for repudiating the whole contract on grounds of breach of condition. In fact they later bought exactly the same cargo at well below half the original contract price from a third party who had obtained it from the original sellers. The buyer then used it to make cattle food, exactly what they had bought it for in the first place. The Court of Appeal held the term to be an intermediate one, and damages rather than repudiation was an appropriate remedy. Lord Denning commented *"if a small portion of the whole cargo was not in good condition and arrived a little unsound, it should be met by a price allowance. The buyer should not have the right to reject the whole cargo unless it was serious or substantial."* In the later case of *Bunge Corporation, New York v. Tradax Export SA Panama* 1981 the House of Lords emphasised that parties cannot artificially create intermediate terms. Whether a term is to be regarded as intermediate is a matter of construction.

Express terms

These are the terms which have been specifically agreed by the parties. They can classify them as conditions or warranties when they are made if they wish. If they fail to do so the court has to decide how significant a particular breach is by looking at the term in relation to the contract as a whole. Even where the contract itself classifies a term or terms, the court still reserves the right to construe the meaning of the term by looking at the contract as a whole.

> In *L Schuler AG v. Wickham Machine Tool Sales* 1973 the German appellant company, granted sole selling rights over their panel presses in England to the respondents, Wickham. Their agreement provided that Wickham's representatives should visit six named firms every week for the purpose of seeking orders. Clause 7(6) indicated the status of this particular term stating that *"it shall be a condition of this agreement"*. On certain occasions Wickham's employees failed to satisfy the term. Schulers responded by claiming repudiation of the contract, arguing that a single failure would be sufficient to constitute a breach. The House of Lords rejected this argument. Such a construction was so unreasonable that the parties could not have intended it.

A question sometimes faced by the Court is whether statements made during contractual negotiations, referred to as representations, have become incorporated into the contract as actual terms. The test usually applied is whether the person making the statement was promising its accuracy. If so, the statement is usually treated as a term.

If the parties to a contract of employment have included their respective rights and obligations under it in a signed document called the contract of employment, then this document will contain the express terms of the agreement. In many cases however the express term of a contract of employment can only be determined by establishing the content and status of the various documents transferred during the *recruitment* process and what the parties orally agreed at the inteview. Express terms will be found in the statutory statement of the main term and conditions of employment, the details contained in the job application form and in rare cases even a job advertisement.

> In *Holliday Concrete v. Wood* 1979 a job advertisement indicated that a fifteen month contract was available and this was held to be the period of employment.

> In *Joseph Steinfeld v. Reypert 1979* the fact that a post was advertised as *"sales manager"* indicated the contractual status of the successful applicant.

Usually a clearly worded job offer will override conflicting statements made in the job advertisement. In the event of conflict between oral statements and writing the writing will normally have primacy but it is the intention of the parties which must be determined.

In *Hawker Siddeley Power Engineering Ltd. v. Rump* 1979 the complainant was employed as a heavy goods vehicle driver in 1973 and signed a contract of employment which stated that he would be liable to travel all over the country. This obligation was confirmed in a later statement of terms of employment issued in 1976 and signed by the employee. In fact the complainant had made it clear when he took the job that because of his wife's illness he would not travel beyond the south of England and that had been orally agreed by a manager when he signed the contract. When finally in 1978 the complainant refused to obey an instruction to travel to Scotland and this led to his dismissal, one issue before the tribunal was whether he was contractually obliged to do so. The tribunal held that the promise to work only in the south was an oral contractual term. Here *"there was a direct promise by the employers which must have become part of the contract of employment because it was following upon the promise that the employee signed the contract"*. Even the subsequent written statement which included a mobility clause signed by the employer was insufficient to exclude the oral term previously agreed. Here the employee *"had no notice that the oral term he had secured was going to form no part of his new contract. The mere putting in front of him a document and invitation for him to sign it could not be held to be a variation by agreement so as to exclude the important oral term which he had previously secured. Rather if there was a variation at all to the contract, it was a unilateral variation which was not binding upon the employee"*.

Terms implied by the courts

It is not the task of the courts to insert new terms into contracts, but rather to interpret those that already exist. But they will sometimes imply a term to give a contract *business efficacy*. The rationale underlying such an approach is that since the parties clearly intended to create a binding agreement, they must have intended to include terms to make the contract function.

In *The Moorcock* 1889 a term was implied by the court in a contract between a ship owner and a firm of wharfingers. The contract was to use their wharf on the Thames for the discharging and loading of his vessel, the Moorcock. He was going to pay a charge for the use of the cranes alongside the wharf. While the vessel was moored there she was damaged when the tide ebbed and she came to rest on a ridge of hard ground. The Court of Appeal held that the wharfingers were liable for breach of an implied term that the mooring was safe for the vessel. *"In business transactions such as this,"* said Bowen LJ, *"what the law desires to effect by implication is to give such business efficacy to the transaction as must have been intended at all events by both parties who are businessmen."*

In *Irwin v. Liverpool City Council* 1977 the defendant council let a flat in an upper floor of a block of flats to the plaintiff tenant. A term was implied by the court into a tenancy agreement between the plaintiff and the defendant council to the effect that the defendants had an obligation to keep in repair the stairs and the lift in the block of flats which they owned, thus ensuring that the plaintiff could gain effective access to his property.

In *Baylis v. Barnett* 1988 the plaintiff lent the defendant a sum of money. The defendant knew this involved the plaintiff in borrowing the money from a bank. Although the parties did not discuss the question of interest the court held there was an implied term that the defendant would indemnify the plaintiff for any interest he owed to the bank.

A field in which the courts have been active in implying terms is in the relationship between employers and employees. The common law implies a number of important terms into the contract of employment; for instance that the *employee* owes a duty of good faith to the employer, and that the *employer* has an obligation to provide for the employee's safety.

In *Woods v. W H Car Services Ltd.* 1982 the court acknowledged that in every employment contract there is an implied term of great importance, that of trust and confidence between the parties. Such a term requires that employers *"will not without reasonable and proper cause, conduct themselves in a manner calculated or likely to destroy the relationship of trust and confidence between employer and employee".*

Malik v. BCCI 1997 is an extremely significant case in employment law involving a claim by the ex-employees of a bank following it's much publisised collapse. The fact that the business of the bank had been carried on fraudulently led the ex-employees to claim that their future prospects in the employment market had suffered as a result of the stigma attached to being a BCCI employee. The House of Lords, in particular Ld Steyn, was given its first opportunity in this case to rule on the implied term of trust and confidence. The court confirmed that mutual respect and trust and confidence is the fundamental feature of an employment relationship and takes effect as a significant term in the contract of employment.

By implying a term into employment contracts that employees should be flexible and adaptable and react positively to change, an employer is authorised to implement quite sweeping changes in job functions provided staff are given sufficient training to enable them to cope with the different demands placed upon them.

> In *Cresswell v. Board of Inland Revenue* 1984, employees sought a legal declaration that their employers had broken the terms of their contract of employment by introducing new technology and expecting them to adapt to it. The High Court declared, however, that, provided they received adequate training, employees were expected to adapt to new methods and new techniques. There is a general contractual duty on employees to adapt to changing working methods. There was also a right for the employer to withhold pay for those employees who refused to conform to the new methods, for they are in breach of their contractual obligations.

Contractual terms are often implied by tribunals and courts into employment contracts when the employee is alleging that he terminated the contract because of his employers repudiatory breach of contract and has been constructively dismissed.

> In *Hilton International Hotels (UK) Ltd. v. Protopapa* 1990 an employee resigned when she was subjected to an officious and insensitive reprimand not justified by her conduct. The industrial tribunal held that she was *"humiliated intimidated and degraded to such an extent that there was breach of trust and confidence which went to the root of the contract"*. The employer nevertheless appealed against the finding of constructive dismissal arguing that the person who had carried out the reprimand, while a supervisor, had no authority to effect a dismissal. This the tribunal found was an irrelevant consideration and restated the general principle that an employer is bound by acts done in the course of a supervisory employee's employment. *"Therefore, if the supervisor is doing what he or she is employed to do and in the course of doing it behaves in a way which if done by the employer would constitute a fundamental breach of the contract between the employer and employee, the employer is bound by the supervisor's misdeeds."*

Statutory implied terms

Parliament has been particularly active during the last thirty years or so in the use of legislation to introduce specific terms into certain types of contractual agreement. Statutory implied terms are nowadays found in an enormous range of different kinds of contract. Being statutory terms they are specific about the obligations being imposed. In many cases statutory terms are implied as a legislative attempt to counter-balance the inequalities that exist in a particular bargaining situation. In other cases statutory terms can be seen as a vehicle for effecting profound social and economic change, such as the insertion of the *equality clause* in contracts of employment. While it is unusual for employment statutes to imply terms into contracts of employment the right to holidays and maximum working hours are implied terms from the Working Time Regulations 1998. Yet again, there are those statutory terms which simply represent a codification of judicially recognised mercantile custom, for example those within the Sale of Goods Act 1979. Detailed examples of statutory implied terms can be found in Chapters 11 and 12 on buying goods and services and consumer law.

Exclusion Clauses

Legal liability can arise in a variety of different ways, for example through misrepresentation, breach of contract or negligence. One way of trying to reduce or extinguish this liability is by the use of exclusion or limitation clauses. An *exclusion clause* in a contract is an express term which attempts to exempt one party from all liability for failure to perform some part of the contract.

A *limitation clause* on the other hand is slightly different for it aims to *reduce* rather than extinguish the liability. These clauses may be drafted to place an overall financial limit on the liability of one party for breach of contract, or to limit liability to the replacement of goods supplied, or to deprive the other of a particular remedy for the breach. For convenience, references made to exclusion clauses used here can be taken to mean both total or partial exclusion of liability.

The principle of freedom of contract permits the use of exclusion clauses. The courts however have developed a number of common law principles designed to rob such clauses of effect in certain circumstances. These principles were developed because the courts recognised that the use of exclusion clauses could result in unfairness to one of the contracting parties. Judicial controls were developed largely by the application of existing principles of contract law and are limited in scope. It was not until the 1970's that legislation was introduced. The Unfair Contract Terms Act 1977 now provides a comprehensive set of rules which regulate both the use of exclusion clauses in contracts and the use of non-contractual notices. These rules have been supplemented by the Unfair Terms in Consumer Contracts Regulations 1994 (1999) which were introduced to give effect to the 1993 European Council Directive on Unfair Terms in Consumer Contracts. The Regulations do not alter the operation of the 1977 Act, which remains unchanged, but provide an additional set of rules designed to strengthen consumer protection in this area. The 1977 Act is dealt with here and you will find the supplementary regulations in Chapter 12.

In determining the validity of an exclusion clause, several legal principles have to be applied. The first step is to make sure that legal liability of one type or another would arise if the exclusion were not present. Next the common law rules of incorporation and interpretation (discussed below) must be applied. If the exclusion survives the application of the common law rules, we must then apply the provisions of the 1977 Act and the 1994 Regulations are then applied. The figure below summarises these steps in diagrammatic form.

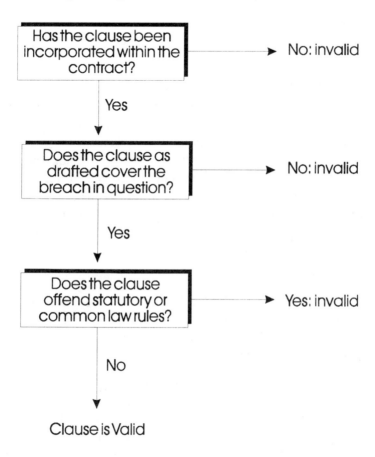

Figure 9.2   *Legal control over exclusion and restriction of contractual liability*

Incorporation – Is the Term Part of the Contract?
Signed documents

A person who signs a document containing an exclusion clause will be bound by the terms it contains whether or not they have actually been read or understood. The only exceptions are where the signature is induced by fraud or misrepresentation. Otherwise the exclusion clause will automatically be part of the contract.

In *Spriggs v. Sotheby Parke Bernet and Co. Ltd.* 1984 the plaintiff handed over to Sothebys a diamond which they were to auction for him. They gave him a document to sign, which he signed without reading. Immediately above the space for signature a printed declaration in bold type said "*I have read and agree to the instructions for sale as detailed on the reverse of this form*". The reverse of the form contained an exclusion clause. It was held that the clause had been validly incorporated into the contract.

If the contents of a contract have been misrepresented before it is signed, an exclusion clause in the document will be ineffective to the extent of the misrepresentative effect of the clause.

In *Curtis v. Chemical Cleaning and Dyeing Co.* 1951 the plaintiff took a wedding dress to the defendant company for cleaning. An assistant asked her to sign a receipt. Before she did so she was told that her signature on the receipt excluded the company's liability for any damage to the beads and sequins on the dress. The dress was stained during cleaning, however no damage was done to the beads and sequins. The signed receipt actually excluded the defendants' liability for any damage to the dress "*howsoever caused*". The Court of Appeal held that the defendants were liable for the damage to the dress and could not rely on the full exclusion clause because they had misrepresented its effect to the plaintiff.

Unsigned documents

A term contained in an unsigned document, or displayed on a notice, is only effective if the person relying on it took reasonable steps to bring it to the attention of the other party, and where the document or notice might reasonably be regarded as likely to contain contractual terms.

In *Chapelton v. Barry U.D.C.* 1940 the plaintiff hired a deck chair from the defendant for use on a beach. He paid an attendant and was given a ticket in return. He was injured when the chair collapsed as he sat down on it. There was an exclusion clause printed on the back of the ticket which the plaintiff had not read. The Court of Appeal held that the ticket was merely a receipt and not the sort of contractual document which a reasonable person might have expected to contain contractual terms. The exclusion clause was therefore ineffective and the defendants were liable.

Where a term is particularly onerous or unusual, then even if it has been incorporated within a contractual document, the party seeking to enforce it must nevertheless show that it has fairly and adequately been drawn to the other party's attention.

Terms introduced after the contract is made

An exclusion clause will not be effective unless it is adequately brought to the attention of the other party before the contract is made. It must be part of the contractual offer, and the rules of offer and acceptance can be used to determine whether the clause is actually part of the contract.

> In *Olley v. Marlborough Court Hotel Ltd*. 1949 the plaintiff booked into an hotel and paid for the room in advance. She went up to her hotel room where there was a notice which stated *"The proprietors will not hold themselves responsible for articles lost or stolen unless handed to the Manageress for safe custody"*. The plaintiff left her fur coat in the room and it was stolen. The Court of Appeal held that the defendant was not entitled to rely on the exclusion clause as it was not a term of the contract. The contract was concluded at the reception desk and the plaintiff had no notice of the clause at that stage.

> In *Thornton v. Shoe Lane Parking* 1971 the plaintiff drove into a car park which he had not used before. At the entrance there was a machine which issued a ticket to him before raising a barrier to allow entry. On the back of the ticket there was a statement that it was issued subject to terms and conditions displayed within the car park. One of these conditions purported to exclude the defendant's liability for injury to customers howsoever caused. The plaintiff was injured by the defendant's negligence when he came to collect his car. The Court of Appeal held that the exclusion clause was ineffective because it had been introduced after the contract was concluded. Lord Denning analysed the process of contract formation in the following way. *"The customer pays his money and gets a ticket. He cannot refuse it. He cannot get his money back. He may protest to the machine, even swear at it; but it will remain unmoved. He is committed beyond recall. He was committed at the very moment when he put his money into the machine: the contract was concluded at that time. It can be translated into offer and acceptance in this way. The offer is made when the proprietor of the machine holds it out as being ready to receive the money. The acceptance takes place when the customer puts his money into the slot. The terms of the offer are contained in the notice placed on or near the machine stating what is offered for the money. The customer is bound by these terms as long as they are sufficiently brought to his notice beforehand, but not otherwise. He is not bound by the terms printed on the ticket, if they differ from the notice, because the ticket comes too late. The contract has already been made"*

Where there is a previous course of dealing between the parties the court may be prepared to recognise the incorporation of an exclusion clause into a contract even though it was not specifically referred to at the time the contract was made. This will occur where the past dealings between the parties have consistently been made on the same terms and with the exclusion clause.

> In *Spurling v. Bradshaw* 1956 the plaintiffs were warehousemen who had dealt with the defendant for many years and always on the plaintiff's standard contractual terms. These terms excluded the plaintiff's liability for *"negligence, wrongful act of default"*. The defendant delivered eight barrels of orange juice to the plaintiff for storage and a few days later received an acknowledgement which referred to the standard terms of contract. When the defendant came to collect the barrels they were found to be empty. He refused to pay the storage charges and the plaintiff sued. It was held that the exclusion clause, although on this occasion introduced after the contract was made, was part of the contract. This was because the parties had regularly dealt with each other in the past and had done so consistently on the same contractual terms. The defendant was therefore well aware of these terms when he deposited the goods. The exclusion of liability was valid and the plaintiff's claim for storage charges succeeded.

The Unfair Contract Terms Act 1977

The Unfair Contract Terms Act 1977 was the first attempt by Parliament to deal with exclusion and limitation of liability in a comprehensive way. There are provisions in the Act which control attempts to exclude or limit liability in relation to negligence, contractual obligations, indemnities, guarantees, implied terms in contracts to supply goods and misrepresentation. For the purposes of the 1977 Act, exclusion or restriction of liability is widely defined so as to include:

- making enforcement of a remedy subject to restrictive conditions, for example a requirement that notice of loss or damage must be given within a specified time or in a specified manner;

- excluding or restricting any right or remedy, for example taking away the right to reject goods for breach of condition and confining the buyer's remedy to damages only;

- restricting the liability, for example to a maximum amount recoverable;

- restricting the time within which the remedy may be claimed, for example by specifying that no claim may be made more than 28 days after the date of the contract; and

- preventing liability arising in the first place, for example by including a term which provides that the seller does not give any warranty or undertaking that the goods are fit for any purpose.

The Act only applies to a *business liability*. This is defined as liability for breach of obligations arising from things done in the course of a business or from the occupation of premises used for business purposes. The meaning of the term *business* is discussed elsewhere. For the purposes of this Act it includes a profession, and the activities of any government department or local or public authority. The Act provides varying degrees of protection against exclusion clauses and notices. Some are totally invalidated, others are subjected to a test of reasonableness, and there are others to which the Act does not apply at all.

The reasonableness test

Where the Act subjects an exclusion clause to the *reasonableness* test, the burden of proving that the contract term or notice is reasonable lies with the party seeking to rely on the exclusion. The test in relation to a contract term is that the term shall have been a fair and reasonable one to be included in the contract, having regard to the circumstances which were or should have been known to the parties at the time when the contract was made. In relation to a non-contractual notice the test is whether it would be fair and reasonable to allow reliance on it, having regard to all the circumstances at the time when the liability arose. An example of a non-contractual notice would be a notice displayed at the entrance to a public park.

Schedule 2 of the Act lays down guidelines which the court can take into account in determining whether a contract term satisfies the requirement of reasonableness. The guidelines include the bargaining strength of the parties, any inducement to agree to the term, and the customer's knowledge of the existence of the term.

Section 3 of the Act applies where one of the parties to a contract deals as a consumer, or where the contract is made on written standard terms of business. In either of these situations, the section subjects to the test of reasonableness any term in which the other party:

"*(a)   when himself in breach of contract, excludes or restricts any liability of his in respect of the breach; or*

(b)   claims to be entitled -

   (i)   to render a contractual performance substantially different from that which was reasonably expected from him, or

> *(ii)   in respect of the whole or any part of his contractual obligation, to render no performance at all".*

This section is extremely wide in its application covering all types of business contract, and all manner of exclusion or limitation of liability clauses. In the case of contracts for the supply of goods, even tighter controls are applied under the provisions of s.6 and s.7, examined below. Many of the exclusion clauses considered in previous cases, such as *Curtis v. Chemical Cleaning and Dyeing Company* 1951, *Olley v. Marlborough Court Hotel* would be caught by s.3.

In addition to straightforward exclusion clauses, the section applies to contract terms in which one party claims to be entitled to give *substituted performance*, for example in a holiday contract where the travel operator reserves the right to change the destination. It also applies to contract terms in which one party claims to be entitled to render no performance at all.

The application of s.3 can be seen in the following cases involving contracts for the development and printing of photographs.

> In *Woodman v. Photo Trade Processing Ltd.* 1981 the plaintiff sent a reel of film of wedding photographs to the defendant for processing. The film was lost by the defendant. The contract contained the following clause *"all photographic materials are accepted on the basis that their value does not exceed the cost of the material itself. Responsibility is limited to the replacement of the films. No liability will be accepted consequential or otherwise, however caused"*. In considering the reasonableness of this clause, the Judge referred to the Code of Practice for the Photographic Industry, which had been approved by the Office of Fair Trading. This code recognised the possibility of a two tier system of trade, the lowest tier of which would be a cheaper service with full exclusion of liability; and the other would be a more expensive service with the processors accepting a greater degree of liability. The Judge concluded that this approach, which had not been adopted by the defendant, would be both reasonable and practicable. On that basis the court held that the defendants had not proved that their arrangements were reasonable and they were held liable.

> In *Warren v. Truprint Ltd.* 1986 photographs of the plaintiff's silver wedding were sent to the defendant for processing. They also were lost and the defendant sought to rely on an exclusion clause printed on their envelope. This limited their liability to the cost of unexposed films plus a refund of the processing charge and postage. The clause went on to say that *"we will undertake further liability at a supplementary charge. Written details on request"*. The court held that this was not sufficient to make the clause

reasonable under the 1977 Act. A reasonable clause would, plainly and clearly, set out the alternative with details of the cost to the consumer. The plaintiff's claim succeeded and he was awarded £50 damages.

Section 4 provides that a person dealing as a consumer cannot by reference to any contract term be made to indemnify another person for liability for breach of contract or negligence unless the indemnity term satisfies the reasonableness test. This is a further restriction on the effective transfer of liability by the use of an indirect exclusion clause.

The effect of the Act upon exclusion of the implied terms in contracts for the sale and supply of goods is considered in Chapter 11.

Assignment - The Premises

Midlands & Northern Property Holdings plc is a company whose business involves the development of industrial and commercial sites for sale and for letting. R & C Enterprises Ltd., a small company based in Northampton, had been seeking commercial premises for some time when one of its directors became aware of an industrial unit that Midlands & Northern had available on a small development just outside town. Following a site visit and a meeting between the director and the representative of the property company, the director, Tom Armstrong raised with the rest of his board the possibility of taking a ten year lease of the premises, which Midlands & Northern were offering.

The company's main business is in coachworks, which involves it building and fitting different types of bodywork to lorry bases. Whilst the existing site was adequate for this work, the company had decided to diversify and use its skills and expertise in the construction of mobile buildings for schools and building sites. It was for this purpose that the new premises were required. Following a further meeting with the representative from Midlands & Northern, a number of questions were raised by Tom Armstrong. In particular he wanted to know if planning permission would be granted to use the premises in the way anticipated by the company; whether the large hard surfaced area to the rear of the site was included in the lease; and whether the premises were suitable for the anticipated use. The representative wrote in reply; *"I can assure you that planning consent for the change of use of the premises will be forthcoming, following a conversation I have had with the Chief Planning Officer of the local authority. I can confirm that the premises include the hard area referred to by you. I would add that the* premises *are entirely suited to the business operations planned by you, and that I see no reason why the business should not operate profitably."*

R & C Enterprises Ltd. leased the premises. A month after doing so planning consent for their proposed change was refused. The lease granted to them makes no reference to the hard area to the rear of the premises, which is now being used by an adjoining owner, and the vehicular access to the premises is about to be cut off for months for major works of repair and improvement to be carried out by sub-contractors acting for Midlands & Northern. You work for R & C Enterprises, and Tom Armstrong has asked you to produce a report for him, which he is anxious to establish whether it is possible to terminate the lease. He has also given you a letter received from Midlands & Northern which states that due to an error by the company surveyor in correctly measuring the internal dimensions of the premises, the quarterly rental being charged is £1,000 less than it should be. The letter adds, *"you were aware that the rental of the premises was based upon the number of square meters of floor space in the factory site, since this was discussed by us during negotiations".* Tom is wondering how to respond to the letter.

Task

Produce a report requested by Tom Armstrong, and draft a reply to the letter from Midlands & Northern, for Mr. Armstrong's approval, which rejects their claim, and contains a statement of the legal grounds for doing so.

Assignment - An Incident at Ashburne Pool

Ashburne District Council owns and operates a sports complex in Ashburne town centre. A notice at the main entrance to the centre states:

> *"The Council can accept no responsibility for loss or damage to visitors personal possessions within this complex, howsoever arising."*

A notice at the bottom of the steps in the main pool leading to the high diving board states:

> *"Divers: you use the diving board at your own risk."*

Peter and his sister Mary visited the leisure complex in order to swim. They paid fifty pence each for keys to the cubicles in the changing rooms and locked the doors when they left. Whilst Mary swam in the pool Peter climbed the ladder to the diving board. The non-slip coating on the board had worn. Peter lost his footing and plunged into the pool injuring himself. He was rushed to hospital.

When Mary subsequently returned to collect their clothes from the cubicles she found the doors open and the clothes gone. She angrily complained to the changing room attendant who explained that he had left his desk to see what was happening when Peter had his accident, and could only assume that during this time someone had used the master keys from behind the desk to gain access to the cubicles. Changing room attendants are under strict instructions from the council never to leave the desk unattended.

Task

You work as a clerical assistant in Ashburne Leisure Services Department. The Director of Leisure Services is seeking your advice concerning the potential legal liability faced by his department for the injury suffered by Peter and the losses sustained by Peter andihis sister. He has asked you to prepare a report which analyses the situation. Produce the report requested by the Director, and in it identify (a) the validity of the notices; and (b) the legal effect of the council's instructions to the changing room attendant.

Chapter 10

The Principles of Contract Law: Discharge and Remedies

In the third chapter on the principles of contract law we consider how the parties to a contract discharge themselves from their respective obligations under it and in the event of a defective performance the potential redress available.

Discharge of Contract

Since a contract gives rise to legally enforceable obligations, contracting parties need to know how and when these obligations have been discharged and cease to be binding on them. Discharge is thus a technical term used to describe the ending of contractual liabilities. No legal claim will lie once a contract is discharged. Discharge can occur in any of the following ways:

Discharge by performance

The general rule is that complete performance, in which both parties comply precisely with the contractual terms they have agreed, is necessary to discharge the contract.

> This common law rule was applied in the case of *Sumpter v. Hedges* 1898, where the plaintiff builder had agreed to erect some houses for a lump sum of £565. Having carried out half the work to the value of £333 the builder was unable to complete the job because of financial difficulties. In an action by the builder to recover compensation for the value of the work he had already carried out, the Court of Appeal confirmed that he was not entitled to payment, Smith, LJ observing that *"The law is that where there is a contract to do work for a lump sum, until the work is completed, the price of it cannot be recovered"*.

This appears to be a very harsh decision, for the builder was unable to recover for any work he had performed, whilst the purchaser obtained a half completed contract for nothing. The difficulty for the court in such a case is that a single sum has been arranged in consideration for the completion of specified works. If these works are not completed in their entirety the court would be varying the clearly expressed intentions of the parties if it was to award payment of a proportionate part of the lump sum. In other words, by agreeing a lump sum the parties have impliedly excluded that possibility of part payment for partially fulfilled building work. Such a contract is said to be an *entire* contract.

The obligation on a contracting party to provide precise, complete performance of the contract before the contractual obligations can be treated as discharged can obviously produce injustice, and there are two exceptions that grant limited relief to the party obliged to perform. These are in cases where the contract is *divisible*, and in cases where there has been *substantial performance*.

A divisible contract

In some circumstances the courts are prepared to accept that a contract is a divisible one, that is a contract which can be broken down into a series of specific parts, so that partial performance of the contract can be set off against partial consideration to be given in return. Had the parties in *Sumpter v. Hedges* agreed a specified sum to be paid on completion of certain stages of the house building, then the builder could have recovered compensation for part of the work done. In practice it is usual in a building contract to provide for payment of parts of the total cost at various stages of completion.

It is not necessary for the parties to formally specify that the contract is a divisible one. The courts seem willing to recognise a divisible contract wherever possible, and will, for example, regard an agreement based upon an estimate or quotation given in advance, which itemises the work to be performed and with a breakdown of the costs, as a divisible contract.

Substantial performance

If a party to a contract has substantially performed his contractual obligations subject only to minor defects, the courts have recognised that it would be unjust to prevent him recovering any of the contractual price. Therefore under this exception the contractual price would be recoverable, less a sum representing the value of the defects. It must be stressed that the exception will only operate where the defects are of a trifling nature, an issue determined by considering not only the character of the defects but also the cost of rectifying them in relation to the total contract price.

A claim of substantial performance of the contract was made in *Bolton v. Mahadeva* 1972. The plaintiff, a heating contractor, had agreed to install a central heating system in the defendant's house for £560. On completion of the work the system proved to be so defective that it would cost £174 to repair. The defendant refused to pay the plaintiff any of the cost of the work and the plaintiff sued. The County Court accepted the plaintiff's claim of substantial performance and awarded him the cost of the work less the cost of the repair. On appeal however, the Court of Appeal held that in the circumstances the plaintiff had not substantially performed the contract and he was not therefore entitled to recover any of the cost of the work. The substantial performance plea would not succeed where there were numerous defects requiring a relatively high cost of repair.

From the consumer's point of view it can be difficult to ascertain whether incomplete performance of the contract is nevertheless sufficient on the facts to amount to substantial performance. Refusal to pay may well be met with a legal action by the contractor to recover the debt owed. Further complications may be caused where the contractor offers to remedy the customer's complaint free of charge and the customer refuses to accept the offer. In the event of a dispute concerning the value of work performed, an offer of reduced payment by the debtor to the creditor will be binding on the creditor, an example of one of the exemptions to *Pinnel's case*.

In *Lawson v. Supasink Ltd.* 1982 the plaintiff's employed the defendants to design, supply and install a fitted kitchen. The total cost was £1,200, and the plaintiffs had to pay a deposit. After the kitchen units had been fitted, but before work on the kitchen was completed, the plaintiffs informed the defendants of their dissatisfaction with the standard of workmanship. In response the defendants undertook to remedy the faults free of charge, but the plaintiffs later rejected this, asked for the units to be removed and for the return of their deposit. The defendants refused. The Court of Appeal, having accepted that the shoddy work did not amount to substantial performance, then considered the offer to remedy made by the defendants. The question was whether they had failed to mitigate their loss, that is minimise the damage they had suffered. In *Fayzu Ltd. v. Saunders* 1919 Scrutton LJ commented, "... *in commercial contracts it is generally reasonable to accept an offer from the party in default.*" In *Lawson* the Court held that the plaintiffs had not acted unreasonably for, in the words of Shaw LJ " *I do not see how the plaintiffs could be required ... to afford the defendants a second opportunity of doing properly what they singularly failed to do adequately in the first instance.*"

The acceptance of partial performance

If a party to a contract partially performs his obligations and the other party accepts the benefit, then he is obliged to pay a reasonable price for it. In such circumstances the courts allow an action on a quantum meruit basis an equitable principle literally meaning as much as he deserves. This exception however will only apply where the party receiving the benefit has the option of whether or not to accept or reject it. In *Sumpter v. Hedges* the owner had no choice but to accept the work done on the half completed houses and was therefore not obliged to pay for it, whereas in *Lawson v. Supasink* the units were capable of being removed and returned.

Where performance is prevented

Obviously if a party to a contract is prevented from fulfilling his contractual obligations by the other party then he will not be in default. In a building contract should the owner prevent the builder from completing, for example by locking him out of the site, the builder can recover a reasonable price for the work done on what is called a *quantum meruit basis* (a concept discussed later in the chapter).

As well as the above exceptions to the general rule that the performance of contractual obligations must be precise, it is well settled that if a party to a contract makes a valid tender (offer) of performance this may be regarded as equivalent to performance. The refusal of the other party to allow performance to take place will discharge any further obligations on the part of the tenderer. Thus if a seller of goods tries to deliver them at the agreed time and place and the goods meet contract description, the refusal of the buyer to accept them will,

- amount to a valid tender of performance; and

- entitle the seller to sue the buyer under s.50 Sale of Goods Act 1979 for damages for non-acceptance of the goods.

Despite the problems that can sometimes occur in performance, most contracts are nevertheless satisfactorily discharged in this way.

Discharge by agreement

This method of discharge occurs where the parties mutually agree to waive their rights and obligations under it. It is called bilateral discharge. To be an effective *waiver* the second agreement must be a contract, the consideration for which is the exchange of promises not to enforce the original contract.

Each party is agreeing to release the other from the original contractual promises and not to use on the grounds of non-performance. The situation however is more complex where one party to a contract has already executed or partly executed his consideration under it. Here for a waiver to be effective it must be embodied within a speciality contract or be supported by fresh consideration. This is called unilateral discharge and can only be achieved by *accord* and *satisfaction*. The accord is simply the agreement to discharge and the satisfaction is the consideration required to support it. An example occurs when a football manager with three years of a £100,000 per year contract still to run is asked by the club after a poor season to leave. If the two sides agree to a new deal (the accord) in which the manager will receive a £200,000 lump sum to go, both sides obtain a new benefit (satisfaction). The manager receives a substantial payment and the club can bring in a new manager. By contrast suppose X contracts to sell goods to Y for £50. X then delivers the goods to Y but hearing of Y's financial difficulties agrees to waive payment. Here the agreement of X to waive payment (the accord) is not enforceable unless supported by fresh consideration furnished by Y (the satisfaction). The fresh consideration of course must be of value but need not be adequate. As we saw in our examination of the principles of consideration, at common law the rule in *Pinnel's case* provides that there is no value in a creditor taking as satisfaction payment of a lesser sum than he was due under the original agreement.

A creditor's promise to accept a reduced amount may however be binding on him, through the operation of the equitable doctrine of promissory estoppel, established in *Hughes v. Metropolitan Railway Co.* 1877 by the House of Lords, and by Denning J as he then was in *Central London Property Trust Ltd. v. High Trees House Ltd.* 1947. In the High Trees case the defendant company took a 99-year lease on a block of flats from the plaintiff company at an annual rent of £2,500. The lease was granted in 1937. By 1940 the evacuation of large numbers of people out of London because of war meant that the defendant company was unable to let all the flats and could not meet the annual rent out of the profits it was making. As a result, the plaintiff company agreed to accept a reduced annual rent of £1,250. By the beginning of 1945 the flats were fully let again. An action was brought by the plaintiff company to recover the difference between the reduced rent and the full rent for the last two quarters of 1945. The action succeeded, for the court considered that the agreement of 1940 would continue only as long as wartime conditions prevailed. The Court also considered whether the plaintiffs could recover the remaining arrears from the defendants, relying on *Pinnel's case*. It took the view that such action would be inequitable, even though permissible at common law. In equity the creditor would be estopped, or denied the right of disowning his promise to accept the reduced amount, where the debtor had to the creditor's knowledge relied on the promise, and acted on it to his detriment. This rule is consequently referred to as promissory estoppel. The doctrine only arises within the context of a pre-existing contractual relationship, and does not remove consideration as a requirement of the contract.

Being a form of equitable relief, promissory estoppel can only be used as defence by those who have acted in an equitable manner themselves.

In *D & C Builders v. Rees* 1965 Mr. & Mrs Rees exacted a promise from D & C Builders to accept a reduced amount than that originally agreed, for building work carried out to the Rees's home. They claimed the building work was substandard, but in fact they were simply attempting to escape the full payment due, using their knowledge that the builders were in financial difficulties and desperate for cash. Sometime after the reduced payment had been made the company sued for the outstanding balance, and the defendants pleaded promissory estoppel. The court refused to allow Mr. & Mrs Rees the equitable defence, on the grounds of their own lack of equity.

The process of mutual termination can also occur in employment relationships.

Mutual termination

If the parties to a contract of employment, without duress and after taking proper advice, enter into a separate contract, supported by good consideration, with the objective of terminating the employment relationship by mutual consent, the contract will be valid and enforceable.

Such was the case in *Logan Salton v. Durham County Council* 1989. Here the complainant was a social worker who, as a result of disciplinary hearings, had been redeployed by his employer. The complainant was given notice of a number of complaints against him and a recommendation that he be summarily dismissed. Prior to that meeting his union representative negotiated on his behalf a mutual agreement to terminate his employment with the Council. By that agreement the employment contract was to terminate in seven weeks' time and an outstanding car loan of £2,750 wiped out as a debt. Despite the fact that the agreement was signed by both parties, the complainant subsequently complained to an industrial tribunal that he had been unfairly dismissed. It was argued that a dismissal had occurred in law, for the mutual agreement to terminate was void as an agreement entered into under duress. The tribunal held that the fact that the employee was aware of the employer's recommendation of dismissal did not constitute duress, bearing in mind the financial inducement. *"In the resolution of industrial disputes, it is in the best interests of all concerned that a contract made without duress, for good consideration, preferably after proper and sufficient advice and which has the effect of terminating a contract of employment by mutual agreement (whether at once or at some future date) should be effective between the contracting parties, in which case there probably will not have been a dismissal."*

Discharge by breach

A party to a contract who completely fails to perform their obligations under it or performs them defectively is in breach of contract. Generally, the remedy of an innocent party to a contract who has suffered as a result of a breach is to sue for damages. For some breaches of contract however, the innocent party is given the additional remedy of treating the contract as repudiated, in other words terminated, thus discharging any remaining obligations arising under it. Terms in a contract have different status and it is only when a condition has been broken that repudiatory breach can occur. Two classic cases from the nineteenth century illuminate the distinction between important terms (conditions) and less important terms (warranties) in a contract. In *Bettini v. Gye* 1876 the plaintiff, an opera singer agreed in writing to sing in various concerts and operas over a period of three and a half months, and to be present at rehearsals for at least six days before the engagements were due to begin. Due to illness he arrived with only two days of rehearsals left, and as a result the defendant terminated the agreement. Looking at the contract as a whole, the court decided that the rehearsal clause was not a condition, but merely a warranty, for which damages alone was the remedy. The contract had been wrongfully terminated and the plaintiff could counter-claim for damages.

> In *Poussard v. Spiers and Pond* 1876 an opera singer was unable to take part in the first week of performances due to illness. In the meantime the management had engaged a substitute and refused the original singer the part when she arrived. They were held to be entitled to do so, for her non-attendance at the performances was a breach of a vital term of the contract.

If a breach of contract takes place before the time set for performance of the agreement it is called an *anticipatory breach*. This will occur where a party to a contract expressly declares they will not perform their part of the bargain. Once an anticipatory breach has arisen the innocent party does not have to wait for the date set for performance but has the option of immediately suing for breach of contract. In such circumstances the injured party has the choice of commencing legal action at the time of the anticipatory breach, or of waiting until performance is due to see if it is in fact carried out, and if it is not, commence action thereafter. Which approach is adopted is likely to have an effect upon the level of any damages awarded. Crucially of course it has to be decided whether the words or actions that have given rise to the assumption of repudiation are in the circumstances sufficient. In *Woodar Investment Development Ltd. v. Wimpey Construction Ltd. 1980*, Lord Willberforce said the test was, " *whether, objectively speaking* (the defendants) *conduct showed an intention to abandon the contract. "*

If a contract of employment is terminated by the employer dismissing the employee then the contractual or· statutory notice must be served or wages paid in lieu. A summary dismissal is a termination instantly without notice and is justifiable under the common law if the employee is in repudiatory breach of contract because of his gross misconduct. By summarily dismissing the employer is accepting the repudiatory breach of the employee and treating the contract as discharged.

> In *Pepper v. Webb* 1969 the action of the head gardener in wilfully disobeying a reasonable order was sufficient to amount to gross misconduct and provide grounds for summary dismissal, despite the contract of employment providing for three months' notice. It should be stressed, however, that the reaction of the gardener in this case represented the culmination of a long period of insolence, and the isolated use of choice obscenities by an employee to an employer may not amount to gross misconduct if there is provocation.

> In Denco *v. Joinson* 1991 an employee who used an unauthorised password to enter a computer file known to contain confidential information was guilty of gross misconduct and could be summarily dismissed.

What about the situation where it is the employee who summarily terminates the contract. In a large number of cases it may seem superficially that the contract of employment has been terminated by the employee's conduct in *walking out* and treating the contract as at an end. Where however, the reason for leaving was due to the conduct of the employer or those under his control, it may be that the employee could show that the employer is responsible for the contractual termination. In such circumstances an employee could claim that there has been a constructive dismissal which is unfair.

The statutory test for determining whether a constructive dismissal had taken place was to judge the reasonableness of the employer's conduct. Since *Western Excavating (ECC) Ltd. v. Sharp* 1978 however, the courts have rejected that approach as being too vague and now the so called 'conduct test' is to be applied based upon strict contractual principles. The aim of the conduct test is to bring some degree of certainty to the law by requiring the employee to justify his leaving as a response to the employer's repudiatory conduct. *"If the employer is guilty of conduct which is a significant breach going to the root of the contract of employment, or which shows that the employer no longer intends to be bound by one or more of the essential terms of the contract then the employee is entitled to treat himself as discharged from any further performance."*

A breach by the employer of the express terms of the contract of employment covering such matters as wages, job location, contractual duties and job description, normally comes about when the employer unilaterally attempts to impose a change on the employee without his consent.

By demoting an employee and failing to provide him with suitable office accommodation an employer could be held to be in fundamental breach of the contract of employment. Such an employee could accept the repudiatory breach and regard himself as constructively dismissed.

> This was the case in *Wadham Stringer Commercials (London) Ltd. & Wadham Stringer Vehicles Ltd. v. Brown* 1983 where a fleet sales director was effectively demoted to no more than a retail salesman. At the same time he was moved from reasonable accommodation to an office 8ft x 6ft with no ventilation, next to the gentleman's lavatory. As a consequence the employee eventually resigned and claimed a constructive dismissal which was unfair. The EAT agreed that there had been a fundamental breach of contract, accepted by the employee, and following *Western Excavating (ECC) Ltd. v. Sharp*, a constructive dismissal. The employer's argument that their actions were the result of economic necessity were relevant, but only in deciding the reasonableness of their conduct for the purposes of the test of fairness or for the purpose of assessing the level of compensation in an unfair dismissal claim.

The need to look for a clear breach of contractual term in applying the conduct test has encouraged both tribunals and courts in the absence of relevant express terms to imply terms into a contract of employment. It is the need therefore to accommodate the doctrine of constructive dismissal that has encouraged judicial ingenuity in applying the business efficacy test to find implied obligations in employment contracts. An excellent example is provided by the need to maintain trust and confidence in the employment relationship.

> In *Courtaulds Northern Textiles Ltd. v. Andrew* 1979 the EAT stated that *"there is an implied term in a contract of employment that the employers will not, without reasonable and proper cause, conduct themselves in a manner calculated or likely to destroy or seriously damage the relationship of confidence and trust between the parties"*. Here a comment made to the complainant by his assistant manager that *"you can't do the bloody job anyway"* which was not a true expression of his opinion was held to justify the

complainant in resigning and treating himself as constructively dismissed. While criticism of a worker's performance would not necessarily amount to repudiatory conduct so as to lead to constructive dismissal, here telling the employee that he could not do his job, when that was not a true expression of opinion, was conduct which was *"likely to destroy the trust relationship which was a necessary element in the relationship between the supervisory employee and his employers"*.

Discharge by frustration or subsequent impossibility

Discharged by frustration occurs where as a result of an event subsequent to making the contract, its performance can no longer be carried out. The event must arise after contracting since if the contract is impossible to perform at the time it is made there can be no contract. Originally the common law did not take such a lenient view of changes in circumstances and required that the parties to a contract should provide for all eventualities. If because of a subsequent event performance of an obligation became impossible, the party required to perform it would be liable to pay damages for non performance. Today however the courts recognise that certain supervening events may frustrate a contract and thus release the parties from their obligation under it.

> In *National Carriers Ltd. v. Panalpina (Northern) Ltd.* 1981 the plaintiffs leased a warehouse in Hull to the defendants. The lease was for ten years, however for a period of twenty months the only access road to the premises was closed by the local authority due to the poor state of a listed building nearby. The defendants refused to pay any further rent to the plaintiffs. The House of Lords accepted the defendant's argument that a lease could, in law, become frustrated, but felt that twenty months out of a ten year period, was not sufficiently substantial to frustrate the contract.

There are a number of grounds upon which a contract may become frustrated. They include:

- *Changes in the law.* If because of new legislation performance of the contract would become illegal this would be a supervening event to frustrate the contract.

- *Destruction of subject matter.* If the subject matter or means of performance of the contract is destroyed this is an event which frustrates a contract.

In *Taylor v. Caldwell* 1863 the plaintiff agreed to hire the defendant's music hall to give some concerts. Prior to performance the hall was destroyed by fire and this event, the court held, released the parties from their obligations under the contract.

- *Inability to achieve main object*. If as a result of change in circumstances performance of the contract would be radically different from the performance envisaged by the parties then the contract is frustrated. It must be shown that the parties are no longer able to achieve their main object under the contract.

In *Krell v. Henry* 1903 the defendant hired a flat for two days to enable him to watch Edward VII's Coronation procession. Due to the King's illness the Coronation was cancelled and the defendant naturally refused to pay. The Court of Appeal held that as the main object of the contract was to view the procession, and this could no longer be achieved, the foundation of the contract had collapsed. The contract was thus frustrated and the parties released from their obligations under it.

A further claim of frustration as a consequence of the cancellation of the Coronation was brought in *Herne Bay Steamboat Co. v. Hutton* 1903. Here a steamboat had been chartered to watch the naval review as part of the Coronation celebrations and also for a day's cruise round the fleet. The Court of Appeal had to determine whether the cancellation of the naval review released the defendant from his obligation to pay the hire charge. The Court held that there has not been a sufficient change in circumstances to constitute a frustration of the contract. Here the defendant could have derived some benefit from the contract and was therefore liable to pay the hire charges. Frustration is not available in a commercial transaction merely because the contract turns out to be less profitable than one of the parties expected.

While the doctrine of frustration should be limited to scenarios where the change of circumstances is caused by an event outside the parties control this is not always the case where the contract is one of employment.

In *Shepherd & Company Ltd. v. Jerrom* 1986 the Court of Appeal considered the position of an apprentice plumber who was sentenced to Borstal training for a minimum period of six months. Failure to dismiss him in accordance with standard procedures for apprentices led the tribunal and the EAT to find that he had been constructively dismissed unfairly and so entitled to compensation. The Court of Appeal disagreed however and held that the four year apprenticeship contract had been frustrated by the six month sentence.

- *Death or illness.* In a contract for personal services the death or illness of the person required to perform will frustrate the contract. Temporary illness or incapacity will generally not release a party from his obligations. The illness must be such that it goes to the root of the contract. This was the case in *Condor v. Barron Knights Ltd.* 1965. In January 1963, Edward Condor, the sixteen year old drummer in the Barron Knights pop group, collapsed at a performance and was diagnosed as suffering severe mental strain due to the strenuous nature of the life style associated with his work. The contract the young drummer had signed with Barron Knights Ltd. was for a five year term and required him to perform up to seven nights weekly, sometimes twice nightly. Coupled with the travelling to one night stands this had contributed to his breakdown. The suggestion was made that Condor should only work three or four nights per week but this was rejected as unacceptable by the groups management, and his engagement was terminated. In a claim for damages for breach of contract and wrongful dismissal the High Court concluded that medical condition of the young drummer was such that he was unlikely to be able to continue to perform the obligations required under his contract and accordingly the contract was terminated by virtue of frustration. Justice Thompson said that *"by reason of the impact upon his health and well being of his life, far too strenuous and exhausting for a boy of 16, talented though he was and ambitious though he was, the impact was such in my judgment that had in a business sense made it impossible for him to continue to perform or for the defendants to have him perform the term of the contract as a member of the group."* Certainly the fact that Condor was more than an instrumentalist and an integral part of a highly synchronised comedy routine meant that it would have been very difficult to employ a substitute for those engagements he could not perform.

Non frustrating events

The common law doctrine of frustration will not apply in the following circumstances:

(a)   If performance of the contract has become more onerous on one party or financially less rewarding.

In *Davis Contractors Ltd. v. Fareham UDC* 1956 the plaintiff building company claimed that a building contract should be regarded as discharged by frustration due to the shortage of available labour and resultant increased costs. The House of Lords rejected the arguments that frustration had discharged the contract. Performance of the contract had simply been made more onerous than originally envisaged by the plaintiffs.

(b)   If the parties to a contract have made express provision for the event which has occurred.

(c)   If it can be shown that a party to the contract caused the supposed frustrating event by his own conduct then there will be no frustration however there may be a contractual breach. This is self induced frustration.

Consequences of frustration of contract

To determine the rights and duties of the parties following frustration it is necessary to consider the position at common law and under statute. As we have seen frustration will terminate a contract. However under common law it does not discharge the contract *ab initio* (from the outset) but only from the time of the frustrating event. Therefore, if before that date work had been done or money transferred, the common law rule is simply that losses lie where they fall. It is thus not possible to recover money due or paid prior to frustrating events, except if there is a total failure or consideration, for example if there has been performance of consideration by one party and non performance of consideration by the other.

This common law position was altered by the Law Reform (Frustrated Contracts) Act 1943. The Act however does not apply to certain contracts such as insurance, charter-parties (shipping contracts) and contracts for the sale of specific goods, so the common law position remains to some transactions relevant. Under the Act the following conditions apply:

*   Money transferred prior to the frustrating event may be recovered.

*   Money due prior to the frustrating event is no longer due.

*   Expenses incurred prior to the frustrating event may be deducted from money to be returned.

*   Compensation may be recovered on a quantum meruit basis where one of the parties has carried out an act of part performance prior to the frustrating event and thus conferred a benefit on the other party.

In *Gamero SA v. ICM/Fair Warning (Agency) Ltd.* 1995 the plaintiffs had agreed with the defendants to promote the defendants rock concert. It was to be held in a Madrid stadium, however a few days before the concert the plaintiff's licence to hold it was taken away by the public authority following safety concerns about the stadium and the concert did not take place. Both the parties had incurred preliminary expenses, and the plaintiffs had made an advance payment to the defendants, which they sought to recover under the 1943 Act. The court found the contract to be frustrated because the stadium could not be used. The plaintiffs could recover the advance payment. The court decided not to deduct the defendants expenses from this sum, as the plaintiffs had also suffered loss and to make the deduction would be unfair.

Remedies for Breach of Contract

Whenever a breach of contract arises the innocent party is likely to seek a remedy against the contract breaker. We saw at the beginning of our study of contract law that the fundamental quality of contracts is their legally enforceability, and in the law on remedies that enforceability is realised. The options available are to claim damages and/or treat the contract as discharged under the common law, or to pursue an equitable discretionary remedy.

Damages

Damages is the technical term used to describe monetary compensation. The usual claim is for *unliquidated* damages under the common law. Unliquidated damages are damages whose level is determined by the court, exercising its own discretion. It is sometimes possible for a plaintiff to quantify the measure of damages being sought concisely, in which event the plaintiff will claim a *liquidated* amount e.g.: three weeks' loss of salary where the salary is of a fixed amount, or loss of profit on a sale.

The aim of awarding damages

Damages awarded under an unliquidated claim should amount to a sum which will put the innocent party in the position he would have been in had the contract been performed properly, that is the loss resulting from the breach directly and naturally. Consequently a plaintiff should not be awarded damages when the result would be to put him in a better position financially than would have been the case if the contract had not been broken. The aim of awarding contractual damages is not to punish the contract breaker.

In *C & B Haulage v. Middleton* 1983 the Court of Appeal refused to grant damages to an engineer who was evicted from the business premises he occupied before the contractual licence he held had expired. The reason for the refusal was that he was working from home, and thus relieved from paying any further charges under the licence. Damages would make him better off.

Damages may be refused where the court is of the view that they are too speculative.

> On this basis the court awarded only nominal damages to the plaintiffs in *Entertainments Ltd. v. Great Yarmouth Borough Council* 1983. The council had repudiated an agreement under which the plaintiffs were to put on summer shows in the town. The judge, Cantley J took the view that as it had not been established as probable that the shows would have made the plaintiffs a profit, to award anything other than nominal damages would be speculative.

If as a result of a breach of contract the innocent party does not obtain what he expected under the contract, but the value of the performance is not affected, what is the level of damages that a court should award to compensate for the loss?

> This was the issue faced by the courts in *Ruxley Electronics and Construction Ltd. v. Forsyth* 1995. Builders had agreed to build a swimming pool with a maximum depth of 7ft 6ins for £70,178. When the work was completed the customer discovered that the maximum depth was only 6ft 9 ins and only 6ft at the point that people would dive in. As is usual in this type of building contract certain sums had been paid by the owner towards the cost of the work during the construction and £39,072 remained outstanding. The builders claimed the balance and the customer counterclaimed for breach of contract. The High Court held that despite the builders breach of contract there had been no reduction in the value of the pool and ordered the customer to pay the balance less £2,500 for the loss of amenity. This decision was reversed by the Court of Appeal who decided that it was appropriate to award £21,560 damages to reflect the cost of replacing the pool to remedy the breach, even though the depth of the pool had not decreased its value. On final appeal the House of Lords held that in this type of case involving defective building work the court was entitled to take the view that it would be unreasonable to insist on reinstatement if the expense of the work involved would be out of all proportion to the benefit obtained. A relevant factor in determining reasonableness was the intention of the customer to rebuild. In this case as the customer did not intend to reinstate, his loss was restricted to the difference in value. The original judgment of £2,500 damages for the loss of amenity was restored and the decision of the Court of Appeal reversed.

Remoteness of damage

The consequences of a contractual breach can often extend well beyond the immediate, obvious losses. A failure to deliver goods may for example result in the buyer being unable to complete the work on a particular job, which will in turn put him in breach with the party who had contracted him to carry out the job. That party may in turn suffer further consequences, thus the original breach leads to a chain of events which become increasingly remote from it. Damages will only be awarded for losses which are *proximate*. The courts take the view that it is unfair to make a contract-breaker responsible for damage caused as a result of circumstances of which he was unaware.

> In *Hadley v. Baxendale* 1854 the plaintiff mill owner contracted with a defendant carrier who agreed to take a broken millshaft to a repairer and then return it. The carrier delayed in delivery of the shaft and as a result the plaintiff sought to recover the loss of profit he would have made during the period of delay. The court held that this loss was not recoverable as it was too remote. The possible loss of profit was a circumstance of which the carrier was unaware at the time of the contract. The result would have been different however had the plaintiff expressly made the defendant aware that this loss of profit was the probable result of a breach of contract.

The decision in *Hadley v. Baxendale* has been approved by the House of Lords on many occasions and knowledge of the circumstances which could produce the damage it still a crucial factor in determining the extent of the liability for the breach.

> In *Czarnikow v. Koufos (The Heron II)* 1969 a shipowner delayed in delivering a cargo of sugar to Basrah. The sugar was to be sold by the cargo owners at Basrah, where there was an established sugar market. During the nine days the ship was delayed the market price fell. The cargo owners successfully sued for their loss. The House of Lords considered that the loss ought to have been within the reasonable contemplation of the shipowners as a consequence of the delay. It was felt that the shipowners should have appreciated that a market for goods is something which by its nature fluctuates over time.

> In *Balfour Beatty Construction (Scotland) Ltd. v. Scottish Power plc* 1994 the defendants were supplying electricity to the plaintiffs under an agreement linked to a construction project the plaintiffs were carrying out. A break in the supply prevented the completion of a concrete pour. As a result prior construction work was rendered useless and had to be demolished, and then rebuilt. On the grounds that the defendants neither were aware, nor ought

reasonably to have been aware of the full effect of interruption to a concrete pour, the House of Lords held the losses to be too remote.

Other principles applicable to a claim for damages

Where a breach has occurred the innocent party, if he accepts that the breach discharges the contract, must take all reasonable steps to mitigate the loss resulting from the breach. There is no requirement for the injured party to act immediately to take on a risky venture but rather act reasonably in order to minimise the loss rather than *sitting on the breach*. For instance an hotel would be expected to try and relet a room that a customer, in breach of contract, had failed to use.

> In *Luker v. Chapman* 1970 the plaintiff lost his right leg below the knee following a motor accident partly caused by the negligence of the defendant. This injury prevented him from continuing his work as a telephone engineer, but he was offered clerical work as an alternative. He refused it, choosing instead to go into teacher training. It was held that he could not recover as damages the loss of income suffered whilst he underwent the teacher training.

Damages are not limited to the pure economic cost of the loss of the bargain but may also be recovered for inconvenience, discomfort, distress or anxiety caused by the breach.

> In *Jackson v. Horizon Holidays* 1975 the plaintiff had booked a month's holiday in Ceylon staying in an hotel. The defendant's brochure described the hotel facilities. These included a swimming pool, a mini golf course and a hair-dressing salon. The hotel in fact had none of these facilities and the food was poor. The plaintiff's children's room was unusable due to mildew and fungus on the walls, and the sanitary facilities were dirty. The Court of Appeal awarded damages of £1,100 to the plaintiff for breach of contract. This was made up of £600 for the reduction in the value of the holiday and £500 damages for mental distress, vexation and disappointment.

> In *Jarvis v. Swans Tours Ltd.* 1973 the plaintiff booked a skiing holiday which was described in the defendant's brochure as a house party in Morlialp. The price included a number of house party arrangements, a welcome party on arrival, afternoon tea and cake, Swiss dinner by candle-light, fondue party, yodel evening, and a farewell party. The brochure also stated that ski packs could be hired in Morlialp, the hotel owner spoke English and the hotel bar would be open several evenings a week. In the first week of the holiday the house party comprised only 13 people, and in the second week the plaintiff was the only guest at the hotel. The hotel owner did not speak English, the bar

was only open on one evening, and the plaintiff was unable to hire full length skis except for two days during the second week. The Court of Appeal held that the quality of holiday provided fell far short of that which was promised in the brochure and awarded damages to the plaintiff. This included damages representing the difference between what the plaintiff had paid for the holiday and what he had been supplied with; as well as damages for mental distress, frustration, annoyance and disappointment.

In substantial contracts involving large sums, such as building contracts, it is usual to attempt to liquidate damages payable in the event of a breach. This is achieved by the parties expressly inserting a clause into the contract providing for a sum of compensation to be payable on a breach. Generally, provided such clauses represent a genuine pre-estimate of the future possible loss rather than amounting to a penalty to ensure performance of contract, they are enforceable by the courts.

The right to treat a contract as discharged will depend upon the nature of the breach. For breaches of condition the innocent party may sue for damages and/or treat the contract as repudiated, whereas for less important terms the innocent party is limited to an action for damages.

Quantification of damages in relation to goods or land is essentially a question of assessing the market price and then determining the actual loss. The Sale of Goods Act 1979 provides for a number of remedies, including damages, available to an injured party to a sale of goods transaction.

Discretionary remedies

Historically these remedies became available through the intervention of the Court of Chancery. They include the injunction, specific performance and the remedy of quantum meruit.

Injunctions

An injunction is an order of the court which directs a person not to break his contract, and is an appropriate remedy where the contract contains a negative stipulation.

This can be seen in *Warner Bros. Pictures v. Nelson* 1937. The defendant, the actress Bette Davis, had agreed to work for the plaintiff company for twelve months, and not to act or sing for anyone else or be otherwise employed for a period of two years, without the plaintiff's written consent. It was held that she could be restrained by injunction from breaking the negative aspects of her undertaking, thus preventing her from working under a new acting contract in England where she was earning more money. The injunction was however confined to her work as an actress, for it was recognised that if the negative terms in her contract were fully enforced it would have the effect of either forcing her to work for Warner Bros. or starve, and this would mean the injunction acting as a device for specific performance of the contract. Equity will not order specific performance of contracts of a personal kind which would involve constant supervision, and which, by their nature, depend upon the good faith of the parties. Similarly in *Page One Records Ltd. v. Britton* 1968 an injunction was applied for to prevent the Troggs pop group from engaging anyone as their manager other than the plaintiff. An injunction on these terms was refused, for to grant it would indirectly compel the pop group to continue to employ the plaintiff.

Types of injunction

There are three types of injunction which may be applied for:

(a) *an interlocutory injunction.* This is designed to regulate the position of the parties pending trial, the plaintiff undertaking to be responsible for any damage caused to the defendant through the use of the injunction if in the subsequent action the plaintiff is unsuccessful. In *American Cyanamid v. Ethicon* 1975 the House of Lords said that an interlocutory injunction should only be granted where the plaintiff can show that the matter to be tried is a serious one and that the balance of convenience is in his favour. One rarely used option for an employee who feels that his employer is unreasonably requiring him to do work which is not part of his contractual obligations is to seek an injunction to maintain the status quo at work.

In certain circumstances a specialised kind of interlocutory injunction, known as a *Mareva injunction*, may be sought. The Mareva injunction takes its name from the case in which it was first successfully applied for, *Mareva Compania Naviera v. International Bulk Carriers* 1980, and it is used when the subject matter of a contract is in danger of being removed from the area of the courts jurisdiction. If the action which is to be heard involves a claim for damages and the sale of the subject matter is likely to be used to pay them, a Mareva injunction can be used to restrict the removal of these assets from the courts' jurisdiction. This is a valuable protection in cases where the defendant is a foreign organisation. Section 37 of the Supreme Court Act 1981 grants the High Court the power to issue such injunctions.

(b)   *a prohibitory injunction.* This orders a defendant not to do a particular thing. The injunction sought in the *Nelson* case (above) was of this kind. Much of the case law concerning prohibitory injunctions is concerned with employment contracts, and as we have seen such an injunction can only be used to enforce a negative stipulation. In addition the remedy of a prohibitory injunction will not be given where a court is of the opinion that damages would be an adequate remedy, although in the words of Sachs LJ in *Evans Marshall v. Bertola SA* 1973 *"The standard question in relation to the grant of an injunction, are damages an adequate remedy? might perhaps, in the light of the authorities of recent years, be rewritten: is it just, in all the circumstances, that a plaintiff should be confined to his remedy in damages."*

A prohibitory injunction was used in *Decro-Wall International v. Practitioners in Marketing* 1971 where a manufacturer was restrained from breaking a sole distributorship agreement by an order preventing him from disposing of the goods to which the agreement related in any other way. The Court was not however prepared to order him to fulfil the positive part of the agreement which was to maintain supplies of the goods to the distributor, for this would have amounted to specific performance of the contract (see below).

(c)   *a mandatory injunction.* This is used to order that a positive act be done, for example that a fence blocking a right of way be taken down.

In *Sky Petroleum Ltd. v. VIP Petroleum Ltd.* 1974 the parties entered into a ten year agreement in 1970 under which VIP undertook to supply all Sky's petrol requirements. Following a dispute in 1973 VIP refused to continue its supplies to Sky, and because of an oil crisis at the time Sky found itself unable to secure any other source of supply. The Court granted a temporary injunction against VIP restraining it from withholding a reasonable level of supplies.

Specific performance

The decree of specific performance is an order of the court requiring a party who is in breach of contract to carry out his promises. Failure to comply amounts to a contempt of court. As an equitable remedy it will only be granted if certain conditions apply. These are:

* *Where damages would not provide an adequate remedy.* Usually in commercial transactions damages will be adequate, and will enable the injured party to purchase the property or obtain the services from some

alternative source. However where the subject matter of the contract is unique, for example a painting, specific performance will lie. The item must however be unique, and in *Cohen v. Roche* 1927 specific performance was not ordered of a contract to sell some rare Hepplewhite chairs since it was difficult, but not impossible, to buy similar chairs on the open market.

Land is always regarded as unique, and it is in the enforcement of contracts for the sale of land that specific performance is most commonly used.

A contract for the purchase of shares or debentures can also be specifically enforced.

- *Where the court can properly supervise the performance.*

- *That it is not just and equitable to grant the order.*

In addition the plaintiff must satisfy the various equitable maxims which demand high standards of behaviour if relief is to be granted. Thus for example it is said that *"he who comes to equity must come with clean hands"*, meaning that the plaintiff's behaviour must be beyond reproach.

Quantum meruit

A *quantum meruit* claim (for as much as is deserved) is available where:

- *damages is not an appropriate remedy.* This could occur where performance of a contract has begun, but the plaintiff is unable to complete the contract because the defendant has repudiated it, thus preventing the plaintiff from obtaining payment.

- *where work has been carried out under a void contract .*

In *British Steel Corporation v. Cleveland Bridge and Engineering Co. Ltd.* 1984 steel had been supplied to the defendants by the plaintiffs whilst the parties were still negotiating terms. The negotiations subsequently failed, and no contract was concluded between them. The court held that the plaintiffs were entitled to claim on a quantum meruit for the price of the steel supplied to the defendants and used by them.

Assignment - Island Tours

In May 1999 Mr. Levine paid Island Tours Limited £3,732 for a two week inclusive holiday for himself, his wife and their four year old child. Their chosen accommodation was the Hotel Sport described in the Island Tours brochure as a four star hotel with a lively atmosphere, a wide range of sporting facilities and fully air conditioned. On arrival at the hotel the Levines were unhappy with the room they were allocated because it was near the swimming pool and was noisy until the early hours. It was also one of the small proportion of rooms at the hotel which had never had air conditioning installed and the humidity at night was unbearable. An alternative room with air conditioning was finally provided for the Levines after three days, but it had a view of the hotel car park. While the sporting facilities at the hotel were first class the Levines never really used them as their child contracted a stomach bug and was poorly throughout the holiday. Mr. Levine thought that the hotel food as to blame for his son's illness as other clients had complained of similar problems, although neither he nor his wife were affected.

In the booking conditions on the booking form signed by Mr. Levine there was a clause which provided that "Island Tours shall not be liable to the client or members of the client's party for any injury, loss, damage or inconvenience caused to the client through the acts or omissions, in negligence or otherwise, of Island Tours, its employees or agents in connection with the holiday".

On returning to the UK the Levines were so disappointed by their holiday that they decided to take legal advice in order to secure redress. As a consequence a letter has been sent to Island Tours Head Office on behalf of the Levines claiming a refund of the holiday cost. The letter indicates that the Levines have a cause of action of breach of contract and if necessary a complaint could be made to Trading Standards.

Task

You are employed as a claims assessor at the Island Tours Head Office and your task is to advise the company on potential liability and how best to proceed with the Levine's complaint.

Chapter 11

Selling Goods and Services

Sale of Goods and Related Transactions

This chapter aims to examine the contractual relationships arising between businesses and all those whom they supply with goods and services. The sale of goods and services is an area of critical importance in developing an understanding of business law, for it lies at the heart of commercial activity.

The primary objective of business activity is the provision of goods and services for consumers. Consumption of goods and services meets the private needs of individuals. All of us act as private consumers in this way. We make regular purchases of goods and services to satisfy our demand for a wide range of necessaries and luxuries, from food and clothing to motor cars, video recorders and holidays. Goods and services are also demanded by business organisations, who acquire them to meet their own internal requirements, as well as for the purpose of resale to other businesses in the chain of production or to consumers. The legal rules relating to inter business contracting are, in many cases, identical to those which apply where a business deals with a private consumer. However the law has increasingly sought to compensate for the relative economic weakness of individual consumers, by developing a framework of consumer protection. This framework is examined here and in Chapter 12

In the previous three chapters we examined the legal rules relating to the formation of business contracts and the discharge of obligations arising under them. The remedies available in the event of non compliance by one of the contracting parties were also considered. We shall now examine in more detail the various types of contract which are encountered in business and identify the features which distinguish them. Some types of contract involving the supply of goods, for example, which appear very similar, are nevertheless governed by different rules. The distinction between them may depend upon the provisions in the contract relating to the transfer of ownership or the time for payment. The transfer of ownership is a fundamental feature of a contract for the sale of goods whereas under a contract of hire goods are supplied with no intention to transfer ownership. Under a hire purchase contract the aim is to transfer ownership in the goods when full payment has been made.

Inevitably in a book of this nature it is necessary to make choices about the types of business contracts we propose to explore. To appreciate how commercial activity is translated it is necessary to examine:

- contracts for the sale of goods;

- contracts for the hire of goods;

- contracts for the sale of services;

- contracts involving consumer credit.

As the most significant commercial contract the main emphasis will be on sale of goods contracts regulated by the Sale of Goods Act 1979.

Contracts for the Sale of Goods

The Sale of Goods Act 1979 regulates all contracts for the sale of goods. The importance of the Sale of Goods Act 1979 to the commercial activity of the United Kingdom cannot be underestimated, for it provides the framework of rights and obligations applicable to all buyers and sellers of goods. The original Sale of Goods Act of 1893 sought to regulate the contract of sale only to the extent that the parties themselves had failed to do so, and as a result subsequently found themselves in disagreement. It was not for Parliament to dictate to a businessperson what the contract should be. This freedom to exclude is still contained in the Sale of Goods Act 1979, but it is now a very limited freedom. This is because it is subject to the provisions of the Unfair Contract Terms Act 1977, which restricts, and in certain cases, prohibits a seller from excluding his potential liabilities which arise under the 1979 Act. The effect of such restrictions is that the 1979 Act is not simply an aid to the business world, it is also a creator and defender of the rights of the economically weaker sections of the community, and thus qualifies for inclusion in the growing body of legislation which grants protection to the consumer and which is consequently referred to as consumer law.

Definition of a Sale of Goods Transaction

The Act defines a contract for the sale of goods as one by which the seller transfers or agrees to transfer the *property* in goods to the buyer for money consideration called the price. To understand this definition and therefore identify those transactions which fall outside the Act, an explanation of the terms *property*, *goods* and *money consideration* is necessary.

Property is ownership. It follows that the Act does not apply to transactions in which ownership does not pass from one party to the other, for example where goods are hired or borrowed, for the hirer or borrower is simply obtaining possession, not ownership. Hire purchase agreements are excluded from the Act. This is because a hire purchase agreement consists of a simple hiring of goods, to which there is attached an option to purchase. Since the hirer is not compelled to purchase the goods he or she is not a 'buyer' for the Act defines a buyer as a person who *buys* or *agrees to buy* goods.

> In *Helby v. Matthews* 1895 the House of Lords made it clear that an option does not give rise to a firm commitment. In that case a piano dealer agreed to hire a piano to a customer for a period of 3 years by monthly repayments. The agreement provided that on completion of all the monthly payments the customer would become the owner of the piano, being liable to pay any arrears of the monthly payments outstanding at the date of termination. During the hire period the customer disposed of the piano to an innocent third party. The Court held that the dealer was entitled to recover the piano from the third party for the customer was not an owner and therefore could not pass a *good title* (i.e. ownership) to the third party.

The expression goods includes all personal property including such things as cars, furniture, tools, and books - but not land which forms a separate category of property. Things which are attached to or form part of the land and which are agreed to be removed from the land either before the sale or under the contract of sale are treated as goods. However such goods must be identifiable from the land itself and not classified as fixtures, such as machinery bolted to the floor.

> In *Morgan v Russell and Sons* 1909 a sale of slag and cinders was considered not to be a sale of goods because these materials had merged into the land upon which they had been deposited.

> In *St Albans District Council v. ICL* 1996 the court held that the sale of computer software to be used by the council administering the community charge (the poll tax) did not constitute a sale of goods because as a program it was intangible. The result would be different however if the program had been supplied on a disk for then the Sale of Goods Act 1979 would imply a term in the contract requiring it to be fit for the purpose for which it was bought.

Annual growing crops such as barley, and industrial growing crops, like pine trees, are also goods within the meaning of the Act. However the following do not constitute goods:

* shares and patents;

- money, unless sold as something other than currency, such as a collector's item;

- contracts whose substance is the supply of labour and materials where the value of the materials supplied under the contract is of lesser value than that of the labour involved. In *Robinson v. Graves* 1935 a commission to paint a portrait was held to be a contract for labour and materials. In contrast the following have been held to the contracts of sale: a contract to supply and lay a carpet, a contract to make a fur coat, and a contract to prepare and supply food in a restaurant.

The expression *money consideration* excludes from the definition of contract of sale gifts, and any transaction where goods are exchanged for other goods - a *barter* - although where the consideration is partly in goods and partly in money the contract will be one of sale.

Price

It might be expected that in a commercial transaction the parties will at very least determine the price of the goods. The Act says that the price may be fixed under the contract or left to be fixed in a manner agreed by the contract, or where the parties have dealt with each other before, by reference to their previous course of dealing. In the event of no price being fixed the buyer must pay a *reasonable* price. Although this is likely to be the *market* price it is necessary to consider the circumstances of each particular case.

The Transfer of Property

The object of a sale is the transfer of property (i.e. ownership) in the goods from the seller to the buyer. The Act lays down a set of rules for determining when this vitally important event takes place, but these rules apply only if the parties have not expressed their own intention as to when property shall pass. The rules are examined later but it is helpful at this stage to identify why the time at which property passes is so important.

(i)   The Act states that *risk* passes with property, unless the parties agree otherwise. This means that it is the owner of the goods who bears the risk of them being stolen or accidentally damaged. A person may be an owner although not in actual physical possession or control of the goods, as for example where a buyer of a painting leaves it at the auction rooms for collection at a later date, or where a seller allows the buyer to take possession of the goods, but provides in the contract that ownership shall only pass to the buyer when all outstanding sums owed by the buyer to the seller have been paid. This is called a *Romalpa clause* (see later in the chapter). A prudent owner will usually insure the goods, and this will be especially important where the goods are not under his or her own control. The Act also provides that if delivery of the goods has been delayed through the fault of one of the parties the goods are then at the risk of the party at fault.

(ii)   It is a general rule of law that a non-owner of goods cannot transfer ownership in them to another. This is expressed by the Latin maxim *nemo dat quod non habet* (no one can give what he has not got). The rule is subject to a number of exceptions, but as a broad principle a seller who is not an owner is unable to transfer a valid title.

(iii)   The seller can sue for the price of the goods only after the property in them has passed, unless the parties have agreed that payment should be made at some other time.

It will be recalled that the definition of a contract for the sale of goods makes reference to the transfer of property. It goes on to add that where property in the goods is transferred at the time the contract is made, there has been a *sale*, whereas if the transfer is to take place at some future time or subject to some condition to be fulfilled later the contract is called an *agreement to sell*. In this connection two points relating to the passing of property are worth noting. Firstly the Act provides that if a seller sells goods to a buyer and is unaware that the goods had *perished* at the time the contract was made the contract will be void on the grounds of *impossibility*. They may for instance have been stolen, or destroyed by fire while in a warehouse, without the seller's knowledge. Secondly the Act provides that where the goods perish *after* the contract has been made, but before the risk was passed to the buyer, then the contract becomes *frustrated* and void, (frustration was examined in Chapter 10). Exactly when the goods reach a stage at which they can be said to have perished is not clear, however in *Asfar v. Blundell* 1896 a consignment of dates that became unsaleable through contamination with sewage were held to have perished.

Conditions and Warranties

Even the most simple type of contract contains promises given by one party to the other. Most will include a variety of mutual undertakings. These undertakings are the contractual obligations which each party owes to the other and they represent the terms of the agreement. They generally arise through express agreement, however certain terms are implied into specific types of contract by statute, and the courts will sometimes be prepared to imply terms which the parties have not expressly agreed. If a term is broken the consequences for the contract will depend upon the importance of the term in relation to the contract. Obviously the more important it is the more serious will be the effect if it is broken. Terms are classified into conditions, warranties and innominate terms.

In relation to sales the Act defines conditions and warranties by looking at the effect on the contract if they are broken. A condition is an undertaking, the breach of which gives rise to a right on the part of the innocent party to treat the contract as repudiated (i.e. rejected) and/or to recover damages. A warranty on the other hand is an undertaking whose breach entitles the innocent party to claim only damages, but the contract still stands. A warranty is therefore of less importance to the purpose of the contract. Where there has been a breach of condition there may still be sound reasons for continuing the contract. For instance the buyer may have no other source of supply than the seller and is unlikely therefore to accept a repudiation when the seller advises that for example the goods cannot be delivered on time. It should be added that the courts will usually regard the delivery date in a commercial transaction as being a condition, or of the essence of the contract as it is sometimes expressed.

> In *Richards (Charles) Ltd v. Oppenheim* 1950 the seller agreed to build the buyer a car. When it had not been completed by the agreed delivery date the buyer requested the seller to complete it as soon as possible. Over three months later the car was still not ready, and the buyer told the seller that if it was not ready at the end of a further four weeks the contract would terminate. It was held that since the car was still incomplete at the end of the period the buyer was under no obligation to buy. He had waived the original delivery date, but had replaced it by serving a reasonable notice on the seller to complete the work.

Whether a particular term is to be treated as a condition or a warranty is a matter of interpretation for the courts. The label placed upon a term by the parties, for instance goods sold *'warranted free of all defects'*, does not mean that the court is bound by that label. In the example above defects in the goods would more likely be regarded as breaches of condition, enabling the buyer to terminate, than warranties limiting the claim to damages alone.

Implied Conditions

Under sections 12-15 of the Sale of Goods Act 1979 a wide range of conditions (and two warranties) are implied into all sales of goods contracts. Taken together these provisions impose upon business sellers stringent trading and quality standards and represent key consumer rights. These occur notably in relation to the descriptions applied in the marketing of goods, in the emphasis placed upon customer reliance on a seller's skill and judgment, and in respect of product standards.

The Right to Sell

Under section 12 a condition is implied into a contract of sale that the seller has *a right to sell the goods*. If there is an agreement to sell it is an implied condition that the seller will have the right to sell by the time ownership is to pass. The words 'right to sell' mean that the seller must have the legal *power* to sell the goods if the seller does not own them (unless the true owner has authorised the seller to sell them) or exceptionally if he or she is the owner but can be prevented by legal means from selling them.

In *Niblett v. Confectioners Materials Co* 1921 a buyer purchased 3000 tons of preserved milk in tins, some of which bore labels marked 'Nissly Brand'. This constituted an infringement of the trade mark used by the Nestlé Company, who could have obtained an injunction restraining the sale of the tins by the purchaser. The purchaser suffered a loss of profits by selling the tins without the offending labels, and it was held that the original sellers were in breach of the condition under s.12. *'If a vendor can be stopped by process of law from selling he has no right to sell,'* said Lord Justice Scrutton.

Section 12 also implies a warranty that the buyer will enjoy *quiet possession* of the goods.

> The meaning of this expression can be seen *in Microbeads v. Vinhurst Road Markings* 1975. Buyers of road-marking machines found that shortly after purchasing them, another company, not the seller, had become the patent holder of such machines, enabling it to bring action against the buyers to enforce the patent. The sellers were held liable in damages to the buyers, since the buyers ownership rights over attempting to exclude the machines were the subject of the rights of the patent holders.

Any clause attempting to exclude s.12 is treated as absolutely void by virtue of the Unfair Contract Terms Act, 1977.

Sale by Description

When goods are sold it is usual to find the seller has described them in some way. The description may be verbal, or by reason of labelling on the *goods 'Low Fat Natural Yoghurt'*. Weight, size, quantity, contents and packing may also constitute part of the description. If goods are sold by description there is an implied condition, under s.13, that the goods shall correspond with the description. The following case illustrates the commercial importance of this condition and demonstrates how liability under it is strict.

In *Re: Moore & Co Ltd and Landauer & Co* 1921 the buyers of a quantity o˙ canned fruit, which the contract required to be packed in cases each containing thirty tins, sought to reject the whole consignment when on delivery it was found that half the consignment was packed in cases containing twenty-four tins. The buyer's action was successful despite the fact that no commercial loss had been suffered by the buyer through the incorrect packing.

However a buyer who purchases on the basis of a *trade* description applied to goods cannot rely on s.13 if the goods correspond to that description while failing to comply with its literal meaning. Thus when buyers of 'safety glass˙ to be fitted into goggles discovered that the glass splintered on impact they were unable to reject the glass since it conformed to the technical trade meaning of safety glass. They had assumed safety glass was glass that would not splinter. In addition microscopic deviations as to size, weight, etc. will in general be disregarded.

Satisfactory Quality

Goods may of course correspond with description but still suffer from some major defect of substance. A leaking washing machine is still a washing machine, even though it is not of sound quality. S. 14(2) assists the buyer in such a situation by implying a condition on the part of the seller that the goods shall be of *satisfactory quality,* an expression introduced by the Sale and Supply of Goods Act 1994 to replace the somewhat old fashioned expression *merchantable quality* contained in the 1979 Act. The 1994 Act seeks to clarify the obligations of a supplier of goods in relation to the quality of the goods and to express the consumers rights in a clear and accessible way using plain English.

Section 14(2) of the 1979 Act, as amended, provides:

> "*Where the seller sells goods in the course of a business there is an implied condition that the goods supplied under the contract are of satisfactory quality*".

Even if the particular goods in question are not regularly sold by a business seller there is still a sale in the course of a business for the purposes of s.14(2) of the Sale of Goods Act 1979.

> In *Stevenson v Rogers* 1998 the Court of Appeal held that a one off sale of a fishing boat by a seller in business as a fisherman was subject to the implied condition of merchantability. This was despite the fact that it was clearly not a sale of trading stock but rather a capital asset, the court stressing the wide protection for buyers that the section was intended to introduce.

Under s.14(2)A, goods are of satisfactory quality if they *"meet the standard that a reasonable person would regard as satisfactory, taking account of any description of the goods, the price (if relevant) and all other relevant circumstances"*.

> In *Rogers v. Parish (Scarborough) Ltd.* 1987 the plaintiff bought a new Range Rover from the defendant's garage. Although it was driveable and roadworthy the car had a number of defects in its engine, gearbox, oil seals and bodywork. The defendant argued that the car was of merchantable quality within the definition as it could be driven in safety on a road and therefore was *"fit for the purpose for which goods of that kind are commonly bought"*. The Court of Appeal rejected the defendant's argument on the grounds that it was based upon too narrow an interpretation of s.14(2)A. *"The purpose for which goods of that kind are commonly bought would include not merely the purpose of driving the vehicle from one place to another but of doing so with the appropriate degree of comfort, ease of handling, reliability and pride in the vehicle's outward and interior appearance.*

It should be stressed that in determining whether goods are of satisfactory quality, price and description are crucial factors. A £1000 used car may have many defects and yet still be of satisfactory quality.

> In *Shine v. General Guarantee Corp Ltd* 1988 a secondhand car which had been submerged in water for 24 hours and written off was nevertheless described by the seller as *"superb, a good runner, and having no problems"*. The Court of Appeal felt that a reasonable purchaser knowing the true position *"would not touch it with a barge pole"* unless it was sold at a substantially reduced price. This secondhand car did not meet the standard of merchantable quality and there was a breach of condition.

The seller is not bound by the condition if the defect has been pointed out to the buyer prior to the contract, or where the buyer has examined the goods before purchasing them, and ought to have discovered the defect.

The case law regarding merchantability is still relevant in deciding whether goods would pass today's test of satisfactory quality. Thus the following have been held to constitute breaches of s.14(2) as non-merchantable items: beer contaminated by arsenic (*Wren v. Holt* 1903), woolen underpants containing a chemical that caused dermatitis (*Grant v. Australian Knitting Mills* 1936), 'Coalite' containing a detonator which exploded when thrown into a fire (*Wilson v. Rickett Cockerell & Co* 1954), and a plastic catapult which splintered on use causing the child who bought it to lose an eye (*Godley v. Perry* 1960).

> Liability under the section is strict. In *Frost v. Aylesbury Dairies Ltd* 1905, the dairy supplied milk containing typhoid germs and was held to be in breach of

the section despite establishing that it had taken all reasonable precautions to prevent such contamination.

Reasonably Fit

An additional benefit to a buyer is granted by s.14(3) which states that where a seller sells goods in the course of a business and the buyer, either expressly or impliedly, makes known to the seller any particular purpose for which the goods are being bought, then there is an implied condition that the goods supplied under the contract are reasonably fit for that purpose. The condition is not implied in circumstances which show that the buyer did not rely, or that it was unreasonable to rely, on the seller's skill and judgment. For instance if goods are purchased by their trade name and in such a way as to indicate that the buyer is satisfied that they will fulfill the purpose, the condition will not apply. Nor will it apply where the buyer has knowledge about particular market conditions which the seller does not possess.

> In *Teheran-Europe Co Ltd v. S T Belton (Tractors) Ltd* 1968 the buyer purchased air compressors from the seller for export and resale in Iran. In fact the goods infringed Iranian import regulations, the buyer was fined, and sued the seller. The action failed. As an Iranian incorporated company, The buyer must have been relying on its own knowledge and judgment of the suitability of the goods for the Iranian market.

However it may happen that the buyer places only partial reliance on the seller. If this occurs the buyer will only have a claim against the seller where the unfitness relates to a matter on which the buyer did rely on the seller.

> In *Cammell Laird & Co Ltd v. Manganese Bronze & Brass Co Ltd* 1934 The buyers supplied the sellers with a specification for ships' propellers which the sellers were to manufacture for the buyers. Reliance was placed upon the sellers regarding matters outside the specification, such as the appropriate thickness of the metal to be used. On delivery the propellers were unsuitable, being too thin. The sellers were held liable, because the unfitness concerned a matter on which the buyers relied on the sellers' skill.

It will be noticed that even if there has been reliance, the standard required of the goods is only that they should be *reasonably fit*, and that like s.14(2) the provisions of s.14(3) apply only where the seller sells in the course of a business. Although a buyer may expressly state to the seller the particular purpose for which the goods are required, it is clear that if the goods have only one usual purpose, for example a CD player, then merely by purchasing the goods the buyer will be implicitly making known that purpose.

Goods may be merchantable under s.14(2) while failing to be fit for their purpose under s. 14(3), although in practice there is considerable overlap between them. The contaminated milk in *Frost v. Aylesbury Dairies* 1905 was both unmerchantable and unfit for its purpose, namely to drink.

The implied conditions imposed upon sellers under the Act, in particular ss.13 and 14, can provide consumers with substantial protection. Many years ago Lord Wright in *Grant v. Australian Knitting Mills* 1935 noted this when he observed that in retail sales *'...a buyer goes to the shop in confidence that the tradesman has selected his stock with skill and judgment'*. This is sometimes expressed by the principle *caveat venditor,* let the seller beware. Sellers are expected to know something of their own business.

The Unfair Contract Terms Act 1977

A breach of the implied conditions will in most cases mean lost profit for the seller, since one remedy for breach of a condition is to terminate the contract by accepting the repudiatory breach. It is hardly surprising that with this in mind the natural reaction of a seller will be, in most cases, to attempt to exclude or restrict liability under ss. 12-15. The seller may do so by trying to exclude the provisions in their entirety, or limit liability to a fixed sum. The seller may impose a time limit upon the buyer's right to reject, or reduce the buyer's remedies (e.g. obliging the buyer to have the defective goods repaired).

The Unfair Contract Terms Act 1977 limits the seller's freedom to exclude and restrict liability. Significantly the Act distinguishes business transactions (non-consumer deals) from consumer deals. Under the 1977 Act a person deals as a consumer if he or she does not make the contract in the course of a business, the other party *does* make the contract in the course of a business, and the contract goods are of a type ordinarily supplied for private use or consumption. If the contract satisfies these criteria any attempt by the seller to exclude or restrict ss.12-15 of the Sale of Goods Act 1979 is void. If the contract does not satisfy these criteria, for example where both parties are acting in the course of business, then the effect is that the seller is unable to exclude or restrict liability under s.12 of the Sale of Goods Act 1979. The seller may however exclude or restrict liability in relation to ss.13-15, provide the term by which it is done satisfies a further test, that of reasonableness. In determining whether this test had been satisfied the 1977 Act lists a number of matters or *guidelines* to which reference must be made in reaching a decision. These are:

- The respective *bargaining strengths* of the parties relative to each other. This involves considering possible alternative sources of supply, hence a monopolist seller may have difficulty in establishing the reasonableness of a widely drafted exclusion clause.

Whether the customer received an *inducement* to agree to the term, or in accepting it had an opportunity of entering into a similar contract with other persons, but without having to accept a similar term. The reference to *other persons* involves account being taken of other suppliers within the market and their terms of trading. Sometimes suppliers combine to produce standardised terms of trading, giving buyers no opportunity of finding improved terms. A customer may receive an *inducement* by an adjustment of the contract price.

*   Whether the customer knew or ought reasonably to have known of the existence of the term. This involves the customer's knowledge of the seller, with whom the customer may have previously traded on the same terms.

*   Where the term excludes or restricts any relevant liability if some condition is not complied with, whether it was reasonable at the time of the contract to expect that it would be practicable to comply with the condition. It might not be practicable, for example, to oblige the buyer to notify the seller of defects occurring in a large consignment of goods within a limited time period and to couple that requirement with a term excluding liability if it is not complied with.

*   Whether the goods were manufactured, processed or adapted to the special order of the customer.

If a contract term excluding or restricting liability under ss.13-15 fails to satisfy the test of reasonableness then it will be void.

A seller may also seek to exclude or restrict liability for failure to comply with other terms of the contract, such as time and place of delivery, delivery of the wrong quantity, or even the rendering of no performance at all.

S.3 Unfair Contract Terms Act 1977 applies in such cases where the seller's liability is a *business liability*. It provides that where goods are purchased by a buyer who either *deals as a consumer*, or who purchases on the seller's written standard terms of business the seller cannot exclude or restrict liability for personal breaches of contract. Nor can the seller claim to be entitled to either,

(i)   render contractual performance substantially different from that which was reasonably expected of him, or

(ii)   in respect of the whole or any part of the contractual obligations, to render no performance at all, unless the exemption clause satisfies the test of reasonableness.

The guidelines used to determine the question of reasonableness are not required to be applied under s.3, although they are likely to be taken into account by the court. The following points arising from the section are worth bearing in mind:

- a buyer who purchases on the seller's written standard terms can of course include business organisations as well as private consumers;

- the meaning of standard terms is not defined, but it seems likely that even if the only standard part is the exclusion clause or clauses that the section will still apply;

- the section will apply to the seller's fundamental breaches of contract. A fundamental breach of contract is a breach which deprives the innocent party of substantially the whole benefit that it was intended should be obtained under the contract, and such breaches have been the object of considerable judicial discussion over the years. Exclusion of fundamental breach of contract is now only valid to the extent that it can be shown to be reasonable, generally something which will be difficult to establish.

The Transfer of Ownership

At some stage after the contract between the buyer and the seller has been concluded ownership will transfer from the seller to the buyer. This transfer of ownership is the principal obligation of the seller under the contract. Earlier, reference was made to the rule under s.20(3) that risk is borne by the owner of the goods. It is obviously important to know who owns the goods for other reasons. For instance if either party becomes bankrupt that person's *trustee in bankruptcy* is obliged to gather all the property belonging to the estate of the bankrupt (in the same way that a liquidator collects the property of a company that is wound up) in order to sell it and pay off debts. The trustee or company liquidator must know which property he can lawfully realise. Also the buyer can be sued for the price of the goods once he or she has become the owner of them.

Section 17 says that if the goods are *specific* or *ascertained*, ownership in them passes when the parties intend it to pass. Specific and ascertained goods are those *identified and agreed upon at the time the contract is made*, such as a motor vehicle by its registration number. The question of intention is determined by looking at the contract itself and all the surrounding circumstances. Because ownership is such a vital concept it will often be expressly referred to under the terms of the agreement.

A good illustration is provided *by Aluminium Industries Vaasen DV v. Romalpa Aluminium Ltd* 1976 where a reservation of title clause was inserted into a contract under which the plaintiffs sold aluminium foil to the defendants. The defendants would use the foil in their manufacturing process for the purposes of resale, and the plaintiffs clause provided firstly that ownership would only pass to the defendants when all payments owing by the defendants had been met, and secondly that if the foil was processed into other articles, that ownership in these articles would pass to the plaintiffs. The Court upheld the validity of the clause.

If the clear intention of the parties regarding the passing of property cannot be found, five rules to ascertain this question come into operation. The rules are contained in s.18.

Rule 1

When there is an *unconditional contract* for the sale of *specific goods* in a *deliverable state* the property in goods passes to the buyer when the contract is *made*, and it is immaterial whether the time of payment or the time of delivery, or both, be postponed. Goods are in a deliverable state when the buyer would be bound to take delivery of them. In *Philip Head & Sons v. Showfronts* 1969 the plaintiffs had sold the defendants a quantity of carpet which the plaintiffs had agreed to lay. After the carpet had been delivered to the defendants' premises in bales, prior to being laid, it was stolen. Since it was not in a deliverable state at the time of the theft it was held that property was still with the plaintiffs under Rule 1 and the defendants were not liable to pay the price. Although Rule 1 enables property to pass even though payment and/or delivery occur at a later date, in the case of sales in supermarkets and cash and carry stores the implied intention is that ownership shall only pass when the price is paid.

Rule 2

In a contract for the sale of specific goods where the seller is bound to do something to the goods to put them into a deliverable state, the property does not pass until that thing is done, and the buyer has notice of it.

In *Underwood v. Burgh Castle Brick & Cement Syndicate* 1922 a 30 ton condensing machine was to be sold under the terms that the seller would be responsible for removing it from its site and loading it on to a train for delivery to the buyer. During the removal it was damaged and the Court held that the seller's action to recover the price must fail since, applying Rule 2, ownership had not passed. This was because something remained to be done to the engine.

Rule 3

In a contract for the sale of specific goods in a deliverable state, but where the seller is bound to weigh, measure or do something to the goods in order to ascertain the price, ownership will not pass until that thing has been done and the buyer has been given notice of it.

Rule 4

When goods are delivered to the buyer on approval or on sale or return property passes to the buyer when he or she either signified his or her approval or acceptance or does some act adopting the transaction, or alternatively if the buyer retains the goods without giving notice that he or she is rejecting them within the time specified (e.g. goods delivered on 14-day approval) or if there is none, within a reasonable time. In cases where the buyer resells the goods he or she will be treated as having *adopted* the transaction. By the resale the buyer is asserting rights of ownership over the goods. In *Kirkham v. Attenborough* 1897 the pledging of goods with a pawnbroker was held to constitute an adopting of the transaction.

Rule 5

This rule applies only to *unascertained goods*, unlike the four previous rules which apply to specific goods. Specific goods, it will be remembered, are those that are identified and agreed upon at the time the contract of sale is made. If the contract of sale is not for specific goods, then it must be for unascertained goods. Examples of such transactions include the purchase of 100 tons of coal, or 500 tons of wheat out of a cargo of 1000 tons of wheat on board a named ship, or animal feedstuff to be produced by the seller according to a formula supplied by the buyer. In each of these examples it is impossible to identify at the time of the contract the particular goods which are to become the buyer's property, even though they have necessarily been described.

Under s.16 in a contract for the sale of unascertained goods no property is transferred to the buyer unless and until the goods are ascertained. If the goods become ascertained then s.17 applies and ownership will pass when the parties intend it to pass. Under the Sale of Goods (Amendment) Act 1995 protection was conferred upon the buyer of an undivided share of goods e.g. 500 computers in a warehouse storing 5000. If the buyer pays for the computers he aquires property in an undivided share of the bulk e.g. 10% of the computers

Under Rule 5 ownership in such goods passes to the buyer when goods as described, and in a deliverable state, are unconditionally appropriated to the contract either by the seller with the buyer's assent or vice-versa. The expression *unconditionally appropriated* is vital.

> In *Carlos Federspiel v. Charles Twigg & Co* 1957 the plaintiffs bought from the defendants a quantity of eighty five bicycles. The contract required the seller to deliver them to the ship they were to be carried in and load them. Before they had left the seller's premises a Receiver was appointed who claimed the bicycles which were packed and marked with the plaintiff's name. The Court held that property had not passed to the plaintiffs, firstly because in a contract of this type (known as an f.o.b. - free on board contract) the intention is that property shall pass when the goods are loaded, and secondly because in any event there had not been an unconditional appropriation. Pearson J stated that *"To constitute an appropriation of goods to the contract the parties must have had, or be reasonably supposed to have had, an intention to attach the contract irrevocably to those goods"*.

Rule 5 requires that the appropriation must be made by one party with the assent of the other. This may be *implied*. A clear illustration is provided in the case of purchasing petrol. It has been held that if petrol is put into a car by a forecourt attendant the petrol is being unconditionally appropriated with the implied assent of the buyer and if it is the buyer who personally fills the car at a self-service petrol station there is an unconditional appropriation with the implied assent of the garage as seller when the petrol is being poured.

Under Rule 5, delivery of the goods by the seller to the buyer, or to a carrier for delivery to the buyer, amounts to an unconditional appropriation.

Remedies Available to Buyers and Sellers

In the event of a breach of the obligations owed by one party to the other under a sale of goods contract the injured party may seek redress against the other. The principal obligations that arise may be summarised as follows:

(a)   *the seller must transfer ownership in the goods to the buyer*; physically deliver them to the buyer unless the contract provides otherwise; and fulfill the implied conditions and warranties contained in ss.12-15 of the 1979 Act.

(b)   *the buyer must accept the goods and pay for them.* Payment and delivery are concurrent obligations, unless the parties agree otherwise. This means they occur at the same time, for instance cash sales in shops.

The Remedies of a Seller

If the seller is owed money by the buyer the Act gives the seller the following rights, even if the buyer has become the *owner* of the goods:

(i)   *a lien over the goods*, i.e. a right to retain possession until he of she is paid;

(ii)   *if the goods are in transit and in possession of a carrier, a right to regain possession of them during the transit if the buyer has become insolvent;*

(iii)   *a right of resale* in certain circumstances, for instance when the goods are of a perishable nature, or where the seller gives the buyer notice of the intention to resell and the buyer does not with a reasonable time pay for the goods. In the event of a resale the seller can claim damages, representing any loss suffered. Such a loss could be the reduced profit on a resale because of a drop in the market price of the goods, including the cost of advertising them, etc;

(iv)   *an action for the price of the goods*;

(v)   *an action for damages* where the goods are still owned by the seller and the buyer refuses or simply fails to accept them. Damages awarded will represent the loss directly and naturally resulting from the non acceptance. Prima facie, this will be the difference between the contract price, and the market price or current price at the time when the goods should have been accepted, assuming of course there is an available market. So if supply exceeds demand and there is a fixed retail price for the goods damages will then represent the loss of profit that would have been made on the sale, but if demand exceeds supply then damages will only be nominal as the goods can be readily resold.

The Remedies of a Buyer

(i)   *an action to recover damages when the seller wrongfully fails or refuses to deliver the* goods. Again damages are measured in the same way as outlined above in a seller's action for non acceptance. It should be stressed that in the case of a non delivery by the seller, or a non acceptance by a buyer it is the market *price when the breach occurs* that is used to determine the measure of damages.

In *Pagnan v. Corbisa* 1970 Lord Justice Salmon made it quite clear that other market fluctuations are not relevant, '*...the innocent party is not bound to go* *on the market and buy or sell at the date of the breach. Nor is he bound to gamble on the market changing in his favour. He may wait if he chooses; and if the market turns against him this cannot increase the liability of the party in default. Similarly, if the market turns in his favour, the liability of the party in default is not diminished'.*

(ii)   *recovery of the price paid* if the goods are not delivered.

(iii)   *rejection of the goods* where there has been a breach of condition, and damages for breach of warranty - the amount being the difference between the value of the goods as delivered, and their value if the warranty had been complied with. A buyer may elect to treat a breach of condition as a breach of warranty.

Contracts of Hire

The essence of a contract of hire is that the hirer, in return for some consideration, usually an agreed fee or the periodical payment of a sum of money, enjoys the possession and the use of goods belonging to someone else, the owner. It is never intended that the hirer shall become the owner of the goods himself under the terms of the contract. Contracts of hire are fairly common in the business world and the period of use by the hirer may range from hours to years. Examples of such contracts include the hire of a mobile crane for a specific task lasting two days; the rental of a household television set over a number of years; the hire of a car for a week whilst on holiday; and the hire of sports equipment at a sports centre. In recent times there has been a growth in the commercial leasing of plant and equipment, particularly motor vehicles, to businesses. Commercial leasing, which is a form of hiring, can be a tax efficient method of acquiring plant and equipment for use in a business.

Contracts of hire are governed partly by the Supply of Goods and Services Act 1982 and may also be regulated partly by the Consumer Credit Act 1974. In order to come within the 1974 Act the contract must be a `consumer hire agreement'. This is defined in s.15(1) of the 1974 Act as:

"an agreement made by a person (the owner) with an individual (the hirer) for the bailment of goods, which:

(a)   is not a hire purchase agreement,

(b)   is capable of subsisting for more than three months, and

(c)   does not require the hirer to make payments exceeding £15,000".

Some of the language of s.15(1) requires explanation:

(a) An agreement made *by a person with an individual*. The Act distinguishes between a person and an individual. Whilst the owner may be a person, the hirer must be an individual before the agreement will be regulated by the Act. An individual is a flesh and blood person or an unincorporated association, such as a partnership. Persons, on the other hand, include, as well as individuals, legally created corporate entities such as limited companies or local authorities.

(b) *for the bailment of goods*. The expression bailment describes a situation in which one person has possession of goods belonging to another. A contract of hire is one of several possible types of contract of bailment. Another example would be a contract under which goods are stored in a warehouse on behalf of a business.

(c) *not a hire purchase agreement*. The nature of a hire purchase agreement is examined below. At this stage it is sufficient to note that an agreement will not be a consumer hire agreement if its real purpose is the eventual acquisition of ownership of the goods by the hirer. The basic idea of any contract of pure hire is that the hirer never becomes the owner of the goods. The goods revert to the possession of the true owner once the period of hire has expired.

Consumer hire agreements are regulated by the Consumer Credit Act 1974 which lays down strict rules as to their form and content. The agreement must be in writing and signed personally by the hirer. If either of these conditions are not fulfilled the owner has no right to sue the hirer under the agreement. The hirer must be given a copy of the agreement containing full information about his rights and duties and about the protection given to him by the 1974 Act. If any of these formalities are not complied with then no legal action can be taken against the hirer without the permission of the court.

Contracts for the Supply of Services

If a consumer contracts for the supply of a service such as car hire, laundry, holidays, financial service, and professional advice, and the service provider does not fulfill their contractual obligations, then the consumer may seek redress for breach of the express contractual term.

The tour operator who fails to provide the agreed holiday and the removal firm that damages the customers belongings could potentially be sued for breach of contract subject of course to any exclusion or limitation of liability.

Usually however the consumer's complaint in relation to the supplying of services relates to the quality of the service provided due to lack of care from the service provider. The claim is that the service has been supplied negligently with insufficient care by the solicitor, hairdresser, surveyor, banker etc. In these circumstances the Supply of Goods and Services Act 1982 may provide assistance by implying terms into service contracts for the benefit of the consumer.

Under section 13 in a contract for the supply of a service where the supplier is acting in the course of a business there is an implied term that the supplier will carry out the service with reasonable skill and care. In all service contracts this term sets the standard of the reasonably competent professional. The lawyer, dentist or hairdresser must exercise a reasonable degree of skill and care. In carrying out their functions this standard of care can be achieved even if the doctor fails to cure your ailment or the lawyer loses the case provided that as suppliers they can demonstrate they have acted competently.

Two holiday cases illustrate how s.13 may be implied to provide the consumer with a remedy.

In *Davey v Cosmos Air Holidays* 1989 the plaintiff and his family contracted diarrhoe and dysentery on a two week package holiday in the Algarve. The evidence established that the illness was caused by a general lack of hygiene at the resort particularly shown by the practice of pumping raw effluent into the sea near the beach. While the tour operators were not the cause of the hygiene risk the fact that they were aware of it and had failed to warn their clients of the danger meant that they were at fault. The court held they were liable for a breach of s.13 by failing to take reasonable care to avoid exposing their clients to a significant risk of injury.

Numerous business contracts involve the supply of a service and goods, in other words a contract for the supply of work and materials.

In *Lawson v. Supasink Ltd.* 1984 the plaintiffs employed the company to design, supply and install a fitted kitchen at a price of £1,200. Plans were drawn up and agreed but the company did not follow them when installing the units. The plaintiffs complained about the standard of work before the installation was complete. After taking independent expert advice the plaintiffs demanded the return of their deposit and asked the defendants to remove the kitchen units. The defendants refused and the plaintiffs sued. The judge found that the kitchen was installed in *"a shocking and shoddy manner"* and that the work was *beyond redemption.* He awarded damages of £500 for inconvenience and loss of the use of the kitchen; damages of the difference between the cost of equivalent units and the contract price; and the return of the deposit. On appeal the defendants argued that they had substantially performed the contract and were therefore entitled to the contract price less the cost of remedying any defects. This was rejected by the Court of Appeal on the grounds that the standard of workmanship and design was so poor that the doctrine of substantial performance could not be applied, having regard to the large sums which would have to be spent to remedy the defects.

The contract in the *Supasink* case was a contract for work and materials. Section 13 of the 1982 Act applies to the work element in such a contract. In some cases it may be important to know whether the defect complained of is due to fault in the materials themselves or the supplier's failure to take care in doing the work. This is because the nature of the liability for each of the two elements of the contract is different. In relation to the supply of materials, the supplier will be strictly liable, even if he is not at fault. If the work is defective the supplier will only be liable if he has failed to take reasonable care.

The Supply and Goods and Services Act 1982 may also imply terms into a service contract in relation to time set for performance of the contract and the prices. These terms are implied into a contract where the parties fail to set a price or the dates for performance. It is not unusual of course in the supply of a service such as car repairs, or professional advice, that the parties will not have fixed the price or the date set for performance. In such cases the Act provides in s.14 that there is an implied term that the supplier will carry out the service within a reasonable time. In section 15 the implied term is that the party contracting with the supplier will pay a reasonable charge. What is a reasonable time and a reasonable charge is a question of fact and will depend on the nature of the service that is provided.

Contracts for the Sale or Supply of Goods on Credit Terms

There are various forms of transaction which provide ways of getting goods on credit, ranging from contracts of hire purchase, credit sale and conditional sale agreements, to the use of *plastic money*. Credit transactions were aptly characterised by one County Court Judge who complained that most of his time was taken up by: *"people who are persuaded by persons whom they do not know to enter into contracts that they do not understand to purchase goods that they do not want with money that they have not got"*.

Contracts of Hire Purchase

A contract of hire purchase, as its name suggests, combines elements of two types of contract. It is in effect a contract of hire which gives one party (the hirer or debtor) an option to purchase goods from the other (the owner or creditor) at the end of a period of hire. During the period of the agreement the debtor pays the creditor by instalments (usually monthly) and the ownership of the goods remains with the creditor. The agreement will contain a term giving the debtor an optional right to purchase the goods at a nominal price once all the instalments have been paid. Ownership of the goods will be transferred to the debtor if and when he exercises the option to purchase. He will invariably do this as soon as he has paid all of the instalments because the real point of the agreement, in practice, it to enable him to acquire ownership.

A hire purchase agreement is not a contract of sale falling within the Sale of Goods Act 1979. Many hire purchase agreements come within the definition of consumer credit agreements and these are regulated by the Consumer Credit Act 1974.

At first sight a hire purchase transaction appears to involve only two parties. In practice, however, the vast majority of hire purchase transactions involve a third party, a finance company. The person who supplies the goods may not be able to wait for his money and may require instant payment, while his customer wishes to have time for payment. The supplier will therefore sell the goods to a finance company, which will supply them to the customer on hire purchase terms under a separate contract.

The supplier will have in his possession a stock of hire purchase forms belonging to the finance company with whom he usually deals. A customer wishing to take goods on credit will be asked to complete one of these forms and thus make a contractual offer to the finance company to take the goods on hire purchase. The supplier will complete a different form which will constitute a contractual offer to sell the goods to the finance company for cash. The supplier will forward both these offers to the finance company which will either accept or reject them both. If accepted, the supplier will be paid immediately by the finance company. The finance company becomes the owner of the goods and the customer will be bound by a contract of hire purchase with the finance company. Usually the customer will take possession of the goods from the supplier at this stage.

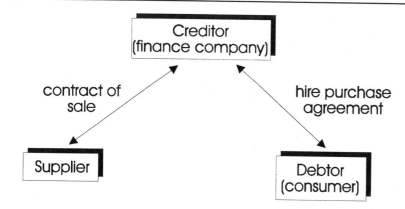

Figure 11.1   *Hire purchase transaction*

It would appear at first sight that there is no contract between the customer and the supplier where the finance company is involved in a credit transaction. If this were so, difficulties could arise for the customer, if, for example, he wished to sue the supplier for making false statements about the goods. The customer cannot at common law (though the position is different under the 1974 Act) rescind the contract with the finance company on the grounds that the supplier made a misrepresentation to him. However, the common law has recognised the existence of a contract between the customer and the supplier in these circumstances. The customer may sue the supplier for breach of this secondary or collateral contract.

> In *Andrews v. Hopkinson* 1956 the defendant car dealer showed a second hand car to the plaintiff and told *him "it's a good little bus. I would stake my life on it"*. As a result the plaintiff entered into a hire purchase contract with a finance company. Soon afterwards he was injured in a collision caused by a failure of the car steering mechanism. It was held that the defendant was liable in damages to the plaintiff for breach of a collateral contract between them. The court was satisfied that each of the parties had given consideration to support the contract. On the part of the defendant, this was his statement, which amounted to a promise that the car was in good condition and reasonably fit for use. On the part of the plaintiff, his entry into the contract with the finance company was the consideration. It had been of direct benefit to the defendant as he was able to sell the car to the finance company as a result.

As we shall see later, where the supplier and creditor have a business connection, the debtor will be able to sue the creditor as well as the supplier in these circumstances.

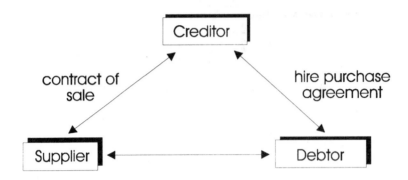

Figure 11.2   *Collateral Contract*

Credit Sale and Conditional Sale Agreements

Credit sale and conditional sale agreements are credit transactions under which the price of goods is payable by instalments. They will often be financed by a finance company in exactly the same way as hire purchase agreements.

At common law the credit sale agreement is broadly similar to the conditional sale agreement. Each is a contract for the sale of goods under which the buyer commits himself at the outset to the purchase. Theoretically, this is not the case with a hire purchase agreement. Here the customer has an option to buy but is not legally bound to exercise that option.

The main difference at common law between credit sale and conditional sale agreements is that:

(i)   in a credit sale agreement ownership of the goods in transferred to the buyer as soon as the contract is made, whereas

(ii)   in a conditional sale agreement ownership of the goods is not transferred to the buyer until some condition (usually the payment of the final instalment) is met.

While the installments are being paid, the buyer is the owner of goods under a credit sale agreement; but the seller is the owner of goods under a conditional sale agreement. In this important respect a conditional sale agreement is similar to a hire purchase agreement. This is why many of the statutory rights of a consumer under a hire purchase agreement such as the right of termination and the protected goods provisions, examined later, also apply to a conditional sale agreement. These rights do not arise in relation to a credit sale agreement.

Consumer Credit Act 1974

The Consumer Credit Act 1974 is the most significant piece of legislation designed to give protection to the consumer in a credit transaction. It sets up a licensing system administered by the Director General of Fair Trading to regulate businesses that supply credit. The Act also contains the rules relating to the supply, formation, content and termination of consumer credit agreements. For the Act to apply and regulate the agreement the creditor who supplies the finance may be a company but the debtor must be an individual and the credit must not exceed £15,000. *'Credit'* includes a cash loan and any other financial accommodation including hire purchase, credit sales and credit cards.

The the rules relating to the formation of credit agreements ensure that the debtor is made aware of the rights and duties imposed under the agreement, in particular

- the amount and rate of the total charge for credit
- the protection and remedies available.

The agreement must be properly signed, contain all the required terms and be in the prescribed form. The debtor must be supplied with a copy of the agreement and given the opportunity to cancel the agreement where the agreement is signed at a place other than the creditor's place of business e.g. at home.

Usually a trader will supply the goods and arrange for a finance company to supply the credit under a hire purchase agreement. This is known as a debtor - creditor - supplier agreement. If the supplier defaults in some way through breach of contract or misrepresentation the creditor may be made equally liable and the debtor can choose to sue either or both of them. By making finance companies potentially liable for the defaults of traders the Act is effectively ensuring that financiers will only deal with suppliers who are reputable. One advantage of purchasing goods with a credit card is that if the supplier breaks the contract the credit card company is also potentially liable.

If the debtor is in default and fails to make the credit payments then the agreement may be enforced against him subject to the provisions of the Act. The creditor in such circumstances is required to serve a *default notice* on the debtor specifying the breach of contract and giving the debtor at least seven days to take remedial action. Under a hire purchase agreement the creditor retains the ownership of the goods until the debtor exercises the option to purchase by payment of the final installment. As owner therefore the creditor may retake the possession of goods if the debtor is in breach of the agreement. However the goods become *protected* once the debtor has paid more than one third of the total price. The creditor can only recover possession of protected goods with the approval of the debtor or the court. Usually possession will be sought because the debtor has defaulted in making payments.

If the debtor has difficulty in making the repayments he can terminate the agreement by giving notice to the creditor and returning the goods. The debtor may also be made liable for further repayments to represent the creditor's loss and this is why formal termination by the debtor is not an advisable course of action. If the court feels that the credit bargain is extortionate in that it is grossly exorbitant or offends the principles of fair dealing then it may reopen the credit agreement and do justice between the parties. Effectively the court could change the agreement by rescheduling repayments and/or set aside the whole or part of the debt.

Standard Form Contracts

In the section on contractual terms in Chapter 9 reference was made to the fact that in the main business organisations conduct their transacting by means of standard form contracts. Having considered some of the rules relating to the sale and hire of goods and services in this chapter it should now be possible to explore the possible content of a standard contract for the sale of goods or services.

The value of expressing the terms of a contract in writing has already been discussed in Chapter 8. In most cases written contracts are of a standard form kind. A standard form contract is a printed document containing a set of uniform terms designed to regulate all aspects of an agreement. Businesses favour them for two reasons:

- firstly because standardising terms avoids the need to negotiate fresh terms each time a new agreement is made; and

- secondly because such a contract can be designed to protect the business against a wide range of contingencies which would otherwise damage it commercially if they were to occur. An obvious example of this is the use of exclusion clauses designed to shield a business from the consequences of breaching its contractual undertakings.

Standard form contracts are found in all fields of commercial activity. Banks, package tour operators, motor vehicle dealers, telephone companies, electricity, water and gas suppliers and train operators are amongst those businesses who always do business with their domestic customers on standardised terms of trading.

If a standard form contract is analysed, it will usually be found to contain terms designed to deal with a range of well recognised eventualities. Of course a standard form agreement under which a service is being provided, such as a package holiday, will not look the same as one in which a product, say a car, is the subject matter of the agreement. These contracts are about very different things. We can however identify the types of standard terms which are most frequently encountered in standard form agreements, and some examples of them are set out below, together with a brief commentary explaining what each term is designed to do.

Standard Form Terms

Exclusion clause (the example given is taken from an agreement between a customer and the supplier of a mobile phone service).

"We have no liability other than the duty to exercise the reasonable care and skill of a competent mobile tele communications service provider. We do not accept liability for indirect loss, such as loss of profits, business, or any other form of economic loss."

The supplier is seeking in this clause to limit any liability which might arise where the customer has suffered a financial loss due to a failure to provide the service. This could occur where, for instance, a business person loses an order being placed over the mobile phone because of poor reception. Such a loss is indirect, or consequential. This limitation of liability is only legally valid if the supplier can show it to be fair - Unfair Terms in Consumer Contracts Regulations 1994. (Chapter 12) The regulations also require all written terms in contracts between sellers and suppliers of goods and services, and consumers, to be expressed in plain English. The reference to reasonable care and skill is a reference to the duty imposed on a supplier under s.13 Supply of Goods and Services Act 1982. This section cannot be lawfully excluded.

Force majeure (the example given comes from an agreement between a holiday company and a customer to provide holiday home accommodation).

"In the event of 'force majeure' we regret we cannot pay any compensation. Force majeure means unusual and unforseeable circumstances beyond our control, the consequences of which neither we nor our suppliers could avoid, for example war, threat of war, riots, civil strife, terrorist activity, industrial disputes, natural or nuclear disaster, fire, adverse weather conditions, level of water in rivers or similar events beyond our control."

Notice that the company, probably as a consequence of the plain English requirement, has set our fully what the technical expression 'force majeure' means. Without excluding force majeure eventualities the company could find itself liable to a holiday maker whose holiday has been affected or prevented by any of items listed. Force majeure eventualities may also frustrate the contract. (see Chapter 10)

Price variation (the example given is taken from a contract of sale).

"Where the date for the delivery of the goods is more than three months from the date of this agreement, the seller reserves the right to increase the price of the goods by an amount not to exceed 2½% of the contract price, to reflect any increase in costs to the seller of materials and labour in the period between the date of the agreement and delivery date."

Using a clause of this type the seller seeks protection from a possible reduction in profits on a sale where additional costs are incurred between the date of the agreement and the date of delivery, by having the capacity to pass these costs on to the buyer such a clause is particularly useful in periods of high inflation.

Retention of title (the example given is taken from a contract of sale).

"Property in the goods subject to this agreement shall remain with the seller until such time as the seller has received payment in full for the goods and all other sums owing to the seller from the buyer on whatever grounds."

Such a term is known technically as a Romalpa clause (from the case in which the validity of such a clause was first upheld). Its effect is to enable an unpaid seller who has physically delivered the goods to the buyer to remain the owner of the goods until they are paid for. In the clause above the seller continues in ownership until all monies owed to the seller from the buyer have been met. S.17 Sale of Goods Act 1979 allows for the parties to a contract of sale to make express provision for the passing of property i.e. the transfer of ownership, in goods, and this is what a Romalpa clause is doing. Often such clauses include additional provisions requiring the buyer to mark the unpaid goods as belonging to the seller and requiring the buyer to seek the sellers approval before dealing with the goods in any way.

Liquidated damages (again the example is taken from a contract of sale).

"In the event of the cancellation of this contract by the buyer for any reason the buyer hereby agrees to pay the seller by way of liquidated damages the sum of 10% of the contract price."

A liquidated damages clause is designed to set in advance the level of compensation payable in the event of a breach of contract, in the above example a failure by the buyer to proceed with the contract. The common law allows such a clause as long as it represents a genuine pre-estimate of the loss that would be suffered if the breach were to occur. If however the figure of compensation set is disproportionate to the loss likely to occur on a breach the clause will be a penalty and void.

In *Dunlop Pneumatic Tyre Co. v. New Garage Motor Co.* 1915, Lord Dunedin stated that a liquidated damages clause:

"will be held to be a penalty if the sum stipulated for is extravagant and unconscionable in amount in comparison with the greatest loss that could conceivably be proved to have followed from the breach."

Assignment - A Swift Exhaust

Task

You work for Swift Exhaust plc and have been assigned to Jane Princetown's office in the Legal Services department for a period of three months as part of your management training programme. Your task is to prepare for her a report setting out the legal basis of the company's claim against Exhaust Systems Supplies Ltd. in relation to the defective exhaust systems, and dealing with the validity of the limitation of liability clause in the standard terms and conditions. In your report you should make reference to decided cases and/or statutes as appropriate. On the basis of the conclusions in your report prepare a draft memo to send from Jane Princetown to Charles Carver, and append it to the report. The memo should be clear and precise, but written in non technical language.

MEMORANDUM

To:	Charles Carver	*Date:* 15 October 1996
	Senior Purchasing Officer	
From:	Bob Paisley	
	Quality Manager, Western Division	
Copy to:	Jane Princetown	
	Legal Services	
Subject:	Consignment No. SE92/4752/JB/VAE	

I have received complaints from a number of Western Division Centres relating to replacement exhaust systems for Vauxhall Astras. The complaints indicate a weakness in the soldered joints between the main exhaust pipe and the rear silencer unit. One of the major fleet customers of the Hereford Centre had replacement exhausts fitted on twenty vehicles during April and May 1995, and eight of these systems are now showing an unacceptable degree of deterioration, two having sheered completely.

It appears that the systems in question were all part of consignment No. SE92/4752/JB/VAE. Of the consignment, comprising 500 systems supplied to Western Division in August 1995, the records show that 280 have been fitted to customers' vehicles and 220 are still in stock. Tests which have just been completed in the quality assurance centre in Birmingham confirmed an inherent weakness in the relevant joints in three of the eight systems which were tested.

In these circumstances I have withdrawn the remainder of the consignment from stock. I have also spoken to Jane Princetown in Legal Services in Head Office in Manchester. She has requested me to refer the matter to you for investigation with a view to legal action against the supplier. Please let her know details of the name and address of the supplier and of any written contract terms or other relevant information in your possession.

Clearly the costs to the Company as a whole, and Western Division in particular, arising from this situation will be high both in financial terms and in terms of customer goodwill. In accordance with our Swift Exhaust customer satisfaction charter, the owners of all vehicles fitted with exhaust systems from this consignment are being invited to attend at their nearest Swift Exhaust Centre for a free quality check. I anticipate that we will ultimately have to replace a very substantial number of these systems, free of charge to the customer, if the results of the Birmingham tests prove to be representative.

I have undertaken to supply details of costs incurred in this connection directly to Jane Princetown, and will copy details to yourself as they become available. Quality Assurance in Birmingham will do likewise in relation to test results etc.

If you require any further information I will be pleased to assist in any way I can. Otherwise please respond directly to Jane Princetown when you have gathered the relevant information.

MEMORANDUM

To:	Jane Princetown	*Date:* 28 October 1996
	Legal Services	
From:	Charles Carver	
	Senior Purchasing Officer	
Copy to:	Bob Paisley	
	Quality Manager, Western Division	
Subject:	Consignment No. SE92/4752/JB/VAE	

I have now established the position with regard to this consignment as requested. It was supplied by Exhaust Systems Supplies Ltd., 104 Western Way, Kings Norton, Birmingham, BH1 4JX in June 1994. It appears to have been supplied under the terms of their standard form contract, a copy of which is enclosed herewith.

The company is a relatively new supplier to Swift Exhaust, and extremely price competitive. Prior to the consignment in question the company had supplied three previous batches of exhaust systems. No problems were reported with the earlier batches.

John Blakeson, the purchasing assistant who handles this account, informs me that when he places an order with this supplier, a simple acknowledgement and acceptance is faxed to him within a few days. When a delivery takes place, a couple of weeks later, an invoice is forwarded to us together with a copy of the standard form contract terms and conditionsI am concerned to note that the `Claims' clause in that contract seems to limit our ability to recover the full losses that we suffer as a result of the defective exhaust systems, and I await with interest your opinion on the legal validity of this clause.

Exhaust System Supplies Ltd.
Terms and Conditions of Contract

Prices

All prices are subject to change without notice.

Unless stated otherwise prices quoted are for individual items.

Prices are quoted in £ Sterling.

Recommended retail prices are shown were available.

All prices quoted are exclusive of Value Added Tax which will be charged at the rate in force at the time of dispatch.

All prices quoted exclude carriage.

Settlement Terms

30 days from the date of invoice. We reserve the right to apply a levy of 3% over bank base rate on all overdue balances.

Damage or Non-delivery

Should damage occur to goods in transit this must be notified to us in writing within 3 days of delivery, non-delivery within 7 days of the date of invoice. Should these conditions not be met we reserve the right to ask for payment in full.

Bulk Discounts

Bulk discounts are available for large orders.

Acceptance of Orders

We reserve the right to accept orders subject to:

    (i)   Our minimum order value of £120.

    (ii)   Availability of raw materials.

    (iii)   Product specification are subject to constant improvement and may alter without prior notice.

    (iv)   Prices ruling at date of dispatch.

    (v)   Correction of errors/omissions on invoices or credit notes.

Claims

If any goods supplied by Exhaust System Supplies Ltd. (the Company) prove on inspection to be defective in material or workmanship the Company undertakes at its option to replace the same or refund to the buyer the price of the goods and in no circumstances will liability exceed the cost of replacement or (at the Company's option) the price paid by the buyer for such goods.

The Company shall not under any circumstances whatsoever be liable for damages whether consequential or otherwise, howsoever caused or occasioned and this undertaking is given in place of and excludes all other warranties and conditions whatsoever whether implied by statute or otherwise.

Retention of Title

    (i)   The risk in respect of any goods supplied under this contract shall pass to the customer on the invoice date, but the property in the goods shall not pass to the customer until the customer has paid all monies due and owing to Exhaust System Supplies Ltd. whether under this contract or otherwise.

(ii)   Until the date of full payment of all monies due and owing to us, you shall keep the goods as bailee in such a manner that they can clearly be identified as being the property of Exhaust System Supplies Ltd.

(iii)   The customer shall be entitled to sell the goods in the ordinary course of business, subject to the conditions that until the date of full payment of all monies due and owing to Exhaust System Supplies Ltd., the customer shall account to us for all monies obtained therefrom. Such account shall be in a form which clearly identifies what money has derived from the sale of our goods as a separate element from any monies derived from the sale of any other products whether the goods are sold separately or mixed with any other products. Such monies are to be held by the customer on trust for the benefit of Exhaust System Supplies Ltd.

(iv)   In the event of any default by the customer in complying with any of the conditions of this agreement including failure to pay to Exhaust System Supplies Ltd. all monies owed to us on the due date, or if a receiver of the customers assets be appointed, or if a petition be presented to wind up the customer or the customer becomes otherwise incapable of trading for whatever reason, the entire sum of money remaining unpaid shall become immediately due and owing to use and we shall be entitled forthwith to stop further delivery of goods and to enter upon the premises of the customer with such transport as may be necessary to remove all property the ownership whereof is retained by us under this or any other contract with the customer without prejudice to our right to claim further monies as remains due and owing to us, nor shall the customer construe this or any other conditions of this agreement as entitling the customer to return the goods or refuse or delay payment therefor.

(v)   The right to recover the possession of goods the ownership whereof is retained by Exhaust System Supplies Ltd. pursuant to the foregoing provisions of this Condition, shall include the right to detach and remove those goods from any other goods to which they may be attached whilst those goods still remain on the premises of the customer.

Removal of the Goods

All goods delivered to the buyer or agent, or person on behalf of the buyer, may be removed from the buyer's premises by the seller at any time after the due date of payment has been passed.

Force Majeur

Exhaust System Supplies Ltd. shall not be liable to any loss or damage caused by non performance due to act of God, war, civil disturbance, government action, strike, lock out, trade dispute, fire accidents, or other causes beyond our control.

Variation of Condition

All quotations and contracts are subject to the above conditions and may only be varied by express permission in writing from the company.

Legal Construction

The contracts shall in all respects be construed and operate as an English Contract and in conformity with English Law. Each individual delivery and invoice is to be regarded as the satisfaction of a separate order.

Chapter 12

Consumer Protection Law

The aim of this chapter is to give you an appreciation of how the law intervenes to protect the consumer when transacting for goods and services. Consumer protection law is now recognised as a distinct legal subject so from the outset you should recognise that the material contained in this chapter will clearly not cover it full breadth. Certainly by exploring the rights of the purchaser in sale of goods, services and consumer credit contracts, in the previous chapter, we have already covered a number of fundamental consumer rights. Statutory intervention by means of implying conditions into contract of sale has a long history and is still an effective way of providing redress to the consumer purchaser of shoddy goods or services. In this chapter it is proposed to move away from breach of contract and consider consumer protection which is non contractual in origin. Legal intervention in the supply of goods and services which we will consider in this chapter includes:

- negligence and the supply of goods;

- the Consumer Protection Act;

- negligence and the supply of services;

- the Trade Descriptions Act;

- the Food Act;

- the Data Protection Act.

On the following page there is a table identifying the sources of consumer law, the potential civil and criminal liability of suppliers and the mode of enforcement.

Consumer Protection Law

Civil Law		
Legal Source	**Unlawful Act**	**Enforcement**
Contract Law	Breach of contract misrepresentation	Contracting party sues in the Civil Courts
Sale of Goods Act 1979 Sale and Supply of Goods Act 1994	Breach of sale of goods contract	Buyer or seller sues in the Civil Courts
Supply of Goods and Services Act 1982	Breach of contract for the supply of service	Buyer or seller sues in the Civil Courts
Package Travel Regulations 1992	Tour organiser falsely describes package causing loss	Consumer sues in the Civil Courts
Consumer Credit Act 1975	Creditors failure to comply with formalities or extortionate credit bargain	Debtor has right of cancellation, termination, and court redress, and possible interest rate deduction
Consumer Protection Act 1987	Defective product put into circulation by producer/supplier	Injured party sues in the Civil Courts
The tort of negligence	Breach of a legal duty of care	Injured party sues in the Civil Courts

Criminal Law		
Legal Source	**Unlawful Act**	**Enforcement**
Trade Descriptions Act 1968 and Consumer Protection Act 1987	False description of goods and services	Trading Standards Officers prosecute in the Criminal Courts
Food Safety Act 1980	Sell, offer for sale food injurious to health	Trading Standards Officers and Environmental Health Officers may serve orders or bring prosecutions
Consumer Protection Act 1987	Supply consumer goods which are not reasonably safe	Trading Standards Officers may serve orders or prosecute in the Criminal Courts
Consumer Credit Act 1974	Failure to comply with duties imposed on the suppliers of credit	Trading Standards Officers
Package Travel Regulations 1992	Tour organiser falsely describes a package holiday or fails to provide information	Trading Standards Officers prosecute in the criminal courts

Negligence and the Supply of Goods

In the last chapter we saw that the right to make a product liability claim in contract is confined to an injured person who actually buys the goods himself. The contract claim can be brought against the supplier of the goods only. The supplier is strictly liable, even if he is not at fault. In negligence anyone injured by the product can sue anyone who has failed to take reasonable care in relation to it thereby causing the injury. To succeed in such a claim it would be necessary to establish the breach of a legal duty of care causing damage. (See Chapter 7)

We shall now examine those elements of negligence liability which are particularly significant in defective product claims:

The duty of care

In relation to liability for manufactured products we saw in Chapter 7 that it was not until as late as 1932 that it was recognised that a general duty of care was owed by manufacturers to consumers. This was established by the decision of the House of Lords in the case of *Donoghue v. Stevenson* the facts of which were described in Chapter 7. The importance of the decision in the field of product liability lies in the fact that, in his judgment, Lord Atkin described the duty of a manufacturer in the following terms *"... a manufacturer of products, which he sells in such a form as to show that he intends them to reach the ultimate consumer in the form in which they left him with no reasonable possibility of intermediate examination, and with the knowledge that the absence of reasonable care in the preparation or putting up of the products will result in an injury to the consumer's life or property, owes a duty to the consumer to take that reasonable care."*

Although this statement has been developed by subsequent interpretation it can still be regarded as the framework within which a court will decide whether a duty of care exists. Four elements within the framework require closer examination:

Who can be sued

Lord Atkin's reference to a manufacturer of products embraces everyone involved in the manufacturing enterprise from design to distribution. It also extends to others who have worked on the goods at any time.

> In *Stennet v. Hancock* 1939, for example, the plaintiff was a pedestrian who was injured when part of the wheel of a lorry broke away whilst the lorry was being driven. The defect in the wheel was the result of a repair which had not been carried out properly. The court held that the repairers were liable under Lord Atkin's manufacturing principle.

What type of defects will give rise to liability

Lord Atkin referred to products which the manufacturer sells in such a form as to show that he intends them to reach the ultimate consumer in the form in which they left him with no reasonable possibility of intermediate examination. This has been interpreted as limiting the application of the duty to products with latent defects. Latent defects are faults which are not apparent on an examination of the goods. Lord Wright in *Grant v. Australian Knitting Mills Ltd.* 1936 stated that *"The principle of Donoghue's case can only be applied where the defect is hidden and unknown to the consumer ... the man who consumes or uses a thing which he knows to be noxious cannot complain in respect of whatever mischief follows, because it follows from his own conscious volition in choosing to incur the risk or certainty of mischance."*

> This interpretation of Lord Atkin's principle was followed in the case of *Crow v. Barford (Agricultural) Ltd. and H.B. Holttum & Co. Ltd.* 1963. The plaintiff bought a rotary lawn mower known as a Barford Rotomo from Holttum after it was demonstrated to him at home. The machine was designed in such a way that the guard for the blades had an opening to allow the grass to be expelled as it was being cut. To start the lawn mower the user's foot had to be placed on the casing containing the blade. While starting the Rotomo the plaintiff's foot slipped into the opening and two of his toes were cut off. The claim against the manufacturer was made on the basis of the principle in *Donoghue v. Stevenson* but the Court of Appeal decided that this did not apply because the danger was *"perfectly obvious"* and not hidden or unknown to the plaintiff. The claim in contract against the retailer was also unsuccessful because the plaintiff had inspected the lawn mower during the demonstration before he purchased it. This brought the case within the exception contained in s.14(2) of the Sale of Goods Act that the seller does not promise that the goods are of satisfactory quality in relation to defects which ought to have been revealed by the buyer's prior examination of the goods.

To whom is the duty owed

Lord Atkin tells us that the duty of care is owed to the ultimate consumer of the product. This expression has been interpreted widely so as to include the purchaser, any person injured while using or consuming the product and any other person, such as the plaintiff in *Stennet v. Hancock*, who is injured by the product in circumstances where injury to him ought reasonably to have been foreseen.

> For example, in *Lambert v. Lewis* 1982 the driver of a car and his son were killed and the plaintiffs, his wife and daughter, were injured when their car was hit by a trailer which had become detached from a farmer's Land Rover and careered across the road into the path of their car. The accident was

caused by a design defect in the towing hitch, which was unable to cope with the stresses to which it was subjected in normal use. The evidence showed that part of the towing hitch had been missing for a number of months before the accident and that the farmer should have realised this.The trial judge decided that the manufacturer was 75% to blame for the accident and that the farmer was 25% to blame and apportioned liability accordingly. The farmer issued third party proceedings against the retailer from whom he had purchased the towing hitch. He was seeking indemnity for the damages for which he was liable and basing his claim in contract on the retailer's breach of the implied terms in s.14 Sale of Goods Act. The retailer in turn issued fourth party proceedings against the manufacturer in contract and in negligence. On appeal the House of Lords decided that the retailer was not liable to the farmer because the farmer's own negligence, rather than the retailer's breach of contract, was the operative cause of his loss. The fourth party proceedings were consequently dismissed because the retailer had no liability to pass on to the manufacturer.

What type of damage is recoverable

In his statement of the duty of care owed by a manufacturer, Lord Atkin confines the scope of the duty to injury to the consumer's life or property. Within this damages are recoverable for death, personal injury or damage to property, excluding damage to the product itself.

One category of loss which cannot always be sued for in negligence is pure financial loss. A 1985 case provides a good illustration of this rule in the context of product liability.

In *Muirhead v. Industrial Tank Specialities (ITT Marlow, third party; Leroy Somer Electric Motors Ltd., fourth party)* 1985, the plaintiff was a wholesale fish merchant who installed in his premises a large sea water tank in which to store lobsters. The sea water had to be filtered, oxygenated and recirculated. This was done by a series of pumps working 24 hours per day. The tank and pumps were installed by I.T.S. Ltd. The pumps were manufactured by Leroy Somer Electric Motors Ltd and supplied to the plaintiff by I.T.S. Ltd. through other suppliers in the chain of distribution. The pumps constantly broke down and on one occasion the recirculation of water was affected so that the plaintiff lost his entire stock of lobsters. The plaintiff successfully sued I.T.S. Ltd. in contract but the company went into liquidation unable to satisfy the judgment against it. The plaintiff then proceeded with action against the manufacturers claiming damages for all of the losses incurred as a result of the defects in the pumps. The vast bulk of the claim was for the loss of profits on intended sales but the Court of Appeal decided that this was pure financial loss and therefore not recoverable in a negligence action. The rest of the plaintiff's claim succeeded.

Breach of Duty

Once it has been established that the manufacturer in a given case owes a duty of care to avoid injury to the plaintiff, the second major element of negligence liability which the plaintiff must prove is that the manufacturer was in breach of that duty. A breach of duty is a failure to take reasonable care and involves a finding of fault on the part of the manufacturer. In many cases the task of proving this may be a difficult one for the plaintiff, involving a detailed investigation of the defendant's processes of manufacture design and testing and a comparison with procedures adopted by other producers in the same field. The plaintiff will need to employ expert witnesses who can analyse these processes and procedures and pin-point any lack of care which may have caused the defect in the product and therefore caused the injury. If the plaintiff is unable to prove a breach of duty he may have to bear the loss himself without compensation, unless there is another available legal basis for his claim.

A breach of the duty of care may occur outside the process of development design and manufacture.

In the case of *Vacwell Engineering v. BDH Chemicals Ltd.* 1971 for example, the manufacturer of a chemical produced for industrial use was held liable in negligence for a failure to give proper and adequate warnings that the chemical would explode when mixed with water. This should have been achieved by clear labelling of the product.

In *Walton v. British Leyland (UK) Ltd.* 1978 the failure of British Leyland to recall the Austin Allegro car after a large number of 'wheel drift' faults had been reported to the company was held to be a breach of the duty of care. Leyland were held liable to the plaintiffs who were severely injured when the wheel of their Allegro came off as the vehicle was travelling at 60 mph on a motorway. The Judge, Willis J., in the High Court stated *"The duty of care owed by Leyland to the public was to make a clean breast of the problem and recall all cars which they could in order that safety washers could be fitted ... The company seriously considered recall and made an estimate of the cost at a figure (£300,000 in 1974) which seems to me to be in no way out of proportion to the risks involved. It was decided not to follow this course for commercial reasons. I think this involved a failure to observe their duty of care for the safety of the many who were bound to remain at risk ..."*

Res ipsa loquitur

In the context of product liability the principle of res ipsa loquitur is of considerable significance. The tendency in recent times has been for the courts to allow the plaintiff to rely on the rule in many cases involving defective products. Res ipsa loquitur is considered in detail in Chapter 7. Here we may note its application in product liability cases.

> In *Chaproniere v. Mason* 1905 the plaintiff broke a tooth when eating a bread bun which was found to contain a pebble. He pleaded res ipsa loquitur and the defendant baker was held to be liable because he was unable to prove that he had not been negligent.

Where the plaintiff pleads res ipsa loquitur, the manufacturer will need to produce strong evidence if he is to satisfy the court that the injuries were not caused by his negligence. It will not be sufficient for him to show that he has a good system of work and provides adequate supervision during the process of manufacture.

> In *Grant v. Australian Knitting Mills* 1936 the plaintiff contracted dermatitis because of the presence in his underwear of excess sulphite after the process of manufacture by the defendant. The defendant's evidence was that he had manufactured over four and a half million pairs of underpants and had received no other complaints. Nevertheless he was held liable because the probability was that someone in his employment for whose acts he was legally responsible had failed to take care.

> In *Hill v. James Crowe (Cases) Ltd.* 1978 the plaintiff, a lorry driver, was injured when he fell off a badly nailed wooden packing case on which he was standing in order to load his lorry. The manufacturer of the packing case gave evidence that the standards of workmanship and supervision in his factory were high and argued that he had not failed to fulfil his duty to the plaintiff to take reasonable care in producing the case. The Court held that the defendant was liable for the bad workmanship of one of his employees even though, in general terms, he had a good production system. He had not proved that the plaintiff's injuries were not due to the negligence of one of his employees.

This case provides an example of the manufacturer's liability for a foreseeable misuse of his product.

The extremely high standard of care which the courts are prepared to impose on a manufacturer can be seen in the following case.

> In *Winward v. TVR Engineering* 1986 the defendants were in the business of producing specialist sports cars. They were responsible for the design and

assembly of the vehicles using components bought in from other sources The car in question incorporated a Ford engine which was supplied to the defendants fitted with a Weber carburettor. The carburettor had a basic design fault which ultimately caused petrol to leak from it. The plaintiff's wife was injured when leaking petrol came into contact with the hot engine. The defendants argued that it was reasonable for them to rely on the expertise of their supplier, particularly as the design fault had never previously manifested itself. The Court of Appeal held that the defendants were in breach of their duty through their failure to test the component and modify its design.

In addition to a potential cause of action under common law negligence a consumer of defective goods may also turn to statute to provide a remedy.

The Consumer Protection Act 1987

Part I of the Consumer Protection Act 1987 provides a framework of strict liability for injury and damage caused by defective products. This part of the Act was introduced in order to give effect to the EC Directive on Product Liability and represents a significant extension of consumer protection in this area by providing an additional basis upon which to obtain compensation for injury caused by unsafe or faulty goods.

Liability under s.2(1) of the Act arises *where any damage is caused wholly or partly by a defect in a product*. In order to succeed in a claim, the plaintiff must prove two things:

- that the product was defective, and

- that the defect caused the injury or damage.

If the plaintiff can prove these things, the defendant will be liable even though he took all possible care in relation to the product. This is the crucial difference between strict liability under the Act and liability based upon negligence which, as we have seen, depends upon proof of fault by the defendant.

Who is liable?

Liability falls upon all or any of the following persons:

- the *producer* – this term is defined in s.1(2) and includes the manufacturer of the product, the producer of any raw materials or the manufacturer of a component part.

- the *own brander* – any person who, by putting his name on the product or using a trade mark or other distinguishing marks in relation to it, has held himself out to be the producer of the product

- the *importer into the EU* – a person importing the product into the Union from a non Union state for the purpose of supplying it in the course of his business.

- *any supplier who cannot identify the person who produced the product, or supplied it to him.* In such circumstances that person will be liable, regardless of whether he was a business supplier, provided he supplied the product to someone else, and the following conditions are met:

  1. he is requested by a person suffering any damage to identify any producer, own brander or importer into the EC;

  2. the request is made within a reasonable time after the damage occurs;

  3. at the time of the request it is not reasonably practicable for the injured party to identify all of the potential defendants; and

  4. he fails, within a reasonable time, to comply with the request or to identify the person who supplied the product to him.

Thus it will be imperative, where litigation is threatened, for businesses to be able to identify the supplier of the products or component parts used in any goods sold by the business. It will be particularly important to differentiate, by product coding for example, between the products of two or more suppliers who are supplying identical components for incorporation into the same type of finished product. This will apply to all component parts ranging from electric motors to nuts and bolts.

Where two or more persons are liable for the injury each can be sued for the full amount of the damage. The party who is sued may be entitled to a contribution or indemnity from anyone else who is liable, under the Civil Liability (Contribution) Act 1978. Of course the injured person can only recover compensation once, regardless of the number of possible defendants or the legal basis of his claim. The injured person will usually choose to sue the defendant against whom liability can most easily be established and who is most likely to be able to afford to pay damages or to have insurance cover.

When is a product defective?

In order to succeed in a claim the plaintiff will have to prove that his injury was caused by a defect in the product. Section 3 tells us that a product will be regarded as defective *when the safety of the product is not such as persons generally are entitled to expect*. It is clear that the lawnmower in the *Crow v. Barford and Holttum* case mentioned earlier would be defective under this definition. The question of when a product is defective is likely to be central to much of the litigation under the Act. Section 3(2) gives us some guidance as to the factors which will be relevant in deciding whether a product is defective. It provides:

> *"In determining what persons generally are entitled to expect in relation to a product all the circumstances shall be taken into account, including:*
>
> *(a)   the manner in which, and purposes for which, the product has been marketed, its get-up, the use of any mark in relation to the product and any instructions for, or warnings with respect to, doing or refraining from doing anything with or in relation to the product;*
>
> *(b)   what might reasonably be expected to be done with or in relation to the product; and*
>
> *(c)   the time when the product was supplied by its producer to another person;*
>
> *and nothing in this section shall require a defect to be inferred from the fact alone that the safety of a product which is supplied after that time is greater than the safety of the product in question."*

Clearly it is very important for any business to ensure that the packaging of their products is such that it does not suggest or imply that the product can be used in a manner or for a purpose which is unsafe. Appropriate warnings of the dangers associated with the use or foreseeable misuse of the product must be amply displayed on the packaging and, where necessary, on the goods themselves. A further precaution which may be taken by the producer of goods is the date coding of products in order to take advantage of the defence suggested by the final part of s.3(2). Thus if a safer product is subsequently developed and put onto the market, the level of safety provided by the original product cannot be judged solely by reference to improved safety features in the new product.

Defences

A number of specific defences are provided for in s.4 of the Consumer Protection Act. These are in addition to the obvious defences that the product was not defective or that it was not the cause of the plaintiff's loss. Thus it is a defence to show:

1. that the defect was attributable to the defendant's compliance with a legal requirement, or

2. that the defendant did not supply the goods to anyone.

In this connection it is interesting to notice s.1(3) which says that where a finished product incorporates component products or raw materials, the supplier of the finished product will not be treated as a supplier of the component products or raw materials by reason only of his supply of the finished product. Thus, for example, a builder using high alumina cement could argue that he was not a supplier of that cement for the purposes of the Act. He could invoke this defence if the building subsequently deteriorated due to defects in the cement.

3. Section 4 also enables the defendant to escape liability if he can show that he had not supplied the goods in the course of his business and that he had not own branded, imported into the EU, or produced the goods with a view to profit.

This defence could be invoked, for example, in relation to the sale of home made jam at a coffee morning in aid of charity.

4. The nature of the fourth defence under s.4 depends upon whether the defendant is a producer, own brander or importer into the EU. If he is, he can escape liability by proving that the defect was not present in the product at the time he supplied it. If he is not, he must show that the defect was not present in the product at the time it was last supplied by any person of that description.

5. Section 4 provides the development risks defence that, given the state of scientific and technical knowledge at the time the product was put into circulation, no producer of a product of that kind could have been expected to have discovered the defect if it had existed in his products while they were under his control.

The development risks defence has provoked much discussion. Its adoption was optional under the terms of the directive. It is argued that the defence reduces the strictness of liability by introducing considerations which are more relevant to negligence. Its main impact will be seen in those areas which are at the forefront of scientific and technical development. The pharmaceutical industry, for example, could benefit from it in relation to the development of new drugs. It may seem ironic that if an event like the Thalidomide tragedy were to re-occur the victims could be prevented from recovering compensation because of the operation of this defence. The tragedy was in fact a major cause of pressure for the introduction of strict product liability laws throughout Europe.

6.   Where the defendant is a producer of a component product, he will have a defence under s.4 if he can show that the defect in the finished product is wholly attributable to its design or to compliance with instructions given by the producer of the finished product.

Damage

Assuming the plaintiff succeeds in his claim, the question arises as to the types of loss he will be compensated for. Under s.5 damages are recoverable for death or for personal injury. This includes any disease or other impairment of a person's physical or mental condition. The plaintiff will also be able to claim compensation for damage to his property. However, exceptions to this provide significant limitations on liability under the Act. There is no liability for loss of or damage to:

(a)   the product itself,

(b)   any property in respect of which the amount of the claim would be below £275,

(c)   any commercial property – property of a type which is not ordinarily intended for private use, occupation or consumption and which is not actually intended by the plaintiff for his own private use, occupation or consumption.

All of these categories of loss are recoverable in a contract claim, although the first category, loss or damage to the product itself, is not recoverable in negligence.Section 7 of the Consumer Protection Act provides for an absolute prohibition on the limitation or exclusion of liability arising under the Act.

Time limits for claims

The limitation period provided for in the Act, regardless of the type of damage, is three years from the date on which the right to take action arises, or, if later, three years from the date on which the plaintiff is aware:

(a)   that he has suffered significant damage,

(b)   that the damage is attributable to a defect in the product, and

(c)   of the identity of the defendant.

There is an overall cut off point 10 years after the product is put into circulation. After the 10 year period has elapsed no new claims can be made although any proceedings which have already been started may continue.

	Contract	Negligence	Consumer Protection Act
who is liable	seller; he may claim an indemnity from the previous seller in the chain of distribution	manufacturer;includes designer, repairer, processor and other persons working on goods	producer, own brander, importer into EC, supplier who refuses to identify previous supplier or producer
who can claim	buyer only	ultimate consumer provided injury to him is foreseeable	any person injured by a defect in the product
basis of liability	strict; if goods not reasonably fit for usual or notified special purposes	fault; failure to take reasonable care in relation to the product	strict; where the product does not provide the safety which persons are entitled to expect
types of loss	personal injury death damage to property financial loss	personal injury death damage to property other than the product financial loss in limited circumstances	personal injury death damage £275 + to consumer property other than product
exclusion of liability	prohibited if buyer dealing as consumer or for death or personal injury othrewise possible if exclusion is reasonable	prohibited if death or personal injury otherwise possible if exclusion is reasonable	prohibited in all cases
time limit for claims	personal injury; 3 years from the date on which the plaintiff had knowledge of the material facts giving rise to the claim Other claims; 6 years from the date on which cause of action arose; or in negligence cases only, (if later) 3 years from the date of plaintiff's knowledge of the material facts if within 15 years of the negligent act		3 years from the date on which the plaintiff was aware of the damage the defect and the identity of the defendant if no more than 10 years since the product was put into circulation

Figure 12.1   *Comparison of Alternative Forms of Legal Liability: Injuries caused by Defective Products*

Criminal Liability for Unsafe Goods

Part II of the Consumer Protection Act 1987 replaces earlier legislation on consumer safety including the Consumer Safety Act 1978 and the Consumer Safety (Amendment) Act 1986.

Under s.10 of the 1987 Act it is a criminal offence to supply consumer goods which are not reasonably safe. An offence is also committed by offering or agreeing to supply unsafe goods or exposing or possessing them for supply.

In deciding whether goods are reasonably safe, the court must examine all the circumstances, including:

- the way in which the goods are marketed;

- the use of any mark, for example indicating compliance with safety standards;

- instructions or warnings as to the use of the goods;

- whether the goods comply with relevant published safety standards;

- whether there is a way in which the goods could reasonably have been made safer.

The offence in s.10 can be committed only in relation to *consumer goods*. Consumer goods are goods which are ordinarily intended for private use or consumption, with the exception of food, water, gas, motor vehicles, medical products and tobacco.

The Secretary of State has power, under s.11, to make regulations for the purpose of ensuring that goods of any particular type are safe. Safety regulations can cover the design, composition or finish of goods; and ensure that appropriate information is given in relation to them. They may also restrict the distribution of particular types of goods or prohibit their supply or exposure for supply.

A considerable number of regulations, made under previous legislation, are still in force. These relate for example to aerosols, babies' dummies, balloons, cosmetics, electrical goods, night-dresses, toys and many other types of product. Breach of safety regulations is an offence under s.12 of the 1987 Act.

Under s.41 of the 1987 Act any person who suffers injury or loss as a result of a breach of safety regulations has the right to sue the trader for damages for *breach of statutory duty*. This right cannot be restricted or excluded by any term or notice in any contract.

The Secretary of State also has a number of other powers under the 1987 Act. He may, for example, serve a *prohibition notice* on a trader requiring him to stop trading in unsafe goods of a particular description. Alternatively, where a trader has distributed goods which are unsafe, the Secretary of State may serve on him a notice to warn. This requires the trader, at his own expense, to publish warnings about the unsafe goods to persons to whom they have been supplied.

Power is also given to local authorities under the Act, to serve a *suspension notice* on any trader. This in effect freezes the goods in the hands of the trader for up to six months. The power to serve a suspension notice arises if the authority has reasonable grounds for suspecting that goods are not reasonably safe under s.10, or are in breach of safety regulations. A trader who fails to comply with a suspension notice is guilty of a criminal offence.

A Magistrates Court has power to order the forfeiture of goods where there has been a contravention of the safety provisions of the 1987 Act.

Negligence and the Supply of Services

The vast majority of claims for injury or loss caused by defective services are made by customers of the service provider rather than by third parties who have no contractual relationship with him. Most claims will therefore be based on an allegation of breach of contract, often on a breach of the implied duty to use reasonable skill and care in the performance of the contract. This is usually referred to as contractual negligence. Where the plaintiff has no contractual relationship with the service provider, he will have to establish that the service provider owes him a duty of care under the general principles of the law of negligence examined in Chapter 6. Without a contract he will obviously be unable to rely on s.13 of the 1982 Act. (See Chapter 11) The term *third party negligence* may be used to distinguish this situation from one of contractual negligence.

In either case the term professional negligence may be used where the defendant has failed to take care in providing professional services.

	CONTRACT	**TORT**
who can sue	client only	client or third party
type of loss recoverable if not too remote	all types of loss	all types except that pure financial loss is recoverable only in very limited circumstances
test for remoteness of damage	*Hadley v. Baxendale* (i) damage arising in the ordinary course of events (ii) unusual loses if known to be likely at time of contract	*The Wagon Mound* damage of a type which was reasonably foreseeable at the time of the breach of duty
time limits for claims	(i) time runs from breach (ii) Latent Damage Act 1986 does not apply	(i) time runs from damage (ii) Latent Damage Act 1986 does apply
exclusion of liability	s.2 and s.3 Unfair Contract Terms Act 1977	s.2 Unfair Contract Terms Act 1977

Figure 12.2   *Main differences between contractual and third party negligence*

One important difference between contractual negligence and third party negligence lies in the range of types of loss or damages which may be sued for. It is well settled law that the contractual duty of care is owed in respect of the full range of losses, including personal injury, death, damage to property and financial loss. Whilst these are all recoverable in a contractual negligence claim, the rules governing third party negligence cases are more restrictive. Where the plaintiff suffers personal injury or damage to property, the neighbour principle laid down by Lord Atkin in *Donoghue v. Stevenson* 1932 will be applied by the court to determine whether a duty of care is owed by the service provider in a third party negligence claim. Many claims against members of the medical profession, for example, arise as a result of personal injuries suffered by patients in their care. In the case of NHS patients, where there is no contract with the practitioner, third party negligence will be the basis of any such claim. In such cases the existence of a duty of care can readily be shown. Applying the neighbour principle, the practitioner can reasonably foresee that carelessness on his part is likely to injure the patient. The patient is clearly a neighbour as he is closely and directly affected by the practitioner's acts or omissions. Numerous third party claims for this type of loss are covered in Chapter 7 on tortious liability.

You will also see in Chapter 7 that where the claim is based upon third party negligence, the plaintiff may have more difficulty in establishing that the defendant owed a duty of care to avoid causing financial loss. A claim for financial or economic loss usually relates to the loss of profits which the plaintiff would have made but for the defendant's negligence, or the loss of money invested as a result of advice or information given by the defendant. For both physical injury and financial loss the Unfair Contract Terms Act severely restricts the opportunity of the service supplier to exclude potential liability.

Section 2 of the Unfair Contract Terms Act 1977 provides

(1)   *"A person cannot by reference to any contract term or to a notice given to persons generally or to particular persons exclude or restrict his liability for death or personal injury resulting from negligence.*

(2)   *In the case of other loss or damage, a person cannot so exclude or restrict his liability for negligence except insofar as the term or notice satisfies the requirement of reasonableness".*

This gives us two important basic rules. First that it is not possible to exclude liability for death or personal injury resulting from negligence.

The second rule is that liability for loss or damage other than death or personal injury cannot be excluded unless the exclusion is reasonable. This would apply, for example, to clauses which excluded liability for damage to property or financial loss caused by negligence. The application of the rule in situations involving contractual negligence and in providing services can be seen in the following case.

In *Spriggs v. Sotheby Parke Bernet and Co. Ltd.* 1984 the plaintiff, who was a businessman, deposited a diamond with Sotheby's to be auctioned. He signed a document which, among other things, excluded Sotheby's liability for negligence. He was given the opportunity to insure the diamond but did not do so. Whilst the diamond was on view prior to the auction, it was stolen despite the defendant's fairly comprehensive security system. The plaintiff sued for negligence and the defendants relied on the exclusion clause. Under s.2(2) the clause is only valid if the defendant can show that it is reasonable. The court held that the clause in this case was reasonable and valid. The plaintiff was a successful and experienced businessman and no doubt was used to contracts containing exclusion clauses. He could not be regarded as having unequal bargaining power. The risk was one which could have been covered by insurance but the plaintiff turned down the opportunity to take this precaution.

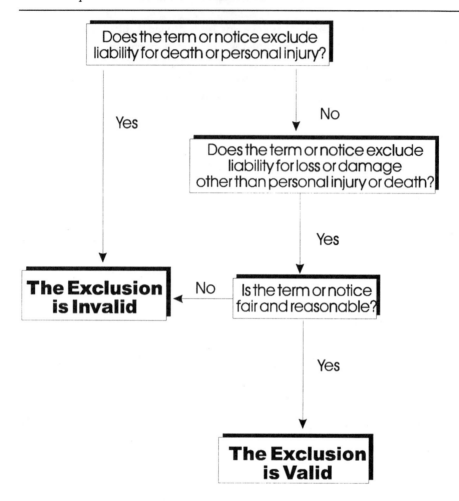

Figure 12.3   *Exclusion of liability for negligence: Section 2 Unfair Contract Terms Act 1977*

Here it is proposed to explore third party claims by consumers against certain service suppliers from the professions (lawyers and accountants) and from the travel industry (tour operators).

Professional Negligence (Accountants)

In recent years there has been some uncertainty as to the precise extent of the accountant's liability in negligence. The uncertainty has centered around the situation in which the accountant, acting as auditor of a limited company, negligently paints too rosy a financial picture of the company in its accounts, and a third party loses money in a transaction entered into on the strength of that financial picture. A limited company's accounts are widely circulated. They are filed with the annual report at the Companies Registry and are available for public inspection.

Consequently a wide range of people may use them for a variety of purposes. Many such people will have no contractual relationship with the auditor. After a period of uncertainty, the legal principles governing the auditor's liability to such people have now been settled by the House of Lords in *Caparo Industries plc v. Dickman* 1990. Before examining some of the relevant caselaw, it may be useful to remind ourselves of the position of auditors of a plc under the Companies Act 1985. This was summarised by Bingham L. J. in the Caparo case as follows: *"The members, or shareholders, of the company are its owners. But they are too numerous, and in most cases too unskilled, to undertake the day-to-day management of that which they own. So responsibility for day-to-day management of the company is delegated to directors. The shareholders, despite their overall powers of control, are in most companies for most of the time investors and little more. But it would, of course, be unsatisfactory and open to abuse if the shareholders received no report on the financial stewardship of their investment save from those to whom the stewardship had been entrusted. So provision is made for the company in general meeting to appoint an auditor whose duty is to investigate and form an opinion on the adequacy of the company's accounting records and returns and the correspondence between the company's accounting records and returns and its accounts . The auditor has then to report to the company's members (among other things) whether in his opinion the company's accounts give a true and fair view of the company's financial position . In carrying out his investigation and in forming his opinion the auditor necessarily works very closely with the directors and officers of the company. He receives his remuneration from the company. He naturally, and rightly, regards the company as his client. But he is employed by the company to exercise his professional skill and judgment for the purpose of giving the shareholders an independent report on the reliability of the company's accounts and thus on their investment.*

There are a large number of claims for professional negligence against accountants in the UK. Such claims are invariably for financial loss and are governed by the rules of contractual negligence or by the principles laid down by the House of Lords in *Hedley Byrne v. Heller* 1964 and *Caparo Industries plc v. Dickman* 1990. In the discussion of the *Hedley Byrne* case in Chapter 7, reference was made to the dissenting judgment of Lord Denning in *Candler v. Crane Christmas* 1951, which has been approved by the House of Lords on a number of occasions.

In *Candler v. Crane Christmas & Co.* 1951 the plaintiff proposed to invest £2,000 in a company, but before making the investment he wished to examine the company's accounts. The defendant accountants were in the course of preparing the accounts. They were instructed by the managing director of the company to complete their work quickly and to show the accounts to the plaintiff. On the strength of the accounts the plaintiff invested his money in the company. The accounts were carelessly prepared and gave a wholly misleading picture of the state of the company, which was wound up within a year. The plaintiff lost his investment and sued the accountants for professional negligence. In a majority decision which has since been overruled by the House of Lords, the Court of Appeal held that the defendant owed no duty of care to the plaintiff. The dissenting judgment of Lord Denning was described in the Caparo case by Lord Bridge as a *"masterly analysis, requiring little, if any, amplification or modification in the light of later authority."* Lord Denning stated that a duty to use care in making statements is owed by: *"those persons such as accountants, surveyors, valuers and analysts, whose profession and occupation is to examine books, accounts, and other things, and to make reports on which other people - other than their clients - rely in the ordinary course of business. Their duty is not merely a duty to use care in their reports. They also have a duty to use care in their work which results in their reports."* and he continued *"to whom do these professional people owe this duty? I will take accountants, but the same reasoning applies to the others. They owe the duty, of course to their employer or client; and also I think to any third person to whom they themselves show the accounts, or to whom they know their employer is going to show the accounts, so as to induce him to invest money or take some other action on them. But I do not think the duty can be extended still further so as to include strangers of whom they have heard nothing and to whom their employer without their knowledge may choose to show their accounts. Once the accountants have handed their accounts to their employer they are not, as a rule, responsible for what he does with them without their knowledge or consent..... I can well understand that it would be going too far to make an accountant liable to any person in the land who chooses to rely on the accounts in matters of business, for that would expose him to liability in an indeterminate amount for an indeterminate time to an indeterminate class".*

Candler v. Crane Christmas was followed in 1964 by the decision of the House of Lords in *Hedley Byrne v. Heller* which, in addition to approving Lord Denning's judgment in *Candler*, established the *special relationship of reliance* as the test to be applied in determining whether a duty of care is owed by a person making a careless statement, including an accountant carelessly preparing misleading accounts, and causing financial loss.

Subsequently, however, the Court of Appeal in *JEB Fasteners Ltd. v. Marks Bloom & Co.* 1983 appeared to have abandoned the special relationship test preferring to follow the less restrictive approach outlined by Lord Wilberforce in *Anns v. Merton* 1977.

In *JEB Fasteners Ltd. v. Marks Bloom & Co.* 1983 the plaintiff proposed to take over another company called B.G. Fasteners Ltd. The principal reason for the take-over was that the plaintiff wished to acquire the services of the two directors of the target company. A copy of the audited accounts of the target company had been certified by the defendant accountants, without qualification, as giving atrue and fair view of the state of the company. The accounts were relied upon by the plaintiff, which acquired the entire share capital of B.G. Fasteners. The accounts had been carelessly prepared and gave a misleading picture as to the value of the company. At the time the accounts were audited the defendants had no knowledge of the plaintiff or its intentions, and were not aware that a take-over from any source was contemplated. The Court of Appeal held that the defendants owed a duty of care to the plaintiff even though it was a complete stranger to them at the time of the audit. The defendants ought to have foreseen that B.G. Fasteners would require funds from money lenders or investors in the short term and that such persons were likely to rely on the audited accounts; secondly that the defendants were in breach of the duty of care as the accounts did not provide a true and fair view of the company. In particular there was a gross overvaluation of stock which caused the profit and loss account to show a profit when in reality the company had made a loss in excess of £13,000; and thirdly that the plaintiff's claim failed on the issue of causation of loss. The evidence clearly indicated that, even if the plaintiff had known the true financial position of the target company, it would nonetheless have gone ahead with the take-over. This was because the plaintiff's overriding object was to acquire the services of the two directors of B.G. Fasteners. Therefore the defendant's negligence was not the operative cause of the plaintiff's loss.

This decision caused a good deal of uncertainty because the Court of Appeal approached the question of duty by applying the broad test of reasonable foresight of harm - the neighbour principle - rather than the more restrictive test of whether there was a special relationship of reliance between the parties. The Court of Appeal felt able to do this, despite the considerable authority of the *Hedley Byrne* decision, by applying the two-stage test laid down by Lord Wilberforce in *Anns v. Merton* 1977. This uncertainty persisted until the House of Lords *in Caparo Industries plc v. Dickman* 1990 disapproved the approach adopted in the *JEB Fastners* case, and reaffirmed *Hedley Byrne v. Heller* 1964.

In *Caparo Industries plc v. Dickman* 1990 the plaintiff owned shares in a public company, Fidelity plc, whose accounts for the year ending 31 March 1984 showed profits far short of the predicted figure. This resulted in a substantial drop in the quoted share price. After receiving the accounts for the year, which had been audited by the third defendant, Touche Ross & Co, the plaintiff purchased further shares in Fidelity plc and shortly afterward made a successful take-over bid. The plaintiff sued the auditors in negligence, claiming that the accounts were inaccurate and misleading in that they showed a profit of £1,200,000, when in fact there had been a loss of over £400,000.

The plaintiff argued that the auditors owed it a duty of care either as a potential bidder for Fidelity plc because they ought to have foreseen that the 1984 results made Fidelity plc vulnerable to a take-over bid, or as an existing shareholder of Fidelity plc interested in buying more shares. The House of Lords held that a duty of care in making a statement arises only where there is a relationship of proximity between the maker of the statement (in this case the auditors) and the person relying on it (the plaintiff). A relationship of proximity is created where the maker of the statement knows that the statement will be communicated to the person relying on it specifically in connection with a particular transaction and that person would be very likely to rely on it for the purpose of deciding whether to enter into the transaction. Applying this principle to the case, the House of Lords held that no duty of care was owed by the auditors to the plaintiff as there was no relationship of proximity on the facts as the auditors were not aware of the plaintiff or its intentions at the time the statement was made. Although auditors owe a statutory duty to shareholders, this is owed to them as a class rather than as individuals. The nature of this duty was explained by Lord Jauncey who stated: *"the purpose of the annual accounts, so far as members are concerned, is to enable them to question the past management of the company, to exercise their voting rights, and to influence future policy and management. Advice to individual shareholders in relation to present or future investment in the company is no part of this purpose."*

The principles laid down by the House of Lords in the *Caparo* case have been applied by the Court of Appeal in two further cases within a very short period of time. In the first of the two, *Caparo* was distinguished.

In *Morgan Crucible Co. Plc v. Hill Samuel Bank Ltd. and Others* 1991 the plaintiff announced a take-over bid for a company called First Castle Electronics plc. First Castle recommended it shareholders not to accept the bid, and issued a number of documents to its shareholders intended to encourage them to retain their shares in order to defend the company from the proposed take-over. One of the defence documents forecast an increase in profits of 38% for the financial year and included a letter from the accountants stating that the profit forecast had been properly compiled. Shortly afterwards the plaintiff increased its bid and succeeded in acquiring First Castle. Subsequently the plaintiff sued claiming that the accounting policies adopted in the profit forecast were negligently misleading and grossly overstated the profits. On an appeal relating to the preliminary issue of whether a duty of care could arise in these circumstances, the Court of Appeal held that it could on the basis that if during a contested take-over bid the directors and financial advisers of the target company made express representations after an identified bidder had emerged, intending that the bidder would rely on those representations, they owed the bidder a duty of care not to mislead him.

In the second of the two cases, the Caparo decision was applied.

> In *James McNaughton Papers Group Ltd. v. Hicks Anderson & Co.* 1991 the plaintiff was negotiating an agreed take-over of a loss making rival company, MK Papers. The defendants were accountants for MK. At MK's request draft accounts were quickly prepared for use in the negotiations. During a meeting between the plaintiff and MK, a representative of the defendants stated, in answer to a question, that as a result of rationalisation MK was breaking even or doing marginally worse. After the take-over was completed the plaintiff discovered discrepancies in the draft accounts and sued the defendants in negligence. The Court of Appeal, applying principles laid down in *Caparo*, held that the defendants did not owe a duty of care to the plaintiff, in particular because the accounts were produced for use by MK and not the plaintiff, they were merely draft accounts and the defendants could not reasonably have foreseen that the plaintiff would treat them as final accounts. The defendants did not take part in the negotiations, and the plaintiff was aware that MK was in a poor state and could be expected to consult their own accountant. Further it could not reasonably be foreseen that the plaintiff would rely on the answer given to the question without further inquiry or advice, particularly because the answer was in very general terms.

Professional Negligence (The Legal Profession)

The legal profession in the UK is divided into two distinct branches with solicitors and barristers having different but overlapping roles within in the legal process. In relation to that part of their work which involves the presentation of cases before a court, members of both branches of the legal profession enjoy an immunity from liability for professional negligence, for reasons which we will consider below. This immunity is of particular significance for the barrister, as most of his work will involve advocacy in the courts.

Barristers

> In *Rondel v. Worsley* 1967 the plaintiff, who had been convicted of causing grievous bodily harm, sued his barrister for professional negligence. He claimed that the defendant barrister had failed to take reasonable care in the conduct of his criminal defence and that he would have been acquitted if the case had been properly handled. The House of Lords held that the plaintiff's claim failed. A barrister's conduct of a case in court could never give rise to a claim in negligence.

The decision was made on the grounds of public policy. It would be contrary to the public interest to allow such a claim for the following reasons:

(a)   A barrister owes a duty not only to his client but also to the court, for example he has a duty not to mislead the court. These twin duties could, on occasion, conflict with each other. He should not be placed, under the pressure of a potential negligence claim, in a position in which he might be tempted to disregard his duty to the court.

(b)   A finding of negligence would necessarily involve a finding that the case in question had been wrongly decided. Thus the negligence proceedings would amount to a retrial of the original case and cast uncertainty on the finality of the previous decision.

(c)   The judge in the original case has a duty to ensure a fair trial and will intervene if necessary to ensure that all of the relevant issues are properly considered.

(d)   Barristers operate under the so-called cab rank principle which means that they have no choice but to accept a client provided the proper fee is paid.

The immunity of the barrister in these circumstances was said by the majority of the Law Lords in *Rondel's* case to extend to solicitors engaged in litigation before the courts.

The scope of the barrister's immunity was further considered by the House of Lords in *Saif Ali v. Sydney Mitchell & Co.* 1978. A barrister failed to advise the plaintiff to bring proceedings against the correct defendant in a personal injuries claim within the three year limitation period. The House of Lords held that the barrister was not immune from proceedings in negligence in these circumstances because the immunity only extends to matters of pre-trial work which are intimately connected with the conduct of the case in court.

In relation to work carried out by a barrister which is not connected with litigation, for example giving opinions and drawing up wills, he may be liable for professional negligence under the principles laid down by the House of Lords in *Hedley Byrne v. Heller* 1964. However he cannot be sued for breach of contract as he has no contractual relationship with his client.

Solicitors

The extent of the solicitor's immunity under the principles laid down in *Saif Ali* was considered by the Court of Appeal in *Somasundaram v. Julius*

Melchior & Co. 1989. The plaintiff claimed that the defendant solicitors had been negligent in over persuading him to plead guilty to the malicious wounding of his wife whom he had stabbed during an argument. The defendant argued that advice as to plea of guilty or not guilty in a criminal case is so intimately connected with the conduct of the case in court as to be covered by immunity. The Court of Appeal accepted this argument and recognised that the immunity applied both to barristers and to solicitors when acting as advocates. However the court did not accept that the immunity applied to a solicitor when a barrister had also been engaged to advise. Despite this finding, the plaintiff did not succeed in his action, as the court also held, as a matter of causation, that the barrister's advice as to plea breaks the chain of causation between the solicitor's advice and the client's plea; and in any event an action for negligence against a barrister or a solicitor could not be brought where its effect would be to challenge the decision of a court of competent jurisdiction.

A solicitors may be liable in negligence to a third party with whom he has no contract:

In *Ross v. Caunters* 1979, for example, a solicitor drew up a will and sent it out for his client to sign. The solicitor gave instructions for the signing and witnessing of the will but forgot to warn his client that if the will was witnessed by a beneficiary or the spouse of a beneficiary then the gift would be invalidated. The will was witnessed by the husband of the plaintiff and the mistake was not discovered until after the client's death. The plaintiff, who was a beneficiary under the will, lost her gift and sued the solicitor for the financial loss caused by his negligence. It was held that the solicitor owed a duty of care to the plaintiff and was liable as his failure to take care had caused her loss.

Whether the courts will recognise the existence of a duty of care in tort where there is a contract between the parties is now an open point.

In *Midland Bank Trust Co. Ltd v. Hett, Stubbs and Kemp* 1979 the defendant solicitors carelessly failed to register as a land charge an option to purchase a farm granted to their client. The client's right to exercise the option to purchase was defeated, because of the failure to register, on the sale of the farm to a third party. The client sued in negligence and the court held that the solicitors were in breach of their duty of care to the client both in contract and in tort under the *Hedley Byrne* principle. It was essential to the success of the claim that the court recognised the existence of a duty in tort in addition to the contractual duty. This is because the plaintiff's claim in contract was statute-barred under the Limitation Act as more than six years had elapsed since the breach of contract by the solicitors. The limitation period in the tort of negligence, however, does not begin to run until the damage has occurred, in this case the date on which the farm was sold to the third party. As this was within six years of the commencement of proceedings in this case, the claim in negligence was not time-barred.

In *Tai Hing Cotton Mills v. Liu Chong Hing Bank Ltd.* 1986, a decision of the Privy Council, Lord Scarman stated *"Their Lordships do not believe that there is anything to the advantage of the law's development in searching for a liability in tort where the parties are in a contractual relationship."*

The important decision of the House of Lords in *White and another v. Jones and others* 1995 considered the potential liability of the defendant solicitors who caused the plaintiff's financial loss as a result of a negligent omission. The plaintiffs had originally been cut out of their father's (the testator) will but then reinstated on the testator's instructions to the defendant solicitors. The solicitors had delayed in carrying out the instructions to change the will for over six weeks and unfortunately, meanwhile, the testator died. As there was no contractual relationship between the plaintiffs and the defendants the action for financial loss could only be based on the tort of negligence. The central issue in the dispute was whether a solicitor in drafting a will owes a legal duty of care in the tort of negligence to a potential beneficiary. The High Court thought not. This decision was reversed on appeal and the solicitors then made a final appeal to the House of Lords. By a three to two majority decision their Lordships held that the potential loss to the plaintiffs in these circumstances was reasonably foreseeable and the relationship of a solicitor, called upon to draft a will, and the potential beneficiary, should be brought within the established categories of relationship under which a duty of care arises. This duty of care had been broken by the solicitor's negligence causing financial loss for which the defendants were liable.

Consumer Protection in relation to Package Holidays

The Package Travel, Package Holidays and Package Tours Regulations 1992, which we shall call the Package Travel Regulations came into force in December 1992 and are designed to implement the EC directive on Package Travel, Package Holidays and Package Tours (90/314/EEC). The regulations introduce a fairly comprehensive set of rules covering package travel and package holidays which are designed to protect the consumer. A number of the matters covered by the regulations were previously dealt with in the ABTA codes of practice for travel agents and tour operators, although the new regulations go much further in protecting the consumer.

The regulations apply to packages sold or offered for sale in the United Kingdom and, unlike the ABTA codes, apply to domestic packages as well as overseas travel arrangements. The concept of a package is central to the application of the regulations. Only if the travel arrangements fall within the definition of a package will the many elements of consumer protection contained within the regulations apply. A package is defined as:

"The pre-arranged combination of at least two of the following components when sold or offered for sale at an inclusive price and when the service covers a period of more than 24 hours or includes overnight accommodation:

a.   transport

b.   accommodation

c.   other tourist services not ancillary to transport or accommodation and accounting for a significant proportion of the package, and

i.   the submission of separate accounts for different components shall not cause the arrangements to be other than a package,

ii.   the fact that a combination is arranged at the request of the consumer and in accordance with his specific instructions (whether modified or not) shall not of itself cause it to be treated as other than pre-arranged"

In order to come within the regulations, the travel arrangements must be *pre-arranged*. This would obviously include the packages which can be bought off-the-shelf, for example a fortnight in Majorca selected from a tour operators brochure. It also includes tailor made travel arrangements put together to meet the needs of a particular client, provided that the arrangements are put together before the conclusion of the contract. The package must be sold at an *inclusive price*. If a customer books travel and accommodation through a travel agent, for example, and pays the travel agent for his air ticket, but pays the hotel direct at the end of his stay, this is not a package and the regulations do not apply. As an anti-avoidance measure, the definition makes clear that the separate invoicing of the individual elements does not of itself prevent the creation of a package. Where transport and accommodation are combined, then provided that the arrangements last for at least 24 hours or include overnight accommodation, a package will come into being. However, if one of these elements is missing, the arrangements must include *other tourist services* which are not ancillary to transport or accommodation and which account for a significant proportion of the package. The other services provided here must be tourist services and not, for example, educational services. If a language summer school is advertised including accommodation and modern language tuition, but excluding transport, this combination is not of itself enough to create a package.

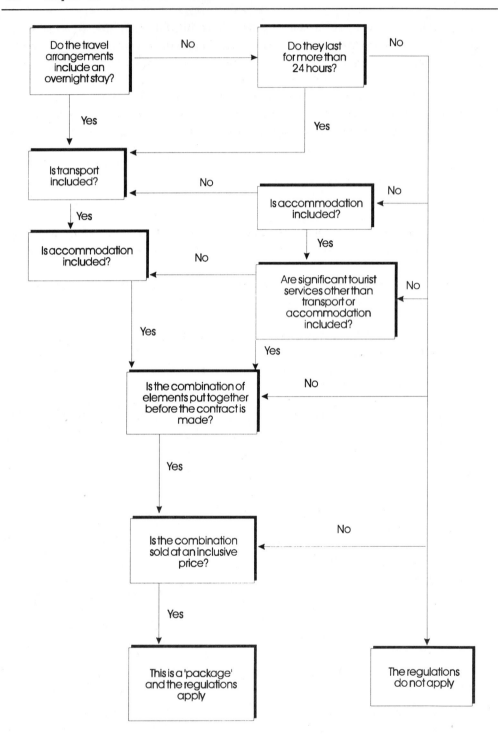

Figure 12.4   *The Package Travel Regulations - When do they apply?*

The other tourist services must account for a significant proportion of the package. This would not be the case, for example, where a guest could use a swimming pool at a hotel as this is a facility which goes with the use of the hotel and not another tourist service. Neither would it usually be significant.

The person or organisation who puts together the package is known as the *organiser*. This will usually be a tour operator, although the travel agent will come within the definition of organiser where he puts together a package for his customers. This will be so even though the customer may end up with individual direct contracts with the providers of the components that make up the package. The expression consumer within the regulations includes the person who takes or agrees to take the package, any person on whose behalf the package is purchased, and any person to whom the package is transferred. This third category of consumer arises because the regulations introduce a new *right to transfer a booking* where the original consumer is *prevented* from proceeding with the package. This may occur for example, due to illness or jury service although the consumer will not be regarded as being prevented from proceeding if he simply changes his mind. The person to whom the package is transferred must satisfy all the conditions applicable to the package, and reasonable notice must be given of the intention to transfer.

Consumer rights contained in the regulations

Regulation 4 gives the consumer the right to sue for compensation where he suffers loss as a result of any misleading description relating to a package or misleading information as to its price. This new right arises in circumstances where an offence would be committed by a trader under s.14 of the Trade Descriptions Act 1968 or s.20 of the Consumer Protection Act 1987, although r.4 is wider in its scope as it applies both to those operating in the course of business and to those who are not. The criminal offences only apply to misleading information which is supplied knowingly or recklessly whereas the regulation applies to information which is misleading even if it is not applied knowingly or recklessly.

Under r.5 it is a criminal offence for an organiser or retailer to make a brochure available to a prospective consumer unless the description of the package in the brochure indicates in an understandable and accurate manner both the price and certain key information relating to the package. This would include:

* the destination and the type of transport used;

* the type of accommodation, its location, degree of comfort and main features;

* the meals which are included;

- the itinerary;

- general information about passports, visas and health formalities;

- when the deposit and balance of the price is due, and

- the arrangements for security for money paid and for repatriation of the consumer in the event of insolvency.

Under r.6 the particulars in a brochure constitute implied warranties for the purposes of any contract to which they relate. Where the brochure states that the information in it may change and the changes are clearly communicated before the contract is made then these will override inconsistent statements in the brochure. Under r.7 a retailer or organiser will be guilty of a criminal offence if they do not provide the intending customer with information in writing or in some other appropriate form about passport and visa requirements, health formalities and the arrangements for the security of money paid over and for the repatriation of the consumer in the event of insolvency. This information must be supplied before the contract is concluded.

It is also a criminal offence, under r.8, to fail to provide the consumer in good time before the start of the journey with written information about the journey and the arrangements for assistance from representatives of the organiser and contact names in the event of difficulties on the tour.

It is an implied condition of the contract that all of its terms should be communicated to the consumer before the contract is made. This does not apply where circumstances make it impracticable, for example in the case of last minute bookings. In any event a written copy of the contract must be supplied to the consumer. The written terms must comply with the regulations and contain certain minimum information. This is similar to, but more detailed than, the information which must be included in a brochure under r.5.

The regulations limit the organiser's ability to increase the price of the package by way of a surcharge. If the contract contains such a clause, it will be void unless the contract allows for the possibility of a price reduction as well as an increase. The contract must state precisely how the revised price is to be calculated. Price changes can only be made to reflect changes in transport or fuel costs, exchange rates, taxes or fees. In any event no price increase may be made in the period of 30 days before departure and the tour operator must always absorb the first 2% of an increase.

If where the organiser, within the terms of the contract, wishes to make a significant alteration to an important term, such as the price, he must notify the consumer as quickly as possible. The consumer will have the option to withdraw from the contract without penalty or to accept the change. If the consumer does withdraw then he is entitled to take an available substitute package of the equivalent quality; a full refund or a lower quality substitute package coupled with a rebate.

Where the organiser is in breach of contract because a significant proportion of the services contracted for are not provided he must make suitable alternative arrangements at no extra cost to the consumer for the continuation of the package. If it is not possible to make such arrangements or if the consumer validly refuses to accept them the organiser must provide the consumer with equivalent transport home or to another destination with the consumers agreement. The organiser may still be liable to compensate the consumer for the difference between the services contracted for and those supplied.

The regulations also make detailed provision for the protection of the consumer in the event of the insolvency of the tour operator or organiser. He is required at all times to be able to provide sufficient evidence of security for the refund of money paid in advance and for the repatriation of the consumer in the event of insolvency. This is important as booking conditions for package holidays will almost invariably require full payment by the consumer eight weeks before departure, and because it provides protection for the holiday maker who would otherwise be stranded abroad if the tour operator becomes insolvent while they are on holiday. This protection is further enhanced by the licensing and bonding requirements in the regulations.

Tour operator's liability

When booking a package holiday, the consumer makes a contract with a tour operator. This contract is usually made through a travel agent, though in the case of direct sell operators the contract may be made without the use of an intermediary. Where a travel agent is involved he will bring together the parties to the contract in return for a commission paid by the tour operator. In accordance with the ordinary principles of the law of agency, the travel agent will not himself be a party to the contract. The tour operator puts together the various elements of the package such as flights, transfers from airport to hotel, hotel accommodation and food; and sells them together as one product. The tour operator will enter into separate contracts with the suppliers of the component parts of the package. In addition to the elements already noted, the package may include other items such as car hire, excursions, tickets for events and holiday insurance, although these may be optional extras.

Where the consumer books a package holiday he is contracting only with the tour operator and has no direct contract with the suppliers of individual components of the holiday. The terms of the contract with the tour operator are set out in the brochure, though not necessarily all on the same page. There will usually be at least one page of general booking conditions, sometimes referred to as a fair trading charter, often towards the back of the brochure. These must be read in conjunction with the information on the booking form itself, and the information in the main body of the brochure about the particular hotel and resort chosen by the consumer which is entered onto the booking form with the holiday dates and the price.

The tour operator may be liable to pay damages to a dissatisfied consumer if facilities described in the brochure are not available, for example where the consumer books a room in a particular hotel which is specified as having a balcony overlooking the sea and bathroom facilities en suite and this turns out not to be the case. The tour operator may incur criminal liability under s.14 Trade Descriptions Act 1968 in these circumstances. (See later in the chapter) The tour operator's civil liability for damages will be based upon the breach of an express term of the contract.

Cases such as *Jackson v. Horizon Holidays* 1975 and *Jarvis v. Swans Tours Ltd.* 1973, considered in Chapter 9 illustrate the contractual liability of tour operators who fail to supply the agreed service.

The tour operator may also be liable for breach of an implied term in the contract. As a provider of services in the course of a business, s.13 of the Supply of Goods and Services Act 1982 applies to the tour operator, and implies a term in the contract between him and the consumer that he will use reasonable care and skill in carrying out the contract.

> In *Davey v. Cosmos Air Holidays* 1989 the plaintiff booked a two weeks' package holiday in the Algarve for himself and his family. During the holiday the entire family suffered diarrhoea and the plaintiff's wife and son both contracted dysentery. The evidence showed that the illness was caused by a general lack of hygiene at the resort and the fact that raw sewage was being pumped into the sea just fifty yards from the beach. The defendant tour operators had resident representatives at the resort who knew of the dangers. It was held that the defendants were liable for breach of the implied duty in the contract to take reasonable care to avoid exposing their clients to a significant risk of injury to their health.

The tour operator will not be liable merely because the consumer has suffered injury, provided the tour operator has taken reasonable care. In the Davey case, for example, Cosmos would not have been liable had they warned the plaintiffs of the risks and advised them as to the steps to take to avoid injury.

A tour operator has a duty to exercise reasonable care and skill in selecting the suppliers of components of the package. In order to fulfil this duty he should, for example, undertake thorough inspections of the hotels, not only to verify the availability of facilities for inclusion in the brochure but also to satisfy himself as to the standards of kitchen hygiene, general safety, sanitary conditions and such things as fire escapes.

In *Wilson v. Best Travel Ltd.* 1993 the plaintiff suffered serious injuries after tripping and falling through glass patio doors at an hotel in Greece. The glass doors were fitted with 4mm glass which complied with Greek safety standards but would not have met equivalent British standards. The plaintiff claimed damages against the defendant tour operators, arguing that the hotel was not reasonably safe for use by the defendants' customers and that they were in breach of their duty of care under s.13 of the Supply and Goods and Services Act 1982. It was held that the tour operators were not liable. They had discharged their contractual duty of care by checking that local safety regulations had been complied with. It was not necessary for them to ensure that the Greek hotel came up to English safety standards provided that the absence of a relevant safety feature was not such that a reasonable holiday maker might decline to take a holiday at the hotel in question. This could be the case, for example, if the hotel had no fire precautions at all even though they were not required under local law.

In *Wall v. Silver Wing Surface Arrangements Ltd. (trading as Enterprise Holidays)* 1981 the plaintiff holiday maker was injured as a result of the fact that the management at his hotel had locked the fire exit. The evidence showed that the fire escape had not been locked when it was inspected by the defendants. It was locked on the occasion in question for security reasons to prevent unauthorised access into the hotel. It was held that the defendants were not liable as they had exercised reasonable care in selecting a suitable hotel and checking that the safety arrangements were satisfactory. The court rejected the plaintiff's argument that the tour operator had an implied contractual duty to ensure that the plaintiff would be reasonably safe in the hotel. The duty to take reasonable care in selecting the hotel had been fulfilled and the tour operator was not liable.

In *Wan (Wong Mee) v. K Wan Kin Travel Services Ltd* 1994 the Privy Council considered the scope of the responsibility of a tour operator who puts a package holiday together by arranging services for the client. Here a tour was arranged of mainland China by a Hong Kong travel company the price to include *"transportation"* as specified in the itinerary. An employee of another travel company engaged as a contractor organised a speedboat to ferry the tour group across a lake and as a result of negligent driving the speedboat crashed and the plaintiff's daughter was drowned. The Hong Kong Court of Appeal agreed with the lower court that the second travel company as contractor and the speedboats owner were liable in negligence, but not the tour operator. The court said that to impose liability for a non-delegatable primary contractual duty would be an intolerable burden on a company putting a package tour together. On further appeal however the Privy Council held that the tour operator was liable. The court drew a distinction between situations where a person agrees as an agent to arrange for services to be provided by some third party and those in which he undertakes to supply the services and then arranges for another to do the work. This was the position here and *"the fact that the supplier of services may under the contract arrange for some or all of them to be performed by others does not absolve the supplier from his contractual obligation"*. He may be liable if the service is performed without the exercise of due care and skill on the part of the subcontractor just as he would be liable if the sub-contractor failed to provide the service or failed to provide it in accordance with the terms of the contract. If a person undertaking to supply the services performs them himself, that he must do so with reasonable skill and care, and if, where the contract permits him to do so, he arranges for others to supply the services, that they should be supplied with reasonable skill and care.

The above decision is a reflection of the Package Tours Regulations 1992 which of course do not apply in Hong Kong. A tour operator who puts together a package by arranging services should require an indemnity from the supplier and/or rely on insurance cover.

In circumstances where the tour operator is not shown to have been negligent, the consumer may be left with the difficult task of suing the hotel. As we have seen there is no contract between the consumer and the hotel. The claim could not therefore be based in contract. A major problem for the consumer is that the hotelier's liability will depend on the national law of the country in which the hotel is situated, and whether an equivalent of the English law of third party negligence exists there. There is the additional expense and inconvenience of having to take legal action in a foreign country with an unfamiliar legal system and perhaps in a foreign language.

The consumer's rights in this situation have been greatly improved as a result of the implementation of the Package Travel Directive by the Package Travel Regulations 1992. Under r.15 the tour operator is legally responsible to the consumer for the proper performance of the obligations arising under the contract, and it does not matter whether the obligations are to be performed by the tour operator or by other suppliers of services. The tour operator is liable to the consumer for any damage caused by the improper performance of the contract by any of his suppliers. This new right to sue the tour operator where, for example, the consumer is injured by the negligence of the hotelier means that the consumer's position is made much easier as he does not have to face the problems involved in suing abroad. If the consumer is successful in his claim, the tour operator will be able to seek an indemnity from his supplier and unlike the consumer who has no contract with the supplier, the tour operator will be able to base his claim on a breach of contract.

Thus in a case such as *Wall v. Silver Wing* the tour operator would be liable to the plaintiff, and in turn would seek an indemnity from the hotel. In *Wilson v. Best*, however, it is probable that the consumer's claim would still fail on the grounds that the supplier had properly performed the contract.

The tour operator will have a defence to a claim by a consumer under r.15 if he can show that the failures in the performance of the contract are attributable to the consumer himself or are unforeseeable or unavoidable and caused by a third party. In such circumstances, except where the problems are entirely due to the consumer, the tour operator still has a duty to render prompt assistance to the consumer.

The tour operator is permitted to limit his liability in line with the levels of compensation provided for in international conventions such as the Warsaw Convention in respect of international flights.

He is also permitted to limit his contractual liability to the consumer for damage other than personal injury, provided that the limitation is not unreasonable. This is in line with the provisions of s.2 Unfair Contract Terms Act 1977, except that the regulations only permit a limitation and not a total exclusion of this liability.

Where the consumer experiences problems when he is actually on the package holiday or tour, he has a duty under r.15 to communicate his complaint to the organiser where he considers that it arises from defective performance of the contract by a component supplier, for example where the hotel room which has been allocated to him is unsatisfactory or is significantly inferior to that which was described in the brochure. The organiser, or his local representative, must then make prompt efforts to resolve the problems in an appropriate way.

Trade Descriptions Legislation

The Trade Descriptions Act 1968 is an early example of the use of the criminal law to promote consumer protection. The Act introduces criminal sanctions which may be imposed on business traders who mislead the public by falsely describing goods and services for sale. The use of the criminal law within the field of consumer protection demonstrate parliaments recognition of harmful effects on market activity unscrupulous and rogue trading can have. It is also acknowledgment of the failure of civil sanctions to provide adequate redress and the desirability of achieving a change in attitude in business suppliers whose trading standards are unacceptable. One of the most important features of the legislation is that there can be no liability under the 1968 Act unless the person applying the false description does so within the course of a trade or business rather than a private sale. This is one reason why the Business Advertisements (Disclosure) Order 1977 requires a trader to identify himself as such when he advertises in the classified advertisements in newspapers.

The fact that a business organisation is the vendor or purchaser does not automatically mean that a sale is in the course of a trade. The transaction must be of a type that is a regular occurrence in that particular business, so that a sale of business assets would not normally qualify as a sale in the course of a trade or business.

> In *Roberts v. Leonard* 1995 veterinary surgeons were held to be carrying on a trade or business, the court deciding that there was no sufficient reason to exclude the professions from the scope of the Act.

Where there is a genuine private sale and, for example, the seller falsely describes the goods, the buyer's remedy will be rescission. He may also claim damages in a civil law action for misrepresentation or breach of the term implied into the contract by s.13 of the Sale of Goods Act 1979. A buyer from a business seller can also exercise these remedies, but in addition may report the trader to the trading standards department with a view to a prosecution for a breach of the criminal law under the 1968 Act. In all trade descriptions cases there is potentially liability under the civil law which illustrates the fact that here consumer protection law is founded upon the interrelationship between civil and criminal activities. Prosecutions for trade description offences are brought in the Magistrates Court and exceptionally in the Crown Court with the possibility of an appeal to the Divisional Court of the Queen's Bench Division of the High Court by way of case-stated on a point of law. There is no requirement for a re-hearing of the evidence, rather the appeal court is concerned with determining the validity of the legal reasoning upon which the decision to convict or acquit is based.

Two principal offences under the Trade Descriptions Act 1968 relate to false description of goods, and making misleading statements about services. A number of defences are also provided for. Further offences of giving misleading price indications were originally contained in s.11 of the Act, and the Price Marking (Bargain Offers) Order 1979 made under the Prices Act 1974. These offences have been replaced by others under Part III of the Consumer Protection Act 1987, and are considered separately below.

False Description of Goods

The 1968 Act provides, in s.1(1) that: *"Any person who, in the course of a trade or business:*

(a)   *applies a false trade description to any goods; or*

(b)   *supplies or offers to supply any goods to which a false trade description is applied;*

shall, subject to the provisions of this Act, be guilty of an offence".

Two different types of conduct will amount to offences under this section. The first is where the trader himself applies the false trade description contrary to s.1(1)(a). This offence could be committed, for example, by a trader who turns back the mileometer of a car to make it appear that the car has not travelled as many miles as it actually has. The second, under s.1(1)(b), involves supplying or offering to supply goods to which a false trade description has been applied by another person, for example where a retailer sells a garment to which the label *pure new wool* has been attached by the manufacturer, where the garment is partly composed of manmade fibres. There is a strict duty therefore not to pass on false trade descriptions applied by another subject to a defence which we will consider later.

In relation to the s.1(1)(b) offence, the trader will not be able to rely on a *Fisher v. Bell* type defence where he displays goods for sale.

> In *Fisher v. Bell* 1961, a shopkeeper who displayed flick knives for sale was acquitted of an offence of *offering to supply* them on the grounds that the display was an invitation to treat rather than a contractual offer.

The 1968 Act, in s.6, closes this loophole by providing that *"a person exposing goods for supply or having goods in his possession for supply shall be deemed to offer to supply them".*

A false trade description may be applied verbally or in writing, for example in a label on goods or in an advertisement, communicated by pictorial representation or even by conduct.

> In *Yugotours Ltd. v. Wadsley* 1988 a photograph of a three-masted schooner and the words "the excitement of being under full sail on board this majestic schooner" in a tour operator's brochure was held to constitute a statement for the purpose of the Act. By providing customers who had booked a holiday relying on the brochure with only a two masted schooner without sails the tour operator was guilty of recklessly making a false statement contrary to the Trade Descriptions Act.

The meaning of the term *trade description* extends, by s.2, to statements relating to quantity, size, composition, method of manufacture, fitness for purpose, place or date of manufacture, approval by any person or other history including previous ownership of goods.

> In *Sherratt v. Geralds The American Jewellers Ltd.* 1970 the defendant sold a watch described by the maker as a diver's watch and inscribed with the word "waterproof". The watch filled with water and stopped after it had been

immersed in water. It was held that the defendant was guilty of an offence under s.1(1)(b).

To constitute an offence under the Act the trade description must be false or misleading to a material degree.

In *Robertson v. Dicicco* 1972 a second-hand motor vehicle was advertised for sale by a dealer and described as *"a beautiful car"*. The car, although having a visually pleasing exterior was unroadworthy and not fit for use. The defendant was charged with an offence under s.1(1)(a). He argued that his statement was true as he had intended it to refer only to the visual appearance of the vehicle. It was held that he was guilty because the description was false to a material degree. A reasonable person would have taken the statement to refer to the mechanics of the car as well as its external appearance.

A similar approach was taken in *Kensington and Chelsea Borough Council v. Riley* 1973 where the trader was convicted of an offence under s.1(1)(a). It was held that the description *"in immaculate condition"* was false when applied to a car which required repairs costing £250 to make it roadworthy.

A trade description applied to goods for sale can be false for the purpose of s.1(1)(b) even when it is scientifically correct if it is likely to mislead a customer without specialist knowledge.

In *Dixon Ltd. v. Barnett* 1989 a customer was supplied with an Astral 500 telescope which was described as being capable of up *to "455 x magnification"*. The evidence showed that the maximum useful magnification was only 120 times, although scientifically 455 times magnification could be achieved. The Divisional Court held that the store was nevertheless guilty of an offence despite the fact that the statement was scientifically sound. An ordinary customer would have been misled by the statement because he would be interested in the maximum useful magnification rather than a blurred image produced at 455 times magnification.

A half truth is false for the purpose of the Act, so that while it was technically true to describe a vehicle as only having one previous owner *in R v. Inner London Justices and another* 1983 the fact that the owner was a leasing company and the car had had five different keepers meant that the statement was grossly misleading and false.

In *Routledge v. Ansa Motors (Chester-le-Street) Limited* 1980 a Ford Escort motor car which was manufactured in 1972 was first registered in 1975. Subsequently it was advertised by the defendant *as "a used 1975 Ford*

Escort". It was held that the defendant had applied a false trade description to the car, contrary to s. 1(1)(a).

In *Denard v. Smith and another* 1990 the Divisonal Court considered whether it is a false trade description to advertise goods in a shop at the point of sale as items offered for sale when they are temporarily out of stock and are not immediately available. The court held that unless customers are informed of the non-availability of the goods at the time of purchase the advertisement constituted a false trade description of offering to supply goods.

In order to be guilty of an offence under s.1, the trader must make the statement in connection with a sale or supply of goods.

In *Wickens Motors (Gloucester) Ltd. v. Hall* 1972 the purchaser of a car from the defendant complained about its performance. The complaint was made 40 days after the car had been supplied to him. The defendant told him that there was nothing wrong with the car, although this was untrue. It was held that the defendant was not guilty of an offence under s.1(1)(a) because there was insufficient connection between the false description and the sale.

An offence under s.1 may be committed by any person. This is not limited to the seller, but may include the buyer, particularly where he is an expert in relation to the subject matter of the contract.

In *Fletcher v. Budgen* 1974 a car dealer bought an old car from a customer for £2 saying that it was only fit to be scrapped. In fact the dealer repaired the car and advertised it for a resale for £135. It was held that he was guilty of an offence under s.1(1)(a) because he applied a false trade description to the car when he bought it in the course of his business.

Where defects in goods are disguised and the trader has no reason to realise or suspect that they are present, he will not be guilty of an offence under s.1(1)(b).

In *Cottee v. Douglas Seaton Ltd.* 1972 the bodywork of a car which had been in very poor condition was repaired using plastic body filler. This was smoothed down and the car repainted before it was sold to the defendant. The defendant was unaware of the fact that the bodywork was defective. He resold the car to a purchaser who subsequently discovered the defect. It was held that the disguised defects amounted to a false trade description as the goods, in effect, told a lie about themselves. The defendant was not guilty of an offence, however, because he was unaware that the description had been applied to the goods.

A person may be guilty of an offence under s.1(1)(b), even though he does rot know the description is false, provided he knows that the description has been applied to the goods by another person. This situation may arise for example where a car dealer sells a car which records an incorrectly low mileage on its mileometer. If a dealer is uncertain as to the accuracy of the recorded mileage, he may try to ensure that a false trade description is not applied by displaying a notice disclaiming the accuracy of the mileage reading.

> In *Norman v. Bennett* 1974 a customer bought a second-hand car with a recorded mileage of 23,000 miles. In fact the true mileage was about 68,000 miles. He signed an agreement containing a clause which said that the reading was not guaranteed. It was held that this was not an effective disclaimer. Lord Widgery, the Lord Chief Justice, stated that, in order to be effective, a disclaimer: *"must be as bold, precise and compelling as the trade description itself and must be as effectively brought to the notice of any person to whom the goods may be supplied. In other words, the disclaimer must equal the trade description in the extent to which it is likely to get home to anyone interested in receiving the goods".*

The use of a disclaimer will be an effective defence provided it complies with the test laid down in *Norman v. Bennett*. The Motor Trade Code of Practice, approved by Director General of Fair Trading in 1976, recommends the use of the following form of wording in these circumstances:

> *"We do not guarantee the accuracy of the recorded mileage. To the best of our knowledge and belief, however the recording is correct/incorrect".*

Clearly a disclaimer will only be an effective defence to a charge under s.1(1)(b). If the trader himself has turned back the mileage he will be unable to rely on this defence.

A disclaimer cannot exclude liability once it has arisen and is only effective to the extent that it prevents the commission of a criminal offence. The disclaimer could:

- prevent an indication being regarded as a trade description; or

- qualify a description so that it does not mislead; or

- qualify a description so that it is not false to a material degree.

Certainly it would be pointless to attempt to disclaim liability after an offence has already been committed.

In *Doble v. David Greig Ltd.* 1972 the defendants displayed bottles of Ribena for sale in their self service store at a particular price with an indication that a deposit on each bottle was refundable on its return. At the cash till however, a different notice stated that in fact no deposit would be charged because in the interest of hygiene the store would not accept the return of empty bottles. The retailer was convicted of the offence of offering to supply goods with a false price indication. The court held that the offence of offering to supply was committed when the goods were displayed and the subsequent notice at the cash till was ineffective in disclaiming liability.

While a disclaimer may prevent the commission of an offence of offering to supply goods, it will not apply to an offence of applying a false trade description.

In *Newham LBC v. Singh* 1988 as the defendant car dealer had not been aware that a car mileometer had been altered and had not been the person applying the false trade description to the car, he could successfully rely on a disclaimer when charged under s.1.

Finally, an important feature of disclaimers is that it is for the prosecution to establish the offence and prove that the disclaimer is ineffective whereas the specific defences under the Act must be established by the defendant.

False Description of Services

Suppliers of services, such as holiday tour operators, hairdressers and dry cleaners will be liable to prosecution under s.14 of the Trade Descriptions Act 1968 if they make false statements knowingly or recklessly in the course of their business.

Under s.14(1):

"It shall be an offence for any person in the course of any trade or business:

(a)   to make a statements which he knows to be false; or

(b)   recklessly to make a statement which is false;as to any of the following matters:

       (i)   the provision ... of any services, accommodation or facilities;

      (ii)   the nature of any services, accommodation or facilities;

     (iii)   the time at which, the manner in which or persons by whom any services, accommodation or facilities are provided;

(iv)   the examination, approval or evaluation by any person of any services, accommodation or facilities;or

(v)   the location or amenities of any accommodation.

The main difference between this offence and the offence in relation to goods is that in order to obtain a conviction under s.14, the prosecution must show *mens rea* (guilty mind) either that the trader knew that the statement was false, or that he was *reckless* as to its truth or falsity. You will remember that in relation to goods, liability is strict.

A statement is made recklessly if it is made regardless of whether it is true or false. It need not necessarily be dishonest. The knowledge or recklessness must be present at the time the statement is made.

In *Sunair Holidays Ltd. v. Dodd* 1970 the defendant's travel brochure described a package holiday in a hotel with *"all twin bedded rooms with bath, shower and terrace"*. The defendant had a contract with the hotel owners under which they were obliged to provide accommodation of that description. A customer who booked the package was given a room without a terrace. The defendant had not checked with the hotel to make sure that its customers were given the correct accommodation of that description. It was held however, that the statement was not false when it was made, and therefore the defendant was not guilty of an offence under s.14.

It must be shown that the trader, at the time the statement is made, either knows that it is false or is reckless as to its truth or falsity; and that the statement actually *is* false. Subsequent developments are irrelevant if these elements are present at the time the statement is made.

In *Cowburn v. Focus Television Rentals Ltd.* 1983 the defendant's advertisement stated: *"Hire 20 feature films absolutely free when you rent a video recorder"*. In response to the advertisement a customer rented a video recorder. The documentation supplied with it indicated that he was entitled only to 6 films, and that they were not absolutely free because he had to pay postage and packing. When he complained, the defendant refunded his postage and packing and supplied 20 free films to him. It was held that the defendant was guilty of an offence under s.14 because the statement in his advertisement was false and recklessly made. The fact that he subsequently honoured the advertisement provided no defence, as this was done after the offence had been committed.

Conduct of the defendant subsequent to the false statement is relevant however to determine whether an inference of recklessness can be maintained.

In *Yugotours Ltd. v. Wadsley* 1988 the fact that statements in a holiday brochure were clearly false and known to be so by the company meant that when the company failed to correct the statement, it was guilty of an offence. The court stated that there was sufficient material before the court to infer recklessness on the part of the maker of the statement. *"If a statement is false and known to be false, and nothing whatever is done to correct it, then the company making the statement can properly be found guilty of recklessness notwithstanding the absence of specific evidence of recklessness"*.

In *Wings Ltd. v. Ellis* 1984 the false nature of a statement in their travel brochure was not known by a tour operator when its brochure was published. Some 250,000 copies of the brochure contained an inaccurate statement that rooms in a hotel in Sri Lanka were air conditioned. The brochure also contained a photograph purporting to be a room in the same hotel which was of a room in a different hotel. When the mistake was discovered, reasonable steps were taken to remedy it by informing agents and customers who had already booked by letter. Despite this, a holiday was booked by a customer on the basis of the false information. It was held by the House of Lords that the tour operator was guilty of an offence under s.14 because the statement was made when the brochure was read by the customer, and at the time the defendant knew that it was false. The fact that the tour operator was unaware that the uncorrected statement was being made to the customer did not prevent the offence being committed. As a result of this judgment the offence under s.1(1)(a) has been described rather crudely as a *"half mens rea offence"*. Knowledge that a statement is false is necessary but there is no need to show mens rea as to the making of the statement.

For corporate liability under s.14 the prosecution must establish that a high ranking official of the company had the necessary mens rea. The Chairman of a company would certainly suffice but not the *"Contracts Manager"* in *Wings Ltd. v. Ellis* who had approved the photograph of the hotel which gave a wrong impression.

Defences under the Trade Descriptions Act 1968

It is a defence to any charge under the 1968 Act that the defendant innocently published a misleading advertisement received by him for publication in the ordinary course of his business. This defence, available for example to newspapers, is provided by s.25.

A number of separate defences are contained in s.24. These are available to a defendant who can prove

(a)   *That the commission of the offence was due to a mistake or to reliance on information supplied to him or to the act or default of another person, an accident, or some other cause beyond his control; and*

(b)   *that he took all reasonable precautions and exercised all due diligence to avoid the commission of such an offence by himself or any person under his control".*

In order to have an effective defence under s.24, the onus is on the defendant to prove any one of the reasons listed in paragraph (a) above and all of the elements in (b). He must also supply to the prosecution, at least 7 days before the hearing, a written notice giving such information as he has to enable the other person to be identified.

In relation to enforcement of the 1968 Act, as we have seen, wide investigatory powers are conferred on local authority trading standards officers. Before a prosecution is brought, however, the local authority is required to inform the Department of Trade. This is to prevent numerous unnecessary prosecutions for the same false trade description.

- The legality of bringing a second prosecution where there are a number of complaints in relation to the same false statement was at issue in *R. v. Thomson Holidays Limited* 1973. In this case a misleading statement in a travel brochure constituted an offence under s.14. The Court of Appeal held that a separate offence was committed every time someone read the brochure, and that it was not necessarily improper to bring more than one prosecution in these circumstances.

Misleading price indications:

Part III of the Consumer Protection Act 1987 .

The provisions of the Consumer Protection Act 1987, s.20 to s.26, replace both s.11 of the Trade Descriptions Act 1968 and the Price Marking (Bargain Offers) Order 1979. The previous provisions had proved to be badly drafted and difficult to enforce.

The offence of giving a misleading price indication is contained in s.20 of the 1987 Act, which provides: *"A person shall be guilty of an offence if, in the course of any business of his, he gives (by any means whatever) to any consumers an indication which is misleading as to the price at which any goods, services, accommodation or facilities are available".*

The types of statements which would be caught by s.20 include:

- false comparisons with recommended prices, for example a false claim that goods are £20 less than the recommended price; or

- indications that the price is less than the real price, for example where hidden extras are added to an advertised price; or

- false comparisons with a previous price, for example a false statement that goods were £50 and are now £30; or

- where the stated method of determining the price is different to the method actually used.

Case law suggests that the courts have interpreted s.20 with consumer protection in mind. In *Toyota (GB) Ltd v North Yorkshire County Council* 1998 a conviction under s.20 against a car dealer was upheld as appeal for a misleading price indication. This was despite the fact that the price indicated was subject to negotiations and invariably reduced. The price was misleading because it did not include a delivery charge which would be added to it and a reference to the charge in small print at the bottom of the advertisement was insufficiently prominent to give a fair indication of the price.

Failure to correct a price indication which initially was true, but has become untrue, is also an offence under s.20.

The Secretary of State, after consulting the Director General of Fair Trading, has issued a code of practice designed to give practical guidance on the requirements of s.20. It aims to promote good practice in relation to giving price indications. Breach of the code will not, of itself, give rise to criminal or civil liability, but may be used as evidence to establish either that an offence had been committed under s.20, or that a trader has a defence to such a charge.

The following cases, decided under previous legislation, illustrate the type of behaviour which will be contrary to s.20.

In *Richards v. Westminster Motors Ltd.*1975 the defendant advertised a commercial vehicle for sale at a price of £1,350. When the buyer purchased the vehicle he was required to pay the asking price plus VAT, which made a total price of £1,534. It was held that the defendant was guilty of giving a misleading indication as to the price at which he was prepared to sell goods.

In *Read Bros. Cycles (Leyton) v. Waltham Forest London Borough* 1978 the defendant advertised a motor cycle for sale at a reduced price of £540, £40 below the list price. A customer agreed to purchase the motor cycle and negotiated a £90 part exchange allowance on his old vehicle. The defendant charged him the full list price for the new cycle, and stated that the reduced price did not apply where goods were given in part exchange. It was held that the defendant was guilty of giving a misleading price indication.

In one significant respect the offence under s.20 is narrower than the offences which it replaced. This is that s.20 only applies to consumer transactions. For the purpose of s.20, the expression *consumer* means:

(a)   in relation to any goods, any person who might wish to be supplied with the goods for his own private use or consumption;

(b)   in relation to any services or facilities, any person who might wish to be provided with the services or facilities otherwise than for the purposes of any business of his; and

(c)   in relation to any accommodation, any person who might wish to occupy the accommodation otherwise than for the purposes of any business of his.

A consequence of the narrowing down of the offence is that misleading price indications to business customers will not be caught by it. On the facts of *Richards v. Westminster Motors*, for example, the defendant would not now be guilty of an offence under s.20 because the customer was not a consumer.

The Property Misdescriptions Act 1991

The Property Misdescriptions Act was passed in 1991 although it did not come into force until April 1993. The Act, which imposes criminal liability for making false statements in relation to the sale of residential and commercial land and buildings, is similar in many respects of the Trade Descriptions Act 1968, although there are several significant differences.

The main offence is set out in s.1(1) which states:

> *"Where a false or misleading statement about a prescribed matter is made in the course of an estate agency business or a property development business... the person by whom the business is carried on shall be guilty of an offence".*

The offence only applies to statements made in the course of an estate agency business or a property development business. Those made by a private seller or a seller in a different line of business are not caught by the Act. Statements made in the course of providing conveyancing services, for example by solicitors or licensed conveyancers, are also outside the scope of the offence. The offence covers statements made by estate agents in advertisements or in written particulars describing a property for sale. It also applies to statements made in the course of a property development business. This covers builders of new commercial and residential premises and those who renovate old properties to sell. The Act does not apply, however, where property is being advertised for rent rather than for sale.

In order for an offence to be committed, the false or misleading statement must be about a prescribed matter.The Property Misdescriptions (Specified Matters) Order 1993 sets out a long list of prescribed matters, including the price, structural characteristics, accommodation, size, outlook or environment, view, proximity to any services, or the results of any survey.The expression *statement* covers pictures as well as written and spoken words. Statements will be regarded false under the Act if they are *false to a material degree*. It will be a question of fact in the circumstances of each case as to whether a statement is materially false. A statement which is not false may nevertheless be misleading if a reasonable person would be likely to draw a false conclusion as a result of it, for example where a half truth is told.

The offence will be committed by the person who carries on the estate agency or property development business. Where the business is carried on by a limited company, the company's senior officers are liable where the offence was committed with their consent or connivance or was attributable to neglect on their part. Where the making of the statement is due to the act of default of an employee the employee is guilty of an offence and may be prosecuted independently of the employer.

It will be a defence under s.2(1) for any defendant to show that he took all reasonable steps and exercised all due diligence to avoid committing the offence. This is similar to the defence available under s.24 of the Trade Descriptions Act 1968. The defendant needs to show that he has an effective system in place which is designed to ensure that offences are not committed.

Where the defendant seeks to rely on information given by another person in his defence, s.2(1) provides that he can only do so if it was reasonable in all the circumstances for him to have relied on that other person. In this context regard shall be had to the steps which the defendant took or might reasonably had taken in order to verify the information; and whether he had any reason to disbelieve the information. Thus an estate agent can not safely take at face value statements which are made by his client about the property where he ought reasonably to take steps to verify the information.Where the defendant is found guilty he may be punished by a fine of up to £5,000 in the Magistrates Court, or an unlimited fine in the Crown Court. In 1993 Mr. Ian Sinclair, an estate agent in Great Yarmouth, was the first person to be prosecuted under the Property Misdescriptions Act. He was fined £500 with costs of £570 after advertising a property for sale in both a newspaper advertisement and his window at a lower price than that actually quoted in the sales particulars.

Regulatory Agencies

To ensure high standards and consumer protection where there is potential for abuse by unscrupulous traders there are some fields, in particular, where statutory licenses are required to enable suppliers to trade. Only advisors licensed under the Financial Services Act 1986 may provide consumers with financial advice and those who provide credit in the course of a business are required to be licensed under the Consumer Credit Act 1974. Withdrawal of a license would be an effective sanction against a trader guilty of abuse.

In addition most professionals are members of professional bodies who administer compliant procedures against their members. Such bodies control solicitors, accountants, surveyors, doctors etc. and can exercise disciplinary powers over their members.

Trade Associations can also be very powerful and often exercise a high degree of control. Membership of the Association of British Travel Agents (ABTA) is a mark of status in the travel industry and conflict between consumers and tour operators is usually dealt with by the ABTA arbitration scheme rather than legal action in the courts. Trade Associations also lay down codes of practice for their members giving guidance as to good practice in straightforward terms. They are self regulatory providing a quick inexpensive means of setting high standards and possible a means of redress for the consumer.

Both central and local governments have important roles to play in consumer protection. The Department of Trade and Industry has responsibility for the promotion and implementation of consumer legislation in conjunction with a number of national consumer protection bodies such as:

- The Office of Fair Trading

- The National Consumer Council

- The Consumer Protection Advisory Committee

- The Directors-General in consumer fields such as electricity and gas.

Enforcement of consumer legislation is in the hands of local authority trading standards officers usually based in consumer protection departments.

The Office of Fair Trading

The Office of Fair Trading, created by the Fair Trading Act 1973, has a significant national role in relation to the broad task of protecting the interests of the consumer. The 1973 Act created the post of Director General of Fair Trading. The Director has wide powers under the 1973 Act and other legislation, notably the Consumer Credit Act 1974 and the Estate Agents Act 1979.

The duties of the Director are:

- to review commercial activities and report to the Secretary of State;

- to refer adverse trade practices to the Consumer Protection Advisory Committee;

- to take action against traders who are persistently unfair to consumers;

- to supervise the enforcement of the Consumer Credit Act 1974 and the administration of the licensing system under that Act;

- to arrange for information and advice to be published for the benefit of consumers in relation to the supply of goods and services and consumer credit;

- to encourage trade associations to produce voluntary Codes of Practice; and

- to superintend the working and enforcement of the Estate Agents Act 1979.

Referral of adverse trade practices to the Consumer Protection Advisory Committee

The Director has power to refer to the Consumer Protection Advisory Committee any consumer trade practice which in his opinion adversely affects the economic interests of consumers. The type of activity which can give rise to such a reference include trade practices relating to:

(i)   the terms or conditions on which goods or services are supplied,

(ii)   the manner in which those terms or conditions are communicated to the consumer,

(iii)   promotion of goods or services by advertising, labelling or marking of goods, or canvassing,

(iv)   methods of salesmanship employed in dealing with consumers,

(v)   the way in which goods are packed, or

(vi)   methods of demanding or securing payments for goods or services supplied.

A reference by the Director may include proposals for the creation of delegated legislation by the Secretary of State.

Examples of regulations made under this procedure include the Consumer Transactions (Restrictions on Statements) Order 1976 and (Amendment) Order 1978, and the Business Advertisements (Disclosure) Order 1977. Another example is the Mail Order Transactions (Information) Order 1976, which applies to goods sold by mail order which have to be paid for in advance. Under the regulations, any advertisement for such goods must state the true name or company name of the person carrying on the mail order business, as well as the true address of the business. Thus, for example, an advertiser giving only a P.O. Box number would be committing an offence if he required payment in advance.

Taking action against persistently unfair traders

The Director has power to bring proceedings in the Restrictive Practices Court against any person who persistently maintains a course of conduct which is unfair to consumers. Before making a reference to the Court, the Director must first attempt to obtain a written assurance from the trader that he will refrain from the unfair trade practice. If the trader refuses to give an assurance, or breaks an assurance once it has been given, the Director must apply for an order restraining the continuance of the unfair conduct. If the trader does not comply with the order, he will be in contempt of court and liable to imprisonment.

A course of conduct will be regarded as being unfair to consumers if it involves a breach of any legal obligations, either criminal or civil, by the trader. Examples of unfair conduct include persistently giving short measure or applying false trade descriptions, or repeatedly delivering unmerchantable goods.

Unfair Terms in Consumer Contract Regulations 1999 (originally 1994)

These regulations were first made in 1994 and came into force on 1st July 1995. They were introduced to implement the directive on Unfair Terms in Consumer Contracts. The Regulations cover a wide variety of contract terms within a broad range of different types of contract. There are, however, a number of exceptions.

These are contracts of employment, contracts relating to the creation and operation of companies or partnerships and contracts dealing with succession rights or rights under family law.

The Regulations apply when a seller or supplier of goods or services, acting in the course of a business, makes a contract with a consumer. The expression *consumer* in this context covers any natural person purchasing goods or services other than for business purposes.

The Regulations introduce three major changes to the present law on unfair contract terms by:

- invalidating any terms in consumer contracts which are unfair and which have not been individually negotiated;

- requiring that plain English is used when consumer contracts are drawn up in writing; and

- providing a mechanism for preventing the continued use of unfair terms by allowing the Director General of Fair Trading to challenge particular contract terms before the courts.

A term in a standard form contract between a business supplier and a consumer will be held to be unfair, under reg. 4(1) where:

> "...*contrary to the requirement of good faith the term causes a significant imbalance in the parties' rights and obligations under the contract to the detriment of the consumer.*"

In determining the fairness of a contract term account must be taken of the nature of the goods or services supplied; the other terms of the contract and any related contract and all of the circumstances at the time the contract was made. Schedule 2 of the regulations sets out a number of factors to which the court shall have regard, including the strength of the bargaining positions of the parties, whether the consumer had an inducement to agree to the term and the extent to which the supplier has dealt fairly and equitably with the consumer.

Schedule 3 of the Regulations contains an indicative list of terms which may be regarded as unfair. The list is not exhaustive, and the following examples are drawn from it:

(a)   terms which make an agreement binding on the consumer when it is not binding on the seller or supplier;

(b)   terms requiring any consumer who fails to fulfil his obligations to pay a disproportionately high sum in compensation;

(c)   terms enabling the seller or supplier to alter the terms of the contract unilaterally without a valid reason which is specified in the contract;

(d)   terms authorising the seller or supplier to dissolve the contract on a discretionary basis where the same facility is not available to the consumer;

(e)   terms allowing the seller or supplier to increase the price without allowing the consumer the right to withdraw if the final price is too high as compared to the agreed price;

(f)   terms limiting the seller or suppliers' obligation to respect commitments undertaken by his agent; and

(g)   terms obliging the consumer to fulfil all his obligations where the seller or supplier does not perform his.

Where a term is found to be unfair it is not be binding upon the consumer although the contract will continue to be binding provided that it is capable of continuing in existence without the unfair term.

Where the supplier uses a standard form contract in relation to the transaction, it is clear that the terms are not individually negotiated. They have been drawn up in advance and the consumer has not been able to influence their content. Where the contract contains some terms which have been individually negotiated and others which are standard, the standard terms will be subject to challenge. Where the supplier claims that a particular term has been individually negotiated, the burden of proving this rests with him.

Certain contract terms, however, cannot be challenged as unfair even where they have not been individually negotiated. These are:

(a)   terms reflecting mandatory, statutory or regulatory provisions, for example terms which are implied by statute into particular types of contract. This means that the substance of such terms cannot be challenged as unfair;

(b)   terms reflecting the principles contained in international conventions, such as the Warsaw Convention which limits the liability of international air carriers for death or personal injury to passengers and for damage to or loss of luggage. There are a number of such conventions particularly in the area of international transport and travel;

(c)   terms defining the main subject matter of the contract and the price to be paid. This exception is in line with the common law rule relating to the adequacy of consideration, discussed in Chapter 7 in the context of the formation of contracts. Under this rule the courts will recognise a contract as valid where some element of consideration is provided by each contracting party to the other, but the court is not concerned to see that the value provided by each is equal or fair;

(d)   terms in insurance contracts which define the risks insured and the insurers liability.

Plain English

Where all or part of the terms of contract with a consumer are in writing, the Regulations provide that these terms must always be drafted in plain intelligible language. Where there is doubt about the meaning of a term, the interpretation most favourable to the consumer shall be given.

Member states were required by the Directive to introduce adequate and effective means to prevent the continued use of unfair terms in contracts concluded with consumers by sellers and suppliers. This was to be achieved by the introduction of rules enabling consumer protection organisations to apply to the court for a declaration as to whether contractual terms drawn up for general use were unfair. The UK government has interpreted this provision narrowly in its implementation of the Directive, and the UK Regulations provide a power only to the Director General of Fair Trading to such action.

Under the regulations as they are currently drawn, where the Director General of Fair Trading considers that a contract term is unfair, he may either seek an injunction to prevent its further use, or accept an undertaking that a supplier or trade organisation will not use or recommend the use of a particular term in the future.

In February 1999 the Director General of Fair Trading wrote to the *Guardian newspaper* and stressed the extent to which the Unfair Terms in Consumer Contracts Regulations 1995 had been enforced by his Office. Following 3400 complaints from consumers over 2000 unfair terms had been modified or dropped from contracts for the supply of goods and services to the advantage of the consumer. He answered the criticism that no court actions had been pursued by emphasising the fact that the Office of Fair Trading is empowered to accept undertakings from suppliers in lieu of court proceedings. The lack of contested cases did not indicate inertia on behalf of his office which stood *"ready to take action against any unfair terms in standard contracts which meet the criteria of the regulations."*

> *Director General of Fair Trading v. First National Bank* 2000 is the first reported case where the Court of Appeal is called upon to interpret the Regulations. The case arose out of an application by the Office of Fair Trading to have a clause in the First National Bank's standard conditions declared invalid. The material part of the relevant conditions related to the right to charge interest until payment is made of money owed to the bank on a loan contract following a court judgment. In the County Court post judgment interest is rarely available. In the High Court the judge felt that the term was not unfair adopting the following test *"As a first step in answering the question whether the provision is unfair, it seems to me appropriate to stand back and without reference to statute or authority consider whether had a potential borrower had the effect of the provision brought to his attention immediately after entering the loan agreement he would reasonably have replied that they were unfair"*. Here he felt the borrower would not have regarded the term unfair. Importantly this approach to testing the validity of such terms was rejected by the Court of Appeal. "The test of unfairness is not to be judged by personal concepts of inherent fairness and we are far from convinced that a borrower would think that it is fair that when he is taken to court and an order for installments has been tailored to meet what he could afford and he complied with that order, he should then be told that he has to pay further sums by way of interest.... in our view the relevant term does not create unfair surprise and so does not satisfy the test of good faith." Breach of these requirements was sufficient to persuade the Court of Appeal that the term should be modified.

The Role of Local Authorities in Consumer Protection

Responsibility for the enforcement of most consumer protection legislation, other than that which gives the consumer a right to sue for damages, rests with local authorities. It is carried out by trading standards or consumer protection departments. In practice, these departments see their major role as one of giving guidance to traders. This is done by a combination of education and persuasion. Prosecution for criminal offences is seen as a last resort when other measures fail.

Trading standards officers have wide investigatory powers to enable them to carry out their enforcement functions effectively. They can make sample purchases of goods or services; enter premises; require suppliers to produce documents; carry out tests on equipment; and seize and detain property. A person who obstructs a trading standards officer, or makes a false statements to him commits a criminal offence.

Many Acts of Parliament and regulations made under them are enforced by trading standards officers including the Consumer Credit Act 1974, the Food Safety Act 1990, the Trade Descriptions Act 1968, the Unsolicited Goods and Services Act 1971, and the Consumer Protection Act 1987.

Most, but not all, of the criminal offences designed to protect the consumer apply only to persons supplying goods or services in the course of a trade or business. Traders who are charged with criminal offences will be prosecuted in the Magistrates or the Crown Court. If convicted, they will be liable to a fine or, in some cases, imprisonment. Following a conviction the criminal courts also have power to make a *compensation order* to the victim of the crime. In this context the victim will be the consumer who has suffered loss as a result of the offence. The power to make a compensation order is contained in s.35 of the Powers of Criminal Courts Act 1973. This provides that any court convicting a person of an offence may, in addition to its sentencing power, make an order requiring the offender to pay compensation for any personal injury, loss or damage resulting from the offence or any other offence taken into consideration.

The power to make compensation orders is particularly useful from the point of view of the consumer. It saves him the trouble and expense of bringing proceedings in the civil courts. It will be used only in relatively straightforward cases, however. It is not designed to deal for example with complicated claims involving issues of causation or remoteness of damage.

The Food Safety Act 1990

The Food Safety Act 1990 is designed to strengthen consumer protection in relation to food safety, an area of increasing concern in recent years. The Act consolidates existing provision in this areas, adds a number of new regulatory powers and substantially increases the penalties for offences relating to the quality and safety of foods. It is an offense, to process or treat food intended for sale for human consumption in any way which makes it injurious to health. Food is injurious to health if it causes any permanent or temporary impairment of health. The offense can be committed by food manufacturers, food handlers, retailers or restaurants. The offense may be committed, for example, by adding a harmful ingredient, or subjecting food to harmful treatment such as storing it at an incorrect temperature or storing cooked meat alongside uncooked meat. Also, food intended for human consumption must satisfy *the food safety requirement*. It is an offense to sell, offer or have in one's possession for sale, prepare or deposit with another for sale any food which fails to meet this requirement.

In *David Greg Ltd. v. Goldfinch* 1961 a trader was convicted of selling food which was unfit for human consumption (under an equivalent provision in the

Food and Drugs Act 1955). He sold a pork pie which had small patches of mold under the crust. The fact that the mold was of a type which was not harmful to human beings was held to be no defense to the charge.

It is also an offense for a supplier to sell, to the prejudice of the consumer, any food which is not of the nature, substance or quality demanded.

In *Meah v. Robbers* 1978 an employee of a brewery cleaned the beer pumps and taps in a restaurant with caustic soda. He placed the remaining fluid in an empty lemonade bottle labeled 'cleaner' which he left for use by the restaurant. The caustic soda was mistakenly served to a customer who order lemonade. The customer became seriously ill as a result. It was held that the restaurant proprietor was guilty of the offence because the food was not of the nature demanded.

As with many other statutes creating criminal offences of strict liability, a number of defences are available, for example it is a defence to a show that the commission of the offence was due to the act or default of another or, that it was committed as a result of reliance on information supplied by another. Similarly, if the defendant can show that he exercised all due diligence and all reasonable precautions to avoid the commission of the offence, he will escape liability.

Following a number of food scares in the 1990s with a consequential loss of public confidence in the way food issues were dealt with, the government was persuaded to create an independent food agency in an attempt to restore public confidence and protect the Food Standards Agency with its main objectives of carrying out functions to protect public health from risks which may arise in connection with the consumption of food. The Agency is empowered to exercise influence over and advise the public in relation to the whole of the production chain of food from "plough to plate" and as a consequence will make a significant contribution to food safety.

The Data Protection Act 1998

Inevitably it is in the interests of suppliers of goods and services to collect and store information about their clients/customers. Usually the information is stored on computer files and concerns about its accuracy and the use to which it could be put led to pressure for legislation in the mid 1980s to protect consumers. The Data Protection Act 1984 was passed with the aim of providing a legal framework governing the collection, storage and distribution of personal data about individuals stored on computers. The fact that the vast majority of individuals who are protected by the Act are consumers of goods and services means that the Act can be classified as consumer protection legislation. The 1984 Act has now been repealed and replaced by the Data Protection Act 1998 which is now the principal means by which the law regulates the gathering of information about individuals including employees. It will come into force in 1999.

The 1998 Act goes further than the Data Protection Act 1984, protecting against the disclosure of private information, and may be viewed as an attempt to regulate surveillance at work. There are new possibilities for workers and unions to discover and object to information held on them by their employers. Under the 1984 Act the control of information held on computers was limited to entitling individuals to copies of the information. The Data Protection Act 1998 was passed to implement the Data Protection Directive 1995 aimed at regulating the dissemination and holding of information about individuals. The Directive requires *"Member States to protect the fundamental rights and freedoms of natural persons, in particular their rights to privacy with respect to the processing of personal data"*.

Some matters are categorised as sensitive personal data and that is given special protection. Thus in data consisting of matters such as ethnic origin, political opinion, racial origin, religion beliefs, criminal record, sex life and trade union membership. The 1998 Act follows the line of the 1984 Act by making reference to the Data Protection principles. It is the duty of the data controller to comply with the data protection principles in relation to all personal data with respect of which he is the data controller.

The Data Protection Principles are set out in the Act:

- personal data shall be processed fairly and lawfully;

- personal data shall be obtained only for one or more specified and lawful purposes;

- personal data shall be adequate, relevant and not excessive in relation to its purpose;

- personal data shall be accurate and where necessary kept up to date;

- personal data shall be processed in accordance with the rights of the data subject;

- appropriate technical and organisational measures shall be taken against unauthorised or unlawful processing of personal data and against accidental loss or destruction of personal data; and

- personal data shall not be transferred to a country outside the European Economic Area; unless that country ensure an adequate level of protection for the rights of data subjects.

The 1998 Act gives data subjects access to personal data by making provisions enabling individuals to be informed of and in some circumstances gaining access to personal data being processed by a data controller. Certain personal data is exempt from the rights of access such as that relating to national security, tax or duty collection, criminal activities, mental or physical health. A failure to supply information without good reason is a contravention of one of the data protection principles. An individual who suffers damage or distress as a result would maintain a claim for compensation.

The Data Protection Registrar created under the 1984 Act continues to exist under the new Act but becomes the Data Protection Commissioner. He is required to maintain a register of notified information and make it publicly available for inspection. There is a duty on data controllers to register with the commissioner before processing personal data, and failure to do so is a criminal offence.

The court has power on the application of a data subject to rectify, block, erase or destroy inaccurate personal data about the data subject. This would be because of the incomplete or inaccurate nature of the data held.

Assignment - Les Trois Vallées

Calder Travel plc is a large tour operator specialising in Winter Ski-ing holidays which are sold by retail travel agents throughout the United Kingdom. The company resolves to attempt to increase its share of the market for ski-ing holidays in France, in particular the Trois Vallées. To enable the company to achieve this, a decision is taken to make an offer of a financial inducement to prospective clients. Accordingly in their Winter Holiday 1996 brochure, of which 200,000 are distributed, Calder Travel make the following offer:

Throughout the 1996 winter season for every individual package ski-ing holiday booked at a resort in the Trois Vallées at a cost of £800 or more:

(a)   ski equipment and ski lessons will be provided absolutely free for the duration of the holiday; and

(b)   a voucher will be issued which will entitle the holder to a 20% discount on any ski clothing purchased at *"Sherrats Ski Wear"*, a retailer with outlets all over the UK.

Three weeks after the brochure containing this offer has been circulated to travel agents, Geoffery Swift, the company secretary of Calder Travel, despite having given prior approval for the offer, decided that after a closer consideration the offer should be amended due to its ambiguity.All company staff and sales agents are therefore instructed to inform travel agents that the offer of free ski equipment hire relates to down-hill skis and sticks only and does not extend to ski boots or cross country equipment. The offer of free ski lessons applies to beginners only and not to intermediate or advanced skiers. Travel agents are told to give the information to clients at the time of booking and inform those who had already booked by letter. Unfortunately some travel agents are never informed of the new instructions and a small proportion who are informed fail to pass it on to the clients. Consequently a large number of complaints are made both to Calder Travel, Travel Agents and local authorities by disappointed clients throughout the 1996 season. The main grievances are the fact that ski boots are not provided on free hire to clients who had booked relevant holidays and that lessons are only free for beginners.Also despite the fact that Sherrats Ski Wear shops display notices stating that they accept Calder discount vouchers, the available discount does not extend to clothing which is advertised as *on sale*.

Task

You are employed as a trading standards officer in the South East of England. Numerous complaints have been made to your office regarding the various *'free offers'* made by Calder Travel plc. You are required to present an informal report to your senior officer in which you advise whether any trade descriptions offences have been committed and assess the chances of bringing a successful prosecution.

Assignment - Spicer and Sharp

Spicer and Sharp plc is a company based in the West Midlands. The company is engaged in the production of power tools, D.I.Y. equipment and accessories. Most of its products are actually manufactured by subcontractors and supplied to Spicer and Sharp's main works in Kings Norton, where they are assembled and packaged in the style of the company under their brand name. The company's expansion is based on an aggressive marketing strategy which aims to establish strong product identity and brand loyalty in order to capture a major share of the UK market.

Having been in post as a legal assistant in Spicer and Sharp's legal department for three years, you have been appointed to run the consumer complaints department. Your first task is to deal with a complaint which has recently been received relating to injuries sustained by Andrew Tucker while using a circular saw fitted with a Spicer and Sharp circular saw blade and belonging to his brother Alan. Alan purchased the new blade for his Spicer and Sharp Circular saw from Home Handyman Stores and loaned it to Andrew who was constructing built-in wardrobes in his daughter's bedroom.

While Andrew was using the saw, the blade shattered when it was applied to a piece of second hand timber which contained a number of old nails. Part of the blade flew up hitting Andrew who suffered facial injuries and may be disfigured permanently as a result. It appears likely that the steel used in the blade had been subjected to excessive hardening in the process of production with the result that it was unusually brittle and more likely to shatter in these circumstances.

Home Handyman Stores purchased the saw blade from Spicer and Sharp as part of a larger consignment of the company's products. Unfortunately there is no certain means of establishing the identity of the supplier of the defective saw blade to Spicer and Sharp because three separate suppliers are under contract to supply identical blades to the company. However, records of the initial testing and subsequent random testing of each of the three supplier's products are on file in the quality control department at Kings Norton. Examination of the records gives no indication that this type of defect had ever come to light in respect of any of the blades which had previously been tested.

Task

Prepare a report for circulation to the legal department in which you indicate:

Whether Andrew would have a viable claim against the company in the tort of negligence or under part 1 of the Consumer Protection Act 1987; and the nature of any defences which may be available to the company in the event of any claim. Also indicate whether any steps should be taken in relation to circular saw blades still in the possession of the company or its retails customers, given that three further complaints have been received involving circular saw blades within a month of the complaint by Andrew Tucker.

Index